Religion in Philadelphia

EDITED BY

Elizabeth Hayes Alvarez

Religion in Philadelphia

TEMPLE UNIVERSITY PRESS
Philadelphia • Rome • Tokyo

TEMPLE UNIVERSITY PRESS
Philadelphia, Pennsylvania 19122
www.temple.edu/tempress

Published 2016

∞The paper used in this publication meets the requirements of the American National Standard for Information Sciences—Permanence of Paper for Printed Library Materials, ANSI Z39.48-1992

Printed in the United States of America

9 8 7 6 5 4 3 2 1

Contents

Primary Sources

Section 1. Religion and the City

Section 2. Lenni Lenape

Section 3. William Penn and the Quakers

Section 4. Religious Life in Colonial Philadelphia

Section 5. Jewish Philadelphia

Section 6. Catholic Philadelphia

Section 7. Mid-Century Reform

Section 8. Philadelphia Sports and Religion

Section 9. Religion and Civil Rights

Section 10. Islam in Philadelphia

Section 11. Religious Communities in Philadelphia Today

Section 12. Religious Freedom

Section 13. Temple University

William Penn to His Wife and Children (1682)

WILLIAM PENN

Warminghurst, 4 August 1682
My dear Wife and Children.

My love, that sea, nor land, nor death itself can extinguish or lessen toward you, most endearedly visits you with eternal embraces and will abide with you forever. And may the God of my life watch over you and bless you and do you good in this world and forever. Some things are upon my spirit to leave with you, in your respective capacities, as I am to one a husband, and to the rest a father, if I should never see you more in this world.

. . .

1st. Let the fear of the Lord, and a zeal and love to His glory, dwell richly in thy heart, and thou will watch for good over thyself and thy dear children and family, that no rude, light, or bad thing be committed, else God will be offended, and He will repent Himself of the good He intends thee and thine.

. . .

3dly. Cast up thy income and see what it daily amounts to, by which thou may be sure to have it in thy sight and power to keep within compass. And I beseech thee to live low and sparingly till my debts are paid, and then enlarge as thou see it convenient. Remember thy mother's example when thy father's public-spiritedness had worsted his estate (which is my case). I know thou loves plain things and are averse to the pomp of the world, a nobility natural to thee. I write not as doubtful, but to quicken thee, for my sake, to be more vigilant herein, knowing that God will bless thy care, and thy poor children and thee for it. My mind is wrapped up in a saying of thy father's. "I desire not riches, but to owe nothing." And truly that is wealth; and more than enough to live is a snare attended with many sorrows.

I need not bid thee be humble, for thou are so; nor meek and patient, for it is much of thy natural disposition. But I pray thee, be often in retirement with the Lord and guard against encroaching friendships. Keep them at arm's end; for it is giving away our power, aye, and self too, into the possession of another. And that which might seem engaging in the beginning, may prove a yoke and burden too hard and heavy in the end. Wherefore keep dominion over thyself, and let thy children, good meetings, and Friends be the pleasure of thy life.

4thly. And now, my dearest, let me recommend to thy care my dear children, abundantly beloved of me as the Lord's blessings and the sweet pledges of our mutual and endeared affection. Above all things, endeavor to breed them up in the love of virtue and that holy plain way of it which we have lived in, that the world, in no part of it, get into my family. I had rather they were homely than finely bred, as to outward behavior; yet I love sweetness mixed with gravity, and cheerfulness tempered with sobriety. Religion in the heart leads into this true civility, teaching men and women to be mild and courteous in their behavior, an accomplishment worthy indeed of praise.

5thly. Next, breed them up in a love one of another. Tell them, it is the charge I left behind me, and that it is the way to have the love and blessing of God upon them; also what his portion is who hates, or calls his brother fool. Sometimes separate them, but not long; and allow them to send and give each other small things, to endear one another with once more. I say, tell them it was my counsel, they should be tender and affectionate one to another.

For their learning, be liberal. Spare no cost, for by such parsimony all is lost that is saved; but let it be useful knowledge, such as is consistent with truth and godliness, not cherishing a vain conversation or idle mind, but ingenuity mixed with industry is good for the body and mind too. I recommend the useful parts of mathematics, as building houses or ships, measuring, surveying, dialing, navigation, etc.; but agriculture is especially in my eye. Let my children be husbandmen and housewives. It is industrious, healthy, honest, and of good example, like Abraham and the holy ancients who pleased God and obtained a good report. This leads to consider the works of God and nature, of things that are good and divert the mind from being taken up with the vain arts and inventions of a luxurious world. It is commendable in the princes of Germany, and [the] nobles of that empire, that they have all their children instructed in some useful occupation. Rather keep an ingenious person in the house to teach them than send them to schools, too many evil impressions being commonly received there. Be sure to observe their genius and don't cross it as to learning. Let them not dwell too long on one thing, but let their change be agreeable, and all their diversions have some little bodily labor in them.

When grown big, have most care for them; for then there are more snares both within and without. When marriageable, see that they have worthy persons in their eye, of good life and good fame for piety and understanding. I need no wealth but sufficiency; and be sure their love be dear, fervent, and mutual, that it may be happy for them. I choose not they should be married into earthly covetous kindred. And of cities and towns of concourse beware. The world is apt to stick close to those who have lived and got wealth there. A country life and estate I like best for my children. I prefer a decent mansion of a hundred pounds per annum before ten thousand pounds in London, or suchlike place, in a way of trade.

[To his children]

Let your industry and parsimony go no farther than for a sufficiency for life, and to make a provision for your children (and that in moderation, if the Lord gives you any). I charge you to help the poor and needy. Let the Lord have a voluntary share of your income, for the good of the poor, both in our Society and others; for we are all His creatures, remembering that he that gives to the poor, lends to the Lord. Know well your incomings, and your outgoings may be the better regulated. Love not money, nor the world. Use them only and they will serve you; but if you love them, you serve them, which will debase your spirits as well as offend the Lord. Pity the distressed, and hold out a hand of help to them; it may be your case, and as you mete to others, God will mete to you again.

Be humble and gentle in your conversation; of few words, I charge you; but always pertinent when you speak, hearing out before you attempt to answer, and then speaking as if you would persuade, not impose.

. . .

Next, my children, be temperate in all things: in your diet, for that is physic by prevention; it keeps, nay, it makes people healthy and their generation sound. This is exclusive of the spiritual advantage it brings. Be also plain in your apparel; keep out that lust which reigns too much over some. Let your virtues be your ornaments; remembering, life is more than food, and the body than raiment. Let your furniture be simple and cheap. Avoid pride, avarice, and luxury. Read my *No Cross, No Crown*; there is instruction. Make your conversation with the most eminent for wisdom and piety; and shun all wicked men, as you hope for the blessing of God, and the comfort of your father's living and dying prayers. Be sure you speak no evil of any; no, not of the meanest, much less of your superiors, as magistrates, guardians, tutors, teachers, and elders in Christ.

. . .

And as for you who are likely to be concerned in the government of Pennsylvania and my parts of East Jersey, especially the first, I do charge you before the Lord God and his only angels that-you be lowly, diligent, and tender; fearing God, loving the people, and hating covetousness. Let justice have its impartial course, and the law free passage. Though to your loss, protect no man against it, for you are not above the law, but the law above you. Live therefore the lives yourselves you would have the people live; and then you have right and boldness to punish the transgressor. Keep upon the square, for God sees you; therefore do your duty; and be sure you see with your own eyes, and hear with your own ears. Entertain no lurchers; cherish no informers for gain or revenge; use no tricks, fly to no devices to support or cover injustice, but let your hearts be upright before the Lord, trusting in Him above the contrivances of men, and none shall be able to hurt or supplant.

. . .

If you thus behave yourselves, and so become a terror to evildoers and a praise to them that do well, God, my God, will be with you, in wisdom and a sound mind, and make you blessed instruments in His hand for the settlement of some of those desolate parts of the world—which my soul desires above all worldly honors and riches, both for you that go and you that stay, you that govern and you that are governed—that in the end you may be gathered with me to the rest of God.

. . .

So farewell to my thrice dearly beloved wife and children. Yours, as God pleases, in that which no waters can quench, no time forget, nor distance wear away, but remains forever.

William Penn

Quaker Petition Against Slavery, 1688 (Feb 18, 1688)

Francis Daniel Pastorius, et al.

This is to ye Monthly Meeting held at Richard Worrell's.

These are the reasons why we are against the traffick of men-body, as foloweth. Is there any that would be done or handled at this manner? viz., to be sold or made a slave for all the time of his life? How fearful and faint-hearted are many on sea, when they see a strange vessel,—being afraid it should be a Turk, and they should be taken, and sold for slaves into Turkey. Now what is this better done, as Turks doe? Yea, rather it is worse for them, which say they are Christians; for we hear that ye most part of such negers are brought hither against their will and consent, and that many of them are stolen. Now, tho they are black, we can not conceive there is more liberty to have them slaves, as it is to have other white ones. There is a saying that we shall doe to all men like as we will be done ourselves; making no difference of what generation, descent or colour they are. And those who steal or robb men, and those who buy or purchase them, are they not all alike? Here is liberty of conscience wch is right and reasonable; here ought to be liberty of ye body, except of evil-doers, wch is an other case. But to bring men hither, or to rob and sell them against their will, we stand against. In Europe there are many oppressed for conscience sake; and here there are those oppressed wh are of a black colour. And we who know than men must not comitt adultery,—some do committ adultery, in separating wives from their husbands and giving them to others; and some sell the children of these poor creatures to other men. Ah! doe consider will this thing, you who doe it, if you would be done at this manner? And if it is done according to Christianity? You surpass Holland and Germany in this thing. This makes an ill report in all those countries of Europe, where they hear of, that ye Quakers doe here handel men as they handel there ye cattle. And for that reason some have no mind or inclination to come hither. And who shall maintain this your cause, or pleid for it. Truly we can not do so, except you shall inform us better hereof, viz., that Christians have liberty to practise these things. Pray, what thing in the world can be done worse towards us, than if men should rob or steal us away, and sell us for slaves to strange countries; separating husbands from their wives and children. Being now that this is not done in the manner we would be done at therefore we contradict and are against this traffic of men-body. And we who profess that is is not lawful to steal, must, likewise, avoid to purchase such things as are stolen, but rather help to stop this robbing and stealing if possible. And such men ought to be delivered out of ye hands of ye robbers, and set free as well as in Europe. Then is Pennsylvania to have a good report, instead it hath now a bad one for this sake in other countries. Especially whereas ye Europeans are desirous to know in what manner ye Quakers doe rule in their province;—and most of them doe look upon us with an envious eye. But if this is done well, what shall we say is done evil?

If once these slaves (wch they say are so wicked and stubbern men) should join themselves,—fight for their freedom,—and handel their masters and mastrisses as they did handel them before; will these masters and mastrisses take the sword at hand and warr against these poor slaves, licke, we are able to believe, some will not refuse to doe; or have these negers not as much right to fight for their freedom, as you have to keep them slaves?

Now consider will this thing, if it is good or bad? And in case you find it to be good to handle these blacks at that manner, we desire and require you hereby lovingly, that you may inform us herein, which at this time never was done, viz., that Christians have such a liberty to do so. To the end we shall be be satisfied in this point, and satisfie likewise our good friends and acquaintances in our natif country, to whose it is a terror, or fairful thing, that men should be handeld so in Pennsylvania.

This is from our meeting at Germantown, held ye 18 of the 2 month, 1688, to be delivered to the Monthly Meeting at Richard Worrell's.

Garret Henderich
Derick op den Graeff
Francis Daniell Pastorius
Abraham op den Graef

From George Washington to the Hebrew Congregation in Newport, Rhode Island, 18 August 1790

George Washington

Gentlemen. [Newport, R.I., 18 August 1790]

While I receive, with much satisfaction, your Address replete with expressions of affection and esteem; I rejoice in the opportunity of assuring you, that I shall always retain a grateful remembrance of the cordial welcome I experienced in my visit to Newport, from all classes of Citizens.

The reflection on the days of difficulty and danger which are past is rendered the more sweet, from a consciousness that they are succeeded by days of uncommon prosperity and security. If we have wisdom to make the best use of the advantages with which we are now favored, we cannot fail, under the just administration of a good Government, to become a great and a happy people.

The Citizens of the United States of America have a right to applaud themselves for having given to mankind examples of an enlarged and liberal policy: a policy worthy of imitation. All possess alike liberty of conscience and immunities of citizenship. It is now no more that toleration is spoken of, as if it was by the indulgence of one class of people, that another enjoyed the exercise of their inherent natural rights. For happily the Government of the United States, which gives to bigotry no sanction, to persecution no assistance requires only that they who live under its protection should demean themselves as good citizens, in giving it on all occasions their effectual support.

It would be inconsistent with the frankness of my character not to avow that I am pleased with your favorable opinion of my Administration, and fervent wishes for my felicity. May the Children of the Stock of Abraham, who dwell in this land, continue to merit and enjoy the good will of the other Inhabitants; while every one shall sit in safety under his own vine and figtree, and there shall be none to make him afraid. May the father of all mercies scatter light and not darkness in our paths, and make us all in our several vocations useful here, and in his own due time and way everlastingly happy.

Go: Washington

The Life, Experience, and Gospel Labours of the Rt. Rev. Richard Allen (1793)

Richard Allen

February, 1786, I came to Philadelphia. Preaching was given out for me at five o'clock in the morning at St. George's Church. I strove to preach as well as I could, but it was a great cross to me; but the Lord was with me. We had a good time, and several souls were awakened, and were earnestly seeking redemption in the blood of Christ. I thought I would stop in Philadelphia a week or two. I preached at different places in the city. My labour was much blessed. I soon saw a large field open in seeking and instructing my African brethren, who had been a long forgotten people and few of them attended public worship. I preached in the commons, in Southwark, Northern Liberties, and wherever I could find an opening. I frequently preached twice a day, at 5 o'clock in the morning and in the evening, and it was not uncommon for me to preach from four to five times a day. I established prayer meetings; I raised a society in 1786 of forty-two members. I saw the necessity of erecting a place of worship for the coloured people. I proposed it to the most respectable people of colour in this city; but here I met with opposition. I had but three coloured brethren that united with me in erecting a place of worship—the Rev. Absalom Jones, William White, and Dorus Ginnings. These united with me as soon as it became public and known by the elder who was stationed in the city. The Rev. C—B—opposed the plan, and would not submit to any argument we could raise; but he was shortly removed from the charge. The Rev Mr. W—took the charge, and the Rev L—G—. Mr. W—was much opposed to an African church, and used very degrading and insulting language to us, to try and prevent us from going on. We all belonging to St. George's church—Rev. Absalom Jones, William White and Dorus Ginnings. We felt ourselves much cramped; but my dear Lord was with us, and we believed, if it was his will, the work would go on, and that we would be able to succeed in building the house of the Lord. We established prayer meetings and meetings of exhortation, and the Lord blessed our endeavours, and many souls were awakened; but the elder soon forbid us holding any such meetings; but we viewed the forlorn state of our coloured brethren, and that they were destitute of a place of worship. They were considered as a nuisance.

A number of us usually attended St. George's Church in Fourth street; and when the coloured people began to get numerous in attending the church, they moved us from the seats we usually sat on, and placed us around the wall, and on Sabbath morning we went to church and the sexton stood at the door, and told us to go in the gallery. He told us to go, and we would see where to sit. We expected to take the seats over the ones we formerly occupied below, not knowing any better. We took those seats.

Meeting had begun, and they were nearly done singing, and just as we got to the seats, the elder said, "let us pray." We had not been long upon our knees before I heard considerable scuffling and low talking. I raised my head up and saw one of the trustees, H—M—, having hold of the Rev. Absalom Jones, pulling him up off of his knees, and saying, "You must get up—you must not kneel here." Mr. Jones replied, "wait until prayer is over." Mr. H—M—said "no, you must get up now, or I will call for aid and I force you away." Mr. Jones said, "wait until prayer is over, and I will get up and trouble you no more." With that he beckoned to one of the other trustees, Mr. L—S—to come to his assistance. He came, and went to William White to pull him up. By this time prayer was over, and we all went out of the church in a body, and they were no more plagued with us in the church. This raised a great excitement and inquiry among the citizens, in so much that I believe they were ashamed of their conduct. But my dear Lord was with us, and we were filled with fresh vigour to get a house erected to worship God in. Seeing our forlorn and distressed situation, many of the hearts of our citizens were moved to urge us forward; notwithstanding we had subscribed largely towards finishing St. George's Church, in building the gallery and laying new floors, and just as the house was made comfortable, we were turned out from enjoying the comforts of worshiping therein. We then hired a store room, and held worship by ourselves. Here we were pursued with threats of being disowned, and read publicly out of meeting if we did continue worship in the place we had hired; but we believed the Lord would be our friend. We got subscription papers out to raise money to build the house of the Lord. By this time we had waited on Dr. Rush and Mr. Robert Ralston, and told them of our distressing situation. We considered it a blessing that the Lord had put it into our hearts to wait upon those gentlemen. They pitied our situation, and subscribed largely towards the church, and were very friendly towards us, and advised us how to go on. We appointed Mr. Ralston our treasurer. Dr. Rush did much for us in public by his influence. I hope the name of Dr. Benjamin Rush and Mr. Robert Ralston will never be forgotten among us. They were the two first gentlemen who espoused the cause of the oppressed, and aided us in building the house of the Lord for the poor Africans to worship in. Here was the beginning and rise of the first African church in America. But the elder of the Methodist church still pursued us. Mr. J—M—called upon us and told us if we did not erase our names from the subscription paper, and give up the paper, we would be publicly turned out of meeting. We asked him if we had violated any rules of discipline by so doing. He replied, "I have the charge given to me by the Conference, and unless you submit I will read you publicly out of meeting." We told him we were willing to abide by the discipline of the Methodist church; "and if you will show us where we have violated any law of discipline of the Methodist church, we will submit; and if there is no rule violated in the discipline, we will proceed on." He replied, "we will read you all out." We told him if he turned us out contrary to rule of discipline, we should seek further redress. We told him we were dragged off of our knees in St. George's church, and treated worse than heathens; and we were determined to seek out for ourselves, the Lord being our helper. He told us we were not Methodists, and left us. Finding we would go on in raising money to build the church, he called upon us again, and wished to see us all together. We met him. He told us that he wished us well, and that he was a friend to us, and used many arguments to convince us that we were wrong in building a church. We told him we had no place of worship; and we did not mean to go to St. George's church any more, as we were so scandalously treated in the presence of all the congregation present; "and if you deny us your name, you cannot seal up the scriptures from us, and deny us a name in heaven. We believe heaven is free for all who worship in spirit and truth." And he said, "so you are determined to go on." We told him—"yes, God being our helper." He then replied, "we will disown you all from the Methodist connexion." We believed if we put our trust in the Lord, he would stand by us. This was a trial that I never had to pass through before. I was confident that the great head of the church would support us. My dear Lord was with us.

An Account of the Terrible Effects of the Pestilential Infection in the City of Philadelphia (1793)

Samuel Stearns

With an Elegy on the Deaths of the People. Also a Song of Praise and Thanksgiving, Composed for Those Who Have Recovered After Having Been Smitten with that Dreadful Contagion.

Righteous art thou, O Lord, and upright are thy Judgements. Psal. cxix. 137. But when God's Judgments are abroad in the Earth, let the Inhabitant thereof learn Rightousness.

Preface.

Kind Reader,

How many people have fallen in the city of Philadelphia, by the Pestilential Infection, is unknown to the author—and he believes to the inhabitants of the same place; for the accounts are very different, as some mention four, other five, six, and even more than seven thousand: and the latter has been supposed to be not too large. Some have given the disorder one name, and others another, &c. It has been called a genuine Plague; a putrid malignant fever; a yellow fever, and a Pestilential Infection. It seems that the mortality began about the beginning of August, and raged with great violence till the weather grew colder.

The Author has composed the following lines at his leisure hours, in which he has given a true description of the terrible effects of this contagion, according to the best information he has been able to obtain from recent publications; and as many people have called it a Plague, and as he knows not its proper name, he hopes he shall be excused for calling it so in the subsequent pages.

From, kind reader, your's and the public's most obedient humble servant,

The Author.
November 13, 1793

A Form of Prayer.
Almighty God, wilt thon thy people *spare?*
Deliver them from this *contagious snare!*
This *mortal Plague* at thy command began,
And thou thereby hast *humbled* sinful man!
Thou art the fountain of all good and love,
And dost thy will on earth—in heav'n above!
Thou givest life, thou givest health and ease,
To all thy creatures, just as thou dost please!
In thine own time thou smitest them with death,
Their bodies fall when thou dost take their breath!
Thou hast ordain'd that this shall be the fate
Of *ev'ry creature* in this mortal state!
These works of thine, if rightly understood,
Promote, we find, the universal good;
Remove thy *children* to a better *shore*,
To realms of *joy*, to live for evermore!

A Form of Thanksgiving.
We give thee *thanks*, most good and gracious Lord,
That this *infection*, was not spread abroad;
That to thy people thou hast been so kind,
That this contagion has been much confin'd:Confin'd, indeed, unto a narrow space,
Preventing death amongst the human race!
May all thus favour'd their glad voices raise,
In celebrating the *Creator's* praise,
That he's been pleas'd in dang'roud times to save
Them from *destruction* and the *silent grave!*
That on thy earth they're yet allow'd to dwell,
Whilst thousands by the pestilence have fell!
May all who from the raging Plague recover,
Their thankfulness unto the world discover,
By rend'ring praise to thee, the God above,
For preservation and thy boundless love;
For all the favours that from thee have came,
Especially for health's new kindled flame!
That strength is now to them restor'd again,
Whilst by thy will some of their friends are slain!
Lord, wilt thou *grant* that those who've liv'd in *sin*,
May all refrain, and a new life begin!
Live temperate, be holy, just, and pure,
So long as time with them shall yet endure;
Conduct, indeed, like very righteous men,
Be *blest* by *thee*, for evermore. Amen.

An Elegy, On the Deaths of Citizens of Philadelphia, Who Were Destroyed by a *Pestilential Infection*, In the Year 1793.

In Philadelphia has been slain,
Indeed it is a doleful sound!
Of diff'rent sects, a num'rous train,
Which now lie silent in the ground!
2.
A pestilence, which there did rage
With rapid force, has swept away
An hundred people from the stage,
Within the compass of a day!3.
But sometimes less, and sometimes more,
The daily publications tell,Upon that mournful city's shore,
In that short time, have often fell!4.
The life and vigour they enjoy'd,
Alas. It was their dismal fate!
By this disease have been destroy'd,
And they mov'd from the present state!5.
But happy is their lot indeed!
Their bodies now need no relief;
For in the silent grave they're freed
From trouble, sorrow, pain, and grief!
6.
Some worthy characters are dead!
Young children too, just in their bloom!
The middle-ag'd, the hoary head,
Have hurry'd been into the tomb!
7.
Alas! Alas! We may relate,
That by experience we have found,
These losses truly have been great,
To relatives and all around!
8.
Let not the relatives repine,
Since the great God, who reigns on high,
By death, which is an act divine,
Rais'd their good friends above the sky!
9.
With patience run the heav'nly race,
Trust in the *Lord*, and do not faint;
For the *Almighty*, by his grace,
Supplies the wants of every saint.
10.
In prosp'rous times, or in distress,
You're in the great Creator's care;

As ye pass through this wilderness,
Let nothing lead you to despair.
11.
He saves alive, and he doth kill;
For life and death from him do flow!
In heav'n above he does his will,
And on his footstool here below!
12.
The famine, sword, and pestilence,
He sends to desolate the land!
Against the *Lord* there's no defence;
None can restrain his mighty hand!
13.
As all he doth is good and right,
Let all his servants be content:
Be humble-minded day and night,
Under the troubles he hath sent.
14.
Serve ye the *Lord*, and in him trust;
That when your days on earth shall cease,
Ye may be seated with the just,
In boundless realms of *joy* and *peace!*

A Song of Praise and Thanksgiving, Composed for Those Who Have Recovered of the *Pestilential Infection*, in Philadelphia

Let us praise God, who reigns on high,
The universal King,
Who rais'd the arches of the sky,
And formed ev'ry'thing.
2.
Who gave the human species birth,
And pass'd a firm decree,
That all the sons of men on earth
Should grief and trouble see.
3.
He hath afflicted us with *pain*,
Whilst thousands all around
Have by his *pestilence* been slain,
And level'd with the ground!
4.
But in a time of deep distress,
He rais'd us up again;
And we within his wilderness
As monuments remain!
5.
We give thee thanks, *Almighty God*,

That it was not our doom,
To be cast by thy chast'ning rod
Into the silent tomb!
6.
Assist us, by thy quick'ning grace,
To number so our days,
That we ourselves in every place
May walk in wisdom's ways.
7.
May we to *thee* due homage pay,
Do good to all mankind,
Thy written laws always obey,
Live to thy will resign'd.
8.
And when we die, may we arise
Where thy good saints are blest,
In realms of joy, above the skies,
With happiness and rest!

November 13, 1793

Finis.

Autobiography (1793)

Benjamin Franklin

In 1739 arrived among us from Ireland the Reverend Mr. Whitefield, who had made himself remarkable there as an itinerant preacher. He was at first permitted to preach in some of our churches; but the clergy, taking a dislike to him, soon refus'd him their pulpits, and he was oblig'd to preach in the fields. The multitudes of all sects and denominations that attended his sermons were enormous, and it was matter of speculation to me, who was one of the number, to observe the extraordinary influence of his oratory on his hearers, and bow much they admir'd and respected him, notwithstanding his common abuse of them, by assuring them that they were naturally half beasts and half devils. It was wonderful to see the change soon made in the manners of our inhabitants. From being thoughtless or indifferent about religion, it seem'd as if all the world were growing religious, so that one could not walk thro' the town in an evening without hearing psalms sung in different families of every street. . . .

Mr. Whitefield, in leaving us, went preaching all the way thro' the colonies to Georgia. The settlement of that province had lately been begun, but, instead of being made with hardy, industrious husbandmen, accustomed to labor, the only people fit for such an enterprise, it was with families of broken shop-keepers and other insolvent debtors, many of indolent and idle habits, taken out of the jails, who, being set down in the woods, unqualified for clearing land, and unable to endure the hardships of a new settlement, perished in numbers, leaving many helpless children unprovided for. The sight of their miserable situation inspir'd the benevolent heart of Mr. Whitefield with the idea of building an Orphan House there, in which they might be supported and educated. Returning northward, he preach'd up this charity, and made large collections, for his eloquence had a wonderful power over the hearts and purses of his hearers, of which I myself was an instance.

I did not disapprove of the design, but, as Georgia was then destitute of materials and workmen, and it was proposed to send them from Philadelphia at a great expense, I thought it would have been better to have built the house here, and brought the children to it. This I advis'd; but he was resolute in his first project, rejected my counsel, and I therefore refus'd to contribute. I happened soon after to attend one of his sermons, in the course of which I perceived he intended to finish with a collection, and I silently resolved he should get nothing from me, I had in my pocket a handful of copper money, three or four silver dollars, and five pistoles in gold. As he proceeded I began to soften, and concluded to give the coppers. Another stroke of his oratory made me asham'd of that, and determin'd me to give the silver; and he finish'd so admirably, that I empty'd my pocket wholly into the collector's dish, gold and all. At this sermon there was also one of our club, who, being of my sentiments respecting the building in Georgia, and suspecting a collection might be intended, had, by precaution, emptied his pockets before he came from home. Towards the conclusion of the discourse, however, he felt a strong desire to give, and apply'd to a neighbour, who stood near him, to borrow some money for the purpose. The application was unfortunately [*made*] to perhaps the only man in the company who had the firmness not to be affected by the preacher. His answer was, "At any other time, Friend Hopkinson, I would lend to thee freely; but not now, for thee seems to be out of thy right senses." . . .

He had a loud and clear voice, and articulated his words and sentences so perfectly, that he might be heard and understood at a great distance, especially as his auditories, however numerous, observ'd the most exact silence. He preach'd one evening from the top of the Court-house steps, which are in the middle of Market-street, and on the west side of Second-street, which crosses it at right angles. Both streets were fill'd with his hearers to a considerable distance. Being among the hindmost in Market-street, I had the curiosity to learn how far he could be heard, by retiring backwards down the street towards the river; and I found his voice distinct till I came near Front-street, when some noise in that street obscur'd it. Imagining then a semi-circle, of which my distance should be the radius, and that it were fill'd with auditors, to each of whom I allow'd two square feet, I computed that he might well be heard by more than thirty thousand. This reconcil'd me to the newspaper accounts of his having preach'd to twenty-five thousand people in the fields, and to the antient histories of generals haranguing whole armies, of which I had sometimes doubted.

By hearing him often, I came to distinguish easily between sermons newly composed, and those which he had often preached in the course of his travels. His delivery of the latter was so improved by frequent repetitions that every accent, every emphasis, every modulation of voice, was so perfectly well turned and well placed, that, without being interested in the subject, one could not help being pleased with the discourse; a pleasure of much the same kind with that received from an excellent piece of music. This is an advantage itinerant preachers have over those who are stationary, as the latter cannot well improve their delivery of a sermon by so many rehearsals.

His writing and printing from time to time gave great advantage to his enemies unguarded expressions, and even erroneous options, delivered in preaching, might have been afterwards explained or qualified by supposing others that might have accompanied them, or they might have been denied; but *litera scripta Manet.* Critics attacked his writings violently, and with so much appearance of reason as to diminish the number of his votaries and prevent their increase; so that I am of opinion if he had never written anything, he would have left behind him a much more numerous and important sect, and his reputation might in that case have been still growing, even after his death, as, there being nothing of his writing on which to found a censure and give him a lower character, his proselytes would be left at liberty to feign for him as great a variety of excellences as their enthusiastic admiration might wish him to have possessed.

Religious Experience and Journal of Mrs Jarena Lee, Giving an Account of Her Call to Preach the Gospel (1836)

Jarena Lee

"And it shall come to pass . . . that I will pour out my Spirit upon all flesh; and your sons and your *daughters* shall prophesy"—*Joel 2.28*

I was born February 11th, 1783, at Cape May, State of New Jersey. At the age of seven years I was parted from my parents, and went to live as a servant maid, with a Mr. Sharp, at the distance of about sixty miles from the place of my birth.

My parents being wholly ignorant of the knowledge of God, had not therefore instructed me in any degree in this great matter. Not long after the commencement of my attendance on this lady, she had bid me do something respecting my work, which in a little while after she asked me if I had done, when I replied, Yes—but this was not true.

At this awful point, in my early history, the Spirit of God moved in power through my conscience, and told me I was a wretched sinner. On this account so great was the impression, and so strong were the feelings of guilt, that I promised in my heart that I would not tell another lie.

But notwithstanding this promise my heart grew harder, after a while, yet the Spirit of the Lord never entirely forsook me, but continued mercifully striving with me, until his gracious power converted my soul.

The manner of this great accomplishment was as follows: In the year 1804, it so happened that I went with others to hear a missionary of the Presbyterian order preach. It was an afternoon meeting, but few were there, the place was a school room; but the preacher was solemn, and in his countenance the earnestness of his master's business appeared equally strong, as though he were about to speak to a multitude.

At the reading of the Psalms, a ray of renewed conviction darted into my soul. These were the words, composing the first verse of the Psalms for the service:

> Lord, I am vile, conceived in sin, /
> Born unholy and unclean. /
> Sprung from man, whose guilty fall /
> Corrupts the race, and taints us all.

This description of my condition struck me to the heart, and made me to feel in some measure, the weight of my sins, and sinful nature. But not knowing how to run immediately to the Lord for help, I was driven of Satan, in the course of a few days, and tempted to destroy myself.

There was a brook about a quarter of a mile from the house, in which there was a deep hole, where the water whirled about among the rocks; to this place, it was suggested, I must go and drown myself.

At the time I had a book in my hand; it was a Sabbath morning, about ten o'clock; to this place I resorted, where on coming to the water I sat down on the bank, and on my looking into it, it was suggested that drowning would be an easy death. It seemed as if some one was speaking to me, saying put your head under, it will not distress you. But by some means, of which I can give no account, my thoughts were taken entirely from this purpose, when I went from the place to the house again. It was the unseen arm of God which saved me from self-murder.

But as yet I had not found Him of whom Moses and the prophets did write, being extremely ignorant: there being no one to instruct me in the way of life and salvation as yet. After my recovery, I left the lady, who, during my sickness, was exceedingly kind, and went to Philadelphia. From this place I soon went a few miles into the country, where I resided in the family of a Roman Catholic. But my anxiety still continued respecting my poor soul, on which account I used to watch my opportunity to read in the Bible; and this lady observing this, took the Bible from me and hid it, giving me a novel in its stead—which when I perceived, I refused to read.

Soon after this I again went to the city of Philadelphia, and commenced going to the English Church, the pastor of which was an Englishman, by the name of Pilmore, one of the number who at first preached Methodism in America, in the city of New York.

But while sitting under the ministration of this man, which was about three months, and at the last time, it appeared that there was a wall between me and a communion with that people, which was higher than I could possibly see over, and seemed to make this impression upon my mind, *this is not the people for you.*

But on returning home at noon I inquired of the head cook of the house respecting the rules of the Methodists, as I knew she belonged to that society, who told me what they were; on which account I replied, that I should not be able to abide by such strict rules not even one year—however, I told her that I would go with her and hear what they had to say.

The man who was to speak in the afternoon of that day, was the Rev. Richard Allen, since bishop of the African Episcopal Methodists in America. During the labors of this man that afternoon, I had come to the conclusion, that this is the people to which my heart unites, and it so happened, that as soon as the service closed he invited such as felt a desire to flee the wrath to come, to unite on trial with them—I embraced the opportunity. Three weeks from that day, my soul was gloriously converted to God, under preaching, at the very outset of the sermon. The text was barely pronounced, which was "I perceive thy heart is not right in the sight of God," when there appeared to *my* view, in the centre of the heart, *one* sin; and this was *malice* against one particular individual, who had strove deeply to injure me, which I resented. At this discovery I said, *Lord* I forgive *every* creature. That instant, it appeared to me as if a garment, which had entirely enveloped my whole person, even to my fingers' ends, split at the crown of my head, and was stripped away from me, passing like a shadow from my sight—when the glory of God seemed to cover me in its stead.

That moment, though hundreds were present, I did leap to my feet and declare that God, for Christ's sake, had pardoned the sins of my soul. Great was the ecstacy of my mind, for I felt that not only the sin of *malice* was pardoned, but all other sins were swept away together. That day was the first when my heart had believed, and my tongue had made confession unto salvation—the first words uttered, a part of that song, which shall fill eternity with its sound, was *glory to God*. For a few moments I had power to exhort sinners, and to tell of the wonders and of the goodness of Him who had clothed me with *His* salvation. During this the minister was silent, until my soul felt its duty had been performed, when he declared another witness of the power of Christ, to forgive sins on earth, was manifest in my conversion.

. . .

I continued in this happy state of mind for almost three months, when a certain coloure man, by name William Scott, came to pay me a religious visit. He had been for many years the faithful follower of the Lamb; and he had also taken much time in visiting the sick and distressed of our color, and understood well the great things belonging to a man of full stature in Christ Jesus.

In the course of our conversation, he inquired if the Lord had justified my soul. I answered yes. He then asked me if he had sanctified me. I answered no; and that I did not know what that was. He then undertook to instruct me further in the knowledge of the Lord respecting this blessing.

He told me the progress of the soul from a state of darkness, or of nature, was three-fold; or consisted in three degrees, as follows: First, conviction for sin. Second, justification from sin. Third, the entire sanctification of the soul to God. I thought this description was beautiful, and immediately believed in it. He then inquired if I would promise to pray for this in my secret devotions. I told him yes. Very soon I began to call upon the Lord to show me all that was in my heart, which was not according to his will. Now there appeared to be a new struggle commencing in my soul, not accompanied with fear, guilt, and bitter distress, as while under my first conviction for sin, but a laboring of the mind to know more of the right way of the Lord. I began now to feel that my heart was not clean in his sight; that there yet remained the roots of bitterness, which if not destroyed, would ere long sprout up from these roots, and overwhelm me in a new growth of the brambles and brushwood of sin.

By the increasing light of the Spirit, I had found there yet remained the root of pride, anger, self-will, with many evils, the result of fallen nature. I now became alarmed at this discovery, and began to fear that I have been deceived in my experience. I was now greatly alarmed, lest I should fall away from what I knew I had enjoyed; and to guard against this I prayed almost incessantly, without setting faith on the power and promises of God to keep me from falling. I had not yet learned how to war against temptation of this kind. Satan well knew that if he could succeed in making me disbelieve my conversion, that he would catch me either on the ground of complete despair, or on the ground of infidelity. For if all I had passed through was to go for nothing, and was but a fiction, the mere ravings of a disordered mind, that I would naturally be led to believe that there is nothing in religion at all.

From this snare I was mercifully preserved, and led to believe that there was yet a greater work than that of pardon to be wrought in me. I retired to a secret place, (after having sought this blessing, as well as I could, for nearly three months, from the time brother Scott had instructed me respecting it,) for prayer, about four o'clock in the afternoon. I had struggled long and hard, but found not the desire of my heart. When I rose from my knees, there seemed a voice speaking to me, as I yet stood in a leaning posture—"Ask for sanctification." When to my surprise, I recollected that I had not even thought of it in my whole prayer. It would seem Satan had hidden the very object from my mind, for which I had purposely kneeled to pray. But when this voice whispered in my heart, saying, "Pray for sanctification," I again bowed in the same place, at the same time, and said, "Lord sanctify my soul for Christ's sake." That very instant, as if lightning had darted through me, I sprang to my feet, and cried, "The Lord has sanctified my soul!" There was none to hear this but the angels who stood around to witness my joy—and Satan, whose malice raged the more. That Satan was there, I knew; for no sooner had I cried out "The Lord has sanctified my soul," than there seemed another voice behind me, saying, "No, it is too great a work to be done." But another spirit said, "Bow down for the witness—I received it—thou art sanctified!" The first I knew of myself after that, I was standing in the yard with my hands spread out, and looking with my face toward heaven.

. . .

Between four and five years after my sanctification, on a certain time, an impressive silence fell upon me, and I stood as if some one was about to speak to me, yet I had no such thought in my heart. But to my utter surprise there seemed to sound a voice which I thought I distinctly heard, and most certainly understand, which said to me, "Go preach the Gospel!" I immediately replied aloud, "No one will believe me." Again I listened, and again the same voice seemed to say—"Preach the Gospel; I will put words in your mouth, and you will turn your enemies to become your friends."

At first I supposed that Satan had spoken to me, for I had read that he could transform himself into an angel of light for the purpose of deception. Immediately I went into a secret place, and called upon the Lord to know if he had called me to preach, and whether I was deceived or not; when there appeared to my view the form and figure of a pulpit, with a Bible lying thereon, the back of which was presented to me as plainly as if it had been a literal fact.

In consequence of this, my mind became so exercised, that during the night following, I took a text and preached in my sleep. I thought there stood before me a great multitude, while I expounded to them the things of religion. So violent were my exertions and so loud were my exclamations, that I awoke from the sound of my own voice, which also awoke the family of the house where I resided. Two days after I went to see the preacher in charge of the African Society, who was the Rev. Richard Allen, the same before named in these pages, to tell him that I felt it my duty to preach the gospel. But as I drew near the street in which his house was, which was in the city of Philadelphia, my courage began to fail me; so terrible did the cross appear, it seemed that I should not be able to bear it. Previous to my acting out to go to see him, so agitated was my mind, that my appetite for my daily food failed me entirely. Several times on my way there, I turned back again; but as often I felt my strength again renewed, and I soon found that the nearer I approached to the house of the minister, the less was my fear. Accordingly, as soon as I came to the door, my fears subsided, the cross was removed, all things appeared pleasant—I was tranquil.

I now told him, that the Lord had revealed it to me, that I must preach the gospel. He replied, by asking, in what sphere I wished to move in? I said, among the Methodists. He then replied, that a Mrs. Cook, a Methodist lady, had also some time before requested the same privilege; who, it was believed, had done much good in the way of exhortation, and holding prayer meetings; and who had been permitted to do so by the verbal license of the preacher in charge at the time. But as to women preaching, he said that our Discipline knew nothing at all about it—that it did not call for women preachers. This I was glad to hear, because it removed the fear of the cross—but no sooner did this feeling cross my mind, than I found that a love of souls had in a measure departed from me; that holy energy which burned within me, as a fire, began to be smothered.

This I soon perceived.

O how careful ought we to be, lest through our by-laws of church government and discipline, we bring into disrepute even the word of life. For as unseemly as it may appear now-a-days for a woman to preach, it should be remembered that nothing is impossible with God. And why should it be thought impossible, heterodox, or improper for a woman to preach? seeing the Saviour died for the woman as well as for the man.

If the man may preach, because the Saviour died for him, why not the woman? seeing he died for her also. Is he not a whole Saviour, instead of a half one? as those who hold it wrong for a woman to preach, would seem to make it appear.

Did not Mary first preach the risen Saviour, and is not the doctrine of the resurrection the very climax of Christianity—hangs not all our hope on this, as argued by St Paul? Then did not Mary, a woman, preach the gospel? For she preached the resurrection of the crucified son of God.

But some will say that Mary did not expound the Scripture, therefore, she did not preach, in the proper sense of the term. To this I reply, it may be that the term preach in those primitive times, do not mean exactly what it is now made to mean; perhaps it was a great deal more simple then, than it is now—if it were not, the unlearned fishermen could not have preached the gospel at all, as they had no learning.

To this it may be replied, by those who are determined not to believe that it is right for a woman to preach, that the disciples, though they were fishermen and ignorant of letters too, were inspired so to do. To which I would reply, that though they were inspired, yet that inspiration did not save them from showing their ignorance of letters and of man's wisdom; this the multitude soon found out, by listening to the remarks of the envious Jewish priests. If then, to preach the gospel, by the gift of heaven, comes by inspiration solely, is God straitened: must he take the man exclusively? May he not, did he not, and can he not inspire a female to preach the simple story of the birth, life, death, and resurrection of our Lord, and accompany it too with power to the sinner's heart. As for me, I am fully persuaded that the Lord called me to labor according to what I have received, in his vineyard. If he has not, how could he consistently hear testimony in favor of my poor labors, in awakening and converting sinners?

. . .

The Subject Of My Call To Preach Renewed

It was now eight years since I had made application to be permitted to preach the gospel, during which time I had only been allowed to exhort, and even this privilege but seldom. This subject now was renewed afresh in my mind; it was as a fire shut up in my bones. About thirteen months passed on, while under this renewed impression. During this time, I had solicited of the Rev. Bishop, Richard Allen, who at this time had become Bishop of the African Episcopal Methodists in America, to be permitted the liberty of holding prayer meetings in my own hired house, and of exhorting as I found liberty, which was granted me. By this means, my mind was relieved, as the house soon filled when the hour appointed for prayer had arrived.

. . .

I now sat down, scarcely knowing what I had done, being frightened. I imagined, that for this indecorum, as I feared it might be called, I should be expelled from the church. But instead of this, the Bishop rose up in the assembly, and related that I had called upon him eight years before, asking to be permitted to preach, and that he had put me off; but that he now as much believed that I was called to that work, as any of the preachers present. These remarks greatly strengthened me, so that my fears of having given an offence, and made myself liable as an offender, subsided, giving place to a sweet serenity, a holy joy of a peculiar kind, untasted in my bosom until then.

Acres of Diamonds (1913)

RUSSELL CONWELL

. . .

The "Acres of Diamonds" which I have mentioned through so many years are to be found in this city, and you are to find them. Many have found them. And what man has done, man can do. I could not find anything better to illustrate my thought than a story I have told over and over again, and which is now found in books in nearly every library.

In 1870 we went down the Tigris River. We hired a guide at Bagdad to show us Persepolis, Nineveh and Babylon, and the ancient countries of Assyria as far as the Arabian Gulf. He was well acquainted with the land, but he was one of those guides who love to entertain their patrons; he was like a barber that tells you many stories in order to keep your mind off the scratching and the scraping. He told me so many stories that I grew tired of his telling them and I refused to listen—looked away whenever he commenced; that made the guide quite angry.

I remember that toward evening he took his Turkish cap off his head and swung it around in the air. The gesture I did not understand and I did not dare look at him for fear I should become the victim of another story. But, although I am not a woman, I did look, and the instant I turned my eyes upon that worthy guide he was off again. Said he, "I will tell you a story now which I reserve for my particular friends!" So then, counting myself a particular friend, I listened, and I have always been glad I did.

He said there once lived not far from the River Indus an ancient Persian by the name of Al Hafed. He said that Al Hafed owned a very large farm with orchards, grain fields and gardens. He was a contented and wealthy man—contented because he was wealthy, and wealthy because he was contented. One day there visited this old farmer one of those ancient Buddhist priests, and he sat down by Al Hafed's fire and told that old farmer how this world of ours was made.

He said that this world was once a mere bank of fog, which is scientifically true, and he said that the Almighty thrust his finger into the bank of fog and then began slowly to move his finger around and gradually to increase the speed of his finger until at last he whirled that bank of fog into a solid ball of fire, and it went rolling through the universe, burning its way through other cosmic banks of fog, until it condensed the moisture without, and fell in floods of rain upon the heated surface and cooled the outward crust. Then the internal flames burst through the cooling crust and threw up the mountains and made the hills and the valleys of this wonderful world of ours. If this internal melted mass burst out and cooled very quickly it became granite; that which cooled less quickly became silver; and less quickly, gold; and after gold, diamonds were made. Said the old priest, "A diamond is a congealed drop of sunlight."

This is a scientific truth also. You all know that a diamond is pure carbon, actually deposited sunlight—and he said another thing I would not forget: he declared that a diamond is the last and highest of God's mineral creations, as a woman is the last and highest of God's animal creations. I suppose that is the reason why the two have such a liking for each other. And the old priest told Al Hafed that if he had a handful of diamonds he could purchase a whole country, and with a mine of diamonds he could place his children upon thrones through the influence of their great wealth.

Al Hafed heard all about diamonds and how much they were worth, and went to his bed that night a poor man—not that he had lost anything, but poor because he was discontented and discontented because he thought he was poor. He said: "I want a mine of diamonds!" So he lay awake all night, and early in the morning sought out the priest.

Now I know from experience that a priest when awakened early in the morning is cross. He awoke that priest out of his dreams and said to him, "Will you tell me where I can find diamonds?" The priest said, "Diamonds? What do you want with diamonds?" "I want to be immensely rich," said Al Hafed, "but I don't know where to go." "Well," said the priest, "if you will find a river that runs over white sand between high mountains, in those sands you will always see diamonds." "Do you really believe that there is such a river?" "Plenty of them, plenty of them; all you have to do is just go and find them, then you have them." Al Hafed said, "I will go." So he sold his farm, collected his money at interest, left his family in charge of a neighbor, and away he went in search of diamonds.

He began very properly, to my mind, at the Mountains of the Moon. Afterwards he went around into Palestine, then wandered on into Europe, and at last, when his money was all spent, and he was in rags, wretchedness and poverty, he stood on the shore of that bay in Barcelona, Spain, when a tidal wave came rolling in through the Pillars of Hercules and the poor, afflicted, suffering man could not resist the awful temptation to cast himself into that incoming tide, and he sank beneath its foaming crest, never to rise in this life again.

When that old guide had told me that very sad story, he stopped the camel I was riding and went back to fix the baggage on one of the other camels, and I remember thinking to myself, "Why did he reserve that for his particular friends?" There seemed to be no beginning, middle or end—nothing to it. That was the first story I ever heard told or read in which the hero was killed in the first chapter. I had but one chapter of that story and the hero was dead.

When the guide came back and took up the halter of my camel again, he went right on with the same story. He said that Al Hafed's successor led his camel out into the garden to drink, and as that camel put its nose down into the clear water of the garden brook Al Hafed's successor noticed a curious flash of light from the sands of the shallow stream, and reaching in he pulled out a black stone having an eye of light that reflected all the colors of the rainbow, and he took that curious pebble into the house and left it on the mantel, then went on his way and forgot all about it.

A few days after that, this same old priest who told Al Hafed how diamonds were made, came in to visit his successor, when he saw that flash of light from the mantel. He rushed up and said, "Here is a diamond—here is a diamond! Has Al Hafed returned?" "No, no; Al Hafed has not returned and that is not a diamond; that is nothing but a stone; we found it right out here in our garden." "But I know a diamond when I see it," said he; "that is a diamond!"

Then together they rushed to the garden and stirred up the white sands with their fingers and found others more beautiful, more valuable diamonds than the first, and thus, said the guide to me, were discovered the diamond mines of Golconda, the most magnificent diamond mines in all the history of mankind, exceeding the Kimberley in its value. The great Kohinoor diamond in England's crown jewels and the largest crown diamond on earth in Russia's crown jewels, which I had often hoped she would have to sell before they had peace with Japan, came from that mine, and when the old guide had called my attention to that wonderful discovery he took his Turkish cap off his head again and swung it around in the air to call my attention to the moral.

Those Arab guides have a moral to each story, though the stories are not always moral. He said had Al Hafed remained at home and dug in his own cellar or in his own garden, instead of wretchedness, starvation, poverty and death—a strange land, he would have had "acres of diamonds"—for every acre, yes, every shovelful of that old farm afterwards revealed the gems which since have decorated the crowns of monarchs. When he had given the moral to his story, I saw why he had reserved this story for his "particular friends." I didn't tell him I could see it; I was not going to tell that old Arab that I could see it. For it was that mean old Arab's way of going around such a thing, like a lawyer, and saying indirectly what he did not dare say directly, that there was a certain young man that day traveling down the Tigris River that might better be at home in America. I didn't tell him I could see it.

. . .

I say you ought to be rich; you have no right to be poor. To live in Philadelphia and not be rich is a misfortune, and it is doubly a misfortune, because you could have been rich just as well as be poor. Philadelphia furnishes so many opportunities. You ought to be rich. But persons with certain religious prejudice will ask, "How can you spend your time advising the rising generation to give their time to getting money—dollars and cents—the commercial spirit?"

Yet I must say that you ought to spend time getting rich. You and I know there are some things more valuable than money; of course, we do. Ah, yes! By a heart made unspeakably sad by a grave on which the autumn leaves now fall, I know there are some things higher and grander and sublimer than money. Well does the man know, who has suffered, that there are some things sweeter and holier and more sacred than gold. Nevertheless, the man of common sense also knows that there is not any one of those things that is not greatly enhanced by the use of money. Money is power.

Love is the grandest thing on God's earth, but fortunate the lover who has plenty of money. Money is power: money has powers; and for a man to say, "I do not want money," is to say, "I do not wish to do any good to my fellowmen." It is absurd thus to talk. It is absurd to disconnect them. This is a wonderfully great life, and you ought to spend your time getting money, because of the power there is in money. And yet this religious prejudice is so great that some people think it is a great honor to be one of God's poor. I am looking in the faces of people who think just that way.

I heard a man once say in a prayer-meeting that he was thankful that he was one of God's poor, and then I silently wondered what his wife would say to that speech, as she took in washing to support the man while he sat and smoked on the veranda. I don't want to see any more of that kind of God's poor. Now, when a man could have been rich just as well, and he is now weak because he is poor, he has done some great wrong; he has been untruthful to himself; he has been unkind to his fellowmen. We ought to get rich if we can by honorable and Christian methods, and these are the only methods that sweep us quickly toward the goal of riches.

I remember, not many years ago, a young theological student who came into my office and said to me that he thought it was his duty to come in and "labor with me." I asked him what had happened, and he said: "I feel it is my duty to come in and speak to you, sir, and say that the Holy Scriptures declare that money is the root of all evil." I asked him where he found that saying, and he said he found it in the Bible. I asked him whether he had made a new Bible, and he said, no, he had not gotten a new Bible, that it was in the old Bible. "Well," I said, "if it is in my Bible, I never saw it. Will you please get the textbook and let me see it?"

He left the room and soon came stalking in with his Bible open, with all the bigoted pride of the narrow sectarian, who founds his creed on some misinterpretation of Scripture, and he puts the Bible down on the table before me and fairly squealed into my ear, "There it is. You can read it for yourself." I said to him, "Young man, you will learn, when you get a little older, that you cannot trust another denomination to read the Bible for you." I said, "Now, you belong to another denomination. Please read it to me, and remember that you are taught in a school where emphasis is exegesis." So he took the Bible and read it: "The love of money is the root of all evil." Then he had it right.

The Great Book has come back into the esteem and love of the people, and into the respect of the greatest minds of earth, and now you can quote it and rest your life and your death on it without more fear. So, when he quoted right from the Scriptures he quoted the truth. "The love of money is the root of all evil." Oh, that is it. It is the worship of the means instead of the end. Though you cannot reach the end without the means. When a man makes an idol of the money instead of the purposes for which it may be used, when he squeezes the dollar until the eagle squeals, then it is made the root of all evil. Think, if you only had the money, what you could do for your wife, your child, and for your home and your city. Think how soon you could endow the Temple College yonder if you only had the money and the disposition to give it; and yet, my friend, people say you and I should not spend the time getting rich. How inconsistent the whole thing is. We ought to be rich, because money has power.

. . .

But there are ever coming to me young men who say, "I would like to go into business, but I cannot." "Why not?" "Because I have no capital to begin on." Capital, capital to begin on! What! young man! Living in Philadelphia and looking at this wealthy generation, all of whom began as poor boys, and you want capital to begin on? It is fortunate for you that you have no capital. I am glad you have no money. I pity a rich man's son. A rich man's son in these days of ours occupies a very difficult position. They are to be pitied. A rich man's son cannot know the very best things in human life. He cannot. The statistics of Massachusetts show us that not one out of seventeen rich men's sons ever die rich. They are raised in luxury, they die in poverty. Even if a rich man's son retains his father's money, even then he cannot know the best things of life.

A young man in our college yonder asked me to formulate for him what I thought was the happiest hour in a man's history, and I studied it long and came back convinced that the happiest hour that any man ever sees in any earthly matter is when a young man takes his bride over the threshold of the door, for the first time, of the house he himself has earned and built, when he turns to his bride and with an eloquence greater than any language of mine, he sayeth to his wife, "My loved one, I earned this home myself; I earned it all. It is all mine, and I divide it with thee." That is the grandest moment a human heart may ever see. But a rich man's son cannot know that. He goes into a finer mansion, it may be, but he is obliged to go through the house and say, "Mother gave me this, mother gave me that, my mother gave me that, my mother gave me that," until his wife wishes she had married his mother.

. . .

He who can give to this people better streets, better homes, better schools, better churches, more religion, more of happiness, more of God, he that can be a blessing to the community in which he lives tonight will be great anywhere, but he who cannot be a blessing where he now lives will never be great anywhere on the face of God's earth. "We live in deeds, not years, in feeling, not in figures on a dial; in thoughts, not breaths; we should count time by heart throbs, in the cause of right." Bailey says: "He most lives who thinks most."

If you forget everything I have said to you, do not forget this, because it contains more in two lines than all I have said. Bailey says: "He most lives who thinks most, who feels the noblest, and who acts the best."

World's Christian Fundamentals Association Doctrinal Statement (Symphony Hall, Philadelphia 1919)

WILLIAM BELL RILEY, CHARLES BLANCHARD, ET AL.

1. We believe in the Scriptures of the Old and New Testaments as verbally inspired of God, and inerrant in the original writings, and that they are the supreme and final authority in faith and life.
2. We believe in one God, eternally existing in three persons, Father, Son and Holy Spirit.
3. We believe that Jesus Christ was begotten by the Holy Spirit, and born of the Virgin Mary, and is true God and true man.
4. We believe that man was created in the image of God, that he sinned and thereby incurred not only physical death, but also that spiritual death which is separation from God, and that all human beings are born with a sinful nature, and, in the case of those who reach moral responsibility, become sinners in thought, word, and deed.
5. We believe that the Lord Jesus Christ died for our sins according to the Scriptures as a representative and substitutionary sacrifice; and that all who believe in Him are justified on the ground of his shed blood.
6. We believe in the resurrection of the crucified body of our Lord, in His ascension into heaven, and in His present life there for us, as High Priest and Advocate.
7. We believe in "that blessed hope," the personal, premillennial and imminent return of our Lord and Saviour Jesus Christ.
8. We believe that all who receive by faith the Lord Jesus Christ are born again of the Holy Spirit, and thereby become the children of God.
9. We believe in the bodily resurrection of the just and the unjust, the everlasting blessedness of the saved, and the everlasting, conscious punishment of the lost.

The Holy Koran of The Moorish Science Temple, "Circle 7 Koran" (1927)

Divinely Prepared by the Noble Prophet Drew Ali

By the guiding of his father God, Allah; the great God of the universe. To redeem man from his sinful and fallen stage of humanity back to the highest plane of life with his father God, Allah.

The genealogy of Jesus with eighteen years of the events, life works and teachings in India, Europe and Africa. These events occurred before He was thirty years of age. These secret lessons are for all of those who love Jesus and desire to know about his life works and teachings.

Dear readers, do not falsely use these lessons. They are for good, peace and happiness for all those that love Jesus.

Dear mothers, teach these lessons to your little ones, that they may learn to love instead of hate.

Dear fathers, by these lessons you can set your house in order and your children will learn to love instead of hate.

The lessons of this pamphlet are not for sale, but for the sake of humanity, as I am a prophet and the servant is worthy of his hire, you can receive this pamphlet at expense. The reason these lessons have not been known is because the Moslems of India, Egypt and Palestine had these secrets and kept them back from the outside world, and when the time appointed by Allah they loosened the keys and freed the secrets, and for the first time in ages have these secrets been delivered in the hands of the Moslems of America. All authority and rights of publishing of this pamphlet of 1927.

By the Prophet
NOBLE DREW ALI

The industrious acts of the Moslems of the northwest and southwest Africa. These are the Moabites, Hamathites, Canaanites, who were driven out of the land of Canaan, by Joshua, and received permission from the Pharoahs of Egypt to settle in that portion of Egypt. In later years they formed themselves kingdoms. These kingdoms are called this day Morocco, Algiers, Tunis, Tripoli, etc.

. . .

The End of Time and the Fulfilling of the Prophesies

1. The last Prophet in these days is Noble Drew Ali, who was prepared divinely in due time by Allah to redeem men from their sinful ways; and to warn them of the great wrath which is sure to come upon the earth.

2. John the Baptist was the forerunner of Jesus in those days, to warn and stir up the nation and prepare them to receive the divine creed which was to be taught by Jesus.
3. In these modern days there came a forerunner of Jesus, who was divinely prepared by the great God-Allah and his name is Marcus Garvey, who did teach and warn the nations of the earth to prepare to meet the coming Prophet; who was to bring the true and divine Creed of Islam, and his name is Noble Drew Ali who was prepared and sent to this earth by Allah, to teach the old time religion and the everlasting gospel to the sons of men. That every nation shall and must worship under their own vine and fig tree, and return to their own and be one with their Father God-Allah.
4. The Moorish Science Temple of America is a lawfully chartered and incorporated organization. Any subordinate Temple that desires to receive a charter; the prophet has them to issue to every state throughout the United States, etc.
5. That the world may hear and know the truth, that among the descendants of Africa there is still much wisdom to be learned in these days for the redemption of the sons of men under Love, Truth, Peace, Freedom, and Justice.
6. We, as a clean and pure nation descended from the inhabitants of Africa, do not desire to amalgamate or marry into the families of the pale skin nations of Europe. Neither serve the gods of their religion, because our forefathers are the true and divine founders of the first religious creed, for the redemption and salvation of mankind on earth.
7. Therefore we are returning the Church and Christianity back to the European Nations, as it was prepared by their forefathers for their earthly salvation.
8. While we, the Moorish Americans are returning to Islam, which was founded by our forefathers for our earthly and divine salvation.
9. The covenant of the great God-Allah: "Honor they father and they mother that thy days may be longer upon the earth land, which the Lord thy God, Allah hath given thee!"
10. Come all ye Asiatics of America and hear the truth about your nationality and birthrights, because you are not negroes. Learn of your forefathers ancient and divine Creed. That you will learn to love instead of hate.
11. We are trying to uplift fallen humanity. Come and link yourselves with the families of nations. We honor all the true and divine prophets.

Section I

Religion and the City

Richard Kent Evans • World Religions

Lucy Lippard • "The Best-Laid Plans and Public Places" in *The Lure of the Local: Senses of Place in a Multicentered Society*

"World Religions"

Richard Kent Evans

If you sign up for a class in Geology, you probably have a good idea of what you are getting into. You are going to be studying rocks. Yes, some rocks are called minerals, some are dissolved in water, some are surprisingly soft, and some are very old. But they are still rocks. You can hold a rock in your hand. You can touch it. You can feel it. No one doubts that rocks exist. No one argues whether something is rockier than something else. Rocks are real. Religion is very different. You cannot pick up religion or hold it in your hands. Religion is a category that people use to label one cluster of ideas, beliefs, and practices as set apart from other kinds of ideas, beliefs, and practices. The purpose of this essay is to orient students to what it is that scholars mean by the term religion.

When people say *religion* they usually mean something like a "belief in or acknowledgement of some superhuman power or powers (esp. a god or gods) which is typically manifested in obedience, reverence, and worship; such a belief as part of a system defining a code of living, esp. as a means of achieving spiritual or material improvement." This definition from the Oxford English Dictionary is the most common usage of the term, at least in the modern United States. However, if this is what we mean by religion, then it is a very recent and geographically bounded phenomenon. Nobody before the sixteenth century, and very few people outside of Europe through the nineteenth century, thought that believing in superhuman powers, practicing obedience, reverence, and worship, or being a part of a system of living meant belonging to a "religion." What we now call *religion* was inseparable from day-to-day life. Until around four hundred years ago, most human cultures simply did not divide the world into one set of special experiences, beliefs, and practices that are set apart from more ordinary experiences, beliefs, and practices.[1]

The definition of religion that seems familiar to us began to emerge in the mid-sixteenth century after the Protestant Reformation launched a hundred years of warfare between Catholics and Protestants in Europe. The Protestant Reformation began after a German priest named Martin Luther published the Ninety-Five Theses, a document criticizing the Catholic Church. Luther's criticisms launched several schisms that separated groups including the Lutherans, Calvinists, Anabaptists, and others from the Catholic Church based in Rome. Martin Luther was not the first person to challenge the Roman Church. What was different about the Protestant Reformation was that, for the first time, the Church's challengers had enough political support to actually take on the church in Rome and communications technology—notably the Gutenberg printing press—allowed for the easy dissemination of religious tracts and Bible translations. But the Protestant Reformation was not an easy split. Reformers and their supporters took up arms against what was left of the Holy Roman Empire. Secular and religious authorities interested in protecting the power of the Roman Catholic Church cracked down on Reformers, often quite violently. Over the next hundred years, Europe split into nation-states, each with its own official state religion. Catholic countries warred with Protestant ones, Protestant countries warred against other Protestant countries, and the deaths mounted. Historians estimate that the number of people who died in the wars that resulted from the Protestant Reformation may range into the tens of millions.[2]

After the Wars of Religion ended in 1648 with the Treaty of Westphalia, intellectuals and philosophers in Western Europe and the American colonies began to develop new ideas about the role of religion in social life. This intellectual movement, which we today call the Enlightenment, put forth the idea that the constant religious violence in Europe might end if Protestants and Catholics realized that they had more in common than they thought. Many Enlightenment thinkers were Deists. Deists believed that all religions, at their core, featured a single Creator God and offered similar moral codes. Deists argued that there was once a single Original Religion in the world and that the Original Religion changed over time and developed unique expressions in various corners of the globe. Change over time had given rise to the world's religious diversity. Deists rejected the Reformers' and Catholic Church's argument that their respective religions represented the one true religion. Instead, Deists believed, no single religion could claim to have exclusive truth because all of the world's religions were imperfect descendants of the Original Religion. Philadelphia's own Benjamin Franklin played a central role in Deism's study of this Original Religion. His publication, the *Pennsylvania Gazette*, pointed out the similarities between the teachings of Confucius and Jesus and drew parallels between Islam and Christianity. Franklin and the Deists were interested in demonstrating how all religions contained a kernel of truth because they hoped that religious people in Europe would stop killing one another over religious difference.[3]

The study of religion took on a greater urgency in the nineteenth century because Europeans and Americans were increasingly coming into contact with foreign cultures as they expanded their empires. These highly developed civilizations with rich spiritual traditions posed a theological problem for Christian Europeans who were interested in the comparative study of religion: were all of these people going to hell? Nineteenth century Christians read the Bible as presenting a world in which there are four different types of religious people. God first entered into a covenant with the Jews who could receive salvation through following God's Law as given to Moses. The New Testament also speaks about the growing community devoted to following the teachings of Jesus, who would later become known as Christians. In addition to Jews and Christians, the Bible speaks about Pagans, a catchall term that biblical authors used to describe the worship of the Greco-Roman pantheon and those who practiced magic, worshiped nature, and pursued pleasure. The New Testament, especially Paul's epistles, warned of heretics—people who claim to speak on behalf of Christ but who are actually false prophets. While Muslims saw the Prophet Muhammad as the final prophet in a chain that included Abraham, Isaac, and Jesus, many Christians interpreted the rise of Islam in the seventh century A.D. as the development of a Christian heresy. This made sense to many Christians until the Age of Colonialism in the nineteenth century. As Europeans and Americans expanded their empires into Asia, India, Africa, and the American West, they came face-to-face with highly developed cultures with ancient religious traditions. This posed a theological problem for Christians interested in other religions: how is it possible that salvation could be limited to only Christians? Were these ancient religious traditions, some of which were far older than Christianity, mistaken? Were all of these non-Christian people damned to hell?[4]

One approach to solving this dilemma of salvation was the development of the theological approach to comparative religions in the mid-nineteenth century. The scholars who developed this approach, who were mostly Protestant theologians teaching at American and British seminaries, wanted to prove that Christianity was the one true religion. They turned the Deists' theory of Original Religion on its head. Instead of arguing that God had bestowed upon early humankind a perfect revelation that had devolved over time into the religious diversity we see today, nineteenth-century religion scholars applied Charles Darwin's theory of evolution to argue that all of the world's religions were evolving *toward* the one true religion, Protestant Christianity. Their reason for pursing this approach to religion is obvious: they were Christians, themselves, and wanted to teach other Christians why the rest of the world's religions were wrong. In 1852, James Moffat, one of America's first religious studies scholars said that the purpose of studying religion was to compare the different cultures of the world "by the corresponding degrees of Christian knowledge. From the midnight blackness of Hindoosim, through Mohammedanism [Islam], and Romanism [Catholicism], and formal Protestantism, to the humble, intelligent and faithful follower of the Word of God, you may distinctly grade the ascending scale of humanity." Moffat ranked the world religions according to theories of cultural evolution. The most "primitive" religion, in his opinion, was the religion of "Hindooism." The most advanced religion was the kind of evangelical Protestantism he practiced. Moffat's approach to religion was built on the theological assumption that Protestant Christianity was the only true religion. Every other religion, if compared to Protestant Christianity, would come up short.[5]

The next generation of religion scholars sought to replace the theologians' approach to religion with a more "scientific" approach. How could it be that God had given a revelation that was limited to relatively few people on the planet? How could all of the other deeply religious cultures of the world all be gravely mistaken? This group of scholars developed a new way of categorizing religious diversity: World Religions. A classic example of this approach is the 1893 World's Parliament of Religions. The Parliament was meant to offer a corrective to the nativist movements of the time. The dramatic increase in immigration into the United States toward the end of the nineteenth century, most of it from countries outside of Western Europe, led to a fairly robust nativist backlash among some white Protestants. The organizers of the World's Parliament of Religions hoped that increased education about the other religions of the world could counter this nativist backlash. The parliament featured representatives of over a dozen major religions including Buddhism, Islam, Hinduism, Taoism, Confucianism, Jainism, Zoroastriansim, and Shintoism. The representatives of these "World Religions" were asked to demonstrate their religious practices, explain their basic religious philosophy, and demonstrate the typical characteristics shared by adherents to their religion through common dress, diet, music, and ritual. The logic underlying the World's Parliament of Religions—the spiritual unity of all religions, that all religions serve essentially the same purpose, and that *any* religion is better than no religion at all—is the logic of pluralism and is a chief reason why religious studies is considered so important today.[6]

World Religions was a less exclusionary way for scholars of religion to make sense of the world's religious diversity, but it also forced the other major world religions to fit a nineteenth-century Protestant paradigm of what religion should be. For example, scholars hoping to add the religions of India to the pantheon of World Religions sometimes fabricated religions where they had not been before. Hinduism was a term invented by British colonial officials to describe the cultural practices of a wide variety of ethnic groups living near the Indus River.[7] What was once spoken of as "the philosophy of the Hindus" became, over time, a World Religion called Hinduism which was comparable to other World Religions. Similarly, Western colonialists began calling the "religion of the Buddha" by the word Buddhism. Simply by grouping, naming, and studying diverse religious beliefs and practices within these categories of Hinduism, Buddhism, and Confucianism, World Religions scholars invented entirely new religious traditions. This is not to say that these cultures did not have beliefs and practices that we could call religious, but rather, that the nineteenth-century World Religions model consolidated these local beliefs and practices into something more abstract, gave it a catchy name, and suggested that these new additions were analogous to other World Religions.[8]

The World Religions approach to studying religion opened the door for the academic study of religion. In the 1890s, the first religion departments emerged, first at the University of Chicago and then at the University of Pennsylvania. Early religious studies fully embraced the World Religions model of studying religion with the assumption that religion was a universal phenomenon that manifested in various, culturally specific World Religions. A leading figure in the emergence of the field of religious studies was Max Müller, a scholar who studied the religions of India at Oxford University from 1850 to 1875. Müller set out to make the study of religion into a "scientific" pursuit. He believed that science and religion were incompatible. Since science would eventually replace religion, his theologically oriented colleagues' efforts to prove Christianity as the one true religion were based on a false assumption. Instead, he thought scholars of religion should look for the characteristics shared by all of the world's religions. This "scientific" approach to religion was very different from the blatantly theological study of comparative religion that it replaced. Instead of comparing religions, Müller was interested in *categorizing* them. Müller argued that the variety of religions in the world could be explained by a theory he called the "disease of language." All cultures throughout history recognized the profundity of the natural world—the majesty of a sunset, the expanse of the night sky, the miracle of birth—and they tried to come up with words to describe this sense of wonder. Müller used the Greek god Apollo to prove his point. "Apollo" once meant "sun." At some point in ancient pre-history, a Greek person must have been attempting to describe how the sun, which he or she called "Apollo," pointed towards the infinitude of the universe. Over time, "Apollo" became personified. Whereas that theoretical Ancient Greek thinker was once simply referring to a sense of transcendence, later Greek cultures created elaborate backstories and personalities around Apollo. Through the "disease of language," they created a god.[9]

In 1902, a Harvard psychologist named William James developed a new theory of religion that argued against Müller's scientific approach to religion. While Müller's "disease of language" theory could explain why some concepts developed and how certain religious institutions emerged, it could not, James argued, account for the *universal phenomenon* of lived religious experience. Müller made a convincing case as to how Apollo went from meaning "sun" to become a personified deity. But what made Greek people want to believe in a god in the first place? What was it about human nature that makes people religious? James developed a definition of religion that would account for this universality of religious experience. To James, religion was "the feelings, acts, and experiences of individual men in their solitude, so far as they apprehend themselves to stand in relation to whatever they may consider divine." James's definition of religion had two very important consequences. First, it divided religion into an interiorized "faith" and an exteriorized practice. In other words, faith was something that existed in the mind or the "heart" while religious practice was something that that people physically *did*. This division between faith and practice is crucial to the way many people think of themselves today. When people say they are *spiritual but not religious* they are echoing James's division between interior faith and exterior practice. The second consequence of James's definition was that scholars of religion began treating religion as a universal phenomenon. James assumed that everyone throughout history and in all places *experienced* the divine. Though various religions may offer different beliefs and practices intended to orient the believer towards the divine, James believed, every human being shares this desire to experience the divine.[10]

In 1912, a French sociologist named Émile Durkheim revolutionized the field of religious studies. Instead of studying religion as the product of the individual mind, Durkheim studied religion as a product of culture. Durkheim argued that all societies throughout history were built upon a moral foundation, a set of rules that everyone had to follow in order for the society to survive and flourish. These rules of society, he argued, are what we study when we study religion. As evidence, Durkheim used the new anthropologic research on Aboriginal tribes of Australia. Durkheim noticed that these tribes used totems—usually a certain species of animal that was thought to be unusually powerful and special—to represent the clan. Each member of the tribe felt an obligation toward the totem and revered its power. Durkheim used this observation to develop a theory called the Totemic Principle. He argued that the totem serves a function for the tribe. It reminds each member of the tribe of his or her obligations to the greater good. Even though individuals may die, the totem, as the clan, lives on forever. Durkheim believed that this was the essence of religion in every culture—religious symbols, religious rituals, and religious beliefs were all ways of expressing social realities. He believed that a religion was "a unified system of beliefs and practices relative to sacred things, I.e., things set apart and forbidden—beliefs and practices which unite in one single moral community called a Church, all those who adhere to them." To Durkheim, the reason religion exists is to reinforce the social element of life; it serves a social function.[11]

Durkheim's theory was a radical departure from the theories of James and Müller. Both James and Müller thought religion was the product of individual minds. Religion was primarily a collection of *beliefs* about the supernatural world. James and Müller wanted to show how something simple like a belief in God or in something transcendent, became complex religious systems. Durkheim's logic ran the opposite direction. He wanted to show how something that seemed complex (religious systems) were in fact simple social constructions. Though religions *appeared* to be complex webs of ritual and belief, they were simply a culture's way of getting everyone to play by the rules. There was no need, Durkheim argued, to study religion as the product of revelation and invention. When we study religion, we study culture and when we study culture, we study religion. Durkheim made the study of religion historical.

Durkheim's social functionalist definition of religion reigned supreme until 1957 when a religion scholar from the University of Chicago named Mircea Eliade published a book titled *The Sacred and the Profane*. It was Durkheim who first suggested that the essence of religion is dividing the world into those things that are sacred (set apart and special) and those things that are profane (normal, everyday activities with no transcendent meaning). Eliade took this concept of the sacred and the profane and developed a theory of religion that argued against Durkheim's functionalism. To Eliade, the "sacred" was a much more central concept to cultures than Durkheim realized. The sacred was not merely an artificial category that societies created to enforce the rules. Rather, the sacred, to Eliade, was a glimpse into an alternative reality, one with deeper meaning. According to Eliade, the role of religion, in all times and in all cultures, is to promote and enhance connections with the sacred. The sacred is central to day-to-day life in cultures all over the world and throughout every time period. Eliade was struck by what he interpreted as similarities in religious symbols shared by disparate cultures. He found cultures all over the world that had "Son" gods who suffered for mankind's sake, died, and then were resurrected. He found recurring sun and moon deities and supreme sky gods. He also argued that every culture has a sense of a Fall, a primordial event that triggered a separation of our present reality from the infinite. To Eliade, religion was ripe for cross-cultural comparison as long as scholars of religion realized that behind seemingly different religious expressions we can find common notions of the sacred. Eliade's definition of religion brought religious studies full circle. Since Müller, scholars of religion tried to approach religion in a scientific way. This scientific approach assumed that the supernatural was not a *real* phenomenon and that cultures made up gods, spirits, and religions in order to make sense of a confusing world. Eliade, on the other hand, thought that scholars of religion should take the reality of the sacred as a starting point. It doesn't matter to us, as scholars of religion, whether or not the supernatural is a real thing. What matters is that the people we study believe in the supernatural and use it to make sense out of their worlds.[12]

Since the 1970s, the field of religion has grown to encompass a wide variety of definitions of "religion." Many scholars have embraced Geertz's emphasis on studying the relationships people form with religious symbols as a methodology called "lived religion." Contemporary religion scholar Robert Orsi argues that religion is a "network of relationships between heaven and earth" that involve saints, ancestors, demons, gods, and ghosts. In this "lived religion" approach, beliefs, creeds, and institutions are less important than the "things, practices, or presences" that make religion *real* to the devout.[13] Recently, some religion scholars have combined religious studies with neurological and cognition research and in an attempt to identify the biological sources of religious experience. Ann Taves, a pioneer in what has become known as cognitive religion, has argued the human brain is hardwired to consciously and subconsciously interpret some experiences as "special" and that today we call these experiences *religious*, *mystical*, or *spiritual*.[14] Within the last decade, scholars have dramatically expanded the types of beliefs and practices that can be called "religion." For example, a recent, well-received book by religion scholar Kathryn Lofton considers what is gained and lost if we study Oprah as a religion.[15]

After all this, we return to our original question: what is religion? That is a question that might be unanswerable. But if it is unanswerable, it is because there are simply too many beliefs, practices, emotions, sights, smells, sounds, and journeys that we can call "religious." There may be as many varied religious experiences as there are religious people. Religion is a starting point for thinking deeply about many of the most pressing issues in our society today. Through studying religion, you can explore the ways in which space becomes sacred, probe the ultimate meaning human cultures ascribe to death and dying, explore the philosophies and ancient wisdom of faraway places, and develop answers to the social problems of racism and poverty. The study of religion is an exercise in understanding what assumptions, values, and backgrounds we bring to decisions to categorize something as "religious." This is the great value in studying religion and in studying the humanities in general. Whatever career you choose, you will be better at that career if you know how to think deeply, to ask the right questions, and to take no assumption for granted. When we study religion, however we define "religion," we are practicing empathy, widening our scope of knowledge, and—most importantly—learning how to think.

Notes

1. Brent Nongbri, *Before Religion: A History of a Modern Concept* (New Haven: Yale University Press, 2013), 1–24.

2. Daniel L. Pals, *Nine Theories of Religion* (New York: Oxford University Press, 2014), 4–5.

3. James Turner, *Religion Enters the Academy: The Origins of the Scholarly Study of Religion in America* (Athens, GA: The University of Georgia Press, 2011), 12–16; Nongbri, *Before Religion*, 97–99.

4. Jonathan Z. Smith, "Religion, Religions, Religious," in *Critical Terms for Religious Studies*, ed. Mark C. Taylor (Chicago, University of Chicago Press, 1998), 275–280.

5. Turner, *Religion Enters the Academy*, 32.

6. Smith, "Religion, Religions, Religious," in *Critical Terms for Religious Studies*, ed. M. Taylor (Chicago, University of Chicago Press, 1998), 275–82.

7. Julius J. Lipner, "The Rise of 'Hinduism'; Or, How to Invent a World Religion with Only Moderate Success," *International Journal of Hindu Studies* 10 (2006): 93.

8. Wilfred Cantwell Smith, *The Meaning and End of Religion: A New Approach to the Religious Traditions of Mankind* (New York: The Macmillan Company, 1962), 55–67.

9. Max Müller, *Introduction to the Science of Religion: Four Lectures Delivered at the Royal Institution with Two Essays on False Analogies, and the Philosophy of Mythology* (London: Longmans, Green and Co., 1873).

10. William James, *The Varieties of Religious Experience: A Study in Human Nature, Being the Gifford Lectures on Natural Religion Delivered at Edinburgh in 1901–1902* (Edinburgh: Gifford Lectures, 1902), 32.

11. Émile Durkheim, *The Elementary Forms of Religious Life: A Study in Religious Sociology* (New York: The Macmillan Company, 1915), 47.

12. Mircea Eliade, *The Sacred and the Profane: The Nature of Religion* (New York: Harvest, 1957).

13. Robert A. Orsi, *Between Heaven and Earth: The Religious Worlds People Make and the Scholars Who Study Them* (Princeton: Princeton University Press, 2005), 2.

14. Ann Taves, *Religious Experience Reconsidered: A Building-Block Approach to the Study of Religion and Other Special Things* (Princeton: Princeton University Press, 2011).

15. Kathryn Lofton, *Oprah: The Gospel of an Icon* (Berkeley: University of California Press, 2011).

The Best-Laid Plans and Public Places

LUCY LIPPARD

In August 1996, the Bath City Council endorsed four waterfront plans for study, associated with the Carlton Bridge replacement. (The city can ask the state for up to 10 percent of its $]50 million cost, though what is asked will not necessarily be given.) The councillors are discussing what Bath wants to be: "Are we a tourist destination? Do we want light manufacturing? What are we trying to do with our downtown?" Commercial Street, which lies along the water, but has little commerce, is a focal point. Despite its role as gateway into coastal Maine, and roadside signs for the Maine Maritime Museum, Bath has never been much of a tourist town. Since the overhead highway to the bridge split it in two and bridge traffic jams reached epic proportions, people have tended to rush straight through. But now Bath, like every other struggling small town in the country, is revving up its tourist engines. In the 1980s, Front Street was modestly tarted up with brick sidewalks and old fashioned light poles. In 1995, "tourism taskforce" volunteers with the Bath Business Association (B BA) put flowerboxes on downtown sidewalks and street lamps, claiming, "there is a pride in Bath that really is coming to life." (The flowerboxes had been tried before and failed because of lack of involvement; this year's support might be seen as an indication of economic uneasiness.) B BA also sponsors Christmas decoration contests, Halloween window painting competitions, hayrides, scare-crow making and other concocted community exercises.

In 1994 a graduate class at the Harvard School of Design used Bath as a case study and worked on projects with city staff. The Comprehensive Core Planning Committee is still at it, having completed a 200-page document calling for marketing the city as a technological center, developing a hotel or convention center, expanding wharf and waterfront improvements, fixing up rundown neighborhoods and increasing volunteerism. 1996, an architecture professor at the University of Tennessee, son of a Bath city councillor, put in his oar, recommending that the city acquire the Coal Pocket property off Front Street, have a public boat ramp, and create a unified space along the riverfront. Councillors agree that any project that puts more boats on the river will help downtown Bath. Like Bath, Brunswick and Wiscasset have recently fixated on development of or for waterfront recreation. Brunswick, although surrounded on three sides by water—the Androscoggin and New Meadows rivers and some shorefront-has no image as a coastal community. With an eye to tourism and "quality of life" standards, the town is building a fishing park, a wetlands park, bike paths and canoe portages around dams. Wiscasset is planning ahead for the closing of Maine Yankee, which will bring a huge loss of tax revenues. In i995, the expansion of the Bath Savings Institution was described as the "single most important downtown project in 20 years." It will provide Bath's first parking garage—38 spaces. Since there is already a municipal parking lot behind the main street, and I've never had trouble finding a parking place, I assume dreams of commercial growth and tourist hordes fuel this project. For all Bath's attempts to be a tourist town, public tours of the Bath Iron Works have been denied anyone except the occasional group of workers' relatives, schoolchildren or businessmen. Reasons given were safety and military secrets. In the fall of 1996, after months of planning, the precedent was broken and the gates opened for two buses of visitors, sponsored by the Maine Maritime Museum and the Bath Bed and Breakfast Association. Museum director Tom Wilcox said, "The challenge for a history museum is to relate history to the present." The Maritime Museum shows how ships were built in the past, and the Bath Iron Works, showing how they are built now, has been the missing !ink. Not that this will become a common occurrence. A yard spokeswoman said two or three tours a year might be possible now. "It was nice to have people in and show off what we do." The a1w tours may be harbingers of a new "alternative" tourism, which focuses more on respecting what people do in places than on idealized or concocted views of a place.

Planners and designers talk about connecting "iconic" public spaces to "organic" public spaces, or the "formal" with the "informal." Increasingly, our public spaces are neither. Obscured by a certain deceit, they may be disguised as private spaces or they may be private spaces disguised as public. Having tried leafleting and political theater in malls, for instance, I can vouch that they are strictly controlled and patrolled private spaces. "Public" space implies that it is governed by rules, but these should be reached through public consensus, by those who live there. Some reactionaries have argued that the way to get cities under control is to reduce communal spaces, close everyone into their own territories so they will be financially and emotionally forced to defend and maintain them—a bunker mentality.

The contemporary loss of the processional, or ceremonial, aspect of older public buildings built on ancient models to inspire respect or intimidation within daily experience is not always a tragedy. Frequently, though, this aspect has been replaced by a newer aspect that merely reflects all too well the dulling bureaucracies housed within.

When architectural critics bemoan the disappearance of appealing public spaces, they tend to be talking about passive meeting grounds, rather than places where an active social life, even dialogue, can occur. Places that are merely accessible to citizens, rather than controlled by them through use, are not truly public places. If access is minimal, perhaps it threatens to erode power, always best elevated and cut off from those who would share it. Sharon Zukin points out that even those buildings that are owned by taxpayers are now being moved out of towns so they are less and less accessible.

Always settling for too little, grateful for even the most unimaginative open spaces, we become less and less aware of the gap between space perceived and experienced, on the one hand, and space conceived and imagined on the other;

between the way things are (what we actually see) and the way things should be (what they want us to see or what we would like to see)—"they" being the policy-makers, planners, bankers and developers who determine what our public spaces will look like. Henri Lefebvre made this distinction right after the 1968 Paris rebellion, observing that perceived space has been produced, haphazardly, by the process of use, while conceived space is a designed infrastructural product. Places themselves shift functions, sometimes before our very eyes, as when a playground becomes a battleground, or a subway car becomes a theatre with a captive audience. Sometimes the conceptions don't work as expected: malls were not planned as teenage hangouts; heating vents were not planned as homeless campgrounds.

Public space has traditionally been male space, while women are meant to remain secluded in private or domestic places, although places too can be sites of male privilege—as in the proverbial "castle" where men can do anything they want, however violent or abusive. As social relationships between men and women change (although not as fast as we think they have), the nature of public space also undergoes subtle transformations. From spatial division and segregation (in religious, labor, business, and social contexts) to spatial domination and restriction (by law, architecture, custom, class), boundaries in space deprive women of information they need for equality: "For women to become more knowledgeable, they must also change places," writes Daphne Spain. Feminist geographers are demanding a redefinition of public space compatible with feminism's blurring of the boundaries between personal and political, private and public.

Although aware that they are still necessarily defined by exclusion from the male discourse that has defined the discipline, some feminist geographers are trying to go beyond obvious opposition to patriarchy and capitalism and the overgeneralized dichotomies of production/reproduction, public/ private, male/ female (which are themselves social constructs) into the more labyrinthine spaces where class, race and gender intersect. Feminist (and women) artists and writers are also preoccupied with their spatial imaginations, with concepts of inside and outside, expressed from the body to domestic to public to geopolitical spaces.

Feminist analysis of the city tends toward detailed research into the complexity of women's lives. Private spaces, for instance, are not inherently bad places to be, when they are chosen voluntarily. Public spaces can be re-formed by women of all classes who move between public and private, workplace and home—but it is crucial to the process of degendering and decentering that the experience of white middle-class women is not assumed to be the norm. Take, for instance, the ways in which urban spaces differ day and night, weekdays and weekends, the ways they are peopled at different times, reflecting working lives and power relations. Or take the notion of "the other side of the tracks" from both sides of those tracks, as bell hooks writes in her meaningfully tided essay "Choosing the Margin as a Space of Radical Openness." "Feminist geographers are understanding the contemporary city not as the increasing fragmentation of a still coherent whole," writes Gillian Rose, but in terms of "a challenge to that omniscient vision and its exclusions."

By resisting the closure that comes all too often with theorization, feminists are recreating spatial categories on their own terms, including lessons learned from local activism and advocacy planning, from dredging up sources ignored by even the most liberal male geographers. A good example is Christine de Pizan's The Book of the City of Ladies (written between 1399 and 1430) which offers a "new town" created from archaeological and architectural metaphors, using "the pick of understanding," "the trowel of your pen," and "mixing the mortar" to fortify the city. In her critique of planning doctrine, Barbara Hooper cites Pizan as well as Frances Wright's utopian community Nashoba, Charlotte Perkins Gilman's proposals for a feminist housing project, Melusina Faye's contributions to a "domestic revolution," and the settlement house movement, among newly considered antecedents of city planning.

Contemporary urban design is a subject so vast that few experts seem to be able to get a grip on that median strip between reality and desire and have remained incapable of changing the urban karma. Given the fact that city planning has failed so miserably so often, the field itself should be scrutinized more carefully than is possible here. Postmodernist planning seems intellectually aware of the issues and the realities, but it is overtheorized and, when practiced, is too often mired in a blowzy and superficial architectural style.

I'm always being asked why I don't talk more about architecture. Perhaps it's a feminist hangup, or a personal limitation; I just don't respond to most of what is out there as I do to organically evolving forms and less manipulated spaces. Architects and planners can only offer a shell—the more open and flexible, the more likely it is to encourage a built environment that meets its inhabitants halfway. I'd like to see what Stephen A. Kurtz has written about apartments applied to larger contexts: "People are remarkably unaware of how they can alter the basic configurations of their apartments and consequently will spend years accomodating themselves to unnecessary inconveniences. At the same time, because they never touch the shape of the space they have been given, their relationship to it remains passive and alien."

Ralph Waldo Emerson's notion of the city as a "human community" continues to be the stated goal of city planners, but I tend to agree with the (early) Richard Sennett, who wrote in 1970 that "a prohibition on preplanned, functional space is important; because it permits great diversity to arise in city neighborhoods, and because it permits whatever social encounters and conflicts exist in the neighborhood to 'take hold' in the character of the neighborhood itself." In this he reflected the inspiring (and to present-day eyes somewhat naive) optimism of Jane Jacobs, who wrote in 1961, "it is the thousands of individuals who create, by making their own choices and operating without guidance from the planners, the exciting fabric of the cosmopolitan city." Sennett at that time was arguing still more radically for virtual anarchism in order to force people to take control of their own lives, their own cities. Murray Bookchin, in the early seventies, also condemned city planning as primarily remedial, behind the times, and steeped in mistrust of populist spontaneity. A decade later, Colin Ward held that contemporary urban design is a megalomaniacal fantasy; its idealized drawings, he said, bear little relation to social conditions, to class structure, and the influence of design on governmental processes and communal life. "The most grandiose and expensive models for a mechanized future have been imposed on the poorest and most dispirited communities." On the other hand, Ward can be overly fatalistic, insisting that cities have always been "bywords for misery and despair," and their decline, "with their industrial raison d'être, is nobody's fault, it is simply one of the facts of urban history."

Urban planner David Lee suggests the following criteria for "a great public space": It is not anyone's private turf; it should be memorable enough that you would want to have your picture taken there; it is a place you couldn't wait to go to without your parents, a place where there is sunlight sometime every day, and there can be music, poetry, art, and speeches—enough visual drama and/or activity that you can send your out-of-town guests there to amuse themselves while you try to get some work done; it should not cost a lot to get to, and it should be clean, but not too tidy. I'd add to this list that it should include a place where peace and quiet is as available as entertainment—though I know that none of these qualities will enhance anything but the most superficial public interaction. Public spaces created for privacy are too easily transformed into private places that exclude the public. These "great places" are primarily about opportunities for private enjoyment. None of them can replace a main street, regular intergenerational dialogue, local or civic organizations, even a church or a workplace despite all their implied restrictions.

This need to pin down the notion of "great" places seems to obsess us like the equally unnecessary need to identify once and for all a definition of "great art," while forgetting that a vast range of tastes is involved. In May 1995 the results of the Lyndhurst Foundation's "Search for Great American Public Places" were released. (Interestingly, it went without saying that these were human-made places.) Suggestions were solicited here and there from the public, but the sixty- three "winners" were ultimately chosen by "a panel of experts" (consisting of writers, developers, architects, designers, teachers, and politicians) directed by Gianni Longo. The panel responded with "a sense of urgency" to supply models for "the builders, bankers and developers who are generally not exposed to them and yet make all the decisions affecting the appearance of our towns," as panel member James Howard Kunstler put it. (One alternative would be to strategize about how to keep these people from making all our decisions.)

The chosen models range (alphabetically and otherwise) from Acoma Pueblo and the Appalachian Trail to Xenia Avenue (the main street of Yellow Springs, ' Ohio), and something called Yorkship in Camden, New Jersey. It is a fascinating and inevitably eclectic list: a different panel would have come up with a different list, and yet another panel with yet another list, though there are some predictable entries amid the puzzling ones. Many of the obvious great American public places are noted as "endangered," including Santa Fe's Plaza, New York's Coney Island, and Times Square, I can only speak for those places I know, but I would have added many more as "endangered" by well-intended over-redevelopment and tarted-up tourist traps. The list focuses on the East Coast, Southeast, and West/Northwest coast, clearly reflecting the makeup of the panel (with a few exceptions, such as Daniel Kemmis, the astute writer on civic responsibility and mayor of Missoula, Montana). "Nature" as a whole, and the Midwest and the West, in particular, are overlooked: New Mexico is the only South/Mountain Western state represented; there is "nothing" in Arizona, Colorado, Wyoming, Utah, Nevada, the Dakotas, Idaho, or Montana, and "nothing" in Chicago (one of my favorite cities). Surprisingly, not even Charleston, South Carolina, made the list.

Longo is also involved with a more democratically oriented group called Urban Initiatives which holds community meetings with small to large cities and regions all over the country, helping them to identify and then to expedite their local goals for improving their places. The first of these was held in Chatanooga, Tennessee, in 1984, right after it had been voted America's dirtiest city, which jolted its citizens into envisioning what they would rather be. Today, according to good press, Chatanooga's river is full of fish, its air is clean, traffic jams are gone, a freshwater aquarium and teenage pregnancy center have been installed, a downtown park and an old theater renovated, and the country's first "zero-emission" urban industrial park is attracting manufacturing companies downtown.

Busy with our daily lives, few of us are even aware of how our locales are changing until it is too late to affect decisions made elsewhere. In my lifetime, the whole concept of "downtown" as a public space has altered. It is no longer where the action is, where people gather to shop, hang out, show off, promenade, cruise, and meet for a movie, lunch, coffee, or a drink; it has been fragmented and homogenized until big cities function merely as extended shopping malls.

Public spaces have been broken down into those dominated by popular culture (streets), by mass culture (malls), by high culture (museums), by corporate culture (office buildings), and by official culture (government structures). Moreover, popular and mass culture have become almost placeless because of their electronic base. Is the World Wide Web a place? And if so, is it public or private? What about all those "home pages" where the number of "visitors" are avidly courted and counted? Such intangible "places" are all the more susceptible to control—for example, the ongoing, but losing, struggle for public control of public-access TV. Stanley Aronowitz has suggested that talk radio is the new public space, but it too is firmly controlled: dissenting callers are screened or jeered off the air. In a real public space you can debate and communicate with those on the soapboxes. There are no "moderators" except for what unspoken custom and courtesy are left.

In artificially constructed cities, says Bookchin, "neighborliness is mistaken for organic social intercourse and mutual aid; well-manicured parks for the harmonization of humanity with nature. . . . an eclectic mix of ranch houses, slab-like apartment buildings, and bachelor-type flats for spontaneous architectural variety; shopping-mart plazas and a vast expanse of lawn for the agora. . . ." Some days it's hard not to be as cranky as Bookchin sounds here. (My nearest grocery store, on a small plaza in a suburban development town with a Spanish name, is incongruously called "The Agora.") One way to forestall frustration is to map one's own community and its cultural and class interconnections. This process facilitates memory and can raise political and historical consciousness, pointing us in the direction we'd like to act. A student of architect Denise Scott Brown mapped and photographed every site in a local social services directory in Cambridge, Massachusetts, in order to flesh out the terms public and private. From detox centers and ethnic community groups to libraries and schools, said Brown, "the relation each had with its street and with its community, when you saw the whole lot together, was very moving."

It seems that we as a society are beginning to listen more carefully to the echoes from a lost or neglected world of "local attachments," even from churches or sports clubs or other organizations that the ultra cool might ordinarily avoid like poison. But we don't know how to reconstruct them organically in our own contemporary image, and it's pretty clear that the artificial versions don't work. Even as cities become increasingly abstracted from the experiences that form them, "featureless distancing" and "spatial disjuncture" make the urban landscape generally unsatisfying. The need grows for "a truly associational space."

Margo Huxley says cities are "our treasure houses of cultural capital and wisdom, and to destroy them would be to will a state of collective amnesia," and Dolores Hayden recommends that we "learn to design with memory rather than against it." I like that idea, which, I assume, precludes the thoughtless destruction of buildings and neighborhoods, and includes a frenzy of rehabbing, remodeling, and revisioning. Different people will be plugged into different memories, not all sweet or even bittersweet. Some will have short memories, others will cultivate longer ones.

Notes

Henri Lefebvre, *The Production of Space,* Oxford: Basil Blackwell, 1991. Places shift functions: this came up in a student dialogue in Don Mitchell's seminar, 1993.

J.B. Jackson, *Landscapes.* Bath City Council: TR, Aug. 8, 1996.

Jane Flax, "Postmodernism and Gender Relations in Feminist Theory," in L. J. Nicholson, *Feminism/Postmodernism,* New York: Routledge, 1990.

Bath Busines Association, quoted in TR, July 5, 1995.

bell hooks, *Yearning.*

Gillian Rose, *Feminism and Geography,* Minneapolis: University of Minnesota Press, 1993.

David Lee, GSD *News.* Great American Public Places: I have seen only the press release, which listed "Portsmouth, Maine"-presumably either Portland, Maine or Portsmouth, New Hampshire. Bath Savings: TR, Oct. 25, 1995.

Urban Initiatives (run by Gianni Longo, also director of the Great American Public Places, and based in New York) was formerly the Institute for Environmental Action. It focuses on "community awareness, marketing, strategic planning and visioning." Its "Vision 2000" project began in Chattanooga in 1984. The rosy view of Chattanooga is from Diego Mulligan, "Beyond Hope," *The Sun,* November 1995.

Alexander Von Hoffman'S *Local Attachments* (Baltimore: Johns Hopkins Press, 1994) is a study of Jamaica Plain, Massachusetts.

Wilcox and yard spokeswoman Julie Phillips: TR, Oct. 29, 1996.

Denise Scott Brown, *CSD News.*

Margo Huxley, quoted in Elizabeth Wilson.

Suggested Readings

Robert Orsi, "Crossing the City Line," in *Gods of the City: Religion and the American Urban Landscape* (Bloomington: Indiana University Press, 1999): 1–18.

Issac Weiner, "Church Bells in the Industrial City, in *Religion Out Loud: Religious Sound, Public Space, and American Pluralism* (New York: NYU Press, 2013): 40–76.

Robert Bellah, "Civil Religion in America," in *Daedalus* 117, no. 3, (Summer, 1988): 97–118.

Discussion Questions:

1. In "Crossing the City Line," Orsi writes: "Spaces on the urban landscape are both geographical sites where real people live and constructions of terror and desire among those who live elsewhere. . . . Part of the work of city religion is contending with such fantasies" (5). What does he mean? What kind of "fantasies" do people have about the city and city dwellers? How would a religious community go about "contending" with "fantasies" and why would they need to?
2. In "Crossing the City Line," Orsi criticizes "Christian narratives of city redemption" (8). What is he worried about? Do you agree that such "narratives" are problematic?
3. If you have lived outside of a city, describe the attitudes you encountered toward the city in your family, religious community, or town. If you have always lived in a city, describe any preconceived ideas about your city that you have heard or encountered. What does it mean to you personally to attend college in a city?
4. In "Civil Religion in America," Bellah writes "This public religious dimension is expressed in a set of beliefs, symbols, and rituals that I am calling the American civil religion" (100). Do you believe there is such a thing as American civil religion and if so, is it really religion? Give examples of beliefs, symbols, and rituals that could be understood as part of America's "civil religion."
5. What does Weiner's narrative tell us about the way that Philadelphians thought about what religion is and what religions should do?

Section 2

Lenni Lenape

Suggested Readings

M. R. Harrington, *Religion and Ceremonies of the Lenape 1882-1971.* (New York, Museum of the American Indian, Heye Foundation, 1921): 17–43; 127–143.

Terry J. Prewitt, "The Big House Described," in *Voices From the Delaware Big House Ceremony,* ed. Robert S. Grumet (Norman, OK: Oklahoma University Press, 2002): 3–22.

Discussion Questions:

1. In "Religion and Ceremonies of the Lenape," Harrington describes Vision Ceremonies. What purpose do you think they served for the community? Do aspects of the ceremonies remind you of other religious meetings or ceremonies you have witnessed or read about?
2. How do the practices that Prewitt describes compare with those described by Harrington?

Section 3

William Penn and the Quakers

J. William Frost • "The Quest for Holiness" in *The Quaker Family in Colonial America: A Portrait of the Society of Friends*

David M. Krueger • Penn's "Holy Experiment": The Vision and Reality of Religious Pluralism in Colonial Philadelphia

The Quest for Holiness

J. WILLIAM FROST

What school is more profitably instructive than the death-bed of the righteous, impressing the understanding with a convincing evidence, that they have not followed cunningly devised fables, but solid substantial truth.

A Collection of Memorials Concerning Divers Deceased Ministers (Philadelphia, 1787), pp. iii–iv.

Few outsiders joined the Society of Friends for purely intellectual reasons. It was far more likely for a person to be converted while in a meeting for worship, after recognizing the moral actions of Quakers, than during an involved study of theological tenets. Thomas Story, an educated man whose journal contains evidence of many theological disputes, recorded that, when attending his first meeting, he heard an attack on predestination

> Yet I took not much notice of it; for as I did not doubt but, like all other Sects, they might have something to say, both for their own, and against the Opinions of others; yet my Concern was much rather to know whether they were a People gathered under a Sense . . . of the Presence of GOD in their meetings.[1]

Only after experiencing in the meeting the corporate presence of the Lord, which he had known before individually, did he become a Quaker. Even Robert Barclay, certainly the prime example of a theologically oriented Friend, noted that he was persuaded to become a member not by arguments but by being "secretly reached" by the power of God in meeting.[2] When Quakers thought about their faith, they expressed their thoughts in terms used by Barclay or Fox or Penn, but to discuss the impact of religion upon them one must go to individual experiences of grace. The various journals of ministering Friends are the best sources for information on how Quakers lived their faith.

The writing of spiritual autobiographies was common among Quakers from the middle of the seventeenth until the beginning of the twentieth century. George Fox and John Woolman were the two most famous journalists, but many other ministers and some ordinary laymen recorded the progress of their devotional lives.

These works were meant, much like the biographies by the Puritan Cotton Mather in the *Magnolia Christi Americana,* to be edifying entertainment and to picture the Christian way of life. The writers thought that the temptations they met and the exaltations they received should be handed down as a medium for posterity to participate in their spiritual life. Howard H. Brinton called the diaries the "most characteristic form of Quaker composition."[3]

No systematic study of family life can be made from Quaker spiritual journals because the writers' children were usually mentioned only when they died. Although intensely introspective, these books contain almost no details of actual living. A tradition records that John Woolman once gave his uncompleted journal to a Friend to read. Upon returning the manuscript, the Quaker wondered why Woolman had never mentioned his wife. So Woolman added one sentence saying that he had married and that the Lord "was pleased to give me a well inclined Damsel."[4] Whether true or not, the story is illustrative of the way in which Friends structured their autobiographies. Thomas Story (1662–1742) was married to Ann Shippen, daughter of a mayor of Philadelphia, from 1706 until her death in 1712. Story lived in Pennsylvania from 1705 until 1709; between 1720 and 1727 he became involved in an acrimonious dispute concerning the Pennsylvania Land Company. He was also extraordinarily interested in the study of natural history.[5] Although his journal ran to nearly 500 pages, none of these personal details appeared in the work. His book contained long religious debates, but some other journals included little systematic theology.

A reader should not expect the diaries to contain objective portraits of the subjects. A late eighteenth-century English Friend, James Jenkins, wondered why Quakers "above others have been . . . given 'to build the tombs of the Prophets, and to garnish the sepulchres of the righteous?'" His answer was that to expose guilt or personal weakness would "militate against the Doctrine of *Perfection in this life.*"[6] The hagiographic character of the journals also resulted from their intended use as a preaching aid; that is, they showed lives transformed by the inward light of Christ.

Most prominent in these books were the religious exercises of the subjects. When the Friend experienced a sense of opening and could give a weighty discourse in meeting, he rejoiced, but he acquiesced in silence if there were no message from the Lord to deliver. Many journals concentrated almost exclusively on detailing the itineraries of the traveling ministers and describing states of the meetings. Since the journals were always edited by committees of Friends before publication, what they said was authoritative. And since the later writers tended to follow a format similar to that found in previous journals, a study of the general characteristics of the journals will reveal a pattern of religious development attained by the elite of Quakerdom and aimed at by the commonality.

II

The writers' childhoods received slight emphasis in these journals. Most were children of pious parents, but little attention was focused on how they were raised. Usually, early life was covered in the first 10 pages of a 200–300 page journal.

Two themes were normally stressed: divine visitations and sin. The child, often before the age of 10 or 12, experienced a sense of divine providence. For example, Thomas Scattergood (1748–1814) at 6 years of age "was favored with seasons of serious thoughtfulness." Joshua Evans (1731–98) recorded that he had received favors from the Divine even in his "tender years" and had "weighty thoughts" about death, eternity, and life. These youthful visitations were never very effective, for the youngster, no matter what he thought or knew to be right, found having fun and playing games to be pleasant diversions from the serious periods of religion. Joshua Evans inclined to "folly and pranks," and Thomas Chalkley (1665–1742) "loved play exceedingly" and delighted in music, dancing, card playing and secretly indulged in "sports and games."[7]

Childhood was followed by a period of "compunction over youthful frivolity"—a time between 12 and 18 when the person was in school and then an apprentice. Today we might call this stage adolescence, but Friends had no conception of a difficult age concerned with the physical and emotional problems of maturation. As in the earlier period, the youth's moments of religious emphasis were closely followed by indulgence in the vanities of life. Thomas Story recorded his experience of

> the common Temptations among Youth. . . . And tho' was preserved from Guilt, as in the Sight of Men, yet not so before the Lord. . . . The Lust of the Flesh, and of the Eye, and the Pride of Life, had their Objects and Subjects presented: The Airs of Youth were many and potent: Strength, Activity, and Comeliness of Person were not a-wanting and had their Share; nor were natural Endowments of Mind.

Joshua Evans between 11 and 14 was tempted and joined "unsuitable company." He had a "libertine spirit" and would jest and talk lightly, speak falsely, use "you" to a single person, and even curse. David Cooper (1745–95) while a student was "much addicted to play and mirth" and had few equals either in scholarship or "mischief." He felt "two Spirits of Strife," one which inclined him to "sadness and Sorrow," resulting in his seeking solitude to weep, and the other a frivolous "endeavouring to persuade that none of my play fellows was like me, nor any body else in the world, others were lively and Merry, and I was better than they." While most of the journalists recorded how desperately sinful they were, almost all wrote that they were preserved from gross pollutions and maintained a good reputation with parents and Friends. John Woolman (1720–72) confessed, "I was not so hardy as to commit things scandalous, but to Exceed in Vanity, and promote mirth, was my chief study." John Griffith (1713–76) was afraid to tell lies (except to embellish a pleasant story), never swore an oath or uttered a curse, never departed from the plain speech, kept "much love and regard" for those whom he regarded as truly religious, and commonly attended first day meetings. Yet he was "hardened in evil" and in a "Carnal degenerate state."[8] Clearly, the theological separation before and after experiencing grace was so absolute that behavior of children was pictured in stark terms.

The next stages were the crucial ones during which the sinner was made into an expectant saint. Howard H. Brinton labeled these periods *search and conflict, convincement,* and *conversion.* The search and conflict consisted of a deepening of the contrast between the good the person knew and the bad he did. When he finally realized what he must do to be saved, he was convinced, and when he eventually reached unity with God he was converted. (Convincement thus defined does not reflect the eighteenth-century Friends' normal usage of the term, by which they meant the procedure that an outsider could follow to become a member of the Society.) Conversion did not necessarily mean a sudden, dramatic renascence as experienced by persons in the Wesleyan revival or the Great Awakening. Quakers rarely used the word conversion to describe what they experienced, perhaps because of its enthusiastic connotations.[9] In more traditional theological terms, what the journalists were undergoing can be described as conviction of sin and the realization of the failure of good works to save, justification, and progression toward sanctification. Since Friends always linked justification and sanctification as a part of the process of becoming a Christian, one should be aware that these stages were a conceptual framework and that the evolution involved a gradual shading from one state into the other. At times the religious experience could be rapid, at other times extraordinarily protracted.

As the youth became a young man, he began to worry about the course of his life. Very often this awakening was precipitated by an external event—sickness, an accident, or the death of a friend. The journalist's attention was thus keenly focused on the inevitability of his own death and his lack of religion. He therefore set out to reform his life and find the truth. In the seventeenth century the journalist might have wandered from sect to sect seeking one that was truly the church. The Friend saw his condition as analogous to Saint Paul's description of inward torment: "For I delight in the law of God after the inward man: But I see another law in my members, warring against the law of my mind, and bringing me into captivity, to the law of sin." Job Scott of Rhode Island (1751–93) described his misery: "My days I spent in vanity and rebellion, my nights frequently in sorrow and distress. I knew myself a prisoner but I hugged my chains." The experience of God under these conditions was not pleasant. Thomas Story knew Jehovah

> only as a Manifester of Evil and Sin, a Word of Reproof, and a Law condemning and judging those Thoughts, Desires, Words, Passions, Affections, Acts and Omissions, which are seated in the first Nature and rooted in the carnal Mind.[10]

Even the stage of convincement, or realisation of the truth of Friends' principles, and the knowledge of what had to be done did not bring peace. Alice Hayes (1657–1720) described the contrast between her expectations and the results

> Instead of Peace, Trouble and Sorrow, Wars and Commotions, with frightful Sights and deeply distressed, fearing that my Condition was such, that never was the like, not knowing that the Messenger of the Covenant was come . . . He whom my Soul had been seeking after, and that he must sit there *as a Refiner's Fire, and as a Fuller with Soap, to clear his own Place.*

John Griffith, in attempting to conquer temptations, first triumphed over the sins of the flesh and then found that Satan became an "angel of light" to make him mortify his body. After going around half-starved, with too little sleep, and attempting to work continually, he fell into a religious depression until a ministering Friend visited and told him that his torturing of the body was a design of Satan.[11] Although the complete acceptance of God ended the struggle, the Quaker would in some sense be engaged in a continuous attempt to feel God's presence for the rest of his life.

The desideratum of religious life was conversion or justification. The primary goal for the Quaker was experiencing conversion daily, and the only difference between the initial and the later encounters with God came from the mature Christian's greater familiarity with the beauty and demands of divine love. In meeting God a paradoxical situation was created in which the person had to undergo the abnegation of his own will and be filled with the will of Christ. Thomas Story experienced a most dramatic conversion in 1689, before he became a professing Friend. At the time, Story had been made conscious of his own sin, had been pursued by the Lord until he was aware of His presence, and had experienced disunity with all churches. While he was worshipping alone one first-day evening, the Lord "brake in upon me unexpectedly" as a "righteous, all powerful, all-knowing, and Sin-condemning Judge."

Before God, Story's soul was filled with "awful Dread" and his mind seemed to separate from the body and plunge into eternal perdition. In his experience of death "a Voice was formed and uttered in me, as from the Center of boundless Darkness, 'Thy Will, O GOD, be done; if this be thy Act alone, and not my own, I yield my Soul to thee.'" These words brought instant "all-healing Virtue" and the vanishing of fear. "My Mind became calm and still, and simple as a little Child; the Day of the LORD dawn'd, and the Son of Righteousness arose in me, with divine Healing, and restoring Virtue in his Countenance; and he became the Center of my Mind." By this experience he lost his "old self," and saw all his sins condemned and forgiven. All his searchings and carnal reasonings and questionings ended. The next day his mind was "calm and free from Anxiety" and toward evening "my whole Nature and Being, both Mind and Body, was filled with the divine Presence, in a Manner I had never known before, nor had ever thought that such a Thing could be." Divine truth was now self-evident. Story experienced insight into the agony of Christ's passion; he was enlightened to see many mysteries of creation and divine redemption, and he could read the Bible with understanding.[12]

The moment of grace was rarely so dramatic and often came as a young man's realization of peace rather than as a sudden encounter. John Woolman had several experiences of seeking and finding God but then turning away. Finally he decided, "I must not go into company as heretofore in my own will, but all the cravings of Sense must be governed by a Divine principle." He then "felt the power of Christ prevail over all selfish desires." James Gough (1712–80) had moved to a new residence where "I was given plainly to see that my safety here and happiness hereafter, depended upon my yielding faithful obedience to his requirings by his light in my heart." This was his "espousal to Christ Jesus," and he was ready to sacrifice anything for Him. His poetry, which earlier he had delighted in composing, now appeared unworthy, and he burnt it. His satisfaction "was in the company of Christ my dear Lord," and he bade farewell to all the world's pleasures. John Griffith, caught between good and evil, realized that he had the power of decision. Afterward the Lord "broke in upon my soul, by his judgments mixed with mercy, in such a powerful manner, as that I was made willing to yield up thereunto, come life or death." John Kelsall (1681–1743), after experiencing the normal turmoil, gradually grew into Quaker customs.

> I made many Rules to myself that when I came among company I would not be light airy nor talkative but have a watch over my words . . . And thus I passed on 'for Some Seasons and by the Help of the Lord . . . I came by degrees to see that Nature that would have been up, in some measure to be subdued, and then there was a Zeal and Fervency begot in me against all such vanity.[13]

Many times during his life the Quaker would feel God's wiping out of his past sins and the creation within him of a new person. After his conversion the Friend witnessed a growth in what he was to do in order to measure up to the increasing demands of God. If the person were not already a plain Quaker, these trials would entail the adoption of a more simple style of dress, the use of the plain style of speech, the refusal to take oaths, the curtailment of business, the embarkation upon the ministry, and even traveling in the service of truth.[14] Friends also found that many times God seemed absent; this resulted either from their own straying from true virtue or from the Lord's unaccountably withdrawing Himself for a season. If the period of barrenness happened to a traveling minister, he might go to a village and appoint a meeting and then find he had absolutely nothing to say. In 1757 Anthony Benezet excused his delay in answering a letter because of a spiritual deadness.

> O my leanness, my leanness—it is beyond expression, and so sensibly felt by me, that I dare not as it were extend any further, lest I should defile God's jewels. Though a beggar may have a prospect of the order and beauty of God's house, and can even at a distance see, and apprehend he can distinguish the furniture of it, yet shall he presume, while clothed in rags, to enter therein?

John Griffith in the midst of his "high career" in the ministry lost his gift to speak for nearly five months. Finally the Lord saw his suffering and restored the ability.[15] These periods might last for weeks or months, but ultimately the Almighty was again pleased to make His presence known.

III

While these experiences of the spiritual elite show the goals of life, the average Quaker's normal religious activities can be seen by focusing on the less dramatic occurrences in the particular meeting for worship. The Friend had a great many opportunities to attend meetings. In Philadelphia there were two weekly meetings—from ten until twelve on Tuesday and Thursday—three meetings on

Sunday, plus special meetings for youth. There were monthly and quarterly meetings for business and several days of sessions at yearly meeting. John Smith, who lived in Philadelphia and traveled often to Burlington where his parents resided, recorded that during 1745 he attended 162 meetings.[16] If one lived in backwoods Virginia or North Carolina, he might have only weekly and first-day meetings in his immediate vicinity except when a traveling minister visited. Any special activity such as serving on a committee as an overseer, helping in a business arbitration, or visiting families took more time. Since the Friends had no professionally trained full-time clergy, the responsibility for all tasks fell upon the laity.

Organized religious devotion took place at the meeting for worship. The meeting house was perfectly plain; no stained glass, ornamentation, or organ music were to distract the person from silently waiting upon God. The benches were hard and might or might not have backs; normally there was a raised platform or gallery at the front with a bench where the ministers and elders could sit facing the congregation. In keeping with what may have been an earlier practice of the English parish churches, men and women sat apart. Unlike the Puritans, the Friends did not buy pews. Except that ministers and elders sat in the gallery, no distinction was made in seating arrangements. Quakers were expected to enter quietly and sit down, filling the seats at the front first.[17]

Friends were supposed to approach the meeting house seriously. Frivolous matters were not to be discussed either just before or after worship. New England's discipline warned against levity in riding a horse away after meeting. The congregation entered, sat down, and waited in silence. Men kept their hats on, except when someone prayed. When a minister felt moved by the Lord, he stood up, removed his hat, and spoke. The meeting ended when a Friend (normally a clerk or an elder) shook hands with the person seated next to him. Behavior within the meeting was strictly regimented. Too frequent excursions to the necessary house, spitting, and chewing tobacco were condemned. The most frequent complaint was that someone was sleeping in meeting. In 1760 Ann Cooper Whitall recorded in her diary, "I thought it my business to tell Kate Andras of Sleeping in meetings so much as She does and her dear husband dead so little awhile." John Kelsall, an English Friend, for a time found it necessary to carry a pin to stick himself when feeling drowsy in order to stay awake. Friends were warned that too large a noon meal on Sundays led to drowsiness in afternoon meetings. A few disturbances of the meeting were allowed. For instance, when the cry of fire was heard, all went. But when a shower of rain came up and Friends left to keep their saddles from getting wet, "a hint was given at the close, touching on the inconsistency with spiritual pure worship, that appears, where small matters are allow'd to interrupt. This was found to touch some members, who shew'd a dislike to their Conduct being faulted."[18]

The best description of a Quaker meeting was written by Peter Kalm, the Swedish traveler, who attended Bank Meeting House in Philadelphia, December 7, 1750.

> Here we sat and waited very quietly from ten o'clock to a quarter after eleven. . . . Finally, one of the two . . . old men in the front pew rose, removed

> his hat, turned hither and yon, and began to speak, but so softly that even in the middle of the church, which was not large, it was impossible to hear anything except the confused murmur of the words. Later he began to talk a little louder, but so slowly that four or five minutes elapsed between the sentences; finally the words came both louder and faster. In their preaching the Quakers have a peculiar mode of expression, which is half singing, with a strange cadence and accent, and ending each cadence, as it were, with a half or . . . a full sob. Each cadence consists of two, three, or four syllables, but sometimes more, according to the demand of the words and means; *e.g.* my friends/ /put in your mind/ / we/ / do nothing/ /good of our selves/ / without God's/ / help and assistance/ /etc. In the beginning the sobbing is not heard so plainly, but the deeper and further the speaker gets into his sermon the stronger becomes the sobbing between the cadences. The speaker today made no gestures, but turned in various directions; occasionally he placed one hand on his cheek; and during most of the sermon kept buttoning and unbuttoning his vest with right hand. . . . When he stood for a while using his sing-song method he changed his manner of delivery and spoke in a more natural way, or as our ministers do when they say a prayer. Shortly afterwards, however, be began again his half-singing mode of expression, and at the end, just as he was speaking at his best, he stopped abruptly, sat down, and put on his hat.[19]

This sermon took half an hour. Thomas Clarkson in the first decade of the nineteenth century provided a description of several of the preachers he heard. The ministers spoke in an odd tone of voice which Clarkson called "unpleasant" and likened to the noise made by street vendors. The speakers began very softly and slowly, but their speech became louder and faster as the discourse progressed. As fuller involvement came, the minister spoke "beyond the quickness of ordinary delivery," and some were "much affected, and even agitated by their subject." The changes of speed in delivery resulted, Clarkson thought, from the minister's caution in outrunning his gift. When he began to talk, he knew neither where his opening would lead him nor what he was to say. As insight grew, the speed of delivery increased. This singing style of preaching became more prevalent as the eighteenth century progressed, and by the middle of the nineteenth century many Quakers did not esteem a minister who did not sing his sermons.[20]

The content and quality of preaching are difficult to judge, since the few surviving sermons of even the most famous ministers were written down by outsiders and often printed without the consent of the Friends. These sermons show amazing ability in organizing extemporaneous discourse and some variety in type: theological disquisitions of Protestant dogmas, defenses of distinctive Quaker tenets, ethical exhortation, scriptural exegesis, personal narratives, and even evangelistic emphasis. Occasionally an ecstatic element entered as a Friend would prophesy or relate a vision. Samuel Bownas maintained that a Quaker could legitimately preach about almost anything, so long as he was careful to speak under God's immediate direction. Speakers rarely used classical allusions or literary flourishes but assumed a minute knowledge of scriptural lore;

prooftexting was common. Sermons invariably had a strong moralistic bent and concluded with some demand upon the listener. Ann Whitall, who attended Haddonfield meeting, recorded that ministers spoke on the final judgment, on the importance of not only listening to sermons but of reforming sins, on spiritual pride, on bringing children to meeting, on education of youth, and on the decline of Friends. Advice to children and youth and preparation for death ranked as the most frequent subjects.[21]

Some opinions that outsiders delivered of Quaker worship tell more about the observers than they do about the Friends. Such is the case with Dr. Johnson's apothegm on a lady preacher: "Sir, a woman preaching is like a dog's walking on its hinder legs! It is not done well; but you are amazed to find it done at all." A more insightful evaluation of Quaker principles was made by Thomas Clarkson. Clarkson found little intellectual merit or variety in preaching in England, for many Friends had "little erudition," and principles forbade premeditation upon the subject. Even Quakers noted the varying abilities of different men, reasoning that one type of sermon might reach the learned and another the illiterate. The sermons were always delivered with 'great seriousness" and were "singularly bold and honest" in rebuking anyone who needed it, no matter how rich or powerful. Because the ministers claimed to be able to discern states, a preacher in the middle of his discourse might feel called to change subjects in order to speak to someone's needs. Since any cultivation of eloquence or preparation was forbidden and inasmuch as all inspiration was to come while the person was actually speaking, a polished discourse was nearly impossible. Yet the best of Quaker ministers, like Rachel Wilson who was compared with George Whitefield, were able to attract large crowds.[22] Friends ministered by fostering a sense of the presence of God rather than by arguing about the truths of Quaker theology.

Brevity was not a necessary quality. In 1710, John Banks stood and preached in Somerton, England, for one hour and a half. George Whitehead spoke in London Yearly Meeting in 1716 for nearly two hours. Sophia Hume, writing from Charlestown in 1767, reported that, although she had been ill, "divine goodness" had so strengthened her that she was able to "exhort the People for at least an Hour at a Time."[23] Friends did not take satisfaction, as did certain Puritan ministers, in how often the hourglass was turned over. One spoke as long as the spirit led him; when inspiration stopped, even if in the middle of a sentence, he sat down.

Some historians have questioned whether the Friend normally heard a sermon in meeting. Rufus Jones, in a two-volume study of the *Later Periods of Quakerism,* found such a decline in the eighteenth century in the amount of preaching in meetings that the worship was often held in complete silence. Two of the better recent histories of Friends, by A. Neave Brayshaw and Elfrida Vipont, echoed Jones's judgment "that for years together many meetings were held wholly in silence."[24]

Direct evidence about speaking in meetings is not easy to find. Journals are a more reliable source for deciphering an individual's feelings about his ministry than for determining the amount of speaking. A diarist discussed his own preaching during a journey but almost never commented upon that of his fellow travelers. One bit of contrary proof comes from the diary of John Smith, who recorded every meeting he attended in the Philadelphia area between January 1745 and January 1746. Of the 162 meetings he went to: 150 had prayers or preaching, 5 were silent, of 7 no information was given. Smith calculated that during the year he heard 657 prayers or sermons, an average of 4 per meeting. Women gave 275. He heard 50 different men and 40 women speak plus a few strangers whose names were not recorded. The most frequently heard men, Michael Lightfoot and Daniel Stanton, spoke 69 times. Next was Benjamin Trotter who preached or prayed 59 times. Sarah Morris, the most frequent woman speaker, appeared 38 times; next was Hannah Hulford who spoke 18 times. Among the men, those who can be identified as ministers constituted 75 percent of the speakers and made 91 percent of the appearances. For the women the comparable figures are 83 percent making 81 percent of appearances. Four men made slightly over one-third of all discourses.[25] Clearly, at most meetings only recognized ministers spoke. Since Smith was in the habit of attending meetings all over Philadelphia, his statistics provide an accurate index to the strength of the ministry in this area, but they should not be taken as applicable to the rest of America. Smith's figures fall in a period of time ten years before the revival of Friends during the French and Indian War.

Comparable figures for other areas are not available, but there is evidence that the frequent laments about the declining state of the ministry were an exaggeration. If there were ministers, then one can legitimately deduce that the probability of speaking increased. There are no statistics on the number of live ministers, but starting in the 1680s London Yearly Meeting recorded the number of ministering Friends who died. From this one can deduce, with a slight time lag, the number of preachers at any one time. The two tables in appendix C give the total number of Quaker ministers who died and the average deaths per year calculated on a five-year average. The figures indicate that there were more ministers during the eighteenth century in almost all decades than in the period from 1690 to 1700. From 1700 till around 1770 the numbers remain relatively stable; the end of the century shows a decline that continues into the nineteenth century. London Meeting for Sufferings calculated in 1756 that there were 487 particular meetings in England, not counting London and Middlesex. Since there were approximately 19 meetings there, this makes a total of 506 meetings. According to my figures, from 1740 to 1759,486 ministers died; according to Charles Hoyland, 475. If one assumes an average ministerial career of twenty years, then most meetings had one minister.[26] Of course many undoubtedly had several and others none, but English Friends did not appear to be destitute of ministers during this period. Philadelphia Yearly Meeting did not begin making accurate lists of ministerial deaths until 1764. Fortunately for the historian, John Smith compiled memorials of all Quaker ministers before 1762. He searched monthly meeting records, wrote letters to Friends in Virginia, New England, and England, and visited elderly ministers.[27] While his information on ministers before 1720 is often sketchy, it is possible, by coupling Smith's figures from 1720 to 1762 with Philadelphia Yearly Meeting records from 1764 to 1779 to determine numbers of ministers. The ministry in Philadelphia Yearly Meeting did not decline in the eighteenth century; rather, the figures, even including the missing year of 1763, show a marked increase as the Revolution approached. (One cannot discount the possibility that the increase may be in part due to the two sources used for numbers.) Figures for the twenty-year period beginning in 1760 show 106 deaths from 103 meetings. The meeting-minister ratio is slightly better than in England. From the available evidence it is clear that there is no proof that there was a lack of preaching in eighteenth-century Quakerism. When a Friend attended a meeting for worship, he expected to hear a spoken ministry consisting of prayers or preaching.

In theory anyone could speak in meetings, but people were not allowed to infringe upon the captive audience very often. Friends who were not officially recognized as ministers were permitted to talk occasionally, but frequent preaching without the approbation of the monthly meeting was frowned upon. In 1726 Philadelphia Monthly Meeting informed Noble Butter that he was not to speak because "he is not esteemed a minister." In 1747 at the Bank Meeting House, "Sam Pennock made a long story, and would have done much longer, but Anthony Morris told him he had said Enough." Elders removed mentally disturbed people from meeting houses. When an outsider visited and began speaking, Friends had to listen although they could keep their hats on or stand as signs of disunity. During the Keithan controversy, his advocates invaded yearly meeting sessions and harangued assemblies. The Quakers sat in silence until the intruders left.[28]

While overseers and elders were often the older and more wealthy members of the congregation (who had the leisure to carry out the duties), neither age nor riches was of much consideration in the ministry. Howard H. Brinton, in his analysis of 100 Quaker journalists, found that the average age at which they began to speak in meeting was 26. James Jenkins noted that in the Yorkshire village of Highflatts one of the ministers, "Henry Dickinson, was an excellent man, and (his illiteracy and condition in life considered) ministered with great propriety of language, and connection of argument." John Smith recorded that apprentices occasionally spoke in Philadelphia meetings and, in 1741 he met a 10-year-old girl preacher. "Several have told me that She speaks very notably and very much to their Satisfaction."[29]

In the eighteenth century the elders supervised both the speaking and the conduct of the ministry. They were responsible for warning the preacher if he misquoted Scripture or outran his gift and for encouraging young people who were just entering the ministry. The elders were to be as "nursing Fathers and Mothers" to both young and old. Historians have tended to find in the growth of the institution of eldership a repressive influence upon the creativity of the ministers.[30] However, no journalist mentioned struggling against elders who suppressed the truth and, occasionally, a preacher who was rebuked by the elders commented on the help he had thereby received. The most scathing comments on preachers came from ordinary laymen and from diaries written by other ministers. Elders should not be held responsible for the theological conservatism that Quakers espoused throughout the eighteenth century. The whole Society stood against doctrinal innovation and the most devout—minister, elder, or ordinary Friend—assumed responsibility for continuing the old ways. Criticism and analysis of what was said in meeting were popular pastimes. Ann Whitall, after hearing people belittle a minister, commented, "I wonder if good men in that day [Bible times] did talk against one another as they do now." Nathaniel Greene, more noted for his Revolutionary War role than his earlier Quakerism, compared one sermon to a meal called "Whistle Belly Vengeance," the more you ate the worse it became.[31] Since some writers were often critical and rarely commendatory and others reversed these tendencies, a person's subjective state undoubtedly had much to do with his opinion of the sermons. Because the light within was involved in judging meetings and sermons, in theory no other criterion except internal feelings could be used. John Griffith seldom had much good to say about a meeting or another's sermon. George Churchman infrequently had praise for any minister except his father, John Churchman, while John Smith rarely blamed or censured a sermon.[32] If learning and polished discourses had been criteria, John Smith, an intelligent and well-educated Friend, was far better qualified to judge than George Churchman. Friends believed that God favored some ministers more than others and esteemed highly those individuals who were eloquent speakers and could bring variety to their sermons without distorting the Scripture.

IV

Quaker religious life was a preparation for the next world. The title of William Penn's very popular *No Cross, No Crown* shows the linkage between mortification in this life and glorification after death. Friends were to "be as strangers and pilgrims to the world, and all things therein, possess as though you did not possess them," for this earth was only a place of travail on the road to a final destination."[33] A devout Quaker lived every day as if it were his last. The small town flavor of colonial life and the degree of involvement of Friends with the meeting meant that an individual would be frequently exposed to people dying. Undoubtedly the ambivalent feelings of Friends toward death—desiring heaven yet dreading the unknown—occasioned the constant preoccupation with health that one finds in letters.

The fear of death and the hope of eternal life motivated not only the initial conviction of sin but the perseverance in the Christian path. Ann Whitall mused in her diary on January 11, 1762:

> I find it an excellent Thing to be as much as we can, always ready, and by being frequently thinking upon Death, it is not so surprizing when it does come: This is a great Point of true wisdom, to number our Days so, as to remember our latter end.[34]

Death was the climax to life, and the period just before the end was supposed to reveal either the righteous prevailing and triumphant or the wicked filled with fear and hesitancy. The journals and the testimonials or memorials to ministers and elders drawn up by the monthly meetings showed how pleasant death could be to a saintly Friend. In 1701 John Tomkins compiled a collection of the dying sayings and deathbed scenes of young and old Friends under the title *Piety Promoted* (which, with additions, was republished 29 times before 1800. The last American edition appeared in 1854.) In England, at the end of the eighteenth century, Friends assembled special editions made up of the death scenes of young persons from age 6 or 7 to the early twenties which were designed for the edification of children and youth.[35] Friends were not unique in their interest in death. In the seventeenth century, Catholics and Protestants issued collections of the dying sayings of children. In 1700 Cotton Mather added several stories to the anthology of James Janeway, an Englishman. Mather published the book under the title *A Token for Children Being an Exact Account of the Conversion, Holy and Exemplary Lives and Joyful Deaths of Several Young Children.*

Typical of this form of Quaker literature were the unpublished accounts of the death of Charles Pemberton, aged 19, drawn up by his mother, Rachel, and his brother, Israel Pemberton, Jr. The mother's account was an extraordinarily impersonal history of the events; the brother's was a very emotional story designed to be placed at his bedside for frequent reading. After Charles had been ill for some time and seemed near death, Israel Pemberton, Sr., warned him that "there Seemed little hopes of his recovery and that he hoped in this long time of Illness he had not been unmindful to prepare for his change." The father informed the youth that both his parents had been praying for him and had petitioned the Lord "to be near to him and grant him resignation of mind to his holy will" and to bring "Some assurance of his mercy and favour." After being informed by Charles of his submission to whatever God demanded, Israel, Sr., told the boy of his own religious experiences and of the Lord's mercy when undergoing "great affliction of body and mind." He offered to have any Friends that Charles wanted visit him. Some were paying him a religious visit five days later when he died.[36]

Unlike the mother, Israel Pemberton, Jr., stressed "The Great Love and Affection which Subsisted between me and my Dear Brother" and also the character of Charles as a "Youth favored of the Lord with a Good Capacity, great memory, good delivery, and a tender spirit." Israel thought that he could not survive the "Loss of him but the Lord was mercifully pleased to assist and help. Wherefore Let my Soul bless his name."[37]

Friends who survived the death of others stressed in Job-like fashion the necessity of submitting to the will of God. When John Reynell's only surviving child was about to die, the girl, age 15, "desired her Mother to give her up, and said She should be better provided for than any thing I could do for her." The father mourned but believed that it was better to "part with them while young, than to have them live to take bad Courses . . . the Lord sees not as Man seeth, He gives and takes away. Blessed be his Name forever and may [we] be Resigned to his Will, for he knows what is best."[38]

Complete resignation was expected not only from the survivors but also from the dying person who was not to desire life or death but was to welcome whatever the Lord brought. If death came, he welcomed it as a deliverance from this world of tribulation. If health returned, the person's submissiveness was seen as being rewarded by God.

The Friends' assurance of knowing the will of God carried over into the experience of death. When Charles Pemberton was dying, Sarah Morris, a ministering Quaker, was told by the Lord "not to be Concerned for him, for that he had a mind to take him unto himself and that his End should be peace, and that was enough." Israel Pemberton, Jr., recorded, quite naturally, how "greatly Comfortable" this testimony was to him. At times the knowledge came directly to the person. When Elizabeth Allinson lay dying, she told her sister that "since she had been on that Bed the Almighty had kindly favoured her and given her to see that all her former transgressions were forgiven and that if it should be his will to take her at that time, she had reason to believe she should be accepted."[39]

An entire household gathered in the death chamber to hear the final words of exhortation. If the Friend were very prominent many visitors, including young children, would come. There was nothing private about the final expiration. The individual was in his closest relationship with God, and the advice and pious expressions he gave were often taken down and kept as family memorials. At Samuel Allinson's death, his wife regretted that he had no opportunity to give final counsel to his children. Her father, Peter Cooper, did not trust to chance but left directions in writing that his coffin was to be perfectly plain pine and that the expense saved thereby should be given to the poor. He wrote out the reasons for his plainness and concluded with an address to his neighbors to suppress their desire for pomp. The paper was read at his funeral.'[40]

The religious exercises of children were not often recorded except when they were dying. One 10-year-old boy bore a testimony to simplicity by asking his mother to remove from the house a (pair of gilt teapots, a chimney piece shaped like a lion, and an ornamental china dish. After he had given to the assembled company a short speech on salvation, the grandmother returned thanks by saying, *"Oh Lord! That* this young Branch, should be a Teacher unto *us old Ones."* The lad agreed that this was his role. Quaker children customarily gave advice to those around them, whether adults, playmates, or brothers and sisters. When Hannah Hill, aged 11, was on her deathbed, she, rebuked those who wished for her recovery. Before dying she exhorted her sister and cousin to obey their parents and trust in the Lord.[41] Hannah Hill's religious exercises went through three editions between 1715 and 1717 and were later incorporated into *Piety Promoted.*

In order not to distract from the religious significance of the occasion and to guard against superfluities, the meeting approved only those burial customs that were free from embellishment. The Society opposed all outward signs of mourning. Normal clothing was correct funeral attire, and the wearing of black was an unseemly formality. The homage paid to the deceased was of no more significance than the opportunity it provided for the living to reflect upon their own deeds. Since there were few undertakers in colonial days, the care of the dead was strictly a family affair. After death the corpse was left at home until the time of burial. Although George Fox had testified against wakes as a heathen custom, by the time of the Revolution the practice had been revived, at least among Philadelphia Friends.[42]

Funerals were generally held within two or three days of death but, if the weather were hot, the burial might take place the next afternoon. Friends were given notification either by an announcement at the close of a meeting, or by personal invitation, or by both. The invitation meant that the person was privileged to partake of refreshments and dinner. The corpse, wrapped in wool in England but in a linen sheet in America, was buried in a wooden coffin. The wealth or strictness of the Friend or his family would determine the degree of ornamentation. John Woolman insisted that his coffin be made perfectly plain and from ash rather than oak because the latter "is a wood more useful than ash for some other purposes." More worldly Friends' coffins were made of mahogany with silver handles and lined with flannel.[43]

Friends disapproved of elaborate funeral processions. In early Pennsylvania the coffin was placed in the ground and then a meeting held. The format was the same as at a regular meeting for worship. Sometimes the meeting was held and then the coffin carried to the graveside. Friends believed that seeing the corpse in the meeting and then carrying the coffin to the cemetery and watching the burial was useful "for the propagation of truth."[44] Philadelphia Monthly Meeting adopted regulations on how the procession was to go from the meeting house to the cemetery. Friends were to follow "orderly . . . not exceeding four in breadth." At the graveside after a short pause during which members had an opportunity to speak, the coffin was placed in the ground. Friends permitted no marker of any kind on the grave, but, since having a tombstone was not a disownable offense, some appeared. If the meeting was large, families would not be buried together; rather, there would be a systematic filling up of the burial ground. An occasional grave site might be lined in bricks, but most Friends preferred to have the wood coffin placed next to earth.[45] Since the person was dust in the beginning and would return to dust shortly, elaborate care of the physical remains was sacrilegious.

Frequent references in yearly meeting disciplines to violations of the simplicity of funerals indicate that moderation was more easily advised than enforced. The most prevalent abuses were found in the serving of refreshments. Friends saw the necessity of providing some repast for people who came from far away, but they objected to the size and lavishness of entertainments that debased a solemn occasion into a "festival." The 1719 Philadelphia discipline listed the offenses:

> Friends are desired'. . . to break from and avoid that offensive and, unsuitable Custom of large provision of strong Drink, Cakes etc. and the formal and repeated servings and offers thereof. This indecent, and indiscreet custom, and practice has run to such excess, That invitations being made to greater number, than their own or Neighbours houses can contain the very Street and open places, are made use of for the handing about burnt wine, and other strong Liquors etc.

It was customary to provide cake and wine before a burial and a meal afterwards. An unverified Quaker practice was to pass the bottle around only twice at a funeral.[46] This was supposedly to prevent early guests from eating and drinking more than was compatible with the solemnity of the occasion. But even in the eighteenth century there were no records of elaborate formalities in the meeting or of the giving of gloves or rings to pallbearers.

V

The shared experience of the inward light in meeting for worship, private prayer, and Scripture or devotional reading shaped Quaker religious life. People converted and remained Friends because they believed that in silence God was found. The encounter with God first brought turmoil and anguish as the person measured his life by the divine standard, but eventually, as the Holy Spirit came to dominate the person's will, the godly enjoyed peace, consolation, and assurance. By reading the journals of weighty members and listening to ministers preach, Friends gained confidence that only the meeting provided pure and true religion.

Quaker ministers did not prepare a message but waited expectantly in meetings for the Holy Spirit to inspire them and the resulting "openings" could be a few words or a long discourse. The belief in divine afflatus did not preclude laymen from grumbling about the content of sermons or from occasional drowsiness. Publishing the journals of prominent Friends provided a method of proselytizing as well as reassuring the faithful, for a holy life stood as an affirmation of the power of God in Quaker religion. The narratives of dying Quakers, which occupy so prominent a position in *Piety Promoted,* testify to the belief that in the moments before his decease the person was in his closest relationship to God and could receive insight into realms beyond the grave. Emphasizing the closeness of eternity also served as a reminder that unrepentant evildoers went to hell and goaded lukewarm Friends to more diligence in religious observances.

The outward forms of worship did not change in the colonial period, but after 1690 the Friends' conception of themselves did evolve. Before the Act of Toleration, Quakers struggled to survive in a hostile environment. The Society saw its religion as a new spiritual phenomenon that would sweep all forms of apostasy from the earth. In the eighteenth century the emotional quality of Quakerism changed. Friends believed just as fervently as before in the truth of their doctrines, but they lost the hope of conquering the world for Christ. The novelty was ended and the excitement completed. The Friends' task became to preserve what was already established rather than to build anew. Any enthusiastic tendencies were disciplined and disappeared, for grace flowed in stable, well-defined channels. In short, the children of light became a respectable Protestant denomination. Frederick Tolies has argued that Quakers were unable to respond favorably to the fervor kindled in the Great Awakening because conservatism, wealth, and stability had sobered the meeting. An early sign of this change can be seen in Benjamin Coole's *Discourse on Inspiration,* printed in 1712, in which the author maintained that the Friend's experience of the grace of God was both "*safe* respecting the Sobriety it leads to, and *sound* respecting its Orthodoxy."[47] The hardening of a universal truth as preached by Fox, Barclay, and Penn into a creed professed by a small denomination made the Society of Friends into a conservative body. The eighteenth century was for them an age of orthodoxy in which tradition governed.

Notes

1. Thomas Story, *A Journal of the Life of Thomas Story* (New Castle, England, 1747), pp. 32–33.

2. Robert Barclay, *An Apology for the True Christian Divinity,* 13th ed. (Manchester, England, 1860), prop. 11, pg. vii, 223.

3. Howard Brinton, "Stages in Spiritual Developments as Recorded in Quaker Journals," in *Children of Light* (New York, 1938), p. 384; see also Luella Wright, *The Literary Life of the Early Friends* (New York, 1932), pp. 165–97.

4. John Woolman, *Journal and Essays of John Woolman,* ed. Amelia M. Gum- mere (New York, 1922), p. 173; Janet Whitney, *John Woolman* (Boston, 1942), pp. 150–51.

5. See the Preface to Story, *Journal,* pp. ii-iii.

6. James Jenkins, "The Records and Recollections of James Jenkins Respecting Himself, and Others from 1761, to 1821," ed. Mildred Campbell, Typed transcript, p. 8, FHL.

7. William Evans and Thomas Evans, eds., *Memoirs of Thomas Scattergood,* in *Friends' Library* (Philadelphia, 1844), 3: 3; Joshua Evans, *A Journal of Joshua Evans,* ed. George Churchman (Byberry, Penn., 1837), p. 5; Thomas Chalkley, *The Works of Thomas Chalkley* (London, 1791), pp. 3–4; Brinton, "Stages in Spiritual Development," p. 387.

8. Story, *Journal,* p. 11; Evans, *Journal,* p. 7; Woolman, *Journal,* p. 155; David Cooper, "Diary of David Cooper," p. 3, QC; John Griffith, *A Journal of the Life, Travels, and Labours in the Work of the Ministry, of John Griffith* (Philadelphia, 1780), pp. 8–9.

9. Brinton, "Stages of Spiritual Development," pp. 390–95; London YM, Christian and Brotherly Advices, pp. 271–72, FHL; William Penn, *Works of William Penn* (London, 1726), 2: 867; John Griffith, *Some Brief Remarks* (London, 1764), p. 36. In 1692 John Banks equated convincement with the first awakening and conversion with sanctification. See *A Journal of the Life . . . of John Banks* (London, 1712), pp. 247–62.

10. Jane Hoskins, *The Life of that Faithful Servant of Christ, Jane Hoskins,* in Friends' Library, 1: 460; Story, *Journal,* p. 12; Job Scott, *Journal of the Life, Travels and Gospel Labour of . . . Job Scott* (New York, 1797), pp. 26–27; Brinton, "Stages of Spiritual Development," p. 390; Romans 7: 15–23; George Churchman, *Journal of George Churchman, in Friends' Library,* 6; 180.

11. Alice Hayes, *A Legacy, or Widow's Mite* (London, 1723), pp. 27–28; Griffith, *Journal,* pp. 17–19.

12. Story, *Journal,* pp. 13–15.

13. Woolman, *Journal,* p. 156; James Gough, *Memoirs or The Life, Religious Experiences and Labours in the Gospel, of James Gough,* ed. John Gough (Dublin, 1802), pp. 21–22; Griffith, *Brief Remarks,* pp. 27–29; John Kelsall, "Diary," *1: 34–35,* FHL.

14. Brinton, "Stages of Spiritual Developments," pp. 400–06.

15. Anthony Benezet to Samuel Fothergill, 10/1/1757, in George S, Brookes, *Friend Anthony Benezet* (Philadelphia, 1937), p. 222; Griffith, *Journal,* p. 31; John Pemberton to Israel Pemberton, Jr., 5/23/1751, PP, 7: 89, HSP.

16. John Smith, "Diary," vol. 2, Jan. 1745- Jan. 1746, Smith Mss, LC.

17. Eleanor Trotter, *Seventeenth Century Life in the Country Parish* (Cambridge, 1919), p. 50; *BFHA* 31 (1941): 29; Mary Leadbeater, *Annals of Ballitore, The Leadbeater Papers* (London, 1862), 1: 175–76.

18. New England YM, Discipline, 1708–38, 10, QC; *The Book of Discipline Agreed on by the Yearly Meeting of Friends for New- England* (Providence, 1785), p. 19; Ann Cooper Whitall, "Diary," 7/27/1760, 30, QC; Kelsall, "Diary," 1: 21–22; Churchman, *Journal* 1: 88, QC.

19. *BFHA* 31 (1942): 28–29.

20. Thomas Clarkson, *Portraiture of Quakerism* (London, 1807), 2: 281—83; Jenkins, "Records and Recollections," 1: 197, 214–15, FH.

21. *Concurrence and Unanimity of the People Called Quakers* (London, 1694), pp. 17, 55, 73–77, 111; Samuel Fothergill, *Two Discourses and a Prayer* (New York, 1768), pp. 1–14, 26; *A Sermon Publickly Delivered At a Meeting of People Called Quakers* (Newport, 1773);

Thomas Story, *Sermons on Following Subjects: 1., Salvation by Christ . . . II. Nature and Necessity of . . . Silence (Leeds, 17.39)*; Samuel Bownas, *A Description of the Qualifications Necessary to a Gospel Minister* (London, 1750), pp. 47–48; [Thomas Letchwork?], *Discourse as Delivered at a Meeting (Supposed at Canterbury) of the People called Quakers, In the Year 1768* (Cork, 1776); Lucia Beamish, "The Quaker Understanding of the Ministerial Vocation" (B. Lit. thesis, Oxford University, 1965): Ann Whitall, "Diary," pp. 36, 39, 57–59, 71, 74, 81, 86–88, 108.

22. Martha Petel to Israel Pemberton 2/21/1770, PP, 21: 116. There is no evidence that Johnson ever heard a lady Quaker preach. G. B. Hill and L. F. Powell, eds., *Boswell's Life of Johnson* (Oxford, 1934), 1:463; Clarkson, *Portraiture of Quakerism, 2:* 284–87.

23. Banks, *Journal,* p. 145; "Peter Briggins' Diary," in *Eliot Papers,* ed. Eliot Howard (London, 1895), 2: 68; Sophia Hume to Israel Pemberton, 6mo./1767, Letters of Sophia Hume, Charleston Mss, DR.

24. A. Neave Brayshaw, *The Quakers: Their Story and Message,* 5th (New York, 1938), pp. 249–55; Elfrida Vipont, *Story of Quakerism* (London, 1954), p. 150; Rufus Jones, *Later Periods of Quakerism,* (London, 1921) p. 63. Jones relied upon journalists and John Rutty's description of twenty-two silent meetings in Dublin in 1770. While one does find references to occasional silent meetings in various sources, the evidence from most localities indicates that total silence was exceptional and journalists who conducted silent meetings reported the disappointment of attenders.

25. Smith, "Diary," vol. 2, Jan. 1745-Jan, 1746. In 1762 Haddonfield had six ministers and a great deal of preaching. Whitall, "Diary," p. 120.

26. For laments of declining strength in the ministry, at a time when the figures show no such phenomenon, see London YM of Ministers and Elders, Minutes, vol. 1 (1757): 8–23 and the epistle sent by Philadelphia Yearly Meeting in 1754, in Epistles Received by London YM, 3: 361. It is not known what records Charles Hoyland based his calculations ,on. I used the deaths of ministers as reported to London, Yearly Meeting, totaled the amounts in five-year periods, and averaged the figures for a per annum death rate. In the memorials collected by John Smith, the average time of service was twenty-seven years, but for many individuals no estimate of time spent as a minister was given.

27. John Smith, "Lives of Ministers Among Friends," 3 vols., QC; Smith Mss, 5: 178, 210, 225, 241, and 6: 91–98, LC.

28. Min. Philadelphia MM, 3 (11/26/1726): 141; Smith, "Diary," vol. 2, 4/22/1746, 11/27/1726; A. C. Myers, ed., *Courtship of Hannah Logan,* (Philadelphia, 1904), p. 120. Min. Philadelphia YM, 1 (7/23/1696): 59. Morris was an elder. Pennock made six appearances in 1746 but was not recognized as a minister.

29. Meetings were often exhorted not to pick their elders by wealth or age, a sign that this was probably done sometimes. Min. London YM, 12 (5/15/1761): 213; Brinton, "Stages of Religious Developments," p. 400; Jenkins, "Records and Recollections," 1:31; Smith, "Diary," 1 (6mo./1741), and 2 (2/27/1746), and 3 (5/16/1747).

30. Arnold Lloyd, *Quaker Social History* (New York, 1950), p. 123; Lucia Beamish, "Quaker Understanding of the Ministerial Vocation," (Bachelor of Letters *thesis,* Oxford, 1965), pp. 107–109; Philadelphia YM, Christian and Brotherly Advices (1723), p. 120. Jones, *Later Periods of Quakerism,* pp. 120–28. Jones has an excellent discussion of the imprecision in functions of elders, overseers, and ministers.

31. Elizabeth Morris to John Smith, 1/20/1756, Smith Mss, 4: 251; Gough, *Memoirs,* pp. 42–43; Whitall, "Diary," pp. 36–37; C. P. Monahon and C. A. Collins, eds., "Nathaniel Greene's Letter to 'Friend Sammy Ward,' " in *Rhode Island History* vol. 15 (1956), p. 52.

32. Griffith, *Journal,* pp. 267–68; George Churchman, *Journal,* 1:10mo./1760,12, 6/1/1760, 9, 10/3–3/1762, 44; Smith, "Diary," 4: 2/26/1748.

33. George Fox, *Works of George Fox* (Philadelphia, 1831), 8: 18.

34. Whitall, "Diary," 1/11/1762. Evidently, a sermon on this subject had been preached in the meeting.

35. William Rawes, Jr., ed. *Examples for Youth in Remarkable Instances of Early Piety* (London, 1797); *Brief Memorials of the People called Quakers* (London, 1781).

36. Rachel Pemberton's undated account of her son Charles' death, ca. 3mo./1748, PP, 4: 112.

37. Israel Pemberton, 3/24/1748, PP, 4:118.

38. John Reynell to Mary Groth, 1756, Letter Book 1756–59, Coates-Reynell Mss, HSP.

39. Israel Pemberton, 3/24/1748, PP, 4:118; Katherine Smith, "Account of the Death of Elizabeth Allinson," 8/20/1768, Allinson Family Mss, QC.

40. *PMHB* 22 (1898): 257; Martha Allinson *to William Allinson,* 11/13/1795, Allinson Family Mss.

41. *A Seasonable Account of the Christian and Dying-Words, of Some Young Men Fit for the Considerations of All: But*

Especially of the Youth of This Generation (Philadelphia, 1700), pp. 13–14; Hannah Hill, *A Legacy for Children* (Philadelphia, 1717), pp. 8–9, 19.

42. Fox, *Journal,* p. 107; Elizabeth Drinker, *Extracts from the Journal of Elizabeth Drinker,* ed. Henry Biddle (Philadelphia, 1889), p. 147; Penn, *Works,* 1: 870–71; Clarkson, *Portraiture of Quakerism,* 2: 39–41.

43. Smith, "Diary," 2 (5/2/1746); Drinker, *Extracts from the Journal,* p. 219; Alton Men and Women Friends, "A Testimony Concerning our deceased Friend, Elizabeth Merryweather," 3/15/1790, Allinson Mss; Woolman, *Journal,* pp. 324–25; *PMHB* 27 (1903): 53–54.

44. Myers, *Hannah Logan's Courtship,* p. 291; *PMHB* 22 (1898): 257, and 17 (1893): 456–58; Min. Philadelphia MM, 2 (12/22/1705).

45. London YM, Christian and Brotherly Advices (1717), p. 199; Min. Philadelphia MM, 1 (8/26/1694): 132; Min. Philadelphia YM, 1 (6/16–20/1732): 360; Clarkson, *Portraiture of Quakerism,* 2: 33–34.

46. Philadelphia YM, Christian and Brotherly Advices (1719, 1729, 1735, 1746, 1750), p. 12; Min. Philadelphia YM, (1719), 1: 223; Watson W. Dewees, "The Meeting at Work," in *225th Anniversary 'of Concord Monthly Meeting of Friends 1686–1911* (Philadelphia, 1911), p. 62.

47. Frederick Tolies, *Quakers and the Atlantic Culture* (New York, 1960), pp. 91- 113; Benjamin Coole, *Miscellanies* (London, 1712), p. 61.

Penn's "Holy Experiment": The Vision and Reality of Religious Pluralism in Colonial Philadelphia

David M. Krueger

The First Amendment states, "Congress shall make no law respecting an establishment of religion or prohibiting the free-exercise thereof." The precise meaning of what has come to be known as the "establishment clause" and the "free-exercise" clause has been vigorously debated in Supreme Court cases ever since the U.S. Constitution and the Bill of Rights were put into effect over two hundred years ago. However, there is broadly-shared consensus among Americans today that citizens should be able to worship, or not worship, as they please. This was not always the case in colonial America. Most colonies operated with a religious establishment and placed strict limits on how its residents could practice religion. In some cases, religious nonconformists faced criminal prosecution or worse.

Pennsylvania stood out as an important exception and it played a pivotal role in how the newly-formed nation came to terms with the reality of religious pluralism. As one historian puts it, "Real liberty of worship in the American republic probably owes more to the fact that William Penn's 'Holy Experiment' worked than to any theory of the separation of church and state articulated and advanced by Thomas Jefferson."[1] This essay examines the radical vision of religious toleration as imagined by the colony's founder, William Penn, and assesses the degree to which this vision was realized as a social, cultural, and legal reality during the colonial period.

The Establishment Status Quo

To better understand how unique Penn's colony was, it is necessary to understand the more typical approach to religious diversity in colonial America. Most American colonies functioned with an established religion, meaning that residents were only permitted to participate in the one religious tradition authorized by the government. In colonies like Massachusetts and Connecticut, Puritans established their religious monopoly through the Congregational Church. In Virginia, Maryland, the Carolinas, and Georgia, the Church of England reigned supreme.

In colonies with a religious establishment, churches and clergymen were supported by public moneys. Only ministers properly credentialed by the state were permitted to conduct church services. These colonies often were quite intolerant of religious difference. In Massachusetts, Quakers like Mary Dwyer were executed and nonconformist thinkers like Anne Hutchinson were exiled. In Virginia, Baptists were put in jail for preaching without a license. Many colonial Americans feared that unless there was a shared religion among the colonists, social chaos would result.

The colony of Pennsylvania took a different approach. From the very beginning, it was a haven for Lutherans, Quakers, Presbyterians, and Pietists from all over Europe. Later on, they were joined by Jews, Catholics, and many others. "While other colonies . . . were still wondering which form of Protestantism to establish . . . Pennsylvania was reveling in its diversity."[2] However, it is important to remember that Pennsylvania was not the first experiment in religious toleration.[3] Roger Williams's "Lively Experiment" in colonial Rhode Island emerged as a haven for religious dissidents several years before William Penn was born. However, what distinguished Williams's colony from Penn's colony was that the former emerged out of immediate necessity, while the latter was founded by design.[4] Williams's writings on religious liberty only took shape after his banishment from Massachusetts Bay Colony for sedition and treason. William Penn actively recruited a wide variety of settlers from throughout Europe, many of whom were oppressed religious minorities, before the colony ever began. From the start, "Penn envisioned a society where different beliefs could dwell together in peace."[5]

William Penn and the Quaker Origins of the "Holy Experiment"

Penn's personal experience as a member of a persecuted religious minority, no doubt, played a role in his thinking about how to deal with religious pluralism. Penn was born in London in 1644, the son of Admiral Sir William Penn. William Penn (the younger) grew up as an Anglican but he became a Quaker at the age of twenty-two after being inspired by the teachings of George Fox. Fox emphasized the innate equality in all people, an inward light that revealed divinity in each person, and a challenge to authority based on wealth, privilege, and militarism. Such assertions were seen as threatening to the Church of England; and many Quakers, including William Penn, were imprisoned. Others were put to death for their beliefs. This led Penn to consider leading his fellow Quakers to a place where they could live without persecution.

The opportunity arose from a debt that King Charles II owed William's father, Admiral Penn. After Admiral Penn's death, the king was faced with the dilemma of owing money to the younger Penn, who was a member of a radical religious sect. Rather than use money, the king paid off his debt to Penn with a large grant of land in colonial America. Spanning 45,000 square miles, the colony was named Pennsylvania or "Penn's Woods" for Admiral Penn, William's father.

By the time that Penn first sailed up the Delaware River in October 1682 on the ship *Welcome*, he had already established the rules for what religious freedom would mean (and would not mean) in the new colony. In the document *Frame of Government of Pennsylvania*, Penn asserted that all

> who confess and acknowledge the one Almighty and Eternal God, to be the Creator, Upholder and Ruler of the world; and that hold themselves obliged in conscience to live peaceably and justly in civil society, shall, in no ways, be molested or prejudiced for their religious persuasion, or practice,

> in matters of faith and worship, nor shall they be compelled, at any time, to frequent or maintain any religious worship, place or ministry whatever.

Penn went on to mandate that residents of the colony were expected to refrain from all labor on Sunday in accord with "the good example of the primitive Christians." Penn also stated that all "offenses against God" would be prohibited by law and "severely punished." A sampling of activities that Penn said would "provoke the indignation of God" included swearing, drunkenness, fornication, sodomy, stage-plays, cock fighting and any activities "which excite people to rudeness, cruelty, looseness, and irreligion."[6]

To modern ears, Penn's rules regarding morality seem archaic and his understanding of religious liberty sounds parochial. Freedom was limited to those who gave deference to "the one Almighty and eternal God." The legal code in his colony was infused with strict Quaker values because he endeavored to establish a virtuous society. Additionally, Penn did not view religious liberty as an end in itself. He viewed religious coercion as a stumbling block for people to discover "true faith" and, therefore, the freedom to follow one's conscience was "an instrument of Christian salvation."[7]

Nonetheless, by the standards of the time, Penn's embrace of religious diversity was indeed quite radical. It would have been almost inconceivable for an American colony to be founded without some unifying notion that God was sovereign over human affairs. Despite their rigid rules for social life, the comparatively-tolerant culture of Quakers welcomed a diversity that was not often experienced in colonial America.

Penn's Colony: Haven for Religious Diversity

The diversity of religious and cultural life was evident in what became known as the Delaware Valley even before Penn's arrival. The Lenape people had lived for thousands of years on the land they called Lenapehoking. They continued to live in the region even after Penn brokered the treaty with Tamanend, a Lenape chief, in 1683. Europeans started arriving in the early seventeenth century. The first enduring European settlement was that of the Swedes, who practiced the Lutheran faith. They established Old Swede's Church 1667. Its current edifice completed in 1700, stands today as the oldest church building in Pennsylvania. Although the Dutch and later the English came to dominate the region politically, the Swedish Lutherans continued to have a presence.

The Quakers, who began arriving in larger numbers in 1680s, came from a wide variety of places, not only England. The Society of Friends (Quakers) sent missionaries throughout Europe during the late seventeenth century. Although most of the early Quakers who came to Philadelphia were from England, many came from Wales, Ireland, and also the German and Dutch-speaking regions of the Rhine Valley, where Penn had actively recruited settlers for his new colony.

Perhaps one of the most religiously-diverse areas of early Pennsylvania was the settlement at Germantown founded in 1683, several miles to the northwest of Penn's city. Germantown became home to Lutherans, Mennonites, Moravians, Dunkards,

Calvinists, and even a few Catholics. It even attracted spirituals seekers such as the Transylvanian mystic, Johannes Kelpius. His religiously-eclectic society, known as the Women in the Wilderness, moved into the woods of the Wissahickon Valley to await the return of Jesus Christ. They even built an observatory on top of their tabernacle for monks to search the nighttime sky for signs of the Second Coming.

Closer to the ground in Penn's city, there was also an array of religious communities. The Church of England established Christ Church in 1695. When it reached 800 members in the 1720s, they constructed the large edifice that still stands near Second and Market Streets today. Presbyterians and Baptists met for worship in nearby commercial buildings. In 1700, Quakers remained the largest minority in the colony at 40 percent of the population.

Although Quakers would remain in political and social control for some time, their numbers were quickly surpassed by new immigrants of other faiths. Some 40,000 German-speaking immigrants arrived between 1726 and 1755.[8] In 1727, Reformed minister George Michael Weiss led a boatload of 400 people from the German Palatinate to found a congregation near Fourth and Race Streets. Although many German Lutherans gravitated to Germantown, they were a significant presence in Philadelphia. When Henry Melchior Muhlenberg arrived in the 1740s, he built and consecrated an impressive edifice with a tall steeple and bells near Fifth and Arch Streets. The more-evangelistic German Moravians succeeded established a church nearby on Race Street.

The Presbyterians flourished in Philadelphia especially due to the large influx of Scottish-Irish immigrants. The Presbyterians were of two varieties. The "Old Lights" were associated with the likes of Reverend Jedidiah Andrews who was a Harvard graduate and advocate of traditionally-educated clergy. William Tennet represented the so-called "New Lights" movement which emphasized the emotional rather than intellectual dimensions of faith. The Old Lights attracted the elite while the New Lights were typically made up of the poor and working class. When the passionate revivalist George Whitefield visited Philadelphia between 1739–1740, he attracted thousands of people to his rallies and the New Light Presbyterians constructed an assembly hall so large that "neither the secular State House nor the latitudinarian Anglicans' Christ Church" surpassed it in size.[9]

The legacy of Philadelphia's religious diversity had an impact on how various institutions developed. When Dr. Thomas Bond and Benjamin Franklin founded the Pennsylvania Hospital in 1755, they established a medical institution intended to serve low-income sick people from "whether Inhabitants of the Province or Strangers." This was a unique approach because most hospitals of the day were charities supported by particular church denomination. Bond envisioned the hospital as a public charity and with the help of Franklin's fundraising prowess, he managed to draw support from donors of many religious backgrounds.[10] In a similar fashion, the predecessor to the University of Pennsylvania was founded as a nonsectarian school and its first trustees were made up of Anglicans, Quakers, and Presbyterians.[11] However, despite these examples of interdenominational collaboration, it is clear that the lived reality of the "Holy Experiment" did not always live up to Penn's ideals.

Exploring the Limits of the Holy Experiment

Despite the remarkable religious diversity of the colonial city, there were still many groups at the fringes of social power. Colonial officials dispossessed the Lenape of a vast section of southeastern Pennsylvania via the dubious Walking Purchase of 1737. However, some Native Americans remained in the region. In the aftermath of the frontier upheaval of the French and Indian War, a group of "Moravian Indians" sought refuge in Philadelphia from both angry white settlers and fellow Native Americans who shunned them due to their pacifist stance. A white vigilante group known as the Paxton Boys descended on Philadelphia in 1754 to attack this group. The unarmed Moravians would have been killed if it weren't for the intervention of a newly-formed militia lead by Benjamin Franklin that stopped the so-called "Christian White Savages" before they got into town.[12] Despite this effort to save the lives of the Moravian Indians, colonial city officials made arrangements to have them sent away from white settlements to remote Western Pennsylvania. Even though this group shared a Christian identity with many of the Philadelphia's residents, it is clear that their racial "otherness" prevented them from being welcomed into Philadelphia society. Although Penn has been lauded for his comparatively benevolent treatment of Native Americans, those who succeeded him had little interest in peaceful coexistence with the Lenape, whether they were Christian or not.

Christianity was also limited in its ability to bridge other racial divides in the city. In 1684, a slave ship arrived in Philadelphia carrying 150 persons from Africa. By the time of the revolution, there were some 1,400 enslaved Africans and around 100 freed men. Despite the religious diversity of the city, Africans had limited choices for where or whether to worship. Traditional African religious practices would not have been permitted by Christian slave owners. However, "Congo Square," what is now named Washington Square, was a known gathering place for Africans at the edge of the city to practice traditional burial customs, dances, and music. Most slaves in Philadelphia were household slaves and if they were permitted to attend church, it would have been at the church of the slave master. An experience of racial discrimination at one church, Old St. George's Methodist, sparked the birth of an autonomous denomination, the African Methodist Episcopal Church, led by Richard Allen.

The English Jesuit Reverend Joseph Greaton founded the Old St. Joseph's Catholic Church in Philadelphia in 1733. Catholics migrated from Maryland after the colony made the decision to establish Anglicanism as its official religion. At the time, Philadelphia was the only place in British North American where it was permitted to hold mass in public. Despite this, the Protestant neighbors expressed concern that a "Romish Chapel" had been established and appealed to the city for it to be closed down. However, due to the religious freedoms guaranteed under the Charter of Privileges, it was determined that the church could remain open.

Although the church was legal, parishioners did not wish to draw unnecessary attention. The chapel was hidden in the middle of the block. Even the present church building, constructed in 1839, is somewhat hidden from the main thoroughfares of the city and it earned the moniker "church in the alley."

Jews also found an early acceptance in Philadelphia. Although the oldest synagogue in North America was founded in Newport, Rhode Island, the second oldest was established in Philadelphia. Jewish businessman Nathan Levy settled in Penn's city in 1735. Within a decade, Levy and other Jews had successfully appealed to the governing authorities to establish a Jewish cemetery and had begun a weekly communal prayer service, which became the Congregation Mikveh Israel.

Although, Mikveh Israel was tolerated in the city and had even earned the financial support of neighboring Christ Church, there were limits to the ability of Jews to achieve political power. Pennsylvania law required that members of the state assembly were required to agree to a religious oath affirming that the New Testament was the word of God. Since Jews do not believe in the divinity of Jesus, the effect of the law was to exclude them from holding political office.

Conclusion

Despite the limitations in both the design and implementation of Penn's "Holy Experiment," the Pennsylvania colony established an important precedent. Social and economic prosperity could flourish in a religiously diverse environment. During Penn's time, few would have predicted that the notion of religious freedom would one day be ensconced in American law. Although we still struggle to be a society where people of different religious beliefs and practices can live together in peace, we can look to history of Penn's Holy Experiment for what it has to teach us today.

Notes

1. James Hudnut-Beumler, "Protestants in the Middle Atlantic Region," in *Religion and Public Life in the Middle Atlantic Region: The Fount of Diversity*, (Lantham, MD: Alta Mira Press, 2006), 68.
2. Hudnut-Beumler, "Protestants in the Middle Atlantic Region," 67.
3. Maryland also had a short-lived policy of religious toleration until the Church of England became the establishment church in 1702. New York was also quite diverse but became so largely due to commercial reasons.
4. Andrew Murphy, "'Livelie Experiment' and 'Holy Experiment': Two Trajectories of Religious Liberty," in *The Lively Experiment: Religious Toleration in American from Roger Williams to the Present*, ed. Chris Beneke and Christopher S. Grenda (Lantham, MD: Roman and Littlefield, 2015) 38.
5. David Hackett Fischer, *Albion's Seed: Four British Folkways in America* (New York: Oxford University Press, 1989) 461.
6. http://avalon.law.yale.edu/17th_century/pa04.asp.
7. Fischer, *Albion's Seed: Four British Folkways in America*, 459.
8. Russell F. Weigley, ed., *Philadelphia: A 300-Year History* (New York: W. W. Norton), 47.
9. Ibid., 49.
10. George W. Boudreau, *Independence: A Guide to Historic Philadelphia* (Yardley, PA: Westholme Publishing), 209.
11. Weigley, *Philadelphia: A 300-Year History,* 83–85.
12. Weigley, *Philadelphia: A 300-Year History,* 108.

Suggested Readings

J. William Frost, "Penn's Experiment in the Wilderness: Promise and Legend" in *Pennsylvania Magazine of History and Biography* 107, no. 4 (October 1983): 577–590.

Dawn Marsh, "Penn's Peaceable Kingdom: Shangri-la Revisited," in *Ethnohistory* 56, no. 4 (2009): 651–667.

Discussion Questions:

1. What specific religious practices does Frost describe in "The Quest for Holiness"? Which of those practices might non-Quakers find most objectionable?
2. Many writers, both popular and academic, romanticize Penn's treaty with the Lenape and the benevolence of the 17th and 18th century Quaker community. How does Marsh's "Penn's Peaceable Kingdom" portray Penn and the Quakers? After reading it do you believe that Pennsylvania was uniquely tolerant and supportive of Native peoples?
3. Marsh writes that "Pennsylvanians struggled to establish a usable Indian past that served their complex needs" (3). What kind of narrative of the past were they trying to construct by erecting a monument to Hannah Freeman? What sorts of "complex needs" did it serve?
4. Marsh writes, "Once the Indian had vanished to the West and was doomed to extinction, American image makers could safely romanticize them from a secure temporal and special distance" (4). What does she mean? How were native people groups "romanticized"? Are Native Americans still "romanticized" today?
5. According to Frost in "Penn's Experiment in the Wilderness," from where did Penn get the name "Philadelphia"? What point does he make about the meaning of the word "experiment"? How does the name "Philadelphia" connect to Penn's "Holy Experiment"?

Section 4

Religious Life in Colonial Philadelphia

Deborah Mathias Gough • "Founding an Anglican Church in a Quaker Colony" in *Christ Church, Philadelphia: The Nation's Church in a Changing City*

John M. Kloos • "Rush's Monument" in *A Sense of Deity: The Republican Spirituality of Benjamin Rush*

Richard S. Newman • "Gospel Labors" in *Freedom's Prophet: Bishop Richard Allen, The AME Church, and the Black Founding Fathers*

Founding an Anglican Church in a Quaker Colony

Deborah Mathias Gough

While the founding of a new congregation was a common and normally routine event in colonial America, there was nothing common or routine about the founding of Christ Church. To Anglicans in Pennsylvania and England it represented the establishment of true Christianity and "English civilization" in a colony that, from an Anglican viewpoint, was ruled by "heathens." To the Quakers it represented a potential threat to their "holy experiment" and an end to religious peace in their colony. The first twenty years of Christ Church history were largely defined by conflicts between these two groups. Yet, remarkably, despite their strikingly different worldviews and longstanding antipathy, by 1720 the two religions had learned to coexist peacefully in Pennsylvania, long before such religious tolerance had been established in other colonies.

It would have been difficult to find a more striking contrast within Christianity at the time than that between members of the Church of England and the Society of Friends, or Quakers. In order to understand the early history of Christ Church, we must understand the basic principles of these two religions. Struggling against great odds to keep the church alive after its glory years were over, finding new and creative missions for the church to fulfill. But it is also the history of ordinary people worshiping in a magnificent building, finding a religious community that fulfilled their needs, and using the strength and inspiration gained at Christ Church to serve God and their neighbors in both common and uncommon ways.

The Church of England was, first and foremost, the established, state- supported church in the mother country. In the seventeenth and eighteenth centuries this meant far more than merely receiving support from tax dollars, although that in itself was important. Most English at the time considered an established church absolutely essential to the orderly functioning of society. To assure correct outward behavior, the state had to promote inward virtue, or religion. Any form of religious freedom would inevitably allow "freedom *from* religion," something an ordered society could not allow.[1]

In seventeenth-century England, church and state were intimately connected. The King or Queen headed the church, appointing the bishops, who were then allowed to serve in the House of Lords. Ecclesiastical laws, including doctrine, had

---

to be approved by Parliament. In return for accepting secular control over certain matters, the church received considerable power and privileges. Ecclesiastical courts, which handled divorces and tried cases involving morals, had coercive power, including the ability to give out jail sentences. Parish churches were supported by taxes. Those not belonging to the Church of England, called dissenters, were banned from holding office, and, while given freedom of worship in 1689, still had to pay taxes to support the state church.[2]

Two characteristics set the Church of England apart from dissenting groups—its episcopal form of government and its adherence to the Book of Common Prayer. Even Anglicans who did not believe that apostolic succession was crucial for a true church did insist that the episcopate was necessary to keep order in the church and to maintain the proper relationship between church and state. Anglicans also firmly believed in the need for a set liturgy; to an Anglican, the Book of Common Prayer was both the symbol and the reality of the national church. No matter what personal or theological controversies might rock the church, the prayers would remain the same, providing continuity with the past and a sense of oneness with Anglicans throughout the realm. While not all Anglicans understood the theoretical justifications for a set liturgy, they did share a devotion to the Book of Common Prayer as a beautiful, awe-inspiring form of worship.[3]

The unity provided by the Book of Common Prayer was intended to include all English men and women, for membership in the Church of England went with citizenship, unless one renounced it. This inclusiveness meant that the characteristics of a congregation mirrored those of society, with people of various socioeconomic groups meeting in church each Sunday. Inclusiveness also meant that members of the Church of England varied greatly in their devotion to the church, their acceptance of its teachings, and their moral behavior. While ecclesiastical courts disciplined certain immoral behavior, excommunications were rare and "moral purity" was not expected.

Despite the efforts of the state to include all citizens in the Church of England, many English citizens renounced their membership, becoming dissenters. Of these dissenting groups, perhaps the most vexing for Anglicans were members of the Society of Friends, because of both their beliefs and their persistence. Founded in 1652 by George Fox, the Society of Friends* or Quakers as they later came to be called, belonged to the left wing of the English Reformation. Accurately called a form of "group mysticism," the Quaker beliefs revolved around the concept of the "Inward Light." Fox preached that all people—not just Christians, and not just those living in the time of the early church—had God or Christ within themselves. God continued to speak *directly* to everyone, and salvation came when a person acknowledged the light within and agreed to live according to its dictates.[4]

Although a simple concept, the doctrine of the "light within" had profound consequences. If God dwelt within each person, then priests were not needed as intermediaries and even churches were superfluous. So, Quakers abolished the ordained ministry, relying instead on lay ministers. They denounced not only liturgical worship but all preplanned worship. Instead, Friends held a "silent meeting," where each individual could join in mystic union with God, and where anyone could speak when he or she felt moved by God to do so.

Quakers were perhaps best known for the actions that resulted from their beliefs. Believing that "the honor which belongs to God he would give to no man, and the honor which belonged to any man he gave to every man," Friends refused to participate in the many contemporary practices that showed more respect for some people than others.[5] They refused to use any titles, did not take their hats off as a sign of respect, and always used "thee and thou" instead of "you," since the latter was used to give distinction. Quakers also refused to take an oath, even in court, believing that such oaths blasphemed God. And, in what would become their most well known belief, Quakers adamantly supported pacifism, arguing that war was against all that was taught by "the Prince of Peace." Moreover, like Puritans, Quakers insisted that their members give up all "vain and empty customs" that "divert the mind from the witness of God," including most kinds of recreation.[6]

Since God spoke to everyone, it followed, according to Fox and his followers, that it was wrong, if not blasphemous, for a government to tell anyone what to believe. When they founded Pennsylvania, an important aspect of their "experiment" was the institution of religious freedom. Among the laws agreed on before the Quakers left England was one assuring all people who believed in God that they would not be "molested or prejudiced for their Religious Persuasion or Practice" or forced to "frequent or maintain any Religious Worship, Place or Ministry whatever."[7]

In 1695 Quakers, not Anglicans, dominated Pennsylvania. In fact, to Anglicans, the entire structure of the new colony seemed a world turned upside down. In government, King William, Queen Mary, and the Anglican parliament had been replaced by the proprietary rule of the Quaker Penn and a colonial Assembly dominated by Quakers, who seemed often to forget that they were, in actuality, still under royal rule.[8] (See Figure 1 for royal coat of arms from Christ Church.) Pacifism had passed from being the absurd belief of an impotent minority to being the dangerous policy of an entire government. Quaker judges refused to administer oaths. The Quaker government also outlawed cards, dice, masques, revels, and the theater, all of which Anglicans enjoyed. Worse still, the Anglicans, who were used to holding all government jobs, were virtually shut out of these by the Quakers. Economically the Anglicans were also at a disadvantage, since the best land in the city belonged to Quakers, and a few wealthy Quakers dominated the commercial life of the city.

While religious freedom ensured Anglicans the right to start a church, the lack of an established church and the total absence of the church hierarchy that so efficiently governed in England made the success of such a church seem doubtful. Christ Church could not depend on revenue from taxes, nor did it have a house and land for its minister; thus its financial situation did not look good. Without a bishop anywhere in the colonies, let alone in Philadelphia, the establishment of a normal church life was also impossible; ministers could not be ordained without going to England, nor could the laity be confirmed.

In 1695 the future of Christ Church may not have seemed promising, but that of Philadelphia did. The city was already established as the Delaware River's chief port, serving Pennsylvania, West Jersey, and what is today Delaware. It was an impressive city, even in these very early days. A visitor in the early 1700s commented that Philadelphia was "most commodiously situated between two navigable Rivers. The

Houses are very stately; the Wharfs and Warehouses numerous and convenient."[9] While there were only around 1,500 people living in Philadelphia in 1695, when Christ Church was founded, it was already a thriving business center. We know that five years earlier the city had 22 shopkeepers and 119 craftsmen, including 34 in the building industry, 26 in the clothing trade, and 14 in food processing.[10]

But Philadelphia in 1695 was still a country town and would remain so for many years to come. Pigs and goats roamed the streets at will. Each morning cows were taken out through the streets to pasture. It was not until the 1710s that householders began paving walks in front of their houses and much later before any streets were paved.[11]

. . .

It was in this environment that a small group of lay Anglicans—without the aid of a minister or other churches—decided to found Christ Church. The founders of Christ Church represented a cross section of the city's population. On both the 1693 and 1696/97 tax list Christ Church members appeared in equal numbers above and below the mean. Included in the twenty-six members for whom we have information were six merchants, one lawyer, one physician, two bakers, three carpenters, two surgeons, and one dyer. Perhaps most interestingly, two men who appeared on the Surveyor General of the Customs 1692 list of pirates were among the founders of Christ Church![12]

The founders did include several wealthy and prominent men. Joshua Carpenter, who listed his occupation as "brewer," was the second wealthiest man in the city in 1693.[13] Robert Quary, another well-to-do Anglican, represented the New Pennsylvania Company, a group of London merchants who were attempting to compete with the established Quaker merchants in Pennsylvania. Quary was perhaps the most politically prominent of the founders; he had served as secretary of council and deputy governor in South Carolina and in 1697 was appointed a vice-admiralty judge for Maryland, Pennsylvania, and West Jersey. Jasper Yeates, another founder, was a wealthy merchant from Wilmington; politically active, he was a leading spokesman for the interests of the three lower counties of Pennsylvania which would eventually form Delaware.[14]

In 1695, while holding services under the leadership of the schoolmaster John Arrowsmith, these Anglicans purchased a lot on Second Street. They completed the building some time in 1696. There is little information about the original church's appearance, but cash books and travelers' accounts indicate that the church apparently was a small brick structure; a belfry was added in 1709. Two travelers' accounts refer to it as a "very fine church" and a "great church," but it could not have been very large; after it was enlarged in 1711 it still had only forty-two pews.[15]

The site chosen for the church was in the heart of Philadelphia. It was the retail center of the young city; two years earlier, in 1693, the public market had been moved to Second and High Street (now Market), one short block from the church. On Wednesdays and Saturdays farmers would bring their varied produce to be sold. Here butchers slaughtered their animals in front of their stalls, bakers and tradesmen of all kinds hawked their wares, and all Philadelphians came to buy the necessities of life. The old prison was also located on High Street, east of Second

Street. On its balcony, in full view of throngs of people, wrongdoers were whipped or executed by hanging. Escapes from this prison were common. The area around Second and High also soon became the governmental center; the city government, the county courts and the Pennsylvania Assembly all met in the County Court House, built down the center of High Street at Second in 1710.[16]

Despite its commercial activity, the area around Christ Church in 1695 retained a certain degree of country atmosphere. It is reported that a large duck pond lay to its rear, where, tradition has it, a great Indian feast took place. To amuse their guest of honor, William Penn, the Indians purportedly held a foot race around the entire pond. To the southeast of Christ Church, between Second and Front Streets, stood a "grassy sward, close cropt by nibbling sheep" that were pastured there until slain and sold. Not too far away on south Second would stand Edward Shippen's house with his "great and famous garden" and a "herd of tranquil deer" on his front lawn.[17]

While they built the church themselves, Philadelphia Anglicans no doubt hoped for help from England in supporting it. After all, the bishop of London, Henry Compton, who had jurisdiction over the Church of England in the colonies, had insisted that the rights of Anglicans be guaranteed in the charter given to William Penn. As a result of his letter to the privy council, the grant of Pennsylvania to Penn stated that whenever twenty inhabitants of Pennsylvania requested a preacher be sent by the bishop of London, "such Preacher or Preachers *shall and may be* [sent] and reside within the said Province without any denial or molestation whatsoever."[18] Moreover, the English church, which had only recently taken an active interest in its colonial branches, was particularly concerned that the Quakers (or "heathens" as they were referred to by some Anglicans of the period) not completely control religious life in Pennsylvania.

The primary champion of Christ Church's cause in England turned out to be the governor of Maryland, Francis Nicholson. In fact, it was probably Nicholson who fulfilled the provision in the charter by asking the bishop to send a minister to Philadelphia. We know that Nicholson, at the urging of Philadelphia Anglicans he met during a visit to the city in 1694, repeatedly asked English authorities to provide an annual subsidy for Christ Church. His efforts paid off in 1697 when the privy council agreed to provide fifty pounds a year for a minister and thirty pounds for a schoolmaster in Philadelphia.[19]

The congregation must have anxiously awaited the arrival of an ordained clergyman. In the interim, the schoolmaster, John Arrowsmith, officiated in the new church, reading the service, but unable to preside at communion. He was reported to be "very well beloved, not only by our own people, but by all in general."[20]

The first ordained minister of Christ Church, Thomas Clayton, about whom we know little, arrived in 1698. He probably graduated from Cambridge University in 1690, and it appears that he was on his way to a parish in Maryland when he stopped in Philadelphia and agreed to remain. His stay in the Quaker city was short; he died in September 1699. Edward Portlock, a former chaplain in the British army on his way to a post in Perth Amboy, New Jersey, served Christ Church for a few months after Clayton's death.

Finally, in November 1700, Evan Evans, an energetic Welshman, took over the Philadelphia church at the direction of the bishop of London. Evans graduated from Oxford University in 1695 and then held positions as a curate and rector of two churches in Wales. Evans served Christ Church with distinction from 1700 to 1717, receiving an honorary doctorate from his alma mater in 1714.[21]

. . .

Once the small band of Philadelphia Anglicans had acquired a permanent minister, they responded to the hostile situation in which they found themselves with the zeal of martyrs and the enthusiasm of crusaders. Compromise and accommodation, attitudes that were becoming increasingly common among Anglicans in England when dealing with dissenters, were not in the vocabulary of Philadelphia Anglicans. As Robert Quary put it, they felt they were "stigmatized with the grim and horrid titles of treacherous and perfidious fellows, dissenters and schismaticks from the Establish't Religions, which is Quakerism."[22] If the members of Christ Church were to establish an environment remotely resembling that which they had known in England, they had to curb the power of the Quakers.

Anglicans addressed the problem of Quaker domination on two fronts—political and religious. From 1700 to at least 1704 the vestry of Christ Church, as well as individual Anglicans, engaged in an almost continual battle with Penn and the Quaker political leaders. The Anglicans' ultimate aim was to make Pennsylvania a royal colony. Once it was, as Portlock put it, "Christianity will flourish in this Province, Quakerism will be rooted out, and the Church will be more than conqueror."[23] While involvement of the Church of England in such politics was not new—after all, bishops in England served in the House of Lords—it was unusual for individual congregations to be so active. The actions of the early Christ Church vestry set the stage for the involvement of that church in the political life of Pennsylvania throughout the colonial period.

Anglicans worked hard to convince the English authorities that the Quaker-dominated government in Pennsylvania was irresponsible, unreasonable, and an actual danger to its citizens. They complained about the refusal of the government to appropriate money to provide a defense for the colony, despite the fact that pirates menaced the coastline as a result of England's war with France and Spain. The vestry wrote to the Board of Trade, the committee that handled all colonial business for the crown, arguing that Anglicans were "expos'd to all the miseries imaginable, not only from a publick enemy, but from pyrates and Indians, the wofull experience of which we have lately felt. . . for want of a Militia."[24]

Anglicans made other accusations which are impossible to prove or disprove, but which were designed to raise suspicions in England. They accused the Quakers of purposely harboring pirates and illegal traders. Moreover, they characterized the Quaker judicial system as inept; they maintained that Quakers protected their own, allowing a woman who admitted killing her baby and a man who raped a servant to go free.[25]

The Anglicans' primary complaint involved a Pennsylvania law that made affirmations as binding as oaths in all court proceedings, contrary to English law. Although judges were allowed to administer oaths, since all judges were Quakers, Anglicans could rarely find a judge willing to do so. The vestry, individual Anglicans, and Anglican ministers in rural parishes surrounding Philadelphia waged a constant battle against each new oath law, even hiring an agent to argue their case in England. Anglicans who were appointed to offices used the issue to disrupt government. Some refused to serve. Others refused to administer oaths to those who wanted to take them or refused to accept affirmations from Quakers, thus halting judicial proceedings. This issue was not completely resolved until 1722 when England changed its law, allowing affirmations without God's name to be used in court.[26]

The Anglicans' efforts in the political arena were ultimately unsuccessful. Each time England disallowed an oath law, the Quaker-controlled legislature passed a new one. English authorities became less and less sympathetic to Anglican complaints as time went on. Moreover, the main goal of making Pennsylvania a royal colony was never achieved, since Parliament refused to rescind any colonial charters. In 1711 it appeared that Penn, who was tired of fighting both the legislature in Pennsylvania and the English government, would give the Anglicans their wish and sell the colony to the crown, but he suffered a debilitating stroke before he could do so. In the end Anglicans had to learn to live with a Quaker proprietor and a government dominated by Quakers.

At the same time that the Anglicans fought the Quakers in the governmental arena, they battled in the religious arena as well. Anglican ministers sought to convert all dissenters, including Quakers. Their first approach, initiated by Thomas Clayton, was to try to convince entire religious groups to rejoin the church. In 1698 Clayton wrote letters to Quakers, Keithian Quakers, a group that had broken away from the Society of Friends, and Baptists, asking each group to end its "schism" and return to the one true church.[27] While this action may appear arrogant, he was following the approach taken by the Church of England in the mother country. As a comprehensive church, the Church of England had never been oriented toward individual conversions. Instead, it had tried to negotiate with whole denominations to bring them back into the fold.[28]

This approach was as unsuccessful in Philadelphia as it had been in England. The Baptists sent a letter that cataloged all the practices of the Church of England that they considered contrary to scriptures, suggested that it was not a "rightly constituted church of Christ," and asked not to be blamed for their "peaceful separation."[29] The Keithian Quakers, whose founder would eventually join the Church of England, were a bit more sympathetic. The author of their reply refused to say anything that would "lessen that love and esteem that we have for each other," but at the same time rejected the suggestion that the Keithians join the Church of England.[30]

Evan Evans, who took over as minister in 1700, took a different, more aggressive approach in dealing with dissenters. Evidencing seemingly boundless energy, Evans dedicated himself to converting individual Quakers and to bringing Anglicans, many of whom he considered on the brink of heathenism, back into the fold. He regularly traveled to the surrounding areas up to forty miles away to preach, and in seven years he baptized eight hundred people. He took particular joy in preaching to the Welsh settlements at Merion and Radnor, which he visited every two weeks for four years. In Philadelphia he used evening lectures to try to reach both Anglicans and Quakers. He felt that the "Society of young men" that met together every Sunday after evening prayer "to read ye Scriptures and Sing Psalms" was a particularly effective conversion tool. "Those Quakers, that Durst not appear in the day at the Publiq Service of the Church, for fear of disobligeing their Parents or Masters would stand under the Church windows att night, till many of them pluck't up so much Courage, as to come to ye Church it selfe."[31]

Evans's labors were greatly aided by the establishment in 1701 of the Society for the Propagation of the Gospel in Foreign Parts, or SPG, a private missionary society in England supported by prominent men and women within the Church of England. Having heard that many colonists lacked "the Administration of God's Word and Sacraments, and seem to be Abandoned to Atheism and Infidelity," they joined together to ensure that "a sufficient Maintenance be provided for an Orthodox Clergy to live amongst" these colonists.[32] This marked the first time that officials of the Anglican church in England involved themselves with missionary work.

From the start, the leaders of the SPG made it clear that they intended to do more than provide ministers to Anglicans—they intended to build Anglican congregations by converting dissenters, particularly Quakers. To accomplish this, they went on the offensive, attacking Quakers and their beliefs, rather than merely preaching the doctrines of the Anglican church. They chose as their first two missionaries men whose intemperate views, love of controversy, and hatred of Quakers were well known. George Keith, who by this time had become an Anglican priest, was despised by orthodox Quakers as a traitor to their cause; John Talbot referred to Quakers as "worse than Infidels. . . [serving] no God but Mammon & their own Bellys." In addition, the SPG equipped these men with one thousand copies of the most extreme anti-Quaker tracts available.[33]

The arrival of Keith and Talbot in Philadelphia in November of 1702 ushered in several years of virulent confrontation between Quakers and Anglicans, an approach supported by Christ Church members. The vestry thanked the SPG for sending Keith, "whose unparalleled zeal . . . whose frequent preaching . . . whose strenuous and elaborate writing made him highly and signally instrumental in promoting the Church."[34]

Keith and Talbot spent more than six months in Philadelphia and the surrounding area between November 1702 and April 1704, preaching to crowds that overflowed the church, engaging the Quakers in public debate whenever possible, and even attempting to speak at Quaker meetings. To their apparent surprise, they found the Quakers "generally very uncivil and rude . . . declining all discourse with us, and returning nothing to our kindly offers to inform them but reproaches and railings and gross reflections." Despite his persistence, by Keith's own admission, his efforts at conversion were largely unsuccessful.[35]

Keith's arrival led to an extended and often nasty debate in the press. The most interesting occurred in the competing Quaker and Anglican almanacs of the time. A former Keithian turned Anglican, Daniel Leeds treated readers of his Almanac to anti-Quaker tirades interspersed with information on the movement of the planets and other scientific topics. In 1705 he also included a carefully reasoned explanation of Anglican doctrine and practices, clearly designed to convert Quakers. The Quaker Jacob Taylor countered in his Almanac by defending Quaker practices, arguing that to Anglicans "forms and Distinctions are a Deity," and accusing Leeds of plagiarism. The rancorous exchange continued until 1711 when Taylor decided to "Let spleen depart and this Contention die."[36]

Despite the longstanding hostility between Anglicans and Quakers that led to these exchanges, within fifteen years of the founding of Christ Church, the Anglicans united and aggressive front against the Quakers had disappeared and within twenty-five years the days of confrontation in both politics and religion had come to an end.

Political confrontation between Anglicans and Quakers had declined dramatically by 1710. Once it became clear that Pennsylvania would not become a royal colony, ambitious individuals within the Anglican church realized that they had to cooperate with the Quakers to gain power. Penn and his supporters, in turn, welcomed help in battling a group of Quakers who had turned against the proprietor. Thus, when Evan Evans went to England to attend to some personal business in 1708, he met with Penn and returned with a letter directing Penn's deputy, James Logan, to consult with Evans regarding the new governor, Charles Gookin. In 1713, when Evans once again returned to England, Logan reported that they had "alwayes had a good understanding with each other." Such a statement certainly could not have been made ten years earlier.[37]

At about the same time that individual Anglicans began cooperating with Quakers, Christ Church as an institution withdrew from the political fray. After 1707 the vestry wrote only one letter opposing Quaker policies, and it was written to the Pennsylvania Assembly, not to English authorities, thus recognizing the legitimacy of the Pennsylvania government. Anglican missionaries in the area outside Philadelphia who had often written on political topics wrote their last political letters dealing with the oath issue in 1712.[38]

The decline in Anglican hostility toward Quakers in the strictly religious sphere is harder to trace than the change in the political sphere, but it is clear that open antagonism and vigorous efforts to convert Friends began to lessen just about the same time that tension in the political arena was easing. Evan Evans had initially welcomed the strident methods of Keith and Talbot and in 1704 had written to Keith recounting his own methods and successes in converting the Quakers.[39] But after that year his letters never again emphasized his dealings with Quakers; instead he concentrated on internal problems within Christ Church. Moreover, Evans was the last rector of Christ Church to focus on the conversion of Quakers.

The end of Anglican-Quaker confrontation can also be seen in the Philadelphia press. Not one anti-Quaker pamphlet or article was published in Philadelphia after 1710. The decision of Jacob Taylor and Daniel Leeds to end their battle merely reflected the overall change in Anglican-Quaker relations.

The importance of this change can best be seen in a comparative framework, for Anglicans in other colonies took far longer to accept the legitimacy of other religions, and religious conflict continued in most colonies until the time of the American Revolution. In the 1720s Massachusetts and Connecticut experienced an intense and at times vicious battle between members of the established Congregational church and Anglicans that climaxed with the conversion to the Church of England of Timothy Cutler, the rector of Yale College, and three of his students in 1722. At the same time, the governor of South Carolina, Francis Nicholson, the deeply committed Anglican who had helped Christ Church, tried to strengthen the largely symbolic establishment of the Church of England in that colony; this resulted in battles between Anglicans and the large number of dissenters. New York, where the Church of England had a much disputed establishment in the lower counties, also witnessed religious tensions in the 1720s, with dissenters in Hempstead trying to take over the Anglican parsonage, arguing that their minister should get the support provided by taxes. Then in the 1750s the successful attempt by New York Anglicans to control the newly created King's College created anti-Anglican feeling in that colony. The drive to establish an Anglican episcopate in the colonies in the 1760s, which we will discuss in Chapter 6, led to fierce exchanges between Anglicans and non-Anglicans in New England and New York. Virginia also saw an increase in Anglican-dissenter battles in the 1760s, primarily involving the Baptists.[40]

Pennsylvania experienced less religious conflict than other colonies primarily because it had no state church. While the early leaders of Christ Church believed that having no state church at all was worse than having a dissenting church as the established church, as was the case in New England, in reality the absence of a state church eliminated the main source of tension and conflict among religious groups. "Dissenters" could not attack the church for its domination or persecution of others, and once the Quakers became a minority in their own colony, which they were by the 1730s, Anglicans could no longer complain that they were being discriminated against.

Moreover, once Anglicans came to terms with the reality of all denominations being equal under the law, they began thinking of other denominations as equal, something that was not possible in a colony where one branch of Christianity was officially sanctioned. When it became clear that Pennsylvania was not going to become a royal colony, Christ Church leaders began to deal with the environment that really existed, not that which they hoped for or that which they feared. They found that their church could and did prosper without being established and without having a royal government. Peaceful coexistence, combined with legitimate, vigorous competition proved to be conducive to the health and prosperity of the Church in Philadelphia. This knowledge contributed to a sense of confidence that Anglicans in other colonies did not have.

Notes

1. In the first part of the seventeenth century the argument for an established church had been based on theological grounds, the belief that the Church of England offered the only way to salvation. By the 1690s more practical considerations had taken over. See particularly William Warburton, *The Alliance between Church and State: or the Necessity and Equity of an Established Religion and a Test Law, demonstrated from the essence of Nature and Nations* (London: F. Giles, 1736).

2. The Act of Toleration did allow dissenters to hold office if they could demonstrate "occasional conformity" (taking communion in a Church of England congregation at least once a year), but this loophole was closed in 1710. For a good discussion of the Anglican view on church-state relations see David Little, *Religion, Order and Law; A Study in Pre-Revolutionary England* (New York: Harper and Row, 1969), 132ff.

3. See Horton Davies, *Worship and Theology in England from Watts and Wesley to Maurice, 1690–1850* (Princeton, N.J.: Princeton University Press, 1961), especially p. 29.

Arthur Warne, *Church and Society in Eighteenth Century Devon* (Newton Abott: David and Charles, 1969), 11—21.

4. The term "group mysticism" is used by Howard H. Brinton, *Friends for Three Hundred Years* (Philadelphia: Pendle Hill Publications, 1964), xiii. A good brief summary of Quaker beliefs is found in the introduction by Rufus Jones to *The Journal of George Fox* (New York: Capricorn Books, 1963). The primary contemporary work on Quaker theology was Robert Barclay's *Apology.* I have used *Barclay's Apology in Modern English,* ed. Dean Freiday (privately printed, 1967).

5. Rufus Jones, introduction to *The Journal of George Fox,* 39.

6. *Barclay's Apology,* 389.

7. "Laws agreed upon in England by the Governour and Divers of the Free-Men of Pennsylvania," attached to William Penn's "Frame of Government," *The Papers of William Penn, Volume 2, 1680–1684,* ed. Richard Dunn and Mary Maples Dunn (Philadelphia: University of Pennsylvania Press, 1982), 225.

8. See *Lawmaking and Legislators in Pennsylvania: A Biographical Dictionary,* ed. Craig W. Horle and Marianne S. Wokeck (Philadelphia: University of Pennsylvania Press, 1991—), vol. 1.

9. John Oldmixon, *The British Empire in America Containing the History of the Discovery, Settlement, Progress and Present State of All the British Colonies, on the Continent and Islands of America* (London, 1708) in Nancy Sirkis, *Reflections of 776: The Colonies Revisited* (New York: Viking Press, 1974), 88.

10. Mary Maples Dunn and Richard Dunn, "The Founding, 1681–1701" in Russell Weigley, ed., *Philadelphia, A Three Hundred Year History* (New York: W.W. Norton and Company, 1982), 11,20–21. The Dunns are here summarizing material from Hannah Benner Roach, "Philadelphia Business Directory, 1690," *Pennsylvania Genealogical Magazine* 23 (1964): 95–129.

11. Edwin Bronner, "Village into Town: 1701–1746" in Weigley, ed., *Philadelphia,* 57; Joseph Kelley, *Life and Times in Colonial Philadelphia* (Harrisburg, Pa., 1973), 51.

12. The only source we have for the early supporters of Christ Church is a letter they sent to Governor Francis Nicholson of Maryland, who had contributed to the new church. Thirty-six men signed the letter; they probably represented most if not all of the literate Anglican men in Philadelphia; Robert Quary and others to Governor Nicholson, Jan. 18, 1696/97 in William Perry, ed., *Historical Collections Relating to the American Colonial Church,* 5 vols. (Hartford, Conn,, 1871; reprint ed., New York: AMS Press, 1969), 2: 5–7. (While I will use new style dates in the text, I will use both old and new style dates in the notes.) The 1693 tax list is in *PMHB* 8 (1884): 85–105; the manuscript of the 1696/97 list is in Philadelphia County, Miscellaneous Papers, HSP. Information about the signers of the letter is found in Charles Keith, "The Founders," in Louis Washburn, ed., *Christ Church, Philadelphia: A Symposium* (Philadelphia: Macrae Smith Co., 1925), 94–100.

13. See Roach, "Philadelphia Business Directory, 1690," 103.

14. For information on Robert Quary, see Gary Nash, *Quakers and Politics: Pennsylvania 1681- 1726* (Princeton, N.J.: Princeton University Press, 1968), 195.

15. Keith, "The Founders," 96–97. The earliest reference to the church being completed is Quary et al, to Governor Nicholson, Jan. 18, 1696/97. John Watson in the earliest edition of his *Annals* asserted that the first church was made of wood. But Benjamin Dorr, a rector of Christ Church in the nineteenth century, challenged that version, arguing convincingly that the first church must have been brick. When Willis Hazard revised the *Annals* he accepted Dorr's arguments. *Annals of Philadelphia and Pennsylvania in the Olden Times,* enlarged and revised by Willis Hazard, 3 vols. (Philadelphia: J.M. Stoddard, 1884), 1: 378. Dorr bases his argument on several factors: there are references

in the cash books to buying 37,000 Flemish bond bricks, the type used for the outside of buildings, when the church was enlarged in 1711; the travelers certainly would not have referred to a wooden structure as great, since Philadelphia already had many brick homes; and the present church building was begun as an addition to the first. Benjamin Dorr, *A Historical Account of Christ Church, Philadelphia* (Philadelphia: R.S.H. George, 1841), 7–14; Accounting Warden's Journal, April 1709, May 1711; John Oldmixon, *The British Empire,* 88; Gabriel Thomas, *An Historical and Geographical Account of the Province and Country of Pennsylvania* London: A. Baldwin, 1698), 52.

16. Ellis P. Oberholtzer, *Philadelphia: A History of the City and Its People,* 4 vols. (Philadelphia: J. Clarke Publishing Company, [1912]), 1: 73,103.

17. Watson, *Annals of Philadelphia,* 1:38. Oberholzer, *Philadelphia,* 1:39.

18. Grant of Pennsylvania to William Penn, March 4,1680, Perry, *Historical Collections,* 2:5.

19. Francis Nicholson to Archbishop Thomas Tenison, March 18, 1695/96, February 28, 1696/97, and June 30,1697, Fulham Papers, American Colonial Section, in Lambeth Palace, microfilm, Van Pelt library, University of Pennsylvania (hereafter referred to as Fulham Papers), 2:51–52,87, and 92–93.

20. Ibid., Feb. 28,1696/97, Fulham Papers, 2: 87; Richard Sewell to Francis Nicholson, Oct. 9, *1697,* Fulham *Papers,* 7:11.

21. William B. Sprague, *Annals of the American Pulpit,* 5 vols. (New York, Arno Press, 1969, reprint of 1857–1869), 5: 22–25.

22. Robert Quary, "A Brief Narrative of the Proceedings of William Penn," Perry, *Historical Collections,* 2:4.

23. Edward Portlock to Archbishop of Canterbury, July 12, 1700, Perry, *Historical Collections,* 2:16.

24. Vestry to Board of Trade, Jan. 28,1700/1701, Board of Trade Papers, Proprietary, VI, ptl G13 (printed in *Calendar of State Papers, Colonial Series, America and West Indies 1574–1737* (London: 1860-), 19 (1701), no. 101.

25. Vestry to Board of Trade, October 27, 1701, Board of Trade Papers, Proprietary, VI, pt1 G13, *Calendar of State Papers,* 20, no. 271; Robert Snead to John Houblon, April 25,1698, ibid., 16, no. 403.

26. See Winfred T. Root, *The Relations of Pennsylvania with the British Government, 1695–1765* (New York: D. Appleton and Company, 1912), 234—55 for a good discussion of the oath question. For Anglican efforts to have laws disallowed in England see Board of Trade Papers, Proprietary, VII, pt2,082, transcripts, HSP. For discussions of Anglican efforts to disrupt the government see, for example, James Logan to William Penn, June 24 and Sept. 29, 1703, *Correspondence Between William Penn and James Logan,* 2 vols., ed. Edward Armstrong, in Historical Society of Pennsylvania, *Memoirs, 9* and 10 (1870,1872), 2:193,243—44.

27. The Keithian schism, which tore apart the Society of Friends from 1690 to 1693, started as an attempt by George Keith, a Scottish Quaker, to introduce more doctrinal rigidity into the Society by requiring adherence to a formal Confession of Faith. At least eighty-seven Philadelphia Quaker men were among Keith's followers. Keith himself returned to England and in 1699 converted to the Church of England. While it is unclear how many of his followers followed his example, we do know they had demonstrated sympathy for the Anglicans, allowing them to use their meeting house and housing the Anglican schoolteacher, John Arrowsmith, when he first arrived. For the details of the Keithian controversy see Gary Nash, *Quakers and Politics: Pennsylvania 1681–1726* (Princeton, N.J.: Princeton University Press, 1968), 144–60.

28. See George Every, *The High Church Party, 1688–1718* (London: Church Historical Society, 1956), chaps. 1 and 2.

29. We do not have any of the letters Clayton wrote, but he discusses his efforts in a letter to Governor Nicholson, Nov. 29, 1698, Perry, *Historical Collections,* 2: 14–15. The Baptist reply, John Watts et al. to Thomas Clayton, March II, 1699, is in David Spencer, *The Early Baptists of Philadelphia* (Philadelphia: W. Syckelmoore, 1877), 35–38.

30. For the Keithian reply see Thomas Martin to Thomas Clayton, Sept.16, 1698, Fulham Papers, 7: 18. Perry reprinted the letter (*Historical Collections,* 2: 12–13, 500), but incorrectly identifies the author as Thomas Makin, an orthodox Quaker.

31. Evan Evans, "The State of the Church in Pennsylvania, most humbly offered to ye Venerable Society for the Propagation of the Gospel in Foreign Parts," Perry, *Historical Collections,* 2:33–34.

32. The quote is from the charter of the SPG, which is found in David Humphreys, *An Historical Account of the Incorporated Society for the Propagation of the Gospel in Foreign Parts. . .* (London, 1730; reprint ed., New York: J. Downing, 1969), xvi.

33. See John Nelson, "Anglican Missions in America, 1701–25: A Study of the Society for the Propagation of the Gospel in Foreign Parts" (Ph.D. diss., Northwestern University, 1962), 96. For Talbot's quote see John Talbot to Secretary of the SPG, Sept. 7, 1724, in Edgar Pennington, *Apostle of New Jersey: John Talbot, 1645–1725* (Philadelphia: Church Historical Society, 1935), 184. Talbot's earlier letters are filled with similar quotes.

34. Vestry of Christ Church to Secretary of the SPG, [1704], quoted in Ethyn Kirby, *George Keith, 1638–1716* (New York: D. Appleton and Century Co., 1942), 144.

35. George Keith, "A Journal of Travels from New Hampshire to Caratuck, on the Continent of North America," *HMPEC* 20 (1951): 424, 431.

36. See, for example, Jacob Taylor, *An Almanack for the Year of Christian Account 1709* (Philadelphia, 1708); Daniel Leeds, *An Almanack for the Year of Christian Account 1708* (Philadelphia, 1707). For the end of the dispute see Leeds, *Almanac^, 1711* and Taylor, *Almanack 1711.*

37. For the political situation during these years see Nash, *Quakers and Politics,* 241–273. For a sample of the Penn-Logan correspondence about Quary and Logan see Armstrong, *Correspondence,* 2: 169,195, 277–78,289, 291,313,317. The quote is from James Logan to William Penn, Sept. 7, 1713, William Penn Papers, HSP.

38. The letter from the vestry concerned the oath law of 1723. See Christ Church Vestry Minutes, Nov. 1723. The letters from the missionaries are not extant. They are referred to in James Logan to William Penn, June 29, 1712, Logan Letter Book, 1712—1715, James Logan Papers, HSP, p. 15.

39. Evan Evans to George Keith, Oct. 25, 1704, Perry, *Historical Collections,* 2:20–21.

40. See Gerald Goodwin, "The Anglican Middle Way in Early Eighteenth Century America" (Ph.D, diss., University of Wisconsin, 1967), chap. 2; Joseph Ellis, *The New England Mind in Transition: Samuel Johnson of Connecticut, 1696–1772* (New Haven, Conn.: Yale University Press, 1973), 88–98; Sidney G. Bolton, "The Anglican Church of Colonial South Carolina 1704–1754: A Study in Americanization" (Ph.D. diss., University of Wisconsin, 1973), chaps. 5 and 6; Jean Paul Jordan, "The Anglican Establishment in Colonial New York, 1693–1783" (Ph.D. diss,, Columbia University, 1971), chap. 4; Carl Bridenbaugh, *Mitre and Sceptre* (London: Oxford University Press, 1962), 144–340; Frederick V. Mills, Sr., *Bishops by Ballot: An Eighteenth Century Ecclesiastical Revolution* (New York: Oxford University Press, 1978), 35–1; Rhys Isaac, *The Transformation of Virginia 1740–1790* (Chapel Hill: University of North Carolina Press, 1982).

Rush's Monument

John M. Kloos

Dr. Benjamin Rush (1745–1813), the Philadelphia physician, is remembered as a signer of the Declaration of Independence and for several other contributions to the American Revolution. It was Rush who suggested the phrase "Common Sense" to pamphleteer Thomas Paine. The doctor served as physician-general and toiled on the fields of battle. He is best remembered for healing the petty controversies between John Adams and Thomas Jefferson long after the war was over, a diplomatic act that led to fifteen years of precious correspondence between the two great founders. In 1813 these two old, and now renewed, companions from 1776 rose to eulogize the devoted physician. Jefferson spoke: "A better man than Rush could not have left us, more benevolent, more learned, of finer genius, or more honest." Adams confessed that he knew "of no Character living or dead, who has done more real good in America."[1]

Many of Rush's contributions have been obscured by history. Like Adams, Rush suffered a long period of neglect, and the reputation of each has only begun to be restored. Why was the physician forgotten? Two sins tarnished his image. If Benjamin Rush was signer of the Declaration, he was also the bleeder of Philadelphians during the yellow fever epidemic of 1793. One historian observed, "the deed of the pen alone [has saved] him from the total disgrace of the lancet." Worse, Rush publically criticized George Washington, a sin for which Americans have never forgiven him.

In 1974, Donald J. D'Elia published *Benjamin Rush, Philosopher of the American Revolution* as one of the *Transactions* of Rush's own American Philosophical Society. It was the burden of this revisionary study to demonstrate that Rush, "far from being a secondary historical character, was a leading—perhaps the chief—philosophical exponent of the American Revolution."[2] This development moved contemporary scholarship on Rush beyond the problem of reputation to present a turning point in the historiography of Benjamin Rush. D'Elia claims that Rush was a great philosopher because he integrated Enlightenment reason with his belief in Christian revelation. Although I believe that his argument for Rush's philosophical orientation is overstated, D'Elia's rescue of the doctor's religiosity is crucial to my thesis.[3]

D'Elia ends his story of Rush in 1790, when the doctor fell into "Grave doubts and otherworldly Consolations."[4] The best political biography of Benjamin Rush, by David Freeman Hawke, also ends at 1790.[5] Given the political squabbling between the Federalists and the republicans in the 1790s, Rush became

Kloos, John M. "Rush's Monument" in *A Sense of Deity: The Republican Spirituality of Benjamin Rush*. Carlson Publishing, 1991: 11–34.

disenchanted with the Revolution and its principles. For D'Elia, the doctor's harmonious philosophical system of "reason and revelation" could not hold, and, after the passage of the Constitution, Rush became "otherworldly" and "mystical."[6] But it is my view that Rush's religious orientation informed his understanding of life in America precisely at the moment when this so-called philosophical synthesis faltered.[7] In fact, it was after the federal victory that Benjamin Rush applied his religious view in a practical, middle-colony way. It should be stated at the outset that however mystical the good doctor became after the revolution, he remained a political creature. This was never more true than during the upheavals of the 1790s. His general religious orientation informed his public activity at this time, as it had throughout his life. Indeed, it was after the passage of the Constitution that Benjamin Rush participated in Philadelphia society by taking on an active role in the city's various voluntary moral associations, and this participation became his primary mode of political interaction.

Rush's involvement in voluntary associational activity, which stemmed from his religious orientation, marked his most characteristic political contribution to the early republic. Indeed, through this middle-colony form of social interaction, Rush continued the work of Benjamin Franklin, whose Philadelphia design for increasing virtue in the republic was also aimed at healing the inflammation brought on by factional politics. Rush's prescription for public health read: Take Americans from the Christian sects (which he saw as the stuff and substance of society); mix reasonably well in moral associations; apply thoroughly to the divided and ailing republic.[8] I have, in this rough formula, condensed Rush's view of the associative role of religious groups. His view differed from that of his friend and mentor Franklin in that Rush stressed the importance of the role played by the Christian sects. In short, it made a difference to Benjamin Rush that moral association was based on the substance of traditional religious belief; on this score the deist Franklin was not as committed.

The doctor's remedy achieved moderate success. Societies for educating the poor, for advancing temperance, for resuscitating drowning victims, and for providing humane treatment for the insane were the objects of Rush's plan for public health. The sun was rising on the "Benevolent Empire," casting warm rays on downtrodden Americans. As a signer of the Declaration and the best-known physician of his day, Rush was respected by educators, temperance organizers, popular health advocates, Christian missionaries, politicians, and religious leaders. In the city of Philadelphia the society movement played a vital role in restructuring city politics after the Revolutionary War.

For instance, in 1780, the Humane Society for Recovering Persons from Suspended Animation was founded. Its object was the restoration of drowning victims by way of "hot woolen cloths," "brushes," "frictions" and other stimulants, such as "heated bricks" applied "to the feet, belly, and breast." Directions for treating the body advised against "the usual destructive methods *of banging it by the heels, rolling it on a barrel, or placing it across a log on the belly.*" But more than merely restoring physical life in "suspended victims," the group worked to mend the social fabric and renew the city. Typical of associations in Philadelphia, the Humane Society was made up of individuals from various religious backgrounds. This voluntary association, and others like it, grew by merger and expansion, on the margins of party politics.[9] By the end of the century voluntary moral associations aided the churches in rethinking their new role in a society that separated civil and religious orders.[10]

To say why Rush's antidote of voluntary moral association was so timely, the social and historical conditions out of which it grew must be described. In arguing for a so-called religion of the republic, Sidney E. Mead described the condition of the religion of the churches after the passage of the Constitution as one of "indigestion." Evangelicals could not "digest" the theory of the separation of church and state until it was too late. Of course, Mead was being metaphorical in his description of the problems facing the revivalistic churches. It is my view that the contribution of the revolutionary physician Rush was that he developed a perspective that both allowed evangelical Americans to affirm Christianity and encouraged them to live under the terms of the Constitution. In formulating his prescription for the role of religion in American society, Rush did not suffer the indigestion associated by Mead with the churches in America. In fact, Benjamin Rush knew all about the federal theory of factional politics and he characterized the constitutional system of government in fundamentally religious terms. For Rush, Federalism reflected the reality of human sin; thus the controls of checks and balances were needed. Further, his role in the creation of the republic had much to do with the mediation of common sense and practical reason through his own generous spirit. First, a short sketch of the doctor.

Benjamin Rush was born in Byberry, Pennsylvania, on his father's farm, about fourteen miles northwest of Philadelphia. In 1752 the Gregorian calendar replaced the Julian system in the colonies, which changed Rush's birthdate from 24 December 1745 to 4 January 1746. Raised in a lower-class Presbyterian home, Rush had a Roundhead ancestor of the Quaker religion. Genealogical notes recall that John Rush "embraced the principles of the Quakers in 1660. . . . In 1691 he and his whole family left the Quakers and became Keithians. In 1697 they became Baptists."[11] At the time of Benjamin's birth, the family was Anglican. Upon the death of his father, six-year-old Benjamin was taken by his mother to Gilbert Tennent's Second Presbyterian Church in Philadelphia. In 1800, when Rush wrote his "Travels Through Life," he described the strong influence of the new side Presbyterians on his character:

> The religious impressions that were made upon my mind at this time were far from issuing in a complete union to God by his Son Jesus Christ, but they left my mind more tender to sin of every kind, and begat in me constant desires for a new heart, and a sense of God's mercy in the way of his Gospel. Religious company now became most agreeable to me and I delighted in public worship, and particularly in hearing evangelical ministers of all denominations. I made conscious of secret prayer from that time, nor do I recollect to have passed a day without it while in health to the present year 1800.[12]

I will return to the profound influence of revivalistic Christianity upon the young Benjamin Rush.

After graduation from the College of New Jersey (Princeton) and an apprenticeship in "physick," Rush sailed for Edinburgh, Scotland. Once there, he wrote to Benjamin Franklin, who was in London, and the young man requested of his fellow Philadelphian letters of introduction to Edinburgh friends. Franklin obliged, introducing Rush to some of the first characters of Europe. In fact, Franklin wrote to his friend Sir Alexander Dick, and within one month of Rush's arrival he dined with David Hume at Sir Alexander's house. The American artist Benjamin West also served as a European guardian, arranging for Rush to meet Sir Joshua Reynolds, Samuel Johnson, and Oliver Goldsmith. London reviewers had severely criticized a recent work by Goldsmith. Rush recalled Johnson's words: "What then, where is the advantage of having a great deal of money, but that the loss of a little will not hurt you, in like manner where is the advantage of having a great deal of reputation but that the loss of a little will not hurt you, you can bear the censures of the reviewers." Indeed, historians are indebted to Rush for his recollection of Samuel Johnson, as well as for his anecdotes from a dinner meeting with David Hume. Also while abroad, Rush visited Mrs. Catherine Macaulay, the Whig historian, and he attended the House of Commons to see Edmund Burke in action.[13]

In Edinburgh Rush moved in the evangelical circles defined by Jonathan Edwards's old friend and correspondent John Erskine. Rush had first met George Whitefield in Gilbert Tennent's Second Presbyterian Church. In Scotland he renewed his acquaintance with the Reverend Whitefield, "the Grand Itinerant." It was here that young Rush met John Witherspoon, the man he later helped bring to the presidency of Princeton.[14]

By 1783, the year of Boerhaave's death at Leyden, Edinburgh was fast becoming the rising star of European medicine. Between 1765 and 1800, 113 Americans received M.D.s from Edinburgh and as many more probably studied there but did not complete the master's thesis, perhaps because it had to be written in Latin.[15] In the medical school, Rush studied with the two giants of late-eighteenth-century chemistry, William Cullen and Joseph Black. That he studied with the discoverer of carbon dioxide (Black), and was acquainted with the discoverer of oxygen (Joseph Priestley), suggests the magnitude of the innovations taking place in the world of early-modern chemistry as well as Rush's location in that nascent world. William Cullen, colleague and friend of Adam Smith, was highly admired by young Rush, and it has been said that Rush's classroom manner, as well as his bedside manner, was derived from Dr. Cullen.

In Europe, Rush was exposed to new ideas and he recast old ones. This was especially true in the area of politics. Rush's political activities have been well documented.[16] At Edinburgh, Rush honed political ideas embraced in the middle colonies, where he had opposed the Stamp Act in 1765. Republicanism grew out of the moral doctrine of "public spirit" proclaimed by the new side Presbyterian Samuel Davies, who was president of the College of New Jersey. Rush first refined this doctrine abroad; then he polished it in the heat of America's revolution. Of the midsummer day of 1776 when Rush "subscribed a copy upon parchment of the Declaration of Independence," he later recalled "the pensive and awful silence which pervaded the house when we were called up, one after another, to the table of the President of Congress to subscribe what was believed by many at that time to be our own death warrants." The silence was broken once, by the hefty Virginian Benjamin Harrison, who said to the New Englander Elbridge Gerry: "I shall have a great advantage over you, Mr. Gerry, when we are all hung for what we are now doing. From the size and weight of my body I shall die in a few minutes, but from the lightness of your body you will dance in the air an hour or two before you are dead." Rush recollected well that "this speech procured a transient smile, but it was soon succeeded by the solemnity with which the whole business was conducted."[17]

As one of the earliest American physicians to advocate humane treatment for the insane, to point toward the benefits of exercise, to concoct a "republican" diet (temperate and vegetable), and to experiment with hydrotherapy, Rush represents much of America's curiosity with British empiricism. Although he rejected mesmerism and animal magnetism, Rush dabbled in a variety of strange and new psychological techniques, which led one writer to compare Rush to France's Philippe Pinel.[18] One year before Rush's death, an extraordinary treatise entitled *Medical Inquiries and Observations on Diseases of the Mind* was published. This first comprehensive text on mental illness in the United States has led some to dub Rush the Father of American Psychiatry.[19]

An array of constructive work grew out of his republicanism. A tireless educator, he was the prime mover behind the founding of Dickinson College, and he took on the tough political work of selecting and organizing the trustees. The doctor was particularly adept at fund-raising, and he crafted the curriculum at Dickinson. Franklin College was another object of the doctor's energy, as was the Pennsylvania backcountry in general.[20] In this regard, Benjamin Rush's *Manners of the German Inhabitants of Pennsylvania* is something of a masterpiece in late-eighteenth-century ethnology.[21] It exhibits familiarity and concern with the backcountry Germans, their traditions, and their needs. Until recently, Rush's commitment to women's status, including especially the education of women in the new republic, was less well documented.[22] His *Thoughts upon Female Education*, delivered at Philadelphia's Young Ladies' Academy, is a remarkable document.[23] Rush's educational and political work with Africans was primarily ecclesiastical, rather than specifically pedagogical. This was due to the fundamental problem of the Africans' status under the law. Rush, an avid abolitionist, had been part of the antislavery movement before the American Revolution broke out. He worked for and with the African community, both slave and free, in a way that was appropriate to its primary condition under the law. The doctor's own teaching cannot be overlooked. It is estimated that he instructed over 3,000 medical students during his tenure at the University of Pennsylvania, well above that of any other teaching physician of his day, and so instruction was an important source for the doctor's influence.[24]

Outside the new political institutions of the new republic that Rush helped to found, it is difficult to characterize the doctor's politics. Lyman H. Butterfield wrote in his Introduction to *The Letters of Benjamin Rush*

> that it is a serious mistake to classify him with deists like Franklin, Paine, and Jefferson, even though he worked with these associates for certain common objectives. If the contradiction seems glaring between his scientific aims and his Christian piety, it is no more so than some others in his

> career, notably in his politics. To contemporaries he must have seemed a very weathercock as he veered from radicalism in the early Revolutionary years to arch-conservatism in the late 1780s (when he denounced as absurd the popular demand for a bill of rights in the Constitution), and then, within two or three years, became an ardent supporter of Jefferson.[25]

When, after extracting himself from political life in 1790, Benjamin Rush was appointed treasurer of the United States Mint, the political fury on the part of Federalists and republicans alike testifies to the problem of classifying the doctor's political allegiance.[26]

Throughout life, Benjamin Rush was a man of affairs. An active layman in the Presbyterian church and a political reformer in the public life of the new nation, Rush cannot be dismissed as a mystical gadfly, especially in the 1790s when his associational politics addressed genuine problems in the republic. But when Rush is compared exclusively to a conservative political theorist like Adams or a liberal like Jefferson, the doctor will always come out second best. In the realm of politics, Rush cannot compete. His star shone brightest elsewhere. In fact, the source of Benjamin Rush's authority was religious.

At the end of a fascinating life, Benjamin visited the grave of his grandfather, James Rush.

> While standing near his grave and recollecting how much of my kindred dust surrounded it, my thoughts became confused, and it was some time before I could arrange them. Had any or all my ancestors and kinsmen risen from their graves and surrounded me in their homespun and working dresses (for they were all farmers or mechanics), they would probably have looked at each other with some surprise and said, "What means that *gentleman* by thus intruding upon us?"—"Dear and venerable friends! Be not offended at me. I inherit your blood, and I bear the name of most of you. I come to claim affinity with you and do homage to your Christian and rural virtues. It is true my dress indicates that I move in a different sphere from that in which you passed through life, but I have acquired and received nothing from the world which I prize so highly as the religious principles I inherited from you, and I possess nothing that I value so much as the innocence and purity of your characters."[27]

Benjamin Rush was a leading figure of the revolutionary period not for his political theory or his moral philosophy. It was his associational activity based on a religious orientation that qualifies Rush as a leading figure in American revolutionary history. That is, his concern with "innocence and purity," his deep and abiding moral commitments, his prophetic dreams, and his intense quest to redeem himself and the American republic embody a religious orientation. This is the best explanation that can be given for Rush's last contribution to the republic: the reconciliation of John Adams and Thomas Jefferson.

Of the many deeds or firsts by which we remember Benjamin Rush, his greatest contribution to the creation of the American republic involved two of the nation's premier founders. It is important to note that Rush's skills at association played a valuable part in this contribution. Also, one need not stretch the imagination to see these men as representative of common sense and reason. Such types, and Rush's relationship to them, have been central to the ordering of the America pantheon. I ask the reader's pardon for lengthy quotations, but I know of no better way to introduce Rush's greatest contribution, to point to his associative style, and to mark his role as mediator. On the reconciliation of Adams and Jefferson, Lyman H. Butterfield wrote:

> Injured pride overcoming old ties of affection is a commonplace in human relations, but magnanimity overcoming injured pride, like man biting dog, is more worthy of notice. John Adams and Thomas Jefferson provide an example of such magnanimity. This much is well known. . . . But the steps by which their reconciliation came about have been vaguely known, because they can be traced only in the unpublished correspondence of a third highly interested party, Dr. Benjamin Rush of Philadelphia.[28]

Butterfield went on to retrace Rush's methodical steps. In a series of letters Rush prepared Adams and Jefferson for the possibility of a renewed friendship. In a letter to John Adams, Rush spun out his vision of the future.

> "What book is that in your hands?" said I to my son Richard a few nights ago in a DREAM. "It is the history of the United States," said he. "Shall I read a page of it to you?" "No, no," said I. "I believe in the truth of no history but in that which is contained in the Old and New Testaments." "But, sir," said my son, "this page relates to your friend Mr. Adams." "Let me see it then," said I. I read it with great pleasure and herewith send you a copy of it.

1809

> "Among the most extraordinary events of this year was the renewal of the friendship and intercourse between Mr. John Adams and Mr. Jefferson, the two ex-Presidents of the United States. They met for the first time in the Congress of 1775. Their principles of liberty, their ardent attachment to their country, and their views of the importance and probable issue of the struggle with Great Britain in which they were engaged being exactly the same, they were strongly attracted to each other and became personal as well as political friends. They met in England during the war while each of them held commissions of honor and trust at two of the first courts of Europe, and spent many happy hours together in reviewing the difficulties and success of their respective negotiations. A difference of opinion upon the objects and issue of the French Revolution separated them during the years in which that great event interested and divided the American people. The predominance of the party which favored the French cause threw Mr. Adams out of the Chair of the United States in the year 1800 and placed Mr.

Jefferson there in his stead. The former retired with resignation and dignity to his seat at Quincy, where he spent the evening of his life in literary and philosophical pursuits surrounded by an amiable family and a few old and affectionate friends. The latter resigned the Chair of the United States in the year 1808, sick of the cares and disgusted with the intrigues of public life, and retired to his seat at Monticello in Virginia, where he spent the remainder of his days at the cultivation of a large farm agreeably to the new system of husbandry. In the month of November, 1809, Mr. Adams addressed a short letter to his friend Mr. Jefferson in which he congratulated him upon his escape to the shades of retirement and domestic happiness, and concluded it with assurances of his regard and good wishes for his welfare. This letter did great honor to Mr. Adams. It discovered a magnanimity known only to great minds. Mr. Jefferson replied to this letter and reciprocated expressions of regard and esteem. These letters were followed by a correspondence of several years, in which they mutually reviewed the scenes of business in which they had been engaged, and candidly acknowledged to each other all the errors of opinion and conduct into which they had fallen during the time they filled the same station in the service of their country. Many precious aphorisms, the result of observation, experience, and profound reflection, it is said, are contained in these letters. It is to be hoped the world will be favored with a sight of them when they can neither injure nor displease any persons or families whose ancestors' follies or crimes were mentioned in them. These gentlemen sunk into the grave nearly at the same time, full of years and rich in the gratitude and praises of their country (for they outlived the heterogeneous parties that were opposed to them), and to their numerous merits and honors posterity has added that they were rival friends.

"With affectionate regard to your fireside, in which all my family join, I am, dear sir, your sincere old friend,

"Benjn: Rush"

Adams, who had been sadly trapped by his own party in the 1790s, had been least willing of the two men to bury the past. But upon Rush's letter, Adams wrote: "A Dream again! I wish you would dream all day and all Night, for one of your dreams puts me in spirits for a Month. I have no other objection to your Dream, but that it is not History. It may be Prophecy."[29] The last sentence communicated to Rush a willingness on the part of Adams to restore the relationship. This was all the doctor needed in order to address the practical problem methodically, in a series of letters to Jefferson.

John Adams and Thomas Jefferson renewed their friendship in 1811. Until their deaths on the 4th of July 1826, these two great founders remembered the events of the revolution and the subsequent creation of the American republic. It is, from the perspective of his religious orientation, no surprise that Benjamin Rush reconciled John Adams, the man of reason, with Thomas Jefferson, the philosopher of common sense. And Lyman H. Butterfield was correct to call this achievement the doctor's "real monument."[30]

Notes

1. Three years later, Adams made this judgment: "Why is not Dr. Rush placed before Dr. Franklin in the Temple of Fame? Because cunning is a more powerful divinity than simplicity. Rush has done infinitely more good to America than Franklin. Both have deserved a high rank, among benefactors to their Country and mankind, but Rush, by far the highest." Adams to Richard Rush, 22 July 1816, "Microfilms of the Adams Papers," Letters, Pt. 2, Box 122, Massachusetts Historical Society, Boston.

2. Donald J. D'Etia, *Benjamin Rush, Philosopher of the American Revolution*, American Philosophical Society *Transactions* 64, new ser., pt. 5 (1974): 8.

3. The only book-length study of Rush's religious thought is D'Elia's, *Rush*, an attempt to systematize Rush's eclectic ideas. D'Elia is most successful at showing the pervasiveness of religious ideas in Rush; Henry May, who arrived

independently at a similar conclusion, in *The Enlightenment in America,* 207–11, views Rush as a Calvinist and an enlightened, but unskeptical, revolutionary.

4. D'Elia, *Rush,* 102–5.

5. David Freeman Hawke, *Benjamin Rush, Revolutionary Gadfly* (Indianapolis: Bobbs-Merrill, 1971), is the most up-to-date political biography, although Nathan G. Goodman's *Benjamin Rush, Physician and Citizen, 1746–1813* (Philadelphia: University of Pennsylvania Press, 1934), remains indispensible. Neither study provides a satisfying assessment of Rush's religiosity.

6. D'Elia's use of these terms conforms roughly to the perspective developed in Ernst Troeltsch, *The Social Teaching of the Christian Churches*, trans. Olive Wyon (Chicago; University of Chicago Press, 1960).

7. By "religious orientation" I follow Mircea Eliade and Paul Tillich's perspectives on general human religiosity. For Eliade, human nature is distinguished by a general religious consciousness. *Homo religiosis* lives primarily in and for the "sacred" as manifested in the variety of myths and cultic practices of the world's religions. Tillich's definition of religion as "ultimate concern" is close to Eliade's view, although it was developed theologically rather than phenomenologically. The formula, culture is the form of religion and religion is the content of culture, is a general proposition that underlies this book.

Paul W. Conner, *Poor Richard's Politicks: Benjamin Franklin and Ilis New American Order* (London: Oxford University Press, 1965), remains an excellent introduction to Franklin's associational activity. "Sect" has taken on more specific meaning since Rush's day. He used the word to refer to all stripes of Christian bodies that had, since the Reformation, been separated.

"Directions for Recovering Persons," in *Do Not Despair* (Philadelphia, n.d.), Humane Society, Soc. Misc. Coll., Historical Society of Pennsylvania, Philadelphia, Pennsylvania. This Society for Recovering Persons merged with the city's skating dub to become the Humane Society of Philadelphia. Ice-skaters on the Delaware were trained to revive drowning victims, but proximity to the river was not the only rationale behind this merger. It was typical of ongoing, expanding association.

10. The need for the churches to rethink their role in the new republic was monumental. Winthrop S. Hudson, *The Great Tradition of the American Churches* (New York: Harper & Brothers, 1953), 27–41; Mead, *The Lively Experiment*, 113–15.

11. Benjamin Rush, *A Memorial Containing Travels Through Life,* ed. Louis Alexander Biddle (Lanoraie, Penn.: Privately printed, 1905), 223; for more background, see the unsigned genealogy of the Rush family addressed to Dr. Geo. W. Corner, M.D., February 1965, Northampton, England. The American Philosophical Society, Philadelphia, Pennsylvania.

12. *The Autobiography of Benjamin Rush,* ed. G. W. Corner (Princeton: Princeton University Press, 1948), 23–37, 164.

13. Benjamin West, a fellow Philadelphian, was the first American artist to achieve a European reputation and to move in London art circles; Joshua Reynolds, the first president of the Royal Society, was knighted during the time that Rush was in London; C. G. Osgood, "An American Boswell," *Princeton University Library Chronicle* 5 (1944): 86; L. H. Butterfield, *Reminiscences of Boswell and Johnson* (Somerville, N.J.: Privately printed, 1946), also treats Rush's encounter with Johnson; Oliver Goldsmith, having published *The Traveller and The Vicar of Wakefield,* was well known by 1768–1769; by the time Rush wrote his "Travels Through Life," he strongly disagreed with Hume's position on moral sense; also see "Contrast between the Death of a Deist and a Christian: David Hume and Samuel Finley," *United States Magazine* 1 (1779): 56–72, an essay Rush hinted he wrote and one that confirms the hint on the basis of internal evidence; *Autobiography of BR,* 33, 34 n. 24; Catherine Sawbridge, the Whig historian, was particularly influential in Rush's republican education; Burke did not speak that day. Notes and impressions were recorded; see Benjamin Rush, 'The Scottish Journal," Special Collections, Lilly Library, Indiana University, Bloomington, Indiana.

14. John Erskine became an important benefactor of Dickinson College. Rush was also drawn to John Wesley's preaching while in England; see *Autobiography of BR,* 42–52, on evangelical circles in Scotland and England; *John Witherspoon Comes to America,* ed. Lyman H. Butterfield (Princeton: Princeton University Press, 1953).

15. Douglas Sloan, *The Scottish Enlightenment and the American College Ideal* (New York: Columbia University Press, 1971), 197,

16. Goodman, *Rush*; Hawke, *Rush.*

17. Rush to John Adams, 20 July 1811, *Letters of Benjamin Rush,* ed. Lyman H. Butterfield, 2 vols. (Princeton: Princeton University Press, 1951), 2:1090.

18. Carl Binger, *Revolutionary Doctor: Benjamin Rush, 1746–1813* (New York: Norton, 1966), 180–81.

19. Benjamin Rush, *Medical Inquiries and Observations into the Diseases of the Mind* (Philadelphia, 1812); Richard H. Shryock, "The Psychiatry of Benjamin Rush," *American Journal of Psychiatry* 101 (1945): 432.

20. The story of his college-founding activity is admirably told by James A. Bonar, "Benjamin Rush and the Theory and Practice of Republican Education in Pennsylvania" (Ph.D. dissertation, Johns Hopkins University, 1965).

21. Benjamin Rush, *An Account of the Manners of the German Inhabitants of Pennsylvania,* with introduction and notes, by Theodore E. Schmauk (Lancaster: Pennsylvania-German Society, 1910; reprint ed., Philadelphia, 1789).

22. Two important exceptions include Linda K. Kerber, "Daughters of Columbia: Educating Women for the Republic, 1787–1805," in *Die Hofstadter Aegis: A Memorial,* ed. Stanley Elkins and Eric McKitrick (New York: Knopf, 1974), 3659, and Jacqueline S. Reiner, "Rearing the Republican Child: Attitudes and Practices in Post-Revolutionary Philadelphia," *William and Mary Quarterly,* ser. 3, 39 (1982): 150–63 (hereafter *WMQ).*

23. Benjamin Rush, *Thoughts upon Female Education, Accommodated to the Present State of Society, Manners and Government, in the United States of America Addressed to the Visitors of the Young Ladies' Academy in Philadelphia, 28 July, 1787* (Philadelphia, 1787); the address was reprinted in Benjamin Rush, *Essays, Literary, Moral and Philosophical* (Philadelphia, 1798), 75–92.

24. Goodman, *Rush,* 132; 162–63.

25. *BR Letters,* l:bdx-lxx.

26. Butterfield, appendix 3 in ibid., 2.1209–12.

27. Rush to John Adams, 13 July 1812, ibid., 2:1151–52.

28. Lyman H. Butterfield, "The Dream of Benjamin Rush: The Reconciliation of John Adams and Thomas Jefferson," *The Yale Review* 40 (1950): 297.

29. Ibid., 301.

30. Ibid., 319.

Gospel Labors

Richard S. Newman

When Richard Allen journeyed to his boyhood home of Philadelphia in 1786, he had just turned twenty-six. Since his manumission, he had traveled to a half-dozen states in the new American nation and worked at well over half a dozen different jobs too. Stability would now become Allen's primary concern. After settling in the City of Brotherly Love, he sought to build institutional homes for the burgeoning free black community—churches, reform groups, educational societies. He also struggled to secure equality for African Americans in the new republic. "Whoever hopes for great things in this world," Allen wrote, "takes pains to attain them."1 He went to great lengths to achieve his dreams.

Allen's efforts soon paid off, as he helped inaugurate two of the most revered black-led institutions in early national America: the Free African Society, a benevolent organization, and Bethel Church, which would become one of the most powerful African American churches in the United States. Achieving equality proved decidedly more difficult, however. The black founder's antislavery sermonizing met with apathy and even anger. But Allen was not deterred. Indeed, he knew that hardship was part of the long, hard road a prophet traveled.

1. Church Roots

Allen's church dated to his itinerant work in Delaware, Maryland, New Jersey, and Pennsylvania. He recalled that few free blacks attended services in Northern locales and that Southern masters tried to keep roaming preachers away from slaves.[2] Yet experience as a Methodist class leader told Allen that both free blacks and enslaved people hungered for the Word. Soon after attending the inaugural Methodist conference in Baltimore in 1784, Allen decided that someone must convert blacks into a powerful Afro-Christian constituency.

In what initially appeared to be a happy coincidence, Philadelphia's Methodist elder pressed Allen to preach to local blacks at St. George's Church. Allen traveled to the Quaker City in February 1786 and began holding services at the very early hour of 5 a.m. The itinerant bug briefly bit, but rising attendance compelled Allen to stay put. "I soon saw a large field open in seeking and instructing my African brethren," he recalled.[3] Allen remained in Philadelphia the rest of his life.

The city that Allen inhabited was not that of his youth. In the 1760s, Allen had been like the majority of his black brethren in British Philadelphia, where

---

Newman, Richard S. "Gospel Labors" in *Freedom's Prophet: Bishop Richard Allen, The AME Church, and the Black Founding Fathers.* New York: New York Univ. Press, 2008: 53–76.

perhaps 90 percent of the roughly eighteen hundred blacks were slaves. By the 1790s, black Philadelphians were overwhelming free, and the City of Brotherly Love had become a capital of free black life. When Pennsylvania abolitionists did the first of several census-style reports on black Philadelphians in the early 1790s, they visited roughly four hundred free families representing nearly thirteen hundred people of color, including ninety-nine homeowners. These numbers grew markedly by the early nineteenth century, when free blacks represented roughly 10 percent of the overall population. Most free blacks, the PAS noted, referring to the rising Allens of the world, "conduct [their lives] reputably and . . . some are very worthy citizens."[4] A sizable contingent of Philadelphia blacks came from outside the city, including those from the Pennsylvania countryside who traded rural life in slavery for urban life in freedom. Others migrated from Chesapeake locales, including runaway slaves who settled in a known abolitionist state with a known abolitionist society (the PAS) ready to aid them.[5]

Philadelphia's growing reputation as an abolitionist capital beckoned blacks along the Atlantic seaboard. The PAS had initially organized as a lobbying group that protested bondage sporadically in legislative halls and courts of law. By 1789, endangered blacks from rural Pennsylvania, Maryland, New Jersey, and Virginia had flooded the group with so many appeals for legal aid that the PAS shifted tactics. It hired more lawyers and represented more blacks in court at the close of the eighteenth century than any other abolitionist organization. Some black litigants were the victims of recalcitrant Pennsylvania masters. No sooner had the state's gradual abolition law been passed in 1780 than slaveholders sought to evade it. The PAS intervened for black freedom. Devious masters beyond Pennsylvania also brought slaves into the state without registering them properly—another violation of the abolitionist law. The PAS again intervened for black freedom (prompting, in some cases, immediate liberation followed by apprenticeship for formerly enslaved people).[6]

Blacks took strong action themselves, both by running *away* from masters and by running *to* white abolitionists for legal aid. In some cases, black runaways proved so irritating and costly to slaveholders inside and outside Pennsylvania that masters ended up striking bargains with slaves. In exchange for pledges against running away again, blacks would turn slavery for life into an indenture contract for a shorter number of years (often seven). White abolitionists officiated many of these indentures, further ensuring black freedom. Of course, PAS members could be paternalistic too—and they certainly did not win every case. They even refused to take some cases involving fugitive slaves for fear of offending Southern masters. But in a new American nation dedicated to liberty for some, and to slaveholders' property rights in man, the PAS was indeed a beacon of hope. In 1790, for instance, the group successfully blocked a proposed revision in the new state constitution separating whites' from blacks' rights. Abolitionist activism ensured that Pennsylvania citizens collectively had only one set of rights. Many freed blacks, as James Forten would later declare, came to view Pennsylvania "as the only state in the union wherein the black man is treated equally to the white."[7]

Allen made his own abolitionist contributions by working as a go-between for PAS activists. On several occasions, endangered blacks contacted the rising black preacher for help. Allen contacted abolitionist lawyers who investigated African

Americans' freedom claims. In 1788, Allen and the PAS sued a white coachmaker who illegally sold his slave to a non-Pennsylvanian.[8] African Americans who claimed to be kidnapping victims or wrongly enslaved former residents of Pennsylvania contacted Allen from as far away as Mississippi.[9] By aiding threatened blacks, Allen helped define the Quaker State as a Northern antislavery borderland that chipped away at slavery's national status.

Philadelphia was no heaven, Allen already knew, but it still proved to be a haven of sorts. Had not Allen himself come north to abolition's home instead of traveling south through the slave countries when he gained his own freedom? Like other people of color, he believed that Philadelphia—and, by extension, the abolitionizing state of Pennsylvania—offered a measure of hope for racial redemption in the new nation.

2. Industry and Uplift

From the moment he arrived in Philadelphia, Allen worked feverishly. "Idle hands do the Devil's work," Poor Richard once told Pennsylvanians. Ben Franklin would have been proud of Allen's work ethic. He did anything to rise in Philadelphia society, laboring as a whitewasher, dry-goods dealer, and cobbler on his way to becoming a master chimney sweep, entrepreneur, and minister supported by his congregation. Allen's chimney-sweeping business was particularly profitable. Ever known as a dangerous trade, chimney sweeps stuffed themselves into the narrowest fireplace chutes, danced on top of sharply slanted roofs, and spent their days face-to-face with ashes and soot. "The business was crowded, unhealthy and dangerous," two modern labor scholars have commented. But free blacks rose in a profession many whites preferred to avoid.[10] Indeed, whereas black sailors in Philadelphia rarely became masters of their own ships, several African Americans became master chimney sweeps.[11]

Allen recognized the potential profitability of chimney sweeping when he started his business in 1785. Philadelphians had established a price index that paid chimney sweepers according to risk—the higher the chimney, the greater the wages. Because Philadelphia was the nation's largest urban center, not to mention a trans-Atlantic trading hub and soon-to-be federal capital, it contained a sizable number of homes with lucrative—or dangerously high—chimneys. And Philadelphia's chimneys had to be cleaned from September through May, when chilly days and nights kept home fires burning. Allen met this demand by doing some of the best and toughest work in the city.

Allen was evidently a tough mastersweep. In 1790 a "boy [named] . . . Tilghman Fitzgerald" complained to white abolitionists about working with the rising black preacher. The PAS sought to investigate the matter but had trouble locating the young lad, "owing to his being employed [by Allen so far] from home." White abolitionists eventually determined that although Allen's mastery did not seriously harm Tilghman Fitzgerald, it did pose risks. The PAS therefore assumed the boy's indenture.[12]

This was not Allen's first problem with an apprentice. In 1789 he placed the first of two runaway ads in the *Pennsylvania Gazette* seeking the return of "an indented Indian mulatto boy named Israel Tolman, whose father was a white man and mother an Indian."[13] Born around 1773, Tolman (alias Tallman) allegedly hailed from Allentown, Pennsylvania. Allen may have acquired Tolman as part of a PAS plan to bind out young people of color. Tolman evidently bolted to escape not only the drudgery of chimney sweeping but Allen's fearsome work ethic. Allen twice offered a reward of four dollars for Tolman's return, indicating his firm belief in the sanctity of indenture work.

These ads tell us something else too: Allen was rising economically. Though no great sum when compared to recapture rewards offered by other masters (escaped slaves fetched up to twenty dollars), four dollars was a significant sum for Afro-Philadelphians. Hiring apprentices like Tolman also meant outlays of capital for food, lodging, tools, and eventually freedom dues. That Allen had disposable income to reclaim an apprentice is therefore revealing. In fact, Allen employed a steady number of apprentices during the 1790s. In February 1793, for instance, he signed an agreement with a young man named Paris. The indenture lasted four years and six months (ending in August 1797), with Allen agreeing to teach Paris the craft of chimney sweep and providing "freedom dues" (perhaps a new suit or some tools).[14] In the late summer of 1793, Allen took on more apprentices for a business he planned with fellow black preacher Absalom Jones: a nail factory. In 1795, he helped several former Jamaican slaves find indenture opportunities in Philadelphia.

Beyond serving as a symbol of his rising status, the practice of apprenticing marked Allen as a black leader in the eyes of many white Philadelphians. Despite Allen's troubles with two indentures, the PAS still viewed him as a key contact in the black community precisely because he could hire young people of color. The 1790s witnessed a brief burst in white demands for apprenticed black labor (European immigrants would cut into this need during the 1800s). Allen and other black leaders worked with the PAS to find apprenticing opportunities for black men and women transiting from slavery to freedom.

Apprenticing also gave Allen an early forum for espousing uplift schemes. According to Allen, by working hard, learning a craft, and remaining humble and pious, freed blacks would rise in American culture. Interestingly, his uplift ideology might have had as much to do with notions of nation-building prevalent in early national Philadelphia as his own religious scruples. For like other working Americans, Allen hoped that his exertions would contribute to the rebuilding of a shattered economy. Pennsylvania abolitionists certainly echoed this line of thinking, noting that black industry and uplift were part and parcel of a national effort to perfect American economies, politics, and the social order itself (albeit with white abolitionists' paternalistic eyes constantly watching them).[15] By the early nineteenth century, Allen's visions of moral uplift seemed a bit didactic to the rising generations of free blacks who encountered more-virulent forms of racism.

For the moment, though, Allen was concerned with rising. By working hard, acquiring land and money, and serving as a master of young apprentices, Allen did just that, and he was undisputedly among black Philadelphia's leadership class by the early 1790s. He soon took that leadership position in challenging new directions.

3. The FAS

Plus ça change: the more things change, the more they stay the same. The French phrase captures perfectly what many black people, including Allen, felt upon arriving in Philadelphia. Slavery might have been on the decline in Pennsylvania, but whites' negative racial attitudes remained entrenched. In fact, emancipation was less a single wave washing over the Quaker State and more an ebb and flow of tides slowly eradicating racial subjugation. For every step forward (the passage of a gradual abolition law), liberated blacks experienced several steps backward: discrimination in the workplace, inadequate public schooling (though free blacks paid equal taxes), and, most seriously for Allen, segregated church pews.

Allen believed that free blacks needed religious guidance to navigate through the rough waters of freedom in late-eighteenth-century Philadelphia. Religion, he argued fiercely, provided the moral discipline necessary to survive white prejudice. Christianity taught piety and compassion, not to mention industriousness and perseverance. Indeed, Allen believed that piety and industriousness went hand in hand—and both were tied to abolitionism's ultimate success. "To you who are favored with freedom," he sermonized, "let your conduct manifest your gratitude toward the compassionate masters who have set you free." Do not be perceived as "lazy and idle," Allen warned, for "the enemies of freedom plead it as a cause why we ought not to be free." Like other black itinerants of the gospel, Allen remained confident that those who followed the pious path of Afro-Christianity—by working hard, forgiving whites' transgressions, and praying daily—would achieve much in American (and Atlantic-world) culture.[16]

Allen's optimism was a vital quality during these years, and it is rather striking considering the small number of black congregants that he initially encountered at St. George's Church: there were five African Americans there when Allen arrived. As even the most naive Sunday-schooler knew, the original Apostles more than doubled that contingent! Black congregants were simply too few to build anything like a black church. According to Allen, black Philadelphians were "long forgotten" by white clerics. In response, he not only increased his preaching activities within the church but also sought out black communities south of Philadelphia's market center, where a vibrant community of former slaves was beginning to rise. He preached up to "five times a day"—in St. George's, on street corners, "wherever I could find an opening," as he put it. The eager Allen also created prayer meetings for black congregants. His incessant activity paid off. Within a year of coming to Philadelphia, he had built "a society of forty-two [black] members" at St. George's.[17]

By 1787, Allen's thoughts turned to finding "a place of worship for the colored people," or perhaps even building an independent "African church." He found a few allies but more skeptics. "Respectable" blacks resisted Allen's overtures about a separate church, possibly for fear of offending white leaders. For their part, white clerics adamantly opposed an autonomous black church. When Allen, Absalom Jones, William White, and Darius Grinnings raised the idea at St. George's, they were lectured and harangued by white leaders who "used very degrading and insulting language to us," as Allen vividly remembered.[18]

From 1787 through 1792, Allen bided his time by further building a black niche within St. George's. He also led "meetings of exhortation" beyond church walls—ecstatic, emotional minirevivals reminiscent of circuit preaching. White elders viewed this rising black presence "as a nuisance," in Allen's words.[19] White derision was a backhanded compliment to a gifted black organizer, for few could deny Allen's key role in attracting more blacks—and thereby, more congregants—to St. George's. In fact, St. George's overall membership grew while Allen was there, and church elders soon planned a second story to accommodate the swelling numbers. Construction of a new wing was funded, in part, by monies collected from Allen's adherents.

Meanwhile, white elders began to circumscribe Allen's activity: he was forbidden to exhort in an ecstatic manner and instructed to give services in a sober, deferential, quiet way. On the surface, Allen complied. In his mind, though, he let the dream of an African church take flight. Just imagine an independent black church not beholden to white officials! "The Lord is with us," Allen told his brethren about the future of this gleaming, autonomous church. "If it was His will, the work would go on." Perhaps someday very soon, black Philadelphians would build their own house of the Lord.[20]

Although he only whispered about it, Allen had planted the idea of an African church in 1787. In that year, Allen and seven other men turned to a related concern: creating a black mutual-aid society. Characterized as a quasi-religious but nondenominational organization from its very inception in April 1787, the Free African Society (FAS) expanded Allen's vision beyond religion.[21] Just as he came to see blacks as an underserved (and often despised) minority within Philadelphia's religious landscape, so too did Allen view them as socially bereft. In a racially prejudiced society, he wondered, where could free blacks turn for financial or educational support? Not to former masters, or to the city council, or even to white abolitionists who scrutinized all loan requests with great rigor. In a time when Philadelphia was turning into a free black capital, mutual aid among blacks assumed particular significance.

The Free African Society was dedicated to community action "without regard to religious tenets," as the group's preamble put it. "We, the Free Africans of the city of Philadelphia and their descendants," the founding document continued, "do unanimously agree for the benefit of each other to advance one shilling . . . monthly . . . to hand forth to the needy of this society." Members would "support one another in sickness, and for the benefit of their widows and fatherless children," provided they live "an orderly and sober life."[22]

Beyond providing financial support to member families, the FAS epitomized black independence in the post-Revolutionary period. Blacks would be known as self-sufficient and prudent, black leaders proclaimed. This was a particularly important statement for Allen and his brethren to make, for a majority of the Free African Society's eight founding members had once been enslaved. Yet the word "slave" never appeared in the Society's early records. These men did not wish to be known as "former slaves," a term that set them apart from the rest of society, but as "free Africans." White abolitionists hailed the organization's self-help initiatives. The Free African Society became a model institution, not just for Afro-Philadelphians but for black communities around the country.[23]

Indeed, although the FAS formed out of the friendship between "Absalom Jones and Richard Allen, two men of the African race, who . . . have obtained a good report among men,"[24] it owed as much to a strong sense of communalism among Afro-Philadelphians. One of the most important social characteristics of African society, communalism served as the foundation for free black culture in early national America. Connections between past and present, between African heritage and American realities, remained omnipresent to black founders like Allen. Nearly every major free black institution created in the urban North following the American Revolution had the word "African" affixed to it, from Masonic lodges to educational groups to benevolent societies. Even though a decreasing number of Northern African Americans had direct contact with African culture by the closing decades of the eighteenth century, emerging black leaders desperately wanted to link their collective uplift to a glorious African past. "The Communal ethic of mutual responsibility that was part of blacks' African heritage," James Horton and Lois Horton observe, "made such cooperative organization a cultural imperative." When combined with the fact that "most white communities denied blacks access to public graveyards," or education, or any number of civic opportunities, communalism became absolutely critical to free blacks.[25]

Yet there is also a distinctly modern political tone in the group's formation. For the Free African Society was not merely a benevolent communal organization but a lobbying group. Created at a moment of political ferment in American society, and taking shape against the backdrop of "nationalist" movements in Western culture, the FAS offers one of the first examples of the idea that free blacks were a nation within a nation. Though diverse, one of the hallmarks of black nationalist thought, according to political scientist Michael Dawson, is the "time-tested skepticism in black communities that, when it comes to race, America will live up to its liberal values."[26] In this sense, the FAS exemplified nationalist as well as Africanist sentiments. In 1790, for example, the group petitioned city leaders for a plot of land in the common cemetery, or Potter's Field. Located southwest of present-day Independence Hall, the African burial ground, as it became known, served as a key site of black communal gatherings and mourning rituals for the following several decades. The lesson for Allen and his brethren was that black organization and politicking got results.

Black leaders in other cities formed similar benevolent organizations by the close of the eighteenth century. The FAS corresponded with groups in Boston and Newport, helping to establish the first national dialogue among free black leaders. As the FAS discovered, free blacks were not a monolithic entity. In the fall of 1789, for example, the Newport Free African Union Society in Rhode Island pledged to support African emigration schemes as a means of repudiating American racism. The FAS countered that peaceable protest *within* America would work better than physical departure. Still, the FAS did not lecture Newport blacks about the folly of their ways. They agreed to disagree.[27]

Despite the FAS's importance, it could not hold Allen's interest. By mid-1789, he had formally departed the group, though evidence indicates that Allen still worked with FAS members on key black initiatives in Philadelphia. Indeed, that Allen spent so little time recounting the successes and failures of the FAS in his autobiography signifies his own devotion to forming a black church. Evidence of Allen's differences with the FAS came in the form of disciplinary action: the FAS accused him of trying to "sow division among us" by politicking for a black church.[28] Allen had attended the group's monthly meetings and given money to the benevolence fund as prescribed by FAS policy. But he also attempted to hold separate religious meetings with an eye toward forming a black Methodist church. Allen's compatriots then learned of his legendary will, for any attempts to reason with him failed. He would not adhere to the FAS's nonsectarian doctrine if it interfered with his attempts to build black Methodism. And so, Allen stopped attending FAS monthly meetings after November 1788. By June 1789, the FAS had actually ejected him from the organization.[29]

Allen's departure from the FAS did not lessen his sense of accomplishment. Every day blacks seemed less dependent on white good will and more confident about voicing their opposition to white prejudice Indeed, Allen himself was emboldened, particularly about building a free black church. Between 1790 and 1792, he helped raise money for an African church from black as well as white figures. Allen recalled that he and Absalom Jones raised $360 in one day alone, "the greatest day's collection that we [ever] met with!"[31] Although the young preacher gave no date, historians estimate that it must have been sometime in 1791. For in the summer of that year, roughly a dozen black men—including both Allen and Jones—met with Benjamin Rush to craft an "Articles of Faith" for the black church. While Jones led a group of black men who addressed wealthy and well-placed white leaders about larger donations to a future African church (none other than George Washington donated money to the cause),[31] Allen negotiated for church land in south Philadelphia.[32]

Talk, hope, endorsements, even money—despite all this, at the start of 1792, black Philadelphians still had no church of their own, nor had they separated from white denominations like St. George's, which increasingly sought to put "uppity" blacks in their segregated place. What would have to be done to make the African church a reality? Allen was done waiting for answers.

4. Head Up, Eyes Open, Fist Clenched

When one sits down to write Allen's life, a single event stands above all others: the founding of the African Methodist Episcopal (AME) Church. Allen certainly thought so, highlighting the AME's establishment as his most cherished accomplishment.[33] Many others have agreed. The distinguished scholar of black religion Albert Raboteau has called the AME "the most important denomination and arguably the most important African-American institution for most of the nineteenth century."[34] Beyond America, the AME has served as a model for black independence movements. When in the 1890s "black Christians in Pretoria, South Africa withdrew from the [white] Wesleyan Methodist Missionary Society," James Campbell writes in his international history of the AME, they joined forces with "the oldest and largest church in black America," the very one founded by Allen a century before.[35]

The signal event of Allen's life also featured one of the great moments of African American reform: black exodus from a segregated white church.[36] One of the first "back of the bus" moments, blacks' departure from St. George's served as an early version of Rosa Parks sitting down on a Montgomery bus in 1955 and standing up to racial injustice. The story began sometime in the early 1790s, when Allen and other black members learned that they could not sit in their normal pews. Rather than comply with what the historian Carol George has called "segregated sabbaths," they bolted.[37] "Here was the beginning and rise of the first African church in America," Allen himself wrote of the walkout.[38] The incident served as a biblical parable. The Reverend Henry McNeal Turner even called it a march to the Promised Land.

Allen's retelling of the incident has become legendary. "A number of us usually attended St. George's church," Allen wrote in both the AME *Doctrines and Discipline* (1817) and his autobiography (1833), "and when the colored people began to get numerous in attending the church, they moved us from the seats we usually sat on, and placed us around the wall." It got worse: blacks were informed one Sunday morning that they must sit in a segregated balcony. Because services had already begun, Allen claimed that blacks misunderstood the hastily given directive and went to the seats on the main floor, "not knowing any better." "Just as we got to the seats," Allen continued, "the elder said 'let us pray.' " Kneeling as they had done countless times before, black parishioners thought only about the Word of the Lord. But, Allen explained, this morning's prayers were drowned out by "considerable scuffling and low talking." Lifting his head, Allen's eyes focused not on the throne of grace at the head of the church but on an unbelievable sight just a few feet away: white trustees "having hold of the Rev. Absalom Jones, pulling him off of his knees, and saying, 'you must get up—you must not kneel here.' " An incredulous Jones admonished the man to "wait until prayer is over."[39]

The commotion intensified. "No," the white official insisted, his hands still clutching Absalom Jones's shoulders, "you must get up now or I will call for aid and force you away." "Wait until prayer is over," Jones pleaded, refusing to rise. "With that," Allen explained, white officials moved in, attempting to banish African Americans to the segregated balconies.[40]

They need not have bothered. According to Allen, "by this time prayer was over," and blacks "all went out of the church in a body." What must have been going through the minds of white ministers and parishioners as this phalanx of blacks marched en masse out of St. George's? "It raised a great excitement and inquiry among the citizens," Allen commented. But white responses mattered little to him. As far as he was concerned, black parishioners now saw that they would never be treated equally unless they formed their own congregation. In Allen's words, whites "were no more plagued with us in [their] church."[41]

If the walkout of St. George's and the subsequent founding of Mother Bethel Church remains Allen's canonical achievement, it is also the subject of a good deal of historical debate. Just when did blacks leave St. George's and form their own church? Earlier Allen scholars, such as Charles Wesley and Carol George, argued that blacks' exodus occurred in 1787, just as Richard Allen had originally claimed. More recently, historians have pushed the date forward to 1792–93, thanks in large part to the wonderful detective work of Milton Sernett of Syracuse University.[42] Sernett mined the records of St. George's for this era, discovering that a new (and therefore segregated) balcony was not even undertaken until 1792. Still, no one knows precisely when black and white parishioners squared off in the City of Brotherly Love. Indeed, one of the leading scholars on early black Philadelphia, Library Company archivist Phillip Lapsansky, wonders why Allen would misrepresent blacks' break from St. George's. It might well have happened in 1787, he claims. "Why would he lie?"[43]

Academic as it sounds, more than historical nitpicking is at stake here. On the one hand, a walkout date of 1787 would mean that racial segregation forced Richard Allen and his black brethren out of a white church before they ever had the chance to claim equality. Moreover, as William Douglass noted in the first full-scale history of independent black churches in 1862, the year 1787 has always had a magical resonance for Americans. Why wouldn't blacks want to claim that year as their own? Douglass saluted African Americans' departure from St. George's as a continuation of the revolutionary spirit that animated American independence. "The Revolutionary struggle," Douglass wrote in galloping prose, "in which was involved the great principles of human rights, was still fresh in the minds of all, from the least to the greatest"—from black leaders like Allen to white worthies like Washington. In short, Douglass believed in a 1787 exodus from the segregated church.[44]

On the other hand, a 1792–93 walkout from St. George's would mean that blacks had planned an independent church all along, with the final confrontation underscoring the predetermined need for black religious autonomy. Blacks did not wait for whites to segregate them, Gary Nash has written in support of this view; they acted boldly and self- assertively in the years leading up to the confrontation with whites to form their own church. The keys to this early black action, according to Nash, were "dignity, self-generated power," and "positive" identifications with an African past.[45]

So were black Philadelphians forced to form their own church after being treated unequally in 1787 or did they seek independence in 1792–93 because they wanted their own church? Beyond this chicken-and-egg question, though, an equally important question lurks: just what was Richard Allen's role in the black exodus? Did he premeditate a confrontation with whites, whenever it occurred? Although many scholars have toyed with this notion, few would answer with an unequivocal yes. There is, however, more than enough evidence to support the claim. To begin, Allen's conspiratorial role in leaving St. George's bears much resemblance to the episode in which he convinced his Delaware master to hear a guilt-producing sermon from Freeborn Garrettson—the same episode that eventually brought Allen his freedom. Recall that Allen basically tricked his master into attending that meeting. Far from demanding freedom, Allen worked behind the scenes to get the same result. He did not even give the fateful sermon that scared his master so. But he knew in advance what his master would do when he heard God calling slaveholders to account.

Likewise, in the St. George's walkout, Allen was no simple bystander. He had been aware of white complaints about blacks' intermingling in so-called white pews for some time. He may have *precipitated* a confrontation in which blacks would either, one, gain acceptance as equals or, two, see once and for all the necessity of an independent church. This was precisely the story passed on by a correspondent to a New York paper, the *Colored American,* in 1837. In an unheralded article entitled "The History of Churches and Ecclesiastical Organization among the People of Color," the unnamed writer described Allen fomenting a rebellion against racial exclusion. "The colored members of [St. George's] Church and congregation had up to that time occupied a seat in the principle floor with white people," he commented. This presumed equality soon gave way to resentment among whites. Didn't blacks know their place? Whites wanted black parishioners pressed against the wall in the back of the church or, even better, planted in the new balcony planned for the second floor. These antiblack "murmurings" predated the formal building of a "Negro pew" but reached a zenith when whites "determined to remove the people of color to the Gallery."[46]

In this version of events—which the correspondent interestingly dates to "1792 or 1793, I forget which"—Allen and black congregants are fully aware of plans to segregate them, not to mention the deeper anxieties over blacks sitting next to whites. Knowing full well that whites might rebuke them, Allen led his people into the main pews. When told to go to "blacks-only" seats in the balcony, Allen then triumphantly led his brethren out of the church. As the correspondent to the *Colored American* put it, despite "hearing of" the proposed seating arrangement, Allen and his congregants still "went into the gallery of their own mind." They sat intently, waiting for services to begin and, when they did, prayed devoutly. "Devotion" gave way to protocol, and blacks were asked to leave. Absalom Jones "begged that the colored people might remain unmolested till the close of services." The white officer only demanded Jones's removal more loudly.[47]

Then the key moment arrived. As soon as the "prayer ceased," the correspondent wrote, "the colored people," led by the wonderfully sure Richard Allen, "got up and left the Church." Fittingly, in the 1837 report, Allen is given the final words upon leaving segregated St. George's: "Said the Bishop—'We never entered it again!' "[48]

Allen's own description of events is much more famous than this one. But tellingly, for he often refrained from trumpeting his own accomplishments, Allen himself assumes a less central role in his own story. Events occur, and he is there to react. In the 1837 history of the incident, however, Allen essentially plots a confrontation with whites over unfair seating practices. The 1837 writer does not say so, but his tale might have been accented by hearing Allen in the confines of the AME Church, a space where Allen felt free to speak more plainly. "Heaven is free for all who worship in spirit and truth," Allen once said.[49] He might have added, as the 1837 correspondent implied, the Lord helps those who help themselves.

But just why would Allen need to work in so crafty a manner to push for a black church? As for his black brethren, Allen knew that some members of the community still hesitated to support an independent black church. True, blacks had held separate services in the Quakers' African School between 1788 and 1791; and by February 1792, black leaders had also negotiated for land dedicated to a future African church. But no structure had since been completed, and Allen surely felt that black Philadelphians needed a galvanizing event to spur independent action. Perhaps, he surmised, blacks moved carefully for fear of white retaliation. Even discussion about creating an independent black church worried some Quakers, traditional friends of black Philadelphians. Decades after blacks walked out of St. George's, Allen could still recall that until that very moment few African Americans felt as strongly as he did about completing an African church. But, as he so wonderfully put if, the walkout of segregated pews "filled" the black community "with fresh vigor to get a house erected to worship God in."[50] Here Allen could essentially say "I told you so" to Philadelphia blacks without actually having to say the words.

As for the white community, the exodus from St. George's provided cover to black actions. No sooner had Allen marched black parishioners out of the segregated church than he and other blacks renewed their efforts to gain white supporters. If he had departed St. George's before any serious conflict arose, then white authorities (friends of Benjamin Rush, say) would likely have refused to help him build a black church. But whites landed the first blow. Shrewd through and through, Allen realized that many white citizens, as he wrote, "were [now] ashamed of their conduct."[51] In other words, Allen's actions made blacks the injured party. And what a difference this made! When Allen, Jones, and others began soliciting white support in 1791, William White, head of Christ Church, derided the cause. He even hectored Benjamin Rush about it. The African church, he told Rush one morning on a Philadelphia Street, was the worst example yet of blacks' newfound sense of racial "pride."[52] But after the St. George's incident, Rush told white benefactor John Nicholson (who provided two thousand dollars in loans to Philadelphia blacks), "you will not—you *cannot* refuse their request for the sake of religion & Christianity."[53]

Seeing Allen as a stealth operator (the architect of blacks' exodus from St. George's Church) perhaps helps us understand why he never set the record straight about the official origination date of the black church. All journeys begin in the mind. Allen may have first envisioned a black church in 1787. After running into opposition from black as well as white figures, he searched for an event that would reinvigorate blacks, put whites on the defensive, and make Allen himself appear to be the visionary that he was. That final confrontation occurred later, sometime in 1792 or 1793. As far as Allen was concerned, though, that five-year period (from first thought until the final break from white Methodists) formed one great episode. In 1837, The *Colored American* put Allen's walkout more boldly in perspective: "By the character of this act, it is unnecessary to speak."[54] But the act did speak, about Allen's incredible head as well as his heart.

5. An African Church

Having left St. George's, black Philadelphians focused on building an African church. They had to stand firm against white backlash. As perhaps the key leader of the St. George's walkout, Allen would bear the brunt of Philadelphians' criticisms. While some whites felt shame over their treatment of black parishioners, others fumed at Allen's actions. When blacks "hired a storefront, and held worship by ourselves," Allen remembered, "we were pursued with threats of being disowned." When "we got subscription papers out to raise money to build the house of the Lord" and received financial and moral support from two distinguished white Philadelphians (one of whom, Benjamin Rush, was a signer of the Declaration of Independence), "the elder of the [Methodist] Church still pursued us." Why, he asked Allen, did black Philadelphians insist on building their own church? A stubborn Allen refused to yield on any point, infuriating the elder. "I have the charge given to me by the [Methodist] Conference," he sternly lectured Allen, "and unless you submit, I will read you publicly out of the Meeting!" "Show us where we have violated any law," the black preacher shot back, and "then we will submit."[55]

Submit! That was a keyword for both Allen and the elder, although each camp viewed the word from diametrically opposed perspectives. For many whites, blacks were supposed to submit to white wills beyond bondage. Slavery may have been a grievous wrong, but postemancipation whites still believed themselves to be "the dominant culture."[56] For black Philadelphians, race-based deference had seen its final days. Allen thus displayed black pride when he replied to a white elder attempting to put the young black preacher in his place. In leaving segregated St. George's and building a black church, Allen knew that no church doctrine had been breached—only the custom of racial exclusion. So when the elder threatened to read Allen "out" of the Methodist Conference, Allen retorted that "we should seek further redress." After all, he continued, "we were dragged off our knees in St. George's Church . . . and treated worse than heathens." After facing such humiliations in a so-called House of the Lord, Philadelphia blacks "were determined," as Allen put it to the elder, "to seek out for ourselves" a true house of worship. Then "you are not Methodists!" the elder bawled before departing in a huff.[57]

Any remaining doubts about the viability of an independent black church must have been quashed when the elder asked for a second meeting with African Methodists. Why would white officials call for another meeting unless they feared that blacks could, and now would, build their own church? This time the white cleric tried a softer appeal. "He told us that he wished us well," Allen observed, "that he was a friend to us." The elder appealed to blacks' sense of propriety, religious scruples, and deference. "He used many arguments to convince us that we were in the wrong in building a church," Allen wrote. Stop raising money for your own church, the elder told blacks, his tone rising; use your funds for the greater glory of St. George's.[58] The appeal went nowhere. African Methodists would not return to St. George's.

Once again, a meeting between the white elder and Allen turned confrontational. Allen now spoke from a position of strength. "If you deny us your name [as Methodists]," he sternly lectured the elder, "remember that 'you cannot seal up the Scriptures from us, and deny us a name in heaven.' " "We will disown you all," the elder yelled, once again leaving in anger. Allen was somewhat shaken. "This was a trial I never had to pass through before," he admitted. Still, he remained sure that Methodist leaders beyond St. George's (such as Francis Asbury) would "support us." And as Allen gathered his brethren, who focused not on "if" a black church could be completed but "when" the first services would be held, his confidence returned. "We met with great success," Allen commented with characteristic understatement.[59]

6. Two Churches

Sometime in March 1793, Richard Allen awoke before dawn, prayed to the Lord, and then prepared to dig the foundation of an African church. Recognizing all Allen had done, the elder Absalom Jones deferred to the younger Allen. "As I was the first proposer of the African church," Allen himself noted with a rare but evident sense of pride, "I put the first spade in the ground to dig a celler for [that church]. This was the first African church or meetinghouse that was erected in the United States of America."[60]

This was not, however, the foundation of Allen's Bethel Church. The ground cleared that day became St. Thomas's African Episcopal Church, located on Fifth between Walnut and Locust streets. Allen's African Methodist Episcopal Church would rise just a few blocks away. Allen's sense of religious certitude led to the division of the two new churches. For the question that once occupied his mind at the Free African Society arose again: which denomination would the African church follow—Methodism or another sect, say, Episcopalianism? Allen said Methodism. His great friend Absalom Jones agreed, though many black parishioners refused to align themselves with Methodism after St. George's. Allen felt that Methodism transcended a segregated church. Methodists often embraced antislavery, affected no airs, and committed themselves fully to the Lord. Conversely, the Episcopal Church had a reputation as being ostentatious and concerned with adornments. For Allen, Methodism was the religion for "plain and simple" (even unlettered) people. "The reason that the Methodist is so successful in the awakening and conversion of the colored people," he explained, was the church's "plain doctrine." It had also been the denomination associated with his liberation. Allen refused to submit to the black majority's wishes.[61]

Allen formed the AME Church, while Jones accepted the offer to head St. Thomas's African Episcopal Church, which did not claim complete independence from the white Episcopal hierarchy. Allen's congregation took root on land he had originally purchased in 1791, thus giving Bethelites legitimate claim to holding "the oldest plot of land continuously owned by blacks" in Philadelphia: the lot at Sixth and Lombard streets. By the summer of 1794, a pack of mules had dragged to that site the physical edifice of what would become Richard Allen's spiritual home: a former blacksmith's shop he had converted into a church. Allen loved this idea of conversion: instead of a nonbelieving bondperson, he became a Christian convert; instead of a suffering slave, he became a successful free person of color; instead of a deferential black man, he become an independent citizen. As Dee Andrews nicely points out, Allen's belief in black uplift may have added fuel to the church-building fire, for he realized that white Methodists would never let black preachers rise in the church hierarchy. Trapped in a middling position, he decided that building an African Methodist church was his only true option.[62]

The church's official dedication occurred on July 29, 1794. White dignitaries, including Methodist bishop Francis Asbury, joined black congregants for the special occasion. Asbury had known Allen for a decade and was glad to give the opening sermon. "Our colored brethren" Asbury excitedly scribbled in his journal that night, "are to be governed by the doctrine and discipline of the Methodists."[63] The name "Bethel" came from a prayer offered by the Reverend John Dickins, another well-known white Methodist whom Allen had known for several years (Dickins officiated at Allen's first marriage).[64] Speaking from the Book of Genesis (28:19), Dickins told black parishioners that the AME Church would serve as a beacon for saving souls. "Amens" echoed throughout the tiny church.

Allen may have liked the name "Bethel" because of its allusion to spiritual destiny. "This is the gate of heaven / And Jacob rose up early in the morning, and took the stone that he had put for his pillows, and set it up for a pillar, and poured oil on the top of it / And he called the name of that place Beth-el" (Genesis 28:17–19). In this section of the biblical story of Genesis, according to a modern scholarly exegesis, the Lord "renews his promise to Jacob as previously he has given it to Abraham (13:14–17) and Isaac (26:1–5)": there is one true God who has anointed a chosen people on earth. Bethel, meaning "temple" in Hebrew, "marked the place where Jacob saw in a dream the gate of heaven and received a manifestation of God. Jacob's great strength, attested in his single-handed erection of this monolith, must have been legendary."[65] Perhaps Allen saw himself as a modern-day Jacob, a "pious, honest" man who carries forth biblical destinies of a chosen people.[66]

Within a year, Allen had attracted over one hundred congregants (at St. Thomas's, congregants initially numbered almost 250 before rising to over 400). By 1796, the savvy preacher sought to solidify the young congregation's future by securing a state incorporation for Bethel Church. On August 23, nine Bethel trustees signed the "Articles of Association of the African Methodist Episcopal Church, of the City of Philadelphia, in the Commonwealth of Pennsylvania."[67] On September 12, 1796, state officials granted corporate status to Bethel AME Church. Joining Allen were trustees John Morris, William Hogan, Peter Lux (each of whom could not sign his own name), Robert Green, Jupiter Gibson, William Jones, Jonathan Trusty, and Prince Pruine (all literate). Few of these men had achieved Allen's economic success, though Green and Trusty had risen above laboring ranks (the former was a waiter and property holder, the latter a mastersweep). While Absalom Jones's St. Thomas's African Episcopal Church attracted some of Afro-Philadelphia's wealthiest families, including black sailmaker and financier James Forten, Allen's AME appealed to a wider cross-section of folks (from day laborers to middling black merchants). By Allen's death in 1831, his AME Church had exploded in membership, claiming over three thousand parishioners in Philadelphia alone.

7. Flora Allen and Sarah Allen

Allen initially counted on forty congregants, a respectable number but barely enough to keep any fledgling church going. Bethelites persevered and then grew, not merely because of a daunting founding figure such as Allen. They also relied on an unheralded band of pious women. With an incident as famous as Allen's walkout from St. George's (including the memorable image of black men being pulled from the pews by white officials), it is easy to lose sight of black women's signal role as church builders. Allen's autobiography does not even mention women's exertions at Bethel.

But soon after Allen departed segregated St. George's, he was joined by perhaps as many as thirteen women whose names are buried deep in dusty church archives. The list includes Allen's first wife, Flora, as well as a young Methodist named Sarah Bass, who later became Allen's second wife (after Flora passed away).[68] Not much is known about these women, save that they usually joined Allen's new church as part of a family network (Esther Trusty, like Flora Allen, followed her husband, Jonathan, to Bethel, where they became longtime congregants). They remained at the church through lean times, filling the pews on Sunday mornings, raising money for church repairs, and spreading the word about the glories of Bethel Church.

The nature of black women's founding role is best illuminated by Flora Allen and Sarah Bass. Richard Allen was a most eligible bachelor by the early 1790s. Pushing into his thirties when he began building African Methodism brick by brick, he was financially secure. Many of his great compatriots were already married. Obviously, Allen's peripatetic nature and deep dedication to an independent black church posed problems for any would-be partner. A potential spouse would have to honor Allen's deepest religious commitments and passions as her own.

His first wife, Flora, was just such a person: a helpmate who assumed his innermost burdens as her own. A former slave who settled in the City of Brotherly Love during the final decades of the eighteenth century, she attended class meetings run by black as well as white preachers. Selfless and dedicated to community uplift, she shared Allen's vision of creating a strong and independent free black church. Indeed, after they wed in October 1790, Flora aided Allen's leadership ascent not only by abiding her husband's commitment to African Methodism but also by establishing a respectable home.[69] For any public persona of this era—a rising black preacher no less than a white politician—there was just no underestimating the importance of having a respectable house for visitors, friends, and the community at large. Creating a virtuous domestic image was especially important for African American leaders, shadowed as they were by stereotypical images as beasts of burden. A stable house registered in the public mind with order and respectability. Before marrying, Allen's compatriot James Forten relied on his mother to keep a respectable home. So too did Absalom Jones's wife guard her husband's image in the public realm.

Flora Allen made sure that Richard Allen appeared to friends and foes alike as a settled and suitable black public man. Visiting white preachers duly took note. "I dined with my good black friend Richard Allen's wife," the Reverend George Cuthbert wrote in his diary in 1797, after a stopover at the Allen residence. "I believe if there is a Christian in Philadelphia this old black woman is one."[70] As Cuthbert's rather blunt prose suggests, he was a white minister dining with Allen and his wife, a quite radical thing to do in early national Philadelphia. Just think back to the incident a few years earlier at St. George's, when white parishioners refused to pray next to black congregants. Now here was a liberal-thinking minister breaking bread with a black founding family. Cuthbert's praise of Flora Allen's piety also conveyed her status as an emerging icon of black virtue. Outside the home, Flora Allen demonstrated her commitment to black church building by praying with her husband at class meetings and Sunday services, cosigning property deeds (indicating that she may have used her own laboring wages for church-building initiatives), and participating in benevolent activities in the black community.[71]

Sadly, on March 11, 1801, Flora Allen died after a nine-month illness. A death notice in *Poulson's Daily Advertiser* the following day indicated her significance to both her husband and a rising Bethel Church.[72] Nevertheless, when Richard Allen married Sarah Bass that same year, the legend of strong black women in the church continued. "The life of Sarah [Allen]," Hallie Brown wrote in her instructional collection of stories of important black women, *Homespun Heroines* (1926), "is indissolubly linked with that of her husband." Like Flora, Sarah Allen was a helpmate and confidante. She too hosted guests, cosigned property deeds, and allowed Allen to serve as a distinguished black public man. "She grieved with him in sorrow and rejoiced with him in the day of his victory and success," Brown observed of Sarah Allen's continuing role as helpmate.[73]

Also like Flora, Sarah Bass had been a slave (she was born in Virginia in 1764) before attaining freedom and settling in Philadelphia. After attending services at St. George's (she sat in Methodist class meetings with her future husband), she became a founding congregant of Bethel Church. Her charitable work during the yellow-fever epidemic of 1793 impressed Richard Allen so much that he highlighted it in a subsequent pamphlet. "Sarah Bass," he observed, is "a coloured widow woman, [who] gave all the assistance she could, in several families, for which she did not receive any thing; and when any thing was offered her, she left it to the option of those she served."[74] After they wed, Sarah Allen became "a household word in the homes of African Methodism." To a growing legion of admirers, she represented black religiosity, virtue, and kindness. As a tribute to her caregiving role at Bethel Church, black Methodists soon took to calling her "Mother Allen."[75] "Her house was the resort of the brethren who labored in the ministry," AME bishop Daniel Payne stated. "Long will her motherly counsel be remembered."[76]

In both Flora and Sarah Allen, one sees the creation of the "black republican mother": the iconic black woman whose domestic-sphere work, religious piety, and self-sacrificing dedication to communal uplift symbolized early African American femininity.[77] Because blackness and hypersexuality were often intertwined in the eyes of many white citizens, the black republican mother was an idealized countertype—a paragon of black virtue. In one sense, the black republican mother functioned very much like her white counterparts. She was responsible for bringing dignity, piety, and moral culture to the home. Bishop Payne would later assert that black women must ever remain in the domestic sphere, for black uplift depended on the proliferation of virtuous black homes.[78]

But in Allen's time, the black republican mother also worked beyond the home for the greater good of black uplift. Church and community building demanded that black women pitch in where they could, either by garnering wages that underwrote church activities or by getting more directly involved in church politics (women helped safeguard Bethel Church during nineteenth-century confrontations with bullying white Methodist officials and rabble-rousing white rioters). Sarah Allen later collected rents from Allen family properties and, in a more daring role, aided fugitive slaves traveling through Philadelphia. "Thoroughly antislavery, [the Allens'] house was never shut against 'the friendless, the homeless, the penniless fugitives from the House of Bondage,' " Bishop Payne once commented.[79] Against the opposition of male church leaders, Sarah Allen even helped female preachers like Jarena Lee speak publicly in the black church.

In short, black founding women did not have the luxury of simply tending home. They worked alongside Richard Allen in any way they could. Without the selfless actions of Sarah and Flora Allen, not to mention countless other black women, Bethel Church may not have survived its rough beginnings.

8. Always Return Home

"Always return home," an African proverb declares. For the rest of his life, Richard Allen's true home remained Bethel Church. Although seemingly the result of a simple dispute over segregated seating at a white church, the formation of Allen's congregation represented a big leap forward in his reform ideology. To redeem African Americans, Allen realized that he would need more than his deep-felt Christian faith. He would need the memory of African communalism and the tools of modernity (in the form of political mobilization and even nationalist thinking) to build an institution capable of galvanizing and protecting free blacks for the duration of their freedom struggle. At this point in his life, Allen did not yet believe that black exodus—that black nationalism—required international migrations. Rather, he was confident that organizing free blacks as a nation within a nation, what we might think of as a nonviolent but confrontational lobbying group, could yield significant results in the American civic realm.

Failing that, Bethel would welcome oppressed blacks in an autonomous space free from white control. As Allen himself called out shortly before his death, "Bethel [was] surrounded by her foes, but not yet in despair."[80] Since that time—save for a short period when Bethel was being rebuilt—Allen's body has resided underneath his beloved Bethel home.

Notes

1. Richard Allen, The Life, Experience, and Gospel Labours of the Rt. Rev. Richard Allen, 1833, p. 31. Hereafter referred to as LEGL.

2. Ibid ., 11.

3. Ibid ., 12.

4. See PAS report on visiting people of color from December 1, I795, in "Committee for Improving the Condition of Free Blacks: Minutes, 1790–1803," PAS Papers, Reel 6.

5. On the rise of black Philadelphia, see Nash, *Forging Freedom; Julie Winch, Philadelphia's Black Elite* (Philadelphia, 1993); and Winch, *A Gentleman of Color.* On slave runaways and abolitionist aid in Pennsylvania, see also Newman, *Transformation of American Abolitionism.*

6. Newman, *Transformation of American Abolitionism*, chap. 3.

7. James Forten, "Series of Letters by a Man of Colour" (Philadelphia, 1813), reprinted in Newman, Rael, and Lapsansky, *Pamphlets of Protest.*

8. See Nash and Soderlund, *Freedom by Degrees*, 127.

9. Newman, *Transformation of American Abolitionism*, chap. 3.

10. Paul A. Gilje and Howard B. Rock, *Keepers of the Revolution: New Yorkers at Work during the Early Republic* (Ithaca, N.Y., 1992), 221–23.

11. On black mariners, see Horton and Horton, *In Hope of Liberty*, 69–70; and W. Jeffrey Bolster, *Black Jacks: African Americans Seamen in the Age of Sail* (Cambridge, Mass., 1997).

12. On the Allen apprentice case, see the PAS's "Committee of Guardians

Report," September 17, 1790, PAS Papers, Reel 6, 47–57.

13. *Pennsylvania Gazette*, August 13, 1788, and September14, 1791; quotation from the second ad.

14 "Committee of Guardians Report," February 16, 1793, PAS Papers, Reel 6, 55.

15. Nash and Soderlund, *Freedom by Degrees*, 192–93.

16. Allen, "To the People of Colour," in Porter, *Negro Protest Pamphlets*, 22. See also Hodges, *Black Itinerants of the Gospel*, introduction.

17. LEGL, 12–13•

18. Ibid.

19. Ibid.

20. Ibid. Andrews, *The Methodists*, 144–50, is particularly good at recounting the meaning of Allen's initial vision of a black church within Methodist religious circles.

21. See Nash, *Forging Freedom*, 98–99.

22. "Preamble and Articles of Association of the Free African Society, April 12, 1787," reprinted in Wesley, *Richard Allen*, 269–71, quotations at 269, 270.

23. See William Douglass, "Annals of the First African Church in United States of America, Now Styled the African Episcopal Church of St. Thomas, Philadelphia" (Philadelphia, 1862). For a terrific treatment of the broader meaning of the FAS and black autonomy, see Craig Steven Wilder, *In the Company of Black Men: The African Influence on African American Culture in New York City* (New York, 2001).

24. "Preamble and Articles of the Free African Society," 269.

25. Horton and Horton, *In Hope of Liberty*, 126–30.

26. Michael C. Dawson, *Black Visions: The Roots of Contemporary African-American Political Ideologies* (Chicago, 2001), 86.

27. The story is told in many places, beginning with Wesley, *Richard Allen*, 66–68.

28. The charges against Allen, brought June 20, 1789, are usefully recounted in Wesley, *Richard Allen*, 66.

29. Ibid , 65.

30. LEGL, 15•

31. On Washington's donation to an African church, see Nash, *Forging Freedom*, 164.

32. Finding precise dates for these activities remains problematic, for documentation is scarce. Allen bought land for the church in 1791, claiming in his autobiography that he had been authorized to do so by the FAS (see LEGL, 15). FAS records note that Allen was no longer a member by this time. But there is no other authoritative documentation on the matter.

33. LEGL, 21.

34. Raboteau, *A Fire in the Bones*, 79.

35. James T. Campbell, *Songs of Zion: The African Methodist Episcopal Church in the United States and South Africa* (New York, 1995), vii-viii.

36. Raboteau, *A Fire in the Bones*, 79.

37. Carol George used the phrase in her book's title, *Segregated Sabbaths.*

38. LEGL, 14.

39. See Richard Allen and Jacob Tapsico, *The Doctrines and Discipline of the African Methodist Episcopal Church* (Philadelphia, 1817). For quotations, see LEGL, 13–14.

40. LEGL, 13–14.

41. Ibid.

42. See Milton Sernett, *Black Religion and American Evangelicalism: White Protestants, Plantation Missions, and the Flowering of Negro Christianity*, 1787–1865 (Metuchen, N.J., 1975), 117–18, 219–20. See also Nash, *Forging Freedom*, 118–19.

43. Phillip Lapsansky, interview with the author, January 21, 2003.

44. Douglass, "Annals of the First African Church," 1–5.
45. Nash, *Forging Freedom*, 118–19.
46. *Colored American* (published in New York), October 14, 1837.
47. Ibid.
48. Ibid.
49. LEGL, 15.
50. Ibid., 3
51. Ibid.
52. Rush, quoted in Nash, *Forging Freedom*, 116; emphasis in original. On Nicholson, see Cynthia Shelton, The Mills of Manayunk (Baltimore, 1986).
53. Ibid., 119.
54. *Colored American*, October 14, 1837.
5 5. LEGL, 14–15.
56. Nash, *Forging Freedom*, 115. 57. LEGL, 14–16.
58. Ibid.
59. Ibid.
60. Ibid., 16. See also Andrews, *The Methodists*, 139–50; and Nash, *Forging Freedom*, 119.
61. LEGL, 16–17.
62. See Andrews, *The Methodists*, 139–40.
63. Asbury, quoted in Wesley, *Richard Allen*, 79.
64. Dickins was a familiar figure during the yellow-fever crisis, working with black as well as white leaders to save the city. He knew Allen, Jones, and James Forten.
65. Charles M. Laymon, ed., *The Interpreter's One-Volume Commentary on the Bible* (Nashville, Tenn., 1971), 21–22.
66. Ibid., 23.
67. For the AME's original charter, see "Articles of Association of the African Methodist Episcopal Church " (Philadelphia, 1799).
68. "A List of the Members of the African Methodist Episcopal Church in the City of Philadelphia," c. 1794, originally in the St. George's Church archives, and now (as a photocopy) in Bethel Archives, Richard Allen Museum. Dee Andrews first publicized the list in *The Methodists*, 147–50. The list, which is only partially legible and may not have correct spellings for all members, includes such names as Esther Freeman, Lucy White, Jane Anderson, Cynthia Bill (Bull?), Esther Claypoole, and Jane Given.
69. Two dates exist for Allen's marriage to Flora: October 19, 1790 (Bethel Church), and October 19, 1796 (documented at St. George's Church). The earlier date seems more probable, for Flora Allen signed property deeds prior to 1796. Still, the latter date may signify an official sanction of the marriage.
70. Quotation from William Culbert's journal, courtesy of Richard Allen Museum display, Bethel Church.
71. Flora Allen was listed as a cosigner of a lot that Richard Allen purchased in 1792 at Sixth and Lombard (adjacent to land he already owned), which would become part of Bethel Church property. See contract between Joseph Lewis and "Richard Allen and his Wife, Flora," August 10, 1792, in Bethel Archives.
72. On Flora Allen's death, see *Poulson's American Daily Advertiser*, March 12, 1901.
73. Hallie Brown, *Homespun Heroines and Other Women of Distinction* (1926; repr., New York, 1988), 12.
74. See Absalom Jones and Richard Allen, "A Narrative of the Proceedings of the Coloured People during the Late Awful Calamity in Philadelphia, in the Year 1793," in LEGL, 35.
75. Brown, *Homespun Heroines*, 12.

76. See Payne, *History of the AME Church*, 87.

77. For the classic definition of "republican motherhood," see Linda Kerber, *Women of the Republic* (Chapel Hill, N.C., 1980).

78. Though it focuses on a later era, Julius H. Bailey 's *Around the Family Altar: Domesticity in the African Methodist Episcopal Church*, 1865–1900 (Gainesville, Fla., 2005) provides insightful treatment of women's public and private roles in the church.

79. Payne, *History of the AM E Church*, 84.

80. LEGL, 24.

Suggested Readings

Jon Butler, "Magic, Astrology and the Early American Religious Heritage" in *The American Historical Review* 84, no. 2 (Apr., 1979): 317–346.

Elizabeth W. Fisher, "Prophesies and Revelations": German Cabbalists in Early Pennsylvania" in *The Pennsylvania Magazine of History and Biography* 109, no. 3 (July 1985): 299–333.

James Campbell, "Chapter 1: Vindicating the Race" in *Songs of Zion: The African Methodist Episcopal Church in the United States and South Africa* (New York: Oxford University Press, 1995): 3–31.

Gary Nash, "To Arise Out of the Dust" in *Forging Freedom* (Cambridge: Harvard University Press, 1998): 101–133.

Discussion Questions:

1. What light does Gough's text shed on the problems that Anglicans encountered while trying to practice Anglican Christianity in a city founded by Quakers?
2. Both Newman and Campbell discuss the origins of the African Methodist Episcopal Church. What role did the first AME Church, Bethel, play in the city of Philadelphia and in the nation? Why do you imagine it took the Bethelites so long to officially split away from the Methodist Episcopal Church?
3. Campbell describes the AME's approach as a program of "race vindication," writing: "By leading unimpeachable lives, by exhibiting industry, intellect, and character, they could vindicate the race's potential and advance the cause of abolition" (26). He also cautioned that "there were hazards here." What are the pitfalls or consequences of a "race vindication" approach?
4. In "Magic, Astrology and the Early American Religious Heritage," Butler writes that we need to "recover noninstitutional religious practices" to understand early American religious life (318). Why? Why is this a "difficult task"? Where does he look and what sorts of sources does he use?
5. According to Butler, was there a strong divide between Christianity and occult practices? How do we know? Cite an example.

Section 5

Jewish Philadelphia

The Founding of the Female Hebrew Benevolent Society: 1817–1830

Dianne Ashton

"In that title ["sister"] I look for such love as has been the most fertile source of comfort to me thro my life."

Rebecca Gratz, 1820

Rebecca Gratz soon faced a new challenge to her mental health, or, as she called it, her spiritual strength. In midwinter 1817, when Rebecca was thirty-six, her sister Sarah died after a long illness. The two sisters, closest in age in a large family, had grown up sharing their bed, clothing, and daily activities.[1] As the sisters who nursed other family members, they shared a unique perspective on domesticity. As their mother aged, Sarah took over the household management and became the home's stabilizing anchor.[2] With Sarah, Rebecca shared special responsibilities, traveling among family households to aid in illnesses and crises. Although sisters Frances, Richea, and Rachel all married and withdrew into their own domestic lives, as long as Sarah lived, Gratz had a partner in her worries. With Sarah's death, she lost the person who understood her best. Without Sarah, Rebecca was left alone in her role and was the only woman, apart from the servants, in the Philadelphia home she shared with Hyman, Joseph, Jacob, and Benjamin. It is hardly surprising that Gratz's "wounded feelings sought retirement."[3]

Jewish mourning rites and the deepening interest in religion she shared with her gentile women friends drew Gratz into religious debates that both eased her personal grief and strengthened her religious convictions. While Rebecca's many non-Jewish friends counseled her to adopt their religious attitudes toward grief, those ideas, based on biblical traditions, were not so far from Gratz's own beliefs, grounded in Judaism. Maria Hoffman and Gertrude Meredith judged religious ideas by two criteria. First, they determined whether an idea could be grounded in biblical sources. For Gratz, this meant the Hebrew Bible and the biblical interpretations she learned from Jewish prayer books and holiday celebrations. Second, they had to find the ideas capable of promoting increased levels of personal piety, to have a real effect on their own experience.

Rebecca assured Maria Hoffman that "tho [I am] far less happy than you have known me, [I] am still too sensible of the blessings I possess to mourn unduly." Nonetheless, she endured a painful daily struggle with grief. Each day was "freighted with fatal remembrances" and she admitted that she was "more than usually depressed," but she assured Hoffman that she did not "reject consolations-and am even cheerful sometimes and always resigned. . . . I exert all my reason and all the strength of my mind to resist depression. I . . . walk every day . . . [and] in our large family I am seldom alone." Yet, she admitted to Maria, "it is not so easy when the elasticity of youth is gone . . . [and] I do not believe I could have parted with the companion and darling of my infant years the sharer of every after scene of my life, and faithful sympathizer of all my cares with greater fortitude than I have done now."[4]

The Rise of Antebellum Evangelism

Gratz's deepened need for both religion and familial companionship following Sarah's death paralleled trends in American society, particularly among women. While some Philadelphians welcomed Shakespearean actor Edmund Kean in 1821[5] and called their city the "Athens of America," others strove to Christianize the city's soul. Historian Jon Butler has argued that at the time of the American Revolution no more than 10 percent of the American population belonged to a Christian church. Widespread interest in alchemy, magical cures, and natural and supernatural lore persisted well into the nineteenth century, and strict denominational allegiance was rare.[6] Spiritualism, efforts to contact the dead, and calculations about the second coming of Jesus drew widespread attention, and religious utopian communities flourished throughout the antebellum period.[7] Christian clergy fought what they saw as magical and utilitarian religion with evangelical societies and revivals, and attempted to use secular laws to fight against what they viewed as false beliefs.

Efforts to Christianize the nation intensified in the early decades of the nineteenth century. For example, in 1814 the Philadelphia Bible Society printed and distributed Christian Bibles and tracts, supplied missionaries nationally, and organized a Female Bible Society (FBS) to raise funds to increase book production. Bible societies were very popular among women, and one year later the FBS listed almost seven hundred contributors.[8] The majority of Philadelphia's religious citizens supported evangelical activities. Between 1780 and 1860, Christian denominations expanded their organizational superstructure, and the growth in number of Christian churches "outstripped the national population growth." The total number of Christian congregations expanded from about 2,500 in 1780 to 11,000 in 1820 and 52,000 in 1860.[9]

Women participated enthusiastically in evangelical work, which was available to all Christians and not confined to seminary-trained individuals.[10] Women evangelists commonly believed that the "primary goal of the church was to evangelize the world."[11] Propriety kept these women from entering male environments to spread Christianity, so they were more likely to approach Jewish women and children than Jewish men. However, antebellum Jews formed less than 1 percent of the country's population, and in 1825 there were no more than three thousand Jews in America![12] Between 1800 and 1860, Philadelphia's Jewish population, second only to that of New York, grew from approximately 200 to 8,000, while the city's population grew from 41,000 to almost 670,000.[13]

Christian evangelists succeeded in converting only a handful of American Jews. In 1816 the *Niles' Weekly Register* ridiculed missionary groups for spending "$500,000 over five years for the conversion, real or supposed, of *five* Jews."[14] Nonetheless, in 1823, missionary-minded Christians established the Philadelphia chapter of the American Society for the Melioration of the Condition of the Jews.[15] Some Americans considered targeting Jews a hopeless waste of evangelical effort. Others were theologically or politically opposed to establishing a national American religious orthodoxy.

Some Americans thought evangelism smacked of illiberalism and intolerance. But, as historian Rasia Diner has noted, "conversionists far outnumbered their opponents."[16]

Because most missionaries targeted poor families, Gratz's wealth and status shielded her from many unwanted visits by strangers hoping to convert her, and her firsthand experience of Christian evangelism was limited to her dialogues with Christian women friends. Gratz and her friends spent most of their time discussing ideas on which they agreed, only probing gently into possible disagreements. Gratz's optimism and confidence that Jews could be fully accepted in America was, in part, confirmed by the largely polite and respectful manner in which these women treated her and conducted their discussions about religion.

When she took over the Gratz household after Sarah's death, Rebecca had yet to develop household skills and found it difficult to control her servants. She wrote to Maria about a project that she called an employment agency, actually a referral system for recording servants' employment histories. Gratz hoped it would assure that only applicants with good letters would be recommended for hire, but the high percentage of immigrants and migrants looking for domestic service positions made the project impossible.[17] Eventually, she mastered her servant difficulties, probably because she preferred sorting letters and visiting her sister Rachel to housework.

Gratz's grief sobered her interests, and she began spending more time doing charitable work and studying religion and less time with what she called "the fashionable world." In 1818 she wrote to Maria that she was "trying to be useful among the orphans," and that year saw her first steps toward running a Jewish school, studying Hebrew with the women and children of her extended family. Hyman Gratz was on the synagogue committee and knew Rebecca wanted a Hebrew teacher, so he brought Solomon I. Cohen, who was hoping to be hired for a position at Mikveh Israel, home to meet Rebecca. After a month of afternoon lessons at her house, Gratz enthusiastically reported to Maria that the school was a success: "Elkalah Cohen, Maria and Ellen Hays and [eleven] little ones . . . have been for the last month outlining pronouns and etc. with as much zeal as success!" she reported. "I expect we shall make out very well if [our teacher] continues here long enough to take us through the grammar."[18] Gratz so admired Cohen that she sent a copy of his book on Judaism to Maria in New York.[19]

Gratz created her informal religious school for the women and children of her family only two years after Joanna Graham Bethune established the first Protestant Sunday school in New York. By the end of the first year Bethune's school had grown to twenty-one schools, with 250 teachers and more than 3,000 pupils.[20] Through her correspondence with Maria Fenno Hoffman and her own visits to family and friends in New York, Gratz knew of Bethune's work. Smaller, congregation-based Sunday schools, usually led by men, first appeared in Philadelphia in the 1790s,[21] and in 1817 Philadelphia's Sunday and Adult School, forerunner to the powerful American Sunday School Union, was formed.[22] Although Gratz's home school never grew beyond her family, it was the only such effort for Jewish children in Philadelphia. Wealthy Jews often hired tutors for their children, but her effort was the first time a group of Jewish children had been brought together in Philadelphia for religious education outside the synagogue. Indeed, formal Jewish religious education in Philadelphia did not extend beyond bar mitzvah tutorials for twelve-year-old boys.

As the evangelical movement gathered momentum, the public use of religious rhetoric increased. By 1819, newspapers printed theological opinions expressed in poems like "To Whom Should We Go But To Thee."

> When rankling sorrows wound the soul,
> and cares invade the breast;
> When DISTANT seems the blissful goal,
> of peace, and lasting rest
> . . .
> Blessed SAVIOUR-'tis to thee alone.[23]

Poulson's American Daily Advertiser of January 1, 1819, included three Christmas poems that likened town watchmen to the angels who, in Christian folklore, announced the birth of Jesus. Framed by a pedestal, two Ionic columns, and an open-winged eagle, the poems asked Philadelphians to give cash gifts to the town watchmen.[24] A few weeks later, the paper described a home Christmas pageant in Pennsylvania. In a home prayer hall draped with evergreens, children played the piano, sang psalms, and questioned adults about the story of Christmas by referring to an oversized painting of the nativity scene. The article assured readers that it was an excellent way to teach children about Christmas, assuming that everyone would want to do so.[25]

These public assertions of Christianity in newspapers, along with Shylock-like images of Jews in theater and folklore, formed a boundary between Christians and Jews in American culture, a boundary that Gratz sought to erase by demonstrating her own usefulness, respectability, and piety and by insisting on her right to equal treatment under American law. If her Christian friends accepted her, she believed, she could influence them to accept all Jews. With this attitude she attended meetings of the Philadelphia Orphan Asylum (POA), which opened with a prayer, often delivered by a Presbyterian minister. The asylum itself required daily Bible readings and mealtime prayers.[26] Indeed, Gratz's interests can be seen as a measure of her thorough participation in American culture and its trends. About 1819, she wrote to Maria Hoffman that she was "much pleased" by a Mr. Everett, a minister she had heard speak, and urged Hoffman to attend his church in New York. Preachers who traveled a circuit of churches throughout the States developed reputations that sometimes attracted large, interreligious audiences. Gratz was often among the listeners. Everett had attracted "several clergymen and a large congregation of different sects of christians . . . and I believe all were gratified and none offended," she wrote. Everett was a Unitarian, yet Gratz thought "an episcopal bishop might have said amen to the whole." She found Everett's "eloquence so simple and touching that his taste as well as his understanding would have [been] approved" by the most conservative sect."[27] Rebecca liked the Unitarian approach, which combined a concept of God that was close to Judaism's principle of unity with lessons about virtue couched in popular language. She developed a close friendship with Unitarian Reverend and Mrs. Furness and attended Reverend Furness's church more than once, as did her nieces and other female relatives.[28] These charitable and religious activities provided friendship and a renewed sense of purpose for Gratz, now left nearly alone at home while her brothers took up new business travels.

Brothers' Business

In the large Gratz family, members diversified in their responsibilities. Simon and Hyman, the eldest sons, followed most closely in the pattern set by Michael and Barnard, entering into many of the same trading and land speculating partnerships begun by their father and uncle and forming many other similar limited partnerships as time went on. The youngest sons, Benjamin and Jacob, both studied trade and business law to protect new ventures begun by their brothers. Benjamin went west to oversee land trading in the Mississippi valley, while Jacob stayed in Philadelphia near the port. Middle brothers Joseph and Jacob also entered into their own trading partnerships, both with their brothers and independently, at times opening their own warehouses in Philadelphia.

While Gratz cultivated her religious life, her brothers traveled the countryside and explored new business ventures in an effort to keep the family's finances attuned to the expanding economy of the country. In November 1817, Jacob traveled around the Pennsylvania countryside examining landholdings.[29] The next year, while Hyman was elected a director of the Pennsylvania Company for Insurance on Lives and Granting Annuities, forerunner to the First Pennsylvania Bank, Benjamin went further west, to Ohio, Indiana, and Kentucky, to look at land his brothers were acquiring and to oversee the negotiations. A few months later, Rebecca lamented to Maria that "brother Hyman soon followed Ben to Kentucky and sister Etting has moved into the country. Her son Edward has gone to Baltimore . . . we have been scattering until only a small portion of the family are left."[30]

In July 1819 Joseph and William Meredith left for an extended tour on horseback, visiting lands in Pennsylvania and New York that the men owned or hoped to acquire. Joseph, the most loquacious of the brothers, understood that his sister longed to be included in her brothers' lives and wrote frequently to Rebecca back home, describing his travels to her in vivid detail.[31]

In August, Joseph found a comfortable tavern in Rochester, New York, after a visit to Niagara Falls, and wrote to Rebecca from there. Like most people, Joseph was astounded by the natural grandeur of the falls and wanted his sister to have the same experience. "You must see them, and it will go hard but you shall visit them next year," he promised. He also visited Painted Post, Chemung River, Lake

Ontario, and Fort Erie, Canada, where he felt he was "treading on sacred ground." "[William Meredith] never expected to see such sights," Joseph told his sister. "Let his family know he is in good health."[32]

By the end of August, Joseph and Meredith were in Saratoga Springs on their way home. Joseph had been thrilled by the mountains in western New York and Pennsylvania. "I would not give one acre of improved mountain land for ten under the same kind of improvement in this level country," he asserted. From the springs they went on to the Genessee River, visiting the villages at the Finger Lakes, and then went a hundred miles beyond into hills. "I was busily employed among our tenants," he reported to his sister. "Many of them are doing pretty well-but the greatest part are poor, bad fellows-however the lands have improved, and I think as I always did that they are valuable, and really a fine estate."[33]

When Joseph returned home from his travels through upstate Pennsylvania and New York, he opened his own shops, first a counting house on South 8th Street and, later, a store on Front Street where he traded in India goods, gunpowder, yarns, and Madeira.[34] Jacob, who hated the countryside, opened a store around the corner from Simon and Hyman's place of business, S. & H. Gratz, selling dry goods, satin, damask, crepe, pongee, and brown Havana sugar.[35] That year, 1819, the Second Bank of the United States opened at 420 Chestnut Street in a white marble building modeled on the Parthenon.[36] But despite the financial confidence implied in its architecture, 1819 ushered in a terrible financial depression. Banknote circulation dropped from $110 million to $45 million.[37] Not surprisingly, the numbers and needs of the city's poor skyrocketed. To meet the needs of many families, Philadelphia's women developed dozens of new charitable societies.

The Female Hebrew Benevolent Society

Gratz and other women of Mikveh Israel believed that because evangelists targeted the poor, Jewish women needed their own charitable society and so established the nation's first nonsynagogal Jewish charity, the Female Hebrew Benevolent Society (FHBS), in 1819. Initially, the FHBS provided food, fuel, clothing, and other necessities and hoped to promote Jewish education when funding increased. In later years the society also arranged for nurses, doctors, traveler's aid, and an employment bureau.[38] To be eligible for aid, a petitioner had to undergo a home visit by an FHBS manager and prove herself truly poor, clean, pious, and industrious.[39] Like most other benevolent societies of this era, the FHBS tried to protect the poor from want without encouraging pauperism.

The records of Philadelphia charitable societies and those of the FHBS give us a profile of poor Jewish women in Philadelphia. They were unmarried, sometimes immigrants, widowed, or dependent on men who could not support them.[40] Desertion posed difficulties for Jewish women at the end of the last century, and we have no reason to believe there were not similar problems earlier on, although organizational records were more circumspect in the antebellum era. The FHBS, for example, kept a special fund for needy women who came from formerly wealthy families holding membership in Mikveh Israel, and the details and names of these cases were never recorded in the minutes.[41] Other recipients were women peddlers who, according to the society's report, "returning with their baskets unemptied at the end of the day," could not feed their children.[42] Although it is impossible to tell who among the poor women defended in paternity suits by the city's Guardians of the Poor, an agency that oversaw the poorhouses, were Jews, at least one Jew, an S. Levy, was a Guardian who did bring suit.[43]

While some Americans believed that charitable societies exacerbated pauperism by encouraging idleness, others pointed out that women had unique, legitimate causes for their poverty.[44] In 1818, for example, the New York Committee on Pauperism admitted that women marshaled fewer resources than men, were more exposed to sudden reversals, and were more likely to require help in finding work.[45] Eleven years later, Philadelphia publisher Mathew Carey wrote that "females are obliged to earn half of what the most stupid of the other sex may earn," and plain seamstresses, who made clothing by hand, earned especially low wages, sometimes as little as eight and a half or fifteen cents per shirt. Ironically, charitable societies, which purchased the shirts to keep the women employed, offered so little for the garments that they drove prices down.[46]

Yet poor women were often suspected of being lazy and immoral. Pauperism was especially troublesome to the religious conscience because, as one minister said, "A virtuous people may expect peculiar interpolations of providence for their defense and prosperity."[47] Because of those assumptions, Philadelphia's poorest Jewish women and children often were subject to Christian preaching. Presbyterian ministers preached in the poorhouse on Sunday mornings, and those of other Christian denominations visited on Sunday afternoons. Private charitable societies dispensed similar Christian lessons with their material aid. In 1824, Philadelphia abolished outdoor relief-welfare paid to people not confined to institutions-claiming that such funds were abused.[48]

Perhaps because it was a woman-led organization and women were not yet counted as synagogue members, the FHBS made no stipulation regarding synagogue attendance or membership for either their members or their clients. Nor did the FHBS, unlike the Female Association (FA), with which Gratz was still involved, require its treasurer to be an unmarried woman. Antebellum American women had no right to own property after marriage, and a treasurer legally could lose her organization's funds to her husband. Jewish law does allow married women to own property, and, whether or not Gratz knew of that law, organizational reports indicate that Jewish women expected their husbands to support their causes. Nonetheless, Gratz, who never married, was the FHBS secretary for its first four decades. Widow Esther Hart, granddaughter of Jacob Cohen, a former hazan at Mikveh Israel, and her unmarried daughter Louisa were among the managers, along with Ellen and Emily Phillips, both unmarried.[49]

Gratz's experience in municipal organizations such as the FA and the POA helped her to take the lead in organizing Jewish groups.[50] Experience made her proposals credible and specific, justified by the failures, as she knew them, of municipal groups to meet the needs of Jews. These organizations addressed different populations with different goals, however, and Gratz remained on the board of managers of each of them for most of her life. The FA served women in Philadelphia's formerly wealthy, but newly poor, families in a period of economic instability, while the POA served the city's orphans during a period of heavy immigration and intense social mobility, the latter often leading to desertion of families by men seeking better financial opportunities elsewhere.

The FHBS, in contrast, strove to care for poor Jewish women, protecting them from both poverty and evangelists. FA veteran Rebecca Phillips was elected "First Directress" and Gratz took her favorite role, secretary. As secretary, Gratz wrote the organization's constitution, kept the minutes of all meetings, and wrote all correspondence and annual reports. These two women's sisters, Arabella Phillips and Richea Gratz Hays, were among the managers, along with Esther Hart and other women of Mikveh Israel.

The FHBS women hoped to be "useful to their indigent sisters of the house of Israel." The managers' domestic and familial metaphors added to the legitimacy of this new endeavor that brought Jewish women into public charity.[51] Antebellum writers cloaked charitable work in romantic notions of women's nature by speaking of benevolence as an extension of home and women's sphere.[52] Like other women of her time, Gratz used rhetoric that linked women's public work to home life and made women's societies an extension of women's kin-work, while making it easier for poor Jewish women to receive charity.[53] By extending the rhetoric of home to the house of Israel, Gratz located the FHBS within both American culture and Jewish tradition. The rhetoric also reveals Gratz's hope that the organizations would replace her diminished family.[54] Instead of establishing her own family to compensate for her losses, Gratz, like her bachelor brothers, preferred communal endeavors to private domesticity. However, the only communal activities available to her were those that promoted domestic life.[55]

As an American Jewish organization, the FHBS drew on both American and traditionally Jewish organizational styles and approaches to charity. Most American women's charitable societies of the era, including the FHBS, framed a written constitution regarding rules about meetings, the uses of money, and the requirements for potential recipients of charity.[56] The preamble to the organization's first constitution reminded readers that *tzedakah* (charity seen as righteousness) is a religious obligation for Jews, but the statement of principles written later in the constitution answered the tenor of Philadelphians' anger over what they saw as misspent charity, promising not to give to the "idle and improvident though their poverty may excite pity." These principles legitimized the FHBS as a vehicle for inculcating middle-class notions of virtue among the poor.[57]

As in nearly every other American charitable society of its day, the FHBS managers circulated their printed constitutions among potential donors and plainly promised that donations would not be wasted. The constitution explained that the managers viewed their organization as a "sacred trust" whose funds would be distributed "only when the purposes of charity can be effected." The women of the FHBS promised to give only to petitioners who were "pining in obscurity" rather than to street beggars, and to the sick and infirm. They promised, too, to act "with delicacy" toward those "who had seen better days," and to offer "secret relief" to "reduced families in our congregation."[58]

Philadelphia's primary municipal charitable agency, the Guardians of the Poor, which divided the city into districts and supervised traffic at the house of refuge and workhouse, provided another model for Gratz's organizations. An organization run by men, it made recommendations to the city and state governments about poor laws and generated funds to cope with disasters. The practice of dividing the city into districts supervised by committees was adopted by later charitable agencies, including the FA and the FHBS.[59]

Although the FHBS women adapted many elements of American organizations in forming their society, they counted on Jewish traditions to ensure its success. In part because of the community ethic inherent in tzedakah, the women of the FHBS expected their menfolk to support their organization financially. Whatever their personal opinions about American individualism, the women of Gratz's Jewish organizations clearly expected all Jews to contribute to their cause, because they hoped to benefit all Jews, directly or indirectly. Jews who did not need the services of the FHBS were provided a means of carrying out a religious commandment, that is, offering charity. They also believed all Jews would benefit: that by caring for indigent Jews they would demonstrate to gentile Americans that Jews were not draining the nation's resources, but were both contributing to America and supporting their own brethren.

Reflecting the Gratz brothers' ideas about sound investments, the FHBS invested all donations "above $10" in municipal and United States bonds and railroad stock to form a permanent fund that would create an operating budget. A visiting committee called on petitioners to "inquire respecting their characters." Visiting committees became the standard way for women to participate in Jewish philanthropies, including those run by men, throughout the century. Like the FA, the FHBS charter assured donors that the society would assist the poor only with "necessaries, rather than money." Finally, the constitution announced the hope that someday the FHBS would be able to educate the children of indigent families, but they were unable to do so for almost twenty years.[60]

Barbara Welter has argued that women's entry into new fields usually followed a change in social conditions that reduced the need for female acquiescence to male leadership. She identified three circumstances that could precipitate this movement: a need to place people in some area barred to men but where women could be admitted; by men's diminishing interest in one type of work when other fields offer greater rewards; or when a general desire to maintain an institution is not matched by an equal desire to fund its operations.[61] All three reasons appear to have been operating in Jewish Philadelphia at the time of the founding of the FHBS. The longevity of women's groups, however, depended on whether or not natural leaders emerged within their ranks.[62]

Before the FHBS was founded, the only other Jewish sources for charity were a synagogue's small alms fund and begging. Because, strictly speaking, only men were members of a synagogue, a widow had little leverage with which to provoke its generosity, despite the religious commandment to protect widows. A wife who wanted aid for her family usually had to convince her husband to ask for help, because synagogue presidents customarily sought to ensure that the funds would not be squandered by men who legally controlled their family's finances. Women hoped to avoid the embarrassment of being named in the synagogue's charity records. Minutes of the FHBS show that women often chose to avoid the synagogue out of concern for their reputations as good housewives.

Itinerant Jewish men were by far the easiest cases for synagogue presidents to deal with, because the accepted response was a donation sufficient to send the petitioner to another Jewish community in another town.[63] From 1820 to 1880 most immigrants were Dorfjuden from Bavaria and Posen—with minimal education in Europe and a smattering of exposure to German culture—who worked as peddlers and tailors.[64] Philadelphia lacked both an independent organization for Jewish welfare and authoritative rabbinic leadership, and Gratz easily stepped into that breach.

As with her early involvement in the FA, Gratz strengthened old ties and forged new ones through management of the FHBS. Most of the members and donors during its first year belonged to only seventeen families, many of whom were linked by marriage. Like synagogue membership, the FHBS was a family activity. The names Levy, Cohen, Nunes, Nones, Etting, Gratz, Hays, Hart, Moss, Marks, Nathan, Phillips, Pesoa, and Peixotto—all members of Mikveh Israel—appear repeatedly on the list of subscribers and members.

Late in 1819, Gratz gained a new sister and colleague when Benjamin married Maria Cecil Gist of Kentucky and settled in Lexington.[65] Maria was the sort of person who would have joined Gratz on the board of the POA, had she lived in Philadelphia. Rebecca immediately established a close relationship with Gist, even though she believed that marriage between people of different religions put too much pressure on both parties to compromise their beliefs and thought that child rearing required religious unity between the parents.[66] The traditional Jewish response to intermarriage, coming from days when there was no way for people to live in the same legal world if they lived in different religious worlds, was to mourn the loss of the Jewish child as if he or she had died. But that behavior was seldom the norm in America, and when Benjamin married Maria, Rebecca decided to do everything she could to make her tie to them as strong as possible. The fact that Maria Gist was just the sort of person whom Rebecca had always preferred in her close friends no doubt influenced her decision. Gist was an educated, genteel, intelligent woman with an active interest in religion that was nonetheless free of dogmatism. Moreover, Gist was the granddaughter of a governor of Kentucky and a niece of Henry Clay. As Gratz had once explained to Peggy Ewing, she expected her brothers' marriages to bring her more sisters. After Sarah's death, her need for close sisterhood was greater than ever.

Gratz told her new sister-in-law in no uncertain terms that she expected intimacy through letters. Telling Maria to "banish reserve now . . . for we are Sisters and with that loved title you have a claim to my warmest affection," she explained both what Maria could expect from her and what she expected from Maria. "In that title too I look for such love as has been the most fertile source of comfort and friends to me thro my life." But Maria did not initially respond with intimacy. Several months later Gratz tried again, using household imagery to convey to Maria exactly what she wanted. Offended that Maria did not "introduce me to your domestic repositories," Rebecca threatened to "in like manner treat you as a parlor visitor[,] but I am getting tired of ceremony."[67] She told Maria that she expected them to be "sincere friends as well as affectionate Sisters to the end of our lives."[68]Rebecca hoped their correspondence would not consist of general small talk, but rather the "minute" details of domestic life along with the emotions and thoughts arising from domesticity. She hoped that as they corresponded, they "may venture to linger on a corner sofa and feel perfectly at our ease."[69] Finally, Rebecca and Maria agreed to write every two weeks, without waiting for special news.[70]

Female Piety and Literary Heroes

America's rapidly growing population was increasingly literate, creating a large reading market for countless new periodicals and volumes.[71] Authorship became one of the few routes to an income available to "respectable women," as the ideology of separate spheres, consigning women to the private sphere, took hold in the 1830s. In Philadelphia, advertisements for books written by women favored historical romances and memoirs of aristocratic or religious women. Wild West tales, boys' adventure stories, mysteries, and textbooks also were often written by women, many under male pseudonyms.[72]

While the Gratz men helped advance secular culture in Philadelphia, Gratz's own activities were increasingly grounded in religious literature. Rebecca remarked to Maria Hoffman that "our ladies are becoming quite literary,"[73] as Sarah Ewing Hall prepared a manuscript called *Conversations on the Bible* in which "a concise and connected history comprising the . . . Pentateuch is contained." Gratz thought the volume "very interesting."[74] From 1820 to 1865, literary magazines addressing domestic and religious issues proliferated.[75] Technological changes transformed publishing into a leading industry, concentrated primarily in New York, but with important publishing houses in Philadelphia and Boston. Women and ministers alike took advantage of this publishing explosion to argue their convictions, demonstrate their talents, and supplement their often meager resources.[76]

By 1820, Gratz wrote her letters from the family's new home on Chestnut Avenue near Seventh Street, about five blocks west of their former home on High Street. An avid reader, she noted new literary activity by women, commented on their work, and promoted these writings among other women readers. In April of that year, Gratz wrote enthusiastically to her sister-in-law Maria about Sir Walter Scott's new book *Ivanhoe,* asking, "Tell me what you think of my namesake Rebecca."[77] Rebecca sent Maria a copy to be sure she read it. Its heroine, Rebecca of York, has been called the first favorable depiction of a Jew in English fiction, and Gratz eagerly sought her sister-in-law's opinion of the character. Most important, she hoped Maria would agree that the character was not only plausible but also "just such a representation of a good girl as . . . human nature can reach." Would her Christian friends and relatives find it believable that so virtuous a female could be, and remain, a Jew as Rebecca did in the tale? Maria responded as Rebecca hoped she would, admitting that she admired the character.[78]

For Gratz, Scott's Rebecca became a test of her friends' opinions about Jews, and Gratz contrasted that book with one published in England only three years earlier by Maria Edgeworth. Titled *Harrington,* the novel traced the cause of prejudice against Jews in Europe and depicted, as Gratz phrased it, "an Israelite without guile." But *Harrington's* fatal flaw, as Gratz perceived it, was that the Jewish heroine, Berenice, married Harrington, a Christian, at the close of the tale, and accepted conversion to her husband's faith. From Edgeworth's perspective, the marriage indicated the ease with which Jews, who did not yet enjoy full equal rights in England, could be integrated into British society.

Both Rachel Mordecai Lazarus of Virginia, daughter of Judaic scholar Jacob Mordecai, and Gratz, however, viewed the marriage as a symbolic assertion that offering equal rights would be an efficient way to convert Jews to Christianity. The book launched an extensive correspondence between Lazarus and Edgeworth, particularly after Scott's *Ivanhoe,* in which a Jewish woman chooses to remain a Jew rather than marry the novel's Christian hero, appeared in 1819. Could such a choice be realistic? In 1821, after *Ivanhoe* reached America, Lazarus wrote to Edgeworth that Gratz was the prototype for Rebecca in *Ivanhoe,* proving the book's authenticity.[79] Intermarriage was a tender issue for Lazarus, for her older sister Ellen had married an Episcopalian and joined that church.

Intrigued, Edgeworth also wrote to Gratz, sending her a signed copy of *Harrington.* In response, Gratz explained that she was indebted to the author for the "manner in which you traced the cause and growth of prejudice against Jews." However, Gratz insisted that Edgeworth's characterization of Berenice was implausible. Depicted as a deeply pious young woman, Berenice "might have died for her religion . . . but . . . she would not have become the wife of Harrington," Gratz argued. Explaining both Jewish piety and literary requirements, Gratz contrasted Scott's work with Edgeworth's. By setting his tale in medieval England, a period when chivalry and tolerance could be romanticized, Scott "placed his heroine in situations to try her faith at the risk of life," Gratz pointed out. Believing that Edgeworth sympathized with Jewish martyrdom in Europe, she asserted, "I . . . believe his picture true to nature." Appealing to Edgeworth's standards as a writer, Gratz argued that marrying Harrington was inconsistent with the character of Berenice, a "consistency of character which Miss Edgeworth never violates in any of her tales." Whatever her disagreement with Edgeworth over Berenice's portrayal, Gratz understood that *Harrington* opposed prejudice against Jews, and for that she was grateful, and she assured Edgeworth that *Harrington* would stand alongside *Ivanhoe* in her library as "heartfelt illustrations of Christian charity towards their elder spiritual brother."[80]

By referring to Judaism as Christianity's "elder spiritual brother," Gratz endowed Judaism with both greater wisdom and more profound spirituality than Christianity. Her letter to the well-known British writer gave her a valuable opportunity to argue for Judaism. After years of religious debate with her Christian women friends, Gratz was ready to seize her opportunity to argue Judaism to an influential Christian woman. Yet however grateful she was to the English writer, Gratz would not give an inch.[81]

Charitable and Religious Obligations

The Gratz family maintained traditional Jewish holidays and Rebecca encouraged her nieces and nephews to develop a sense of Jewish piety. In August 1821, Richea's daughter Ellen Hays wrote to her aunt Rebecca from Long Branch assuring her that they had not forgotten the Jewish mourning day of *Tishah B'Av* that had recently passed. Visiting her aunt Rachel Moses that day, Ellen "found all there as [Gratz] would wish. Isabella [Etting, Fanny's daughter] came in Sunday evening to stay a few days with me and is now in the parlor with Sarah [Hays] reading the Lamentations," an essential part of *Tishah B'Av* observance.[82]

For most antebellum Americans, religious obligations included charitable activities. By the 1820s, hundreds of specialized charitable societies sought to care for the poor among diverse religious, and racial groups. The Daughters of Africa mutual aid society was founded by black women in 1821.[83] In 1829 Mathew Carey counted thirty-three female religious, charitable, and moral reform societies in Philadelphia, and separate orphanages existed for Roman Catholic, African American, and white Protestant children. Quaker, Episcopalian, and Catholic women organized distinct associations for the welfare of their women and children.[84]

Several of the Gratz men involved themselves in community service. In 1820, Richea's son Isaac Hays, a newly graduated opthamologist, opened his office in Philadelphia and offered his services to the FHBS and to Bikur Holim (Visitors of the Sick), the two Jewish charitable organizations in city, and a few years later to the POA.[85] That year fifteen Jews subscribed to the Athenaeum, an arts library in Philadelphia, which Jacob led. In 1821, Jacob travelled to Harrisburg, Pennsylvania, to petition the state legislature to fund a new school for the "deaf and dumb" in Philadelphia.[86] Joseph Gratz was on the first board of managers of the newly formed Apprentices Library, whose holdings were geared to the interests and needs of tradesmen. Nephew Benjamin Etting, who had been associated with the Board of Education, was elected secretary of the Mercantile Library, which served businessmen.[87]

Gratz continued to be looked to for leadership and advice in the organizations in which she was involved. In 1821, the POA board, facing both increased requests for aid and fewer donations, decided to publish a history of their institution that would emphasize its importance to Philadelphia. The Board asked Gratz, its secretary, to work with Baltimore writer Sarah Ewing Hall in compiling the volume, but the collaboration did not go well. Hall thought that Gratz, as the organization's secretary, ought to write it, while Gratz thought the task should fall to Hall, an already published and known author. "My Dear Becky," Hall wrote to her, "the editor is ready for our history of the Orphan House. If you are determined, cross as you are—to throw this business on me, you can I suppose furnish me with the documents." Hall wanted Gratz to at least provide the data from the minute books, which Gratz, as secretary, kept.

Gratz argued that her letters to Hall over the years provided ample detail about the organization's growth, and preferred not to make public all the information in the minutes. Hall responded that she could not find the letters: "I have put away your letters so carefully that it will cost me more time to hunt [them] up than to write the particulars [they] contain. I want however several other particulars which I shall probably obtain from your annual reports." Hoping to convince Gratz to accept at least partial responsibility for the volume, Hall urged her to write about the asylum's founding, limiting Hall's work to discussions of its impact on Philadelphia's poor. "I heartily wish you would write the historical part at least, were it only because you have more time than I have—to say nothing of your ability to do it better than I can," she explained.

Hoping to soften Gratz's opposition, Hall complimented her on the character of Rebecca in *Ivanhoe,* whom Hall firmly believed to be inspired by Gratz herself. "Are you not delighted with your sublime namesake in *Ivanhoe?*" Hall's sister Peggy Ewing had told her about the correspondence between Gratz and Edgeworth, and Hall used that information now, she hoped, to her advantage, "If Miss Edgeworth failed in her good intentions towards you—Walter Scott has made you ample amends. *Ivanhoe* is a misnomer; the title should have been *The Jewess.* Rebecca is completely the heroine of the tale, the only beautiful, and by far the most interesting person in the book. So firm, yet so tender—so heroic, yet so feminine, her character alone would place a wreath of glory on the brow of its author." Hall closed by lamenting that she lived so far from Gratz and asserting her affection for the Philadelphian.[88] Gratz provided information, but Hall, despite her pleadings, wrote the history.

Hall's solicitous praise for *Ivanhoe* was blatantly manipulative, but a failure. After many years of managing organizations, Gratz had grown utterly confident in her own judgments about them. The organizations were her career and she approached them with the dedication and the no-nonsense attitude that historian Lori Ginzberg found common to benevolent society managers in this era.[89] At forty, Gratz had lost interest in balls and gala events. She described a New Year's Eve ball at Mrs. John Sargeant's as "stale, flat, and unprofitable to me—the companions of former days have either passed away or lost interest in my heart and the idea has so much melancholy in it to me, that a ballroom seems more like a memorial of lost pleasures than an incitement to new ones."[90] Those companions who now bored her had not turned their intellectual abilities toward religious and charitable endeavors, the milieu of the developing women's culture. For Gratz, such endeavors carried an urgency that surpassed fancy dress balls. She complained that even her own letters were less interesting to write. Perhaps, as she said, her "cares and dull realities . . . [clipped] the wings of imagination."[91]

Gratz's time was filled with the day-to-day needs of the orphan asylum. In 1822, a fire—begun when two boys filled a clothing trunk with hearth coals—killed twenty-three of the 106 children living in the building. The matron's illness forced Gratz to make daily visits to both the matron and the asylum. The city's newly improved water supply saved most of the children from the fire, but the home was badly burned.[92] Gratz detailed her work: "What with thanking great and small distant and present donors, providing for the [asylum] family and legislating about the new asylum, I have not been a very companionable character to anyone above the rank of the poor orphans."[93] A year later, after the Pennsylvania legislature granted $5,000 and private donors contributed $28,000 more, Gratz was one of four women who furnished the new asylum and moved the residents into it."[94] She worried about long-term financial problems the fire caused: "I do not know that we have anything to complain of more than might be expected by those acquainted with public institutions, [but] . . . misfortunes . . . lose us friends."[95] That winter she kept busy supplying the kitchen, purchasing clothing, and preparing the children for their annual public exam.[96] The board used the children's exams to demonstrate the institution's effectiveness to the public, their donors.

Soon after she put the orphan asylum back in order, Rebecca's own family suffered another severe loss. In the evening of September 29, 1823, Rachel Gratz Moses died. Her infant daughter Gertrude, just thirteen months old, one of nine children born to Rachel and Solomon Moses, died the next morning. Gertrude Meredith wrote an obituary for Rachel, describing her as "sleep[ing] with her fathers in humble trust of a joyful resurrection to the heavenly Jerusalem."[97] Gratz immediately resigned from the FA board and brought Rachel's six remaining children home to live with her.[98]

Thus began a new phase of life for Gratz, who eight years earlier had remarked that "Rachel's children are my favorite toys."[99] Two years after Rachel's death, their father, Solomon Moses, bought a house directly opposite the Gratz home and the older children moved in with him, but Gratz continued to help him raise his children. She not only supervised their education, but was the person most like a mother to them for the rest of their lives. She told Maria Gist Gratz that they were the "objects of my constant and tenderest concern" and that they gave her a "deep interest in life." More than that, Rebecca felt that Rachel's children cheered her own life, whose "many and severe trials . . . might otherwise have made a weary pilgrimmage [sic]."[100]

Gratz found special interest in the lives and accomplishments of her nieces and nephews. One of her older nephews, Richea's son Isaac was selected by city leaders in 1823 to be one of six physicians for Philadelphia's dispensary. Gratz also strove to develop a close relationship with Benjamin and Maria's children in distant Lexington, although she seldom visited them. When their third child, Henry Howard, was born in July 1824, she sought news about her new nephew, who was named for Henry Clay.

Gratz's increased involvement in philanthropic organizations paralleled similar activities on the part of her bachelor brothers. Hyman Gratz was especially involved in guiding their congregation. In 1824 Hyman was elected treasurer of Mikveh Israel, a post he held for more than thirty years.[101] Eager to be part of the city's new cultural face, Mikveh Israel commissioned William Strickland, one of the city's most popular architects, to design a new synagogue building for the congregation. By January 1825, the new building on Cherry Street was ready, largely due to the Gratz family's contributions. Joseph Gratz, treasurer of the building committee, accepted pledges from his siblings totalling two thousand dollars. Simon Gratz alone gave one thousand dollars, and his brothers and Rebecca matched his gift.[102]

The dedication of the new building on January 21, 1825, attracted a large interreligious audience, including a local Christian bishop. Gertrude Meredith had planned to go, but the day's bad weather stopped her, although three of her children attended the ceremony.[103] In the dedication service, nine Torah scrolls were brought from the previous place of worship and placed in the ark of the new building. Rebecca viewed the ceremony lovingly and described the service in detail to Benjamin. "I have never witnessed a more impressive or solemn ceremony or one more calculated to elevate the mind to religious exercises," she wrote. Although the new building was a small, high-ceilinged brick rectangle with Egyptian-inspired marble lintels over the doors and windows, to Gratz it was "one of the most beautiful specimens of ancient architecture in the city."

Beginning just before sundown on Friday evening, the service was performed by lamplight. Moses Peixotto, then hazan of Shearith Israel in New York, assisted Abraham Keys, Mikveh Israel's hazan. Simon Gratz opened the doors and intoned the initial blessing, and "the processions entered with the two Reverends in their robes followed by [men carrying] nine sacred scrolls," Gratz told Benjamin.[104] A choir chanted psalms as the scrolls were carried seven times around the reading desk in the center of the room; then Hebrew prayers were pronounced. According to Gratz, even the Christian bishop agreed that there had never been such fine "church music" sung in Philadelphia. Choirmaster Jacob Seixas and his sister Miriam, who were visiting from New York, led a choir made up of Mikveh Israel members. After the scrolls were placed in the ark, Peixotto and Keys recited more Hebrew prayers. Four different accounts of the event, all remarking on its solemnity, were published in local newspapers. One Christian observer wondered if the chants could have been the same music that Jesus had heard.[105]

The new synagogue reflected other growth in Philadelphia. The 108-mile Schuylkill Canal now brought anthracite coal from Port Carbon, above Reading, to the city's port.[106] The Schuylkill River was lined with wharves and canals connecting it to the Chesapeake Bay and Delaware River. Over one hundred mills in the Manayunk section of Philadelphia would soon ship goods along these canals. Joseph Dennie and the *Port Folio* were forgotten largely because the city's literary output had surpassed Dennie's accomplishments. By 1820, over one hundred thousand dollars in book sales in Philadelphia included science, religion, and literature.[107] The flavor of the town had so changed since its colonial heyday that in 1825 city councillors agreed that Philadelphians needed a reminder of its founders and named the public squares Penn, Logan, Washington, Franklin, Rittenhouse, and Independence. Beginning to develop a sense of its own place in history and to memorialize its early days, in 1827 the city erected a monument in Kensington commemorating William Penn's 1682 treaty with Native Americans.[108] Wealth enabled Philadelphians to display their taste for fine architecture, and in the 1820s and 1830s public buildings as diverse as the new Unitarian church at 10th and Locust, the Arch Street Theater, the Almshouse west of the Schuylkill River and the Merchants' Exchange at Third and Dock Streets all were built of white marble.

Just as Jews from New York traveled to Philadelphia to help make the synagogue dedication a more memorable occasion, so Jews within Philadelphia worked together in new ways for their general benefit. As new charitable societies emerged among Jews in Philadelphia, cooperation between men's and women's societies grew commonplace. For example, in 1825 a Jewish widower left town, abandoning three children. The United Hebrew Beneficent Society (UHBS), a men's charity founded three years earlier, asked the FHBS women to help care for the children, which they did. The UHBS hoped to provide for "unfortunate and indigent brethren" but functioned in many ways as a mutual aid society rather than as a benevolent society. Only men who married according to Jewish ritual and circumcised their male children could be members of the UHBS.

Insisting that "charity . . . strengthens the bonds of society" and intending to "provide for the sick of our persuasion," men of the UHBS also promised to visit the sick and provide a decent burial and a quorum for prayers at the homes of mourners. Additionally, they promised to see that boys were apprenticed with masters who would allow them to observe the Jewish Sabbath and holy days. Like the FHBS women, they hoped to provide for Jewish education as soon as funding permitted. Their "female relatives," they said, would attend to any necessary sewing for the poor. Membership in the UHBS was at first limited to Jewish men in Philadelphia, but because many Jewish men traveled the outlying counties as peddlers, it was soon extended to Jewish men throughout the state.[109]

Although Gratz had argued heatedly that a pious Jewish woman would not marry a non Jew, she knew that since the days of the earliest Jewish settlers, marriages between Jews and non Jews were a fact of life. Yet Judaism prohibited such marriages, requiring many home practices, prayers, blessings, and observances. Dietary restrictions and customs, blessings before and after meals, Sabbath, Passover, Sukkot, and Hanukkah celebrations and observances each included domestic responsibilities for both men and women. Additionally, married Jewish women were required to ritually immerse in water and recite blessings monthly and to confine their sexual activity with their husbands to those "purified" times of each month. Traditional Jewish husbands relied on their wives' observance of both sexual and dietary restrictions. Jewish wives relied on their husbands to lead home worship and to oversee the religious rites relating to their children's development.

But in North America, several circumstances worked against Jewish marriages. First, because most immigrants were men, the ratio of men to women did not equalize until later in the nineteenth century, and then only in areas of high Jewish settlement. In frontier areas, Jewish men heavily outnumbered Jewish women.[110] Second, immigrants came from widely scattered areas of Europe, making knowledge about their family backgrounds uncertain. New immigrants held little status in America, and an American-born individual might be unwilling to marry an immigrant. Finally, American cultural values, which lauded individualism and romantic love, held little regard for other marriage values.

Jewish congregations struggled to pressure their members to abide by Jewish marriage standards. In 1826, Philadelphia's Rodeph Shalom ruled that no member (only male adults were counted as members) who had married a non-Jew could vote on synagogue governance or be called to read the Torah scroll at worship services. Yet the practical needs of Philadelphia's small synagogues, which were wholly dependent on their membership for funds, blunted the force of rulings of this sort.[111] Torn between the desire to promote a high level of Jewish religious observance and the need to keep contributing members, congregations experimented with various postures. Expressing the membership's wishes rather than rabbinic judgment, synagogue constitutions shifted away from prohibitions against intermarriage to procedural rules for proselytes and marriage.[112] In 1829, Rodeph Shalom withdrew rules disallowing full membership to Jewish men married to gentile women. All members were welcome if they raised their children as

Jews. Mikveh Israel, with fewer immigrant members pressing to have things done as they were in Europe, avoided the issue altogether.

Synagogues struggled with intermarriage when American expectations for women's lives were changing. Widespread Christian revivals in the 1820s brought a new attitude toward women's piety and purpose, which was reflected in women's literature. In 1828, Sarah Josepha Hale edited the *Ladies Magazine* and Hale's

opinions about women's place in American society are evidenced in her early work there. "Let the education of women differ ever so much in DETAIL," she explained to her readers, "its END is the same, to qualify them to become wives and mothers." In a rapidly diversifying society, she insisted that linguistic, religious, and ethnic differences counted little against those of sex and gender. Hale wrote that women's "similarity of purpose produces a similarity of thought, feeling, action and consequently CHARACTER, which no uniformity of training could otherwise bestow."[113] For Hale, the lives of all American women were governed by a common framework of events, tasks, crises, and rewards. All women faced lifelong dependency on men for financial support and/or political safety, and most faced repeated childbirths that would leave them progressively weaker and with progressively greater responsibilities. Each hoped to find an old age among people who still cared for her, knowing that the degree of ease she would find depended on the degree of compassion she could arouse in her benefactors.

As Jewish immigration increased in the 1820s and 1830s, Jews' religious standards were more and more influenced by American ideals and attitudes. One was that women were naturally more religious than men. This idea had a number of sources. The literature of romanticism, which drew on the new middleclass fascination with tales of chivalric old aristocrats and virtuous individual upstarts, insisted that religion was ultimately a feeling of devotion of a sort that seemed unlikely to occur among men who were mired in earthly power. A combative, irreligious personality seemed more suited to government, business, and soldiering, all men's tasks. Popular literature by nineteenth-century Protestants portrayed religion as fundamentally emotional, resting on feelings of reverence, awe, gratitude, and dependence on God, feelings that were thought natural to women.

Economic realities also supported the idea that women were more religious and emotional than men. As the production of goods moved out of homes and into factories, women became more financially dependent on men as household economies changed from production to consumption, and as commercial clothing, foodstuffs, candles, medicine, and liquor appeared. Over the course of the century, as women's home nursing and educational responsibilities diminished with the proliferation of hospitals and schools, women's central responsibilities revolved around nurturing the emotional and spiritual lives of their families. Middleclass women increasingly took up activities in all forms of religious life—except the ministry itself, which remained barred to them.[114] While women's piety became a mark of middle-class status throughout western Europe as well, American evangelism gave women's piety an activist cast both at home and in charitable societies.[115] Indeed, these activities and this rhetoric supporting women's religious and charitable activities became the foundation for what Ann Douglas has called the matriarchal culture of nineteenth-century America.[116]

These changes modified republican motherhood into an ideology suitable to the Victorian age. The women of America, as mothers, sisters, wives, and daughters, would influence the character of boys and men toward social virtue by religious education and emotional direction. Through them, women would determine social order and mold the nation's character. Many magazines written for women during this era referred to women's triumph in becoming society's leaders. Their leadership was thought proof of the high degree of civilization America had achieved.[117]

Hale's series, "Sketches of American Character," offered images of women as leaders of civility. In an essay on the village schoolmistress, Hale argued women's suitability for public teaching. "Their influence on the manners is readily and willingly conceded by everyone," she insisted. "Might not their influence on the MIND be made quite as irresistible, and far more beneficial, and that too, without violating . . . the PROPRIETY which, to make their examples valuable, should ever mark their conduct?"[118] Hale's argument was hardly revolutionary, as women had been running private schools for decades. But her goal was to open teaching to women as a profession, not limited to individual women whose family resources supported their venture in academia.

By the third decade of the nineteenth century, two ideas about the nature and role of women began appearing in tandem. As the intensity and number of revivals increased, to women's civilizing and education function emphasized in republican motherhood was added the ability to save the nation. This was a direct result of women's role in teaching religion in the family and acting as the bearers of religion because regular church attendance was becoming an evermore female activity. Since God acts within history to reward good and punish evil, Hale reasoned, there could be nothing more important to the country than God and his power to affect the history of the nation. As religion moved fully into the private sphere, women were no longer just civilizing or refining America, as assumed in republican motherhood; they were also saving it.[119] Eventually, these arguments supported what has been called a domestic feminism, framing a vision of the public good based on women's experience.[120]

Gratz agreed with Hale that among women, differences of opinion, even of religious opinion, could not override women's commonalities, which enabled women to work together effectively. But as women's responsibilities grew more clearly defined as religious, Gratz's relationships with Christian friends and co-workers grew more complex. Although she shared with them a deep, biblically based faith, her belief in the truth of Judaism conflicted with their Christian convictions.

Gratz and other American Jewish women of her era found themselves faced with taking a role in Judaism for which they had not been trained. Typically, Jewish women received little formal religious education, yet in America it was their responsibility to keep Judaism in their homes and Christianity out. Gratz showed Jewish women how to accomplish this task. Through the FHBS, she provided Jewish philanthropic women who hesitated to work in Christian organizations a means to display the values of spirituality and compassion that they shared with their gentile peers. Beginning with the FHBS, Gratz's organizations were founded on ideas shared by educated American women like Hale, Maria Gist, and Gertrude

Meredith. For the organization's leaders, such as Gratz, the FHBS proved their outstanding qualities as American leaders in charitable societies, the arena most respected by influential Christian women. For the needy Jewish women, both immigrant and American-born, who received its assistance, the FHBS provided an avenue for finding the necessities of life, advice on acculturating to America and withstanding evangelical assaults, and contacts within the local Jewish community.

By the late 1820s Philadelphia's economy was again declining. The city's status as the nation's premier location for moving goods from the port to America's western frontier suffered a severe challenge when the Erie Canal opened in 1825. With the new canal, New York merchants could bring goods from the port of New York, which never froze, up the Hudson River, along the canal, and across the Great Lakes, stopping at hundreds of towns along the way. In July 1826, one year after the Erie Canal opened, Simon and Hyman Gratz faced bankruptcy.

The Gratz brothers were not the only Philadelphia merchants to feel the economic blow from New York, and they were treated with sympathy and encountered many small acts of kindness. Simon retained his presidency of the Schuylkill Bank, which he had helped to found in 1811. The Pennsylvania Company for Insurance in Lives and Granting Annuities, an organization Hyman had been associated with since 1818, soon elected him president. Relieved, Rebecca was grateful that they had "shed more tears of gratitude than grief." Abraham Elkin, a younger member of Mikveh Israel, had loaned money to Simon and Hyman. After Simon wrote Elkin a letter promising to pay him as soon as the brothers could do so. Elkin told him the debt was of no consequence and offered to redeem Simon's estate from foreclosure. "Poor Simon wept like a child when he related this anecdote to me," Gratz told her sister-in-law Maria.[121]

In response to their new financial situation, Rebecca, Hyman, Jacob, and Joseph planned their move to a smaller house at 2 Boston Row, behind Richea's house on Chestnut Street. Gratz knew that bankruptcies had destroyed some of Philadelphia's wealthiest families, and she focused on adjusting the household and quieting battles. She soon began to "philosophize on the subject-and examine . . . whether poverty be so great an evil . . . I have implicit faith in Scripture . . . I do not fear.[122] She rolled up the carpets and moved the household to a less auspicious neighborhood than their former large home on High Street (now Market) near Seventh Street. The former home had been twenty-eight feet wide and fifty-six feet deep, with mahogany folding doors, marble mantles, and spacious rooms. Around it were a bathhouse, a cistern, a large stable, and a carriage house.[123] But the new home was far from a hovel. To her sister-in-law Maria she described its two parlours "nearly covered by the mat taken from the floor of the [former] back room," a small dining room, a library, and bedrooms.[124]

Notes

1. RG. to Maria Fenno Hoffman, January 26, 1818, Rebecca Gratz Papers, P-9, AJHS.
2. RG. to Maria Fenno Hoffman, February 14, 1817, Rebecca Gratz Papers, Manuscript Collection no. 236, AJA.
3. RG. to Maria Fenno Hoffman, June 3, 1818, Rebecca Gratz Papers, P-9, AJHS.

4. RG. to Maria Fenno Hoffman, January 26, 1818, Rebecca Gratz Papers, Manuscript Collection no. 236, AJA; same to same, 1817, ibid.

5. Richardson, "Athens of America."

6. Butler, *Awash in a Sea of Faith*, 67–95.

7. Saum, *The Popular Mood, 224.*

8. First Report of the Female Bible Society of Philadelphia (1815), LCP.

9. "By comparison, the overall United States population grew from about 4,000,000 in 1780 to 10,000,000 in 1820 and 31,000,000 in 1860"; Butler, *Awash in a Sea of Faith*, 270–71, 278–79.

10. Reuther and Keller, *Women and Religion in America*, vol. 1; Welter, "She Hath Done What She Could"; Faith Rogow, "Step Right Up: The Attraction of Evangelicalism to Ante-Bellum Southern White Women," unpublished manuscript, 1984.

11. Reuther, *Religion and Sexism*, 242.

12. Diner, *A Time for Gathering*, 56.

13. Ashton, "Souls Have No Sex," 36. Population statistics for Philadelphia are from Weigley, *Philadelphia*, 104–15. Population statistics for Jews in Philadelphia are from Whiteman, "Legacy of IsaacLeeser," 27, and Edwin Wolf II, "The German-Jewish Influence in Philadelphia's Jewish Charities," in M. Friedman, *Jewish Life in Philadelphia, 1830–1940, 125.*

14. Diner, *A Time for Gathering*, 177.

15. WW, 241–42.

16. Diner, *A Time for Gathering*, 86.

17. R.G. to Maria Fenno Hoffman, June 3,1818, Rebecca Gratz Papers, Manuscript Collection no. 236, AJA.

18. RG. to Maria Fenno Hoffman, March 9, 1818, ibid.

19. RG. to Maria Fenno Hoffman, March 3, 1818, Gratz Family Papers, RM; S. 1. Cohen, *Elements of the Jewish Faith*, translated from the Hebrew (Richmond, 1817; Philadelphia, 1823); Hyman Polock Rosenbach, "Notes on the First Settlement of Jews in Pennsylvania," *PAJHS* 5 (1897): 191–98.

20. Miller, "Women in the Vanguard," 312.

21. Moore, *Selling God*, 61.

22. Toll and Gillam, *Invisible Philadelphia*, 278.

23. *Poulson's American Daily Advertiser*, January 21, 1819, LCP.

24. Ibid., January 1, 1819, LCP.

25. Ibid., January 22, 1819, LCP.

26. First Annual Report of the Philadelphia Orphan Asylum (1816), 1718, "Pamphlets no. 992," APS.

27. RG. to Maria Fenno Hoffman, n.d., Rebecca Gratz Papers, Manuscript Collection no. 236, AJA.

28. RG. to Maria Gist Gratz, 1832, excerpted in Philipson, *Letters, 133.*

29. Jacob Gratz to RG., Gratz Family Papers, Collection no. 72, box 16, APS.

30. RG. to Maria Fenno Hoffman, December 13, 1817, Rebecca Gratz Papers, P-9, AJHS.

31. Joseph Gratz to RG., July [1819?], July 31, 1819, Gratz Family Papers, Collection no. 72, box 16, APS.

32. Joseph Gratz to RG., August 1819, ibid.

33. Joseph Gratz to RG., August 26, 1819, ibid.

34. WW,341.

35. Ibid.

36. Wainwright, "The Age of Nicholas Biddle," 282.

37. Richardson, "Athens of America," 249.

38. Bodek, "Making Do," 145, 147.

39. FHBS Constitution, LCP.

40. Glanz, *The Jewish Woman in America,* vol. 2; R.G. to Miriam Moses Cohen, January 24, 1843, Rebecca Gratz Papers, Manuscript Collection no. 236, AJA.

41. R. S. Friedman, "'Send Me My Husband.'"

42. Rebecca Gratz, *Female Hebrew Benevolent Society's Secretary's Report* (1858), Henry Joseph Collection, box 239, AJA.

43. Guardians of the Poor: Records 1822–1824, 4–5, HSP.

44. *Report of a Committee on the Subject of Pauperism* (New York, 1818), 9, APS. Although several causes for poverty were listed, charitable institutions were blamed for the "evils that flow from the expectations they necessarily excite." Mathew Carey, *Essays an the Public Charities of Philadelphia,* 4th ed. (Philadelphia, 1829), "Pamphlets no. 992," APS.

45. *Report of a Committee,* 14, APS.

46. Carey, *Essays, 1–2.*

47. William Ellery Channing, A *Sermon Delivered in Boston, September* 18, 1818 (Boston, 1818),8, "Pamphlets no. 992," APS.

48. Lawrence, *Philadelphia Almshouses,* 9.

49. Minute Book of the Juuto for Congregation Mikveh Israel, April 18, 1824-February 14, 1881, MIA.

50. According to historian Ann Boylau ("Women in Groups"), antebellum women's organizations did not follow a linear development from small auxiliaries to independent, large public agencies. Instead, the groups were organized along distinct networks that often had little contact or communication with each other. While women's local mission societies usually began as small prayer meetings and grew into support systems for male-led church and national mission societies, benevolent societies began with public activities and independent administrations as early as 1800. Benevolent societies usually attracted women from merchant and clergy families and tried to "uplift" individuals among the "worthy poor." Moral reform societies focusing on the environmental causes of poverty appeared in the 1830s and drew their support from a more varied population of women. Finally in the 1840s, when many states adopted the principle of universal white male suffrage, women's rights groups appeared. A crucial handful of women moved from leadership in the abolition movement to leadership in the fight for women's suffrage. As a rule, these different types of organizations existed as parallel sets of societies with little in common. Boylan concludes that antebellum women's social activism is best explained by personal class and religious experiences of the women involved.

51. FHBS Constitution 1820, LCP. D. S. Smith, "Family Limitation," 119–36; Scott, *Natural Allies,* 11–37.

52. Ginzberg, *Women and the Work of Benevolence,* 53.

53. Di Leonardo, "The Female World of Cards and Holidays."

54. FHBS Constitution, LCP. Phillips's granddaughter Ellen Phillips bequeathed over $100,000 to numerous Philadelphia Jewish and municipal philanthropies when she died in 1891. Will of Ellen Phillips, Ellen Phillips Papers, HSP.

55. Byars, *B. & M. Gratz,* 35–55; Bodek, "Making Do," 142.

56. Scott, *Natural Allies,* 13.

57. Ginzberg, *Women and the Work of Benevolence,* 215.

58. FHBS Constitution, 1819, AJA.

59. FHBS, Board Minutes, 1814–1875, FHBS Collection, NMAJH.

60. FHBS Constitution, AJA.

61. Welter, "The Feminization of American Religion."

62. Scott, *Natural Allies,* 15.

63. Welter, "She Hath Done What She Could"; WW, 78.

64. Diner, *A Time for Gathering,* 163.

65. H. Morais, *The Jews of Philadelphia,* 432; WW, 180, 202, 293–99.

66. RG. to Maria Fenno Hoffman, October 20, 1817, to Miriam Moses Cohen, November 14, 1837, and to Maria Fenno Hoffman, October 31, 1819, all in Rebecca Gratz Papers, Manuscript Collection no. 236, AJA.

67. RG. to Maria Gist Gratz, 1820, Rebecca Gratz Papers, P-9, AJHS.

68. RG. to Maria Gist Gratz, 1819, Philipson, *Letters,* 21.

69. RG. to Maria Gist Gratz, 1820, ibid., 27.

70. RG. to Maria Gist Gratz, February 23, 1840, Rebecca Gratz Papers, P-9, AJHS.

71. Butler, *Awash in a Sea of Faith,* 97.

72. *Poulson's American Daily Advertiser,* December 1838, LCP.

73. RG. to Maria Fenno Hoffman, 1817, Rebecca Gratz Papers, P-9, AJHS.

74. Hall's *Port Folio* pseudonym was Constantia. RG. to Maria Fenno Hoffman, ca. 1817, Miriam Gratz Moses Cohen Papers and Books, Collection no. 2639, SHC.

75. Douglas, *The Feminization of American Culture,* 99.

76. Butler, *Awash in a Sea of Faith,* 278.

77. RG. to Maria Gist Gratz, April 4, 1820, Rebecca Gratz Papers, Manuscript Collection no. 236, AJA.

78. RG. to Maria Gist Gratz, May 10, 1820, ibid.

79. MacDonald, *The Education of the Heart,* 28.

80. RG. to Maria Edgeworth, n.d., ca. 1822, APS, box 9.

81. Gratz also wrote to her old friend Maria Fenno Hoffinan about *Harrington* and her concerns about its message. Gratz understood that "religious tolerance . . . [is] the message [Edgeworth] would inculcate," but she disliked Edgeworth's plot. "I think however a more interesting and natural story might have been produced in making the characters of Jew and Christian associate and assimilate in all the respective charities of social life without bringing the passions into contact. I believe it is impossible to reconcile a matrimonial engagement between persons of so different a creed without requiring one or the other to yield. In all instances we have heard of in real life this has been the case & where a family of children are to be brought up it appears necessary that parents should agree." RG. to Maria Fenno Hoffman, October 20, 1817, Rebecca Gratz Papers, Manuscript Collection no. 236, AJA.

82. Ellen Hays to KG., August 7, 1821, Gratz Family Papers, Collection no. 71, box 16, AP8.

83. Scott, *Natural Allies,* 19.

84. Carey, *Essays.*

85. WW, 326.

86. Jacob Gratz to KG., 1821, Gratz Family Papers, Collection no. 72, APS, box 16.

87. WW, 97.

88. S[arah] Hall to KG., ca. 1821, Gratz Family Papers, APS, Collection no. 72, box 16.

89. Ginzberg, *Women and the Work of Benevolence,* 36–45.

90. R.G. to Maria Fenno Hoffmanl n.d., Gratz Family Papersl Collection no. 72, box 16, APS.

91. KG. to Maria Gist Gratz, May 4, 1828, Rebecca Gratz Papers, P-9, AJHS.

92. Richardson, "Athens of America," 208–56.

93. KG. to Maria Fenno Hoffman, March 2,1822, Rebecca Gratz Papers, Manuscript Collection no. 236, AJA.

94. Eighth Annual Report of the Philadelphia Orphan Asylum, 1822, Pamphlet no. 922, APS.

95. KG. to Maria Fenno Hoffman, April 6, 1823, Rebecca Gratz Papers, Manuscript Collection no. 236, AJA.

96. KG. to Maria Fenno Hoffman, n.d., ibid.

97. "Obituary of RachefGratz Moses by Mrs. Gertrude Meredith," Gratz Family Papers, Collection no. 72, box 17, APS.

98. Toll and Gillam, *Invisible Philadelphia,* 348. They comment that after Gratz's resignation the organization's minutes became perfunctory.

99. KG. to Maria Fenno Hoffman, ca. 1815, Rebecca Gratz Papers, Manuscript Collection no. 236, AJA.

100. KG. to Maria Gist Gratz, 1824, Rebecca Gratz Papers, P-9, AJHS.

101. WW, 343–44.

102. Richardson, "Athens of America," 249; WW, 361.

103. Gertrude G. Meredith to William Meredith, January 21, 1825, Meredith Papers Correspondence, box 34, folder 2, HSP.

104. Quoted in WW, 362.

105. WW, 367–68.

106. Richardson, "Athens of America," 208–56.

107. Wainwright, "The Age of Nicholas Biddle"; Weigley, *Philadelphia*, 267–69.

108. Wainwright, "The Age of Nicholas Biddle," 301.

109. United Hebrew Beneficent Society, Annual Reports, 1822, 1825, 1841, UHBS Collection, PJA-BIES.

110. Diner, *A Time for Gathering,* 46–47.

111. WW, 242.

112. Ibid., 240.

113. Sara Hale, "Sketches of an American Character," *The Ladies Magazine* (1828): 202, LC.

114. Douglas, *Feminization;* Welter, "The Feminization of American Religion," 83–102; Houghton, *The Victorian Frame of Mind;* Auerbach, *Woman and the Demon;* Stansell, *City of Women,* 68–75, 7; Bell, *Crusade in the City.*

115. On women's piety as a mark of middle-class status in Europe see Hyman, *Gender and Assimilation,* 28; on a more activist version of that phenomenon in America see Reuther and Keller, *Women and Religion in America,* Vol. 1: The Nineteenth Century; McDannell, *The Christian Home in Victorian America.*

116. Douglas, *Terrible Honesty.*

117. Bloch, "American Feminine Ideals in Transition," 2.

118. Sarah Hale, "Sketches of an American Character: The Village Schoolmistress," *The Ladies Magazine* (1828): 202, LC.

119. See for example Sarah Hale, "A Review of *Religion at Home* by Mrs. William Providence," *The Ladies Magazine* 2, no. 9 (1828): 436–37, LC.

120. G. Matthews, *The Rise of Public Woman,* 72–73; Jane Tompkins, "Sentimental Power: *Uncle Tom's Cabin* and the Politics of Literary History," *Glyph* 8 (1981): 79–102; G. Brown, "Getting into the Kitchen with Dinah," 503–23.

121. WW, 344, 345.

122. RG. to Maria Fenno Hoffman, February 19, 1826, Rebecca Gratz Papers, Manuscript Collection no. 236, AJA.

123. Sarner, "Rebecca Gratz," 6.

124. RG. to Maria Gist Gratz, 1826, Rebecca Gratz Papers, Manuscript Collection no. 236, AJA.

Pioneer Preacher

LANCE SUSSMAN

In 1829, When Isaac Leeser first arrived in town, Philadelphia stood on the verge of a major period of growth. In the course of the next few decades, the "City of Brotherly Love" was transformed from a provincial American town to a large, modem city. It had a rich colonial history and had served as the political capital of the revolutionary struggle. Some of the old charm was still visible, but it was quickly becoming evident that Philadelphia would be a radically different place than the town planned by William Penn in 1682.

The rapid increase in the number of residents and the vast expansion of Philadelphia's boundaries were the most visible signs of change. In 1795, Philadelphia, already a large city by American standards, had a population of 23,700; by 1820, its population had ballooned to 98,000; twenty years later, 258,000 people lived there. The physical growth of the city was just as dramatic. Originally the town was planned as a small grid of streets on the west bank of the Delaware River. In 1854, a consolidation movement resulted in the official amalgamation of twenty-nine separate municipalities into the city of Philadelphia.[1]

The transition of Philadelphia from a town into a city was accompanied by a host of problems. "Most historians agree," writes Michael Feldberg, "that in the rapid expansion of the 1830s and 1840s, citizens of the American city lost social knowledge and physical contact with one another for the first time."[2] As a result, tensions among the myriad class, racial, religious, and occupational communities increased. As early as 1828, tension between German and Irish ethnics resulted in a bloody riot in nearby suburban Kensington. "The series of riots that began in 1834," writes Philadelphia historian Sam Bass Warner, Jr., "rose in intensity to a peak of violence in 1844 and then abated as organized politics assumed the place of fragmentary outbursts of frustration, prejudice, and anger."[3]

In addition to "organized politics," Jacksonian Philadelphia also saw the development of a number of important institutions. "Many of our [current] urban habits and institutions," Warner writes, "are survivals from innovations of the nation's first big city era—hospitals, charities, parks, water works, police departments, and public schools." Moreover, "the mid-nineteenth century was *par excellence* the era of the urban parish, the Lodge, the benefit association, the social and athletic club, the political club, the fire company, and the gang."[4]

In many ways, changes in the broad pattern of urban life in Philadelphia during the Jacksonian and antebellum periods were reflected in the Jewish community. In 1830, Philadelphia had a small Jewish population, between five hundred and one thousand, and had two Jewish congregations and three benevolent societies. Less than twenty-five years later, in their 1854 *Jewish Calendar,* Jacques.J. Lyons and Abraham de Sola reported that Philadelphia had five congregations and seventeen societies.[5] By 1858, it is estimated that the Jewish population had grown to eight thousand.[6]

The early history of the Philadelphia Jewish community is well known. Jews first came to the Delaware Valley area during the 1650s as traders. Permanent Jewish settlement began in 1737 with the arrival of Nathan and Isaac Levy. The best-known Philadelphia colonial Jews, Bernard and Michael Gratz, brothers who developed a lucrative business that specialized in western trade, arrived in 1754. Their family also assumed a leadership role among the city's Jews, whose population finally surpassed one hundred by 1765.[7]

Jewish communal life began in 1740, when Nathan Levy secured a small parcel of land for Jewish burial on Spruce Street between Eighth and Ninth streets. Services, however, continued to be conducted on an informal basis for two more decades. For the High Holy Days in 1761, the local Jewish community obtained a Scroll of the Law from Congregation Shearith Israel in New York. "It may be assumed," write Edwin Wolf and Maxwell Whiteman, "that with a *Sefer Torah* on indefinite loan in Philadelphia, religious services became more regular. There was even a communal employee: Michael Gratz's account book for this period records a payment to a *Shammash,* or beadle." By 1773, the Philadelphia Jewish community had adopted *Mickveh Israel* ("The Hope of Israel") as its corporate name.[8]

The community grew slowly and steadily. Patterning themselves after Shearith Israel, which in turn had modeled itself after the great Sephardic congregations of London and Amsterdam, the Jews of Philadelphia elected a parnass, gabbai (treasurer), and a six-member adjunta (board of directors). At first they met in a rented house on Sterling Alley near Third Street. In 1776, they moved to Cherry Alley, where they assembled in a second-story room in a house owned by a gentile, Joseph Cauffman. According to Wolf and Whiteman,

> Cherry Alley was a little, cobblestone street, about fifteen feet wide, which began at Third Street and ran west between Race and Arch. An occasional tree threw some shade against the two-story brick houses in which some of the congregants lived. There were but few shops along its short length, for while it was surrounded by the business district, it was not part of it.[9]

The Revolutionary War completely transformed the Jewish community of Philadelphia. Following the departure of the British from the city in the spring of 1778, Philadelphia became a safe haven for Jewish civilians on the patriots' side who were fleeing from the ravages of battle. The largest number of refugees came from New York, including Gershom Mendes Seixas, the hazzan of Shearith Israel. Others came from Charleston, South Carolina, and Savannah, Georgia.

Also among the many Jews who sought asylum in Philadelphia during the war was Haym Solomon (1740–85), a patriot who aided the cause of American independence by assisting Robert Morris, superintendent of the Office of Finance, in successfully selling bills of exchange and government notes on the Philadelphia market at a time when fiat continental currency was nearly worthless.[10]

By the end of the War of Independence, approximately one thousand Jews, more than a third of the total Jewish population of the United States, lived in Philadelphia. New quarters had to be found to house the congregation. In March 1782, a decision was made to build a new synagogue. A tiny edifice, erected on Cherry Street between Third and Fourth, was dedicated on September 13, 1782 with little fanfare.[11] Thus, after nearly fifty years of continuous Jewish settlement, Philadelphia's Jews had their own place of worship.

With the surrender of Cornwallis, Jews from New England, New York, and the South began to return home, including Gershom Seixas, who had been the congregation's hazzan since 1780. With great difficulty, the local community struggled to survive. A new hazzan, Jacob Raphael Cohen (1738?-1811), was hired, as were several other religious functionaries. Various parnassim, including Jonas Phillips (1736–1803), Manuel Josephson (1729–96), and Benjamin Nones (1757–1826), served the congregation with distinction. Phillips was the first parnass of Mickveh Israel after its reorganization in 1782. Josephson served as president for six years (1785–91) and spearheaded the drive among the scattered American synagogues to jointly congratulate George Washington on his election as president. Nones, a native of Bordeaux, France, was the head of the congregation for fifteen years (1791–99, 1805–1806, 1808–10, and 1820–1822) and championed a strict approach to Jewish law. He was well known in the general community for his outspoken support of Thomas Jefferson.[12]

The fledgling community established a clear Jewish presence in the political life of the city and in the new nation. In 1787, Jonas Phillips protested the Test Oath in Philadelphia, which prevented Jews from holding public office. The same year, when the new federal Constitution was ratified, the Philadelphia Jewish community furnished a table with kosher food so that its members could join in the public celebration of the event.[13]

Throughout the Early National Period, the Phillips family continued to play an important role in Mickveh Israel. Three of Jonas Phillips's sons served as parnass of the congregation: Naphtali Phillips (1799–1800), Benjamin I. Phillips (1811–15), and Zalegman Phillips (1806–1807 and 1822–34). Naphtali became the first American-born parnass of Mickveh Israel at the age of twenty-six. Thereafter, he moved to New York, where he served as parnass of Shearith Israel for ten years (1804–1805, 1815–24).[14]

Zalegman Phillips (1779–1839) was parnass of Mickveh Israel when Isaac Leeser was first elected hazzan in 1829. Phillips was a native Philadelphian and a graduate of the University of Pennsylvania. He was admitted to the bar in 1799 and was widely respected as a highly capable criminal lawyer with a large clientele. On October 23, 1805, he married Arabella Bush Solomons of Baltimore. Two of their sons, Jonas Altamont and Henry Myer Phillips, also had distinguished legal careers.[15]

Phillips had overseen the hiring of the previous hazzan, Abraham Israel Keys, after a transition period of seven years when the congregation functioned without benefit of a regular hazzan. Phillips was also president of the congregation when Mickveh Israel built its second sanctuary, a neo-Egyptian structure designed by William Strickland, the same architect who designed the Second Bank of the United States in Philadelphia. The new synagogue, completed in the autumn of 1824, had over 350 permanent seats, including a women's gallery. The success of the congregation during Phillips's presidency even resulted in numerous defections from Rodeph Sholom, Philadelphia's Ashkenazic congregation.[16]

As parnass, Phillips understood that one of the most important decisions a congregation faced was the selection of its religious leadership. When Mickveh Israel began searching for a new hazzan in 1829, the parnass opted for the appointment of Eleazar S. Lazarus (17881844), a native-born New Yorker and the grandfather of poet Emma Lazarus. In 1824, Lazarus had already been offered the position of hazzan at Mickveh Israel but refused, because he would not accept a contract "unless it be during good behavior and with a salary not extravagant but sufficient."[17] In other words, Lazarus wanted a life contract and an assurance of financial security. Phillips and the congregation would not meet his terms and instead turned to Keys.

Lazarus's boldness can be explained by the fact that he already had full-time employment in New York as a city assessor. He was also active in the Jewish community. He was affiliated with Shearith Israel and was a patron, but not a member, of B'nai Jeshurun, the city's first Ashkenazic congregation. In 1826 he edited the Hebrew text of Solomon

H. Jackson's *The Form of Prayers According to the Custom of the Spanish and Portuguese Jews.* During the spring of 1829 he was persuaded to come to Philadelphia to lead services during the Passover holiday. However, he had no intention of staying, and returned to New York.[18]

A broad search for candidates for the office of hazzan resulted in three other possibilities: Isaac Leeser of Richmond, twenty-two years old; Abraham Ottolengui of Charleston, twenty years old; and Gompart S. Gomparts, who submitted his name at the last moment without presenting his credentials. Leeser was the most highly recommended of the three, and accepted the invitation from Mickveh Israel to come to Philadelphia "tō perform the services for the Judgement of the Congregation."

The parnass was not impressed with Leeser and resolved to block his election. "Instead of an examination into [myl fitness, by previous study and the due achievements for the office to which [I] was called," Leeser complained, "[I] was merely required to read the service for three successive weeks."[19] "It has been my misfortune," Leeser later wrote to Zalma Rehine, "to have among the congregation a few persons who were opposed to my first coming hither and who left no means untried to prevent my being elected . . . and at every fitting opportunity they showed their darling scheme not to be abandoned, and that they were resolved to either make me retire or to render my stay unpleasant and dishonorable."[20]

Leeser's frie[illegible]d, John Hampden Pleasants, advised him to remain calm and let his merit [illegible] itself. On August 27, 1829, the editor of the *Whig* wrote to Leeser:

I am sorry to hear that the prospect of thy success is not so certain as I was induced to believe, for though I am not personally interested in the result of the election, my feelings are so far excited as to desire the preference of one with whom I am in a measure acquainted, and who I have no doubt is qualified to fill the office in some very essential respects. But I am glad to perceive that thou will be satisfied, however the election may result; and not less so, at thy standing aloof from all interference in it. When promotion is voluntarily offered, there is a charm and gratification in success, which does not fall to our lot if we have used any active means to obtain it. I shall be pleased to hear from thee as soon as the matter is decided.[21]

Why the parnass and his faction opposed Leeser is not fully known. Several factors present themselves as the possible cause. First, Leeser was only twenty-two years old, and had neither experience nor substantial training as hazzan, especially in the Sephardic liturgy. Also, Leeser was ambivalent about the prospect of becoming a religious functionary. A third possibility is that Jacob Mordecai's suggestion that Leeser had the financial support of his uncle was interpreted by Phillips and others to mean that Leeser would be independent-minded and not fully responsive to the authority of the parnass and adjunta. Fourth, Leeser also had ideas about being a writer and an intellectual, prospects not necessarily viewed with favor by some members of the congregation. Fifth, Leeser's opponents might have simply detected something in his personality that they did not like. Finally, it is also possible that there was prejudice against Leeser because he was a German Jew. Phillips might even have found Leeser's close relations with John Hampden Pleasants, a Southern Whig, objectionable.

On September 6, 1829, the congregation met to elect a new hazzan. A motion to postpone the whole matter was quickly overridden. The terms of employment were then debated. Suggestions concerning length of contract ranged from one to five years, and from $600 to $1,000 per annum for salary. After considerable discussion and parliamentary maneuvering, the salary was fixed at $800 for a term of two years. The status of the potential candidates was then reviewed. Lazarus had not consented to stand for election. Ottolengui had withdrawn, and his name was dropped from contention. Only Leeser remained as a bona fide candidate. In the ensuing election, he received twenty-six votes, while seven ballots were cast to Lazarus, as a protest.[22]

Some years later, Leeser wrote to the chief rabbi of England about his bittersweet election: "Knowing my own want of proper qualification, I would never have consented to serve, if others more fitting in point of standing, information, or other qualities had been there; but this not being the case . . . I consented to serve."[23]

On September 7, 1829, Leeser officially accepted the position without questioning the fact that the income originally promised to him by de Cordova had been reduced by 20 percent. He informed the congregation of his decision by writing to two officials involved in the selection process, Joseph S. Cohen and L M. Goldsmidt.

Permit me to transmit through you, to the members of K. K. [holy congregation] Mickveh Israel, my acceptance of the office of hazan, to which office they did me the honor to elect me on yesterday. In accepting this highly

> responsible station, I am fully alive to the various, and in a measure, new duties which devolve upon me. No man can be more aware than myself of my want of qualifications to acquit myself properly; but it shall be my constant aim to merit the indulgence, if not the confidence, of this respectable congregation by attending strictly, as far as lies in my power, to the duties of my office so that I may never be accused of carelessness and negligence. It would be unbecoming in me to be more particular, as I do consider it wrong to make any promises which I might be unable to fulfill.
>
> Accept for yourselves, gentlemen, my sincere thanks of the highly flattering matter in which you announced to me the result of the election; and be assured that your prosperity, and the prosperity of the community you represent, will ever be gratifying to
>
> Yours and the very Obedient Servant Isaac Leeser[24]

Leeser had little time to settle his personal affairs—the High Holy Days were close at hand. After they passed, Zalma Rehine came to Philadelphia to observe, first hand, how his nephew was adjusting to his new situation. Rehine was particularly pleased with the way his friends the Peixotto family, who had been providing Leeser a place to stay, were helping. Upon returning to Richmond, he wrote to Leeser with some sage advice: "My dear Isaac, I hope you will Try to Cultivate the friendship of every body in your Congregation and not mind some few kicks which now and then you might receive, never interfere with any difference between them, but be a peacemaker and make them friends."[25]

Unfortunately, the parnass and those who sided with him against Leeser did not relent in their opposition to the young hazzan. In a letter to the congregation written eleven years later, Leeser recalled that "during the first year of my residence here, various unpleasant things took place, which it is needless to call to mind again, and altho' matters were smoothed over again, *still the report reached a distant congregation,* that my situation was not very pleasant here. Therefore, overtures were made to me by several influential members from that place to take the office of Hazzan vacant there." Leeser, however, decided to stay and make Philadelphia his home. He remained with Mickveh Israel for twenty-one stormy years before resigning in anger and frustration.[26]

The predicament of the young hazzan was viewed sympathetically by Rebecca Gratz (1781–1869), a daughter of Michael Gratz, a leading Philadelphia businessman and early leader of the local Jewish community. She was the outstanding Jewish woman of her time, and exemplar of the "cult of true womanhood." Involved in numerous social welfare activities, in both the Jewish and general communities, she was secretary of the Female Association for the Relief of Women and Children in Reduced Circumstances in 1801, aided in the founding of the Female Hebrew Benevolent Society in 1819, was the moving force behind the establishment of the first Jewish Sunday school in 1838, and helped organize various orphanages in Philadelphia.[27]

Rebecca Gratz immediately recognized the importance of Leeser to the Jewish community and criticized the "horrible spirits" in the congregation who persecuted him. In her private correspondence, she also gives the earliest portrait of the young hazzan. In a letter to her sister-in-law, Maria Gist Gratz, on November 4, 1829, she writes that

> our young pastor is certainly more attractive to those who are indifferent to the *outer Man* looking sage, who in reply to a high born damsel's remark on the freak of nature in placing so much wisdom in so ugly a creature, demanded what kind of vessel her father kept his wine in—she said a common earthen, for wine kept in precious metal became sour—he observed wisdom is safest with ugliness—for there are few provokatives to vanity—which is an enemy to wisdom—this anecdote is most aptly applied to Mr. Leeser—who is ugly and awkward—but so sensible and pleasant as well as pious—that all the old ladies are charmed, while the girls are obliged to persuade themselves to be pleasant.[28]

The following April, she again wrote to her sister-in-law about Leeser and made several critical observations about him.

> Before he came to Phila he had written some essays in "defence of the Jews and Mosaic law," which gained him some reputation among a small circle of friends. It was his first attempt at authorship and he fell in love with his work. . . . I have read it, and although it gives me a good opinion of his talents have advised him not to publish—but some other friends have encouraged him, and he issued proposals to publish it by subscription. . . . With these burthens on his shoulders, before he had got through the first difficulties of his new station, he had taken too much upon himself and does not seem to get along happily as if he had reserved his whole strength and attention to the duties of the reading desk. But youth is apt to be proved, experience will aid in checking, or rather directing enthusiasm to proper channels . . . he is certainly a very pious and worthy man and takes very hard the latitude allowed in matters of religion in this enlightened age. Fortunately he is a beardless youth. Did he wear the chin of a rabbi, he would be scoffed at by his congregation.[29]

Leeser's physical unattractiveness and personal frustrations with his congregation stood in stark contrast to the success of a local Unitarian minister, William Henry Furness (1802–1896), who enjoyed the friendship of many of Leeser's congregants, especially Rebecca Gratz. In January 1825, he had been installed as the minister in the church founded by Dr. Joseph Priestly in 1796. Furness quickly became a highly regarded preacher, scholar, and translator. Various Jews could be found in his congregation on Sunday mornings to hear his sermons. On August 9, 1831, Rebecca Gratz again wrote to Maria Gratz:

> Your favorable opinion of Mr. Furness will be confirmed by a fact which has raised him in the estimation of his congregation, so much that they are at a loss to express their admiration. He had permission to accompany his family to New England and pass July and August away. He preached

> at Boston, and had a unanimous call to a church in that city, at a salary of $2,500—and an allowance of $200 more for fuel, and the perquisites which would add considerably to the richness of living—he receives here but $1,500—yet his love for his own congregation, and sense of duty to them was put in the balance, and outweighed the tempting offer—he returned home last week.[30]

Gratz also admired Furness's skill as a public speaker. In 1838, she again wrote her sister-in-law about Furness:

> Our favorite orator gave a most beautiful lecture the other evening on Genesis—and verily—I thought he illustrated the subject most aptly—the hall was crowded, and the most deep and fixed attention prevailed. I wished you could have heard him, for I never heard him more eloquent in the pulpit, and he managed popular lecture so as to abate nothing from the reverence and dignity of his clerical character.[31]

From the very beginning of his employment at Mickveh Israel, Leeser hoped to elevate the office of hazzan and to remodel it after the best aspects of the Christian ministry. The first and most important change, according to Leeser, was the establishment of regular preaching in the synagogue. Sermons, he wrote in 1845, could "exercise an influence over the mind of society, which we now can hardly have any idea of. What does one think would be the fate of protestant Christianity without the constant appeal to the fear and reason of its professors from the ten thousand pulpits which scatter information and admonition many times during every week."[32] Later, he also advocated the development of an American Jewish theological seminary to train "ministers" and championed substantial changes in the contractual relationship between the hazzan and his congregation.

Historically, preaching had its roots in the ancient synagogue. The need to translate and explain the meaning of the Torah was already felt in synagogues in the land of Israel during the first century. Specific rules of biblical exegesis, a variety of literary structures, and novel illustrative techniques were developed to teach, inspire, and comfort worshippers. During the Middle Ages, the *derashah* or homily was a regular feature of synagogue life. While formal preaching by rabbis was often limited to the Sabbaths before Yom Kippur and Passover, informal and often imaginative discussion of the Torah by *maggidim* (itinerant preachers) was a popular folk custom, especially in Eastern Europe. Even boys who had become Bar Mitzvah, and bridegrooms, were expected to give a *derashah*.[33]

At the beginning of the nineteenth century, interest in modem preaching developed among Jews in Germany and England. German reformers sought to replace the traditional *derashah* with a *predigt*, a vernacular sermon consciously modeled on the pattern of Christian homiletics. They even used Christian guides to the art of preaching. Subsequently, beginning in the 1840s, German Jewish preachers broadly began using rabbinic sources to illustrate their sermons. In England, on the other hand, where vernacular preaching also began among the Sephardim early in the nineteenth century, Jewish homiletics remained Bibliocentric.[34]

Modern Jewish preaching also began in the United States during the Early National Period on a limited basis. "It is true," Leeser wrote in 1841, "that occasionally lectures were delivered . . . by the late Rev. Gershom M. Seixas, of New York, the late Rev. Emanuel N. Carvalho, of Philadelphia, Rev. A. H. Cohen of Richmond, Dr. Jacob De La Motta, of Charleston, and several other ministers, besides occasional volunteer lectures among laymen, if such a word can be with propriety used among Israelites; but no appointment was ever made with a view to sermons."[35] More traditional messages were delivered to American Jews by a handful of "Palestinian messengers" who already began visiting American synagogues in the eighteenth century to raise funds for Jewish communities and activities in the Land of Israel. However, the Saturday afternoon *shiur* (scriptural lesson) and the tradition of the *maggid* did not transplant themselves to America.

By contrast, preaching and public lecturing were important features of American culture in general. Early New England preachers such as Increase Mather (1639–1723), Cotton Mather (1663–1728), and Jonathan Edwards (1703–1750) helped establish the centrality of the sermon in American religion. During the nineteenth century, that tradition was continued by numerous preachers and revivalists including Horace Bushnell (1802–1870), Peter Cartwright (1785–1872), and Charles G. Finney (1792–1875). And, of course, there was Leeser's contemporary, William Henry Furness. Moreover, between 1826 and 1834, the same period when Leeser emerged as a preacher and lecturer, over three thousand lyceums were established in the United States as a form of adult education.[36]

"But even before being in office," Leeser wrote in a note in his first volume of sermons, published in 1837, "it had appeared to me as an incongruity, that words of instruction formed no part of our regular service." Whether Leeser thought the lack of preaching in the American synagogue to be "incongruous" with Jewish tradition or American culture or both is unknown. He certainly believed that American Jews were broadly in favor of restoring the sermon to the synagogue. "It was perfectly clear," he wrote, "that the people desired public instruction." He also received some "kind approbation and encouragement . . . by some intelligent ladies" from Mickveh lsrael.[37]

The parnass and the adjunta, on the other hand, were content with the status quo. The authority to order a sermon on special occasions lay with the parnass. Late in life, Leeser recalled with disdain the original conditions of his employment at Mickveh Israel.

> Our own position for twenty-one years, was simply that of hazzan, in which capacity we were only required to read the prayers in the original Hebrew according to the custom of the Portuguese Jews, on Sabbath Eve, morning and night, and the same on Holy Days and festivals, to attend all funerals and subsequent mourning services and to perform at no time any marriages or funeral rites without the consent of the parnass or the adjunta. . . . It requires little reflection to understand that the ministry under such conditions is one of very limited functions and privileges and likewise demands only a very small amount of talent and information.[38]

Leeser had hoped that on account of his "literary" achievements in Richmond, the board of Mickveh Israel would have requested that "he give discourses on our religion in the language of the country." When they failed to take any such initiative, Leeser was "sadly disappointed." After nine months in office, he recalled, "I was induced to address a circular letter to the several members of the Board of the Adjunta, asking them whether my speaking in Synagogue would meet their consent." Again to his dismay, the board did not act officially on his proposal. Instead, they "signified, in unofficial letters, their approval of my intention." Thirteen years passed before the board formally sanctioned Leeser's work as a preacher.[39]

Leeser targeted the first Saturday in June 1830 *(Shabbat Naso),* as the date for delivering his first sermon. Preparing his first "discourse" was not an easy task for him. He needed nearly two weeks to write it. He began with a verse from the prophet Isaiah (25:9). Appropriately, he called his sermon "Confidence in God."[40] Twenty-two years later, Leeser recalled his anxiety on the Sabbath he began his career as a preacher.

> Few but those who have been placed as I was, can imagine the embarrassment I experienced when I commenced speaking. I will briefly state, that I, in all my life, never had heard but about a half a dozen addresses, either from the pulpit or elsewhere; I knew that I have a considerable heaviness of speech, almost amounting to a stammer, unless I speak very deliberately or rapidly; besides all this, a first attempt before an audience, whose judgements one has to respect, and individuals, whose taste is both refined and experienced, is not an easy or pleasant task.[41]

Waiting until the end of the service, he spoke after the singing of the closing hymn, "Adon Olam" ("Lord of the Universe"). Later in his career, he preached prior to the conclusion of worship.

He began "Confidence in God" with a confession of humility and by revealing "that only in obedience to the repeated solicitations of persons who really feel an interest in the welfare of our [Jewish] nation, I persuaded myself to attempt teaching that, which I deem to be the essential part of our faith." Then he explained why he felt it was necessary to preach at all.

> It is highly probable, that most of you, if not all, may have heard all of which I can advance; but then I must beg of you to consider, that known truths may often be faintly remembered, and that we may derive great and lasting benefits by having them presented to us in a light, in which perhaps we had never before viewed them. It is for this reason expedient, that occasional lectures on religious subjects should be delivered in our Synagogue.[42]

With that, Leeser gave the verse and commenced with his exegesis. Peering through his heavy spectacles, Leeser reminded his congregation that it is "our duty to remain unshaken: in being God's servants. The God of Israel is a faithful God and we should be mindful not to be overcome with a false sense of self-sufficiency. Instead, we should busy ourselves with the care of our souls." In a parable, Leeser illustrated his own pious conviction:

> A certain man had three friends, to one whom he was devotedly attached; to the second he was kind but he did not esteem him by far as much as the first; to the third, however, he paid but little regard, and scarcely ever thought of him. It happened one day, that this man was suddenly summoned to appear before the king; and not knowing the cause of the unexpected summons, or perhaps dreading to appear before the king without a powerful defender to assist him in case of necessity; he applied to the first of his friends, being sure, that he would not refuse him his countenance in the present emergency. The friend, however, did refuse, excusing himself, saying: "I really cannot go; I am so much occupied with my own concerns, that it is impossible for me to assist you now; besides this, I have no influence with the king." He then went to the second, who answered: "I can do but little for you; but as we have been friends so long, I will accompany you as far as the palace-gate; more than this I cannot do." Finding himself so rudely treated by his most intimate friends, he applied to the last, whom he had so long neglected. This one, who in fact had always loved him more than either of the others, received him with open arms, saying: "How glad I am, my dear friend, that you have given me this opportunity of serving you; I will go with you to the king, I will remain with you, and defend you if necessary."

The preacher then gave his interpretation.

> The moral of the foregoing is, that a man generally values his riches more than his relatives and friends, and these again more than his religion, which, alas! like the last friend in the parable, is too often neglected and almost forgotten. He is finally summoned to appear before the King of kings, the Holy One, praised be He; his money avails him nothing—this must be left behind; his friends and relatives accompany him to the grave, there they must leave him, and thus his virtues and good deeds alone remain with him to the tribunal of the Judge of all to defend him and to plead in his favor.[43]

Having defined the "true aim of life," Leeser brought his remarks to a close with a *nehemta* (passage of consolation) and a prayer petitioning for Restoration in Zion.

The style and structure of Leeser's sermons quickly evolved after this first address. He rarely returned to the use of parables and tales from rabbinic literature, a practice soon to be popularized in Europe by the Viennese preacher Adolf Jellinek (1820–93). Instead, he primarily used the Bible to illustrate his talks. An original introductory prayer, often in the petitionary mode, became a standard feature of his preaching. This prayer was of variable length and not strictly tied to the major themes of the subsequent discourse. The place of the verse also shifted from the beginning to the middle or end of the sermon, at least during his first few years as a preacher, probably to distinguish his own remarks from those of contemporary Christian preachers, who often stated their scriptural passage before preaching. In discussing the organization of his sermons, Leeser later wrote:

> In place of giving out a text and stringing a sermon to the same, as is customary with most preachers, I have generally chosen to introduce it in the middle or even at the conclusion of my discourses; because I desired to illustrate a doctrinal point, and then show its consonance with the text of Scripture, believing this course less fatiguing and more interesting to the audience than the usual mode.[44]

The body of Leeser's sermons often did not follow any consistent organization pattern. He was aware of his tendency to ramble. Commenting in the middle of one sermon, he noted "as usual with me, I have wandered away from the subject which I first spoke of." Because the structure of his remarks was not well defined, his sermons were long, requiring thirty to forty-five minutes to deliver, but in the context of America in the mid-nineteenth century, this length was not unusual. An average Leeser sermon consisted of 5,300 words and was slightly over sixteen printed pages.[45]

The literary quality of Leeser's sermons has been a matter of some debate. His friend and assistant Mayer Sulzberger wrote warmly of Leeser's sermonic accomplishments:

> The chief characteristic of his method is simplicity. He is never betrayed into an affectation, if even a show, of learning. There is no straining after rhetorical effect, or startling climaxes, or marvellous theories. He has a message to deliver, which he does straightway in a manner that is relieved from dryness only by his pronounced taste for illustrating what he has to say, for simplifying it to its last elements. Indeed, measured by ordinary standards, he rarely reaches the point which the schools call eloquence. But if true eloquence be to convince and impress, rather than to daze and electrify, he possesses that quality in a high degree. His subject always remains, at bottom, a monition, a warning, an instruction; it is never an essay or a philosophical treatise. It is informed by learning—not filled with it. The element of personality is therefore never prominent. One never stops to wonder at the beauty of the discourse or the eloquence of the preacher. There arises, rather, a feeling of the subject discussed, a realization of short-comings, a resolve to better one's self.[46]

Sulzberger was even more complimentary about Leeser's extemporaneous speaking, to which the hazzan increasingly resorted after leaving Mickveh Israel in 1850: "As a speaker, his command of language and of ideas enabled him to present well-digested thoughts in excellent shape, without previous preparation. Indeed, many of his extemporaneous discourses might well serve as elegant specimens of pulpit oratory."[47] Rosa Mordecai wrote in a similar vein, "These extemporaneous discourses seemed often to be inspired and it is impossible for me to make any one who had not the great privilege of hearing them understand their full force. . . . I never heard such a flow of language or rapidity of utterance, except from the late, lamented Bishop Phillips Brooks."[48]

Modem scholarly opinion, on the other hand, has taken a dimmer view of Leeser's sermons. The views of Joseph Blau and Salo W. Baron are typical:

> At no time in his career, if we may judge by his published volumes of *Discourses*, was Leeser an inspired or inspiring preacher. His sermons, in his maturity as well as . . . in his youth, read like student essays. There is, too, a stiffness, almost a pomposity, in their style and language, with no touch of warmth and color or any originality of conception or freshness of exposition to them. He must have been very dull to hear. Perhaps the redeeming quality of his sermons, for the auditor as well as the reader, is the obvious sincerity with which Leeser struggled to express his simple faith and piety.[49]

During the course of his long career, Leeser published more than 250 sermons and addresses. Most of them appear in his ten-volume work, *Discourses in the Jewish Religion* (volumes 1 and 2 were first published in 1837, volume 3 in 1841, and volumes 4–10 in 1867). Additionally, many of his sermons appeared in his newspaper, *The Occident and American Jewish Advocate* (1843–69). A few of his sermons were also printed separately as pamphlets. To promote Jewish preaching in general, Leeser also published scores of "messages" by other Jewish preachers in America and Europe in the *Occident*, many of which he translated and edited himself.

Leeser did not give Sabbath sermons with great frequency compared to twentieth-century congregational rabbis in the United States. In 1830, the first year of his preaching, he spoke eleven times at Mickveh Israel. The following year, he gave eight sermons. During a three-year period, 1837–40, when his relations with his congregation were at a low ebb, he spoke a total of only six times, mainly during the High Holy Days. His peak year as a preacher was 1847, when he sermonized eighteen times.[50]

Thematically, Leeser limited himself to theological topics reflecting his belief in the strict separation of the spiritual and the temporal parts of existence. His favorite topics were God the Creator, providence, the Covenant, irreligion and sin, the Messiah, and the Restoration of the Jewish people to the Land of Israel. He often emphasized the importance of religious faith and placed a greater value on belief than on the performance of any one particular commandment. He was also careful to delineate the differences between Jewish and Christian doctrines and, beginning in the middle of his career, was critical of Reform Judaism's denial of the coming of a human Messiah and rejection of the hope of Restoration. Only on rare occasions would Leeser talk directly to his congregation about its internal problems or accomplishments.[51]

His sermons, however, were not mere abstractions unconnected to the daily course of events. Rather, Leeser attempted to interpret in a theologically orthodox manner the meaning of daily life. Thus, if the community was suffering from a "plague," he would talk about sin and retribution. If riots broke out in Philadelphia, he would talk about the value of divinely revealed "Law." If a member of the community—or, as happened in 1841, the president of the United States—died, he would offer his congregants the assurance of eternal life. Sometimes, in his published works, he added a note to explain the context of his remarks. His congregants most likely made the connections on their own.[52]

Of all Leeser's accomplishments, his role as the pioneer Jewish preacher in the United States was closest to his heart. On being honored by friends in March 1861, he responded to a tribute by saying, "You have spoken of my sermons; and indeed, if I have any merit, it is to these that I point."[53] When Maimonides College, the first rabbinical seminary in America, finally opened in 1867, Leeser was gratified in being appointed not only provost but also professor of homiletics, belles lettres, and comparative theology. In fact, the last project Leeser undertook was the publication of his *Discourses*. On July 21, 1867, he wrote:

> It is confidently hoped, however, that all the various sermons, addresses, and prayers may be found to have sufficient interest to make them somewhat valuable for future reference and use, and that they may be regarded hereafter as vehicles of information on many points, and be used for private devotion in the family circles of our people. If this wish be realized, I shall be amply compensated for the thought, labour, and care expended in preparing them for press, and presenting them to the public as my humble contribution to Jewish religious literature.[54]

Leeser's dedication to preaching as a form of adult Jewish education was matched by his interest in religious instruction for Jewish youth. During his first year at Mickveh Israel, he clearly established himself as an important Jewish educator. Simultaneously, he tried to resolve two fundamental problems: the need for properly organized Jewish day schools, and the lack of appropriate study materials.

On March 31, 1830, Leeser proposed to the board of Mickveh Israel that the congregation establish a Jewish school for both boys and girls with an enrollment of twenty students. He also requested $1,500 to begin the program. Apparently, the board did not grant him the money. Approximately one year later Leeser tried again and was able to start a small school at the house where he was then boarding. His seven students created all types of problems for him, and even damaged the landlord's furniture. On April 21, 1831, he asked the congregation to supplement his income ($80–100 per quarter) so that he could continue to run the school. The congregation wanted no part of it, and classes were suspended.[55]

Lack of appropriate Jewish study material in English was just as frustrating to Leeser as the refusal of the congregation to give him financial support. Familiar with modern Jewish schoolbooks written in Germany, Leeser decided to translate Joseph Johlson's *Unterricht in der Mosaischen Religion* (Frankfurt am Main, 1819) or *Instruction in the Mosaic Religion* sometime during his first year at Mickveh Israel. Johlson (1777–1851), the son of the rabbi of Fulda, was closely associated with the emerging Reform movement in Germany. His chief works were written in connection with his career as a classroom teacher, and in 1826 he also published a German translation of the twelve minor prophets.[56]

Leeser's willingness to associate himself with the work of a known reformer is not difficult to explain. According to Jakob J. Petuchowski,"the acceptance or rejection of the method of catechism per se had very little to do with the 'assimilationist' (or other) tendencies of the authors. It was primarily a matter of educational technique broadly used among Christians and Jews. Some arch-conservatives, like Salomon Plessner, wrote catechisms, while religious radicals, like Israel Ascher Francolm, preferred other styles of presentation.[57] Leeser himself wrote:

> In an age when science of every kind is pursued with avidity, no astonishment can be manifested at the attempt of an Israelite to give his brethren a clear knowledge of the religion which they have inherited from their ancestors; since, if it is of any importance whatever to any portion of the human family to profess a certain creed, it is also highly necessary that the principal features at least of this creed should be familiar to all who profess the same.[58]

Moreover, Johlson was a relatively obscure figure, and American Jews were not yet polarized into Reform and Orthodox factions except, perhaps, in Charleston. In general, the distance between Reform Judaism and Orthodoxy was still relatively narrow in 1830. The great German philosophical systematizers of Reform, Abraham Geiger and Samuel Holdheim, were only twenty and twenty-four years old, respectively, and neither had, to date, been appointed rabbis. Although Reform and Orthodox rabbis had already exchanged angry words in Germany, they had done so primarily in the form of traditional response, or rabbinic legal briefs written in Hebrew. Separationist tendencies on both sides had not yet fully developed.[59]

In explaining why he should undertake to translate Johlson's catechism, Leeser told his readers:

> Having been appointed lately a fellow-labourer in the vineyard of the Lord, I thought it best to transplant this foreign shoot into that part entrusted to my care. May then its branches spread over a wide surface, to shade and shelter the weary, and may its good fruit be plentiful, and refresh many a hungry traveller in the path of life. This is the sincere wish and only reason of the humble servant of his brethren.[60]

In preparing his translation of *Instruction in the Mosaic Religion,* Leeser generally adhered closely to Johlson's original German text.

> I claim no great literary merit on the account of the present performance; for though the labour bestowed on it has been great, and considerable additions have been made (particularly to the *tenth* ["Of the Duties Towards Our Fellow-Men"] and *eleventh* ["Of the Duties Towards the State"] chapters), yet the road was already so clearly pointed out by the learned author of the original that I had nothing more to do than to make as good a use of the materials as my limited abilities and inexperience would permit.[61]

However, he did make several important changes in the book to give it an Orthodox character. When Johlson declared that "teachers of the people" can "in some cases act even against established customs, which have become of equal force with laws through public opinion," Leeser added a lengthy note of his own.

> As the words of Mr. Johlson may perhaps be misunderstood, I beg leave to subjoin the following in explanation: From the whole tenor of our laws it is apparent, that no old established custom, which has become general, can be abolished for the benefit of *one* particular section of the country; as through such means the uniformity of our institutions would be annihilated. Let us, for instance, name the worship in the Hebrew language, which is now universal throughout all the dispersions of Israel. It is no doubt a great misfortune, that the Hebrew is so little understood by many persons; but it would nevertheless be more injurious to adopt as the sole language of public worship, any of the languages of the countries in which we live . . . . My limits will not permit me to enter at greater length into a discussion of this point, which would, besides, be also out of place here; but this one example will clearly prove that reform, such as our author recommends from time to time, must be confined to *excrescences* only, but should never be extended to *essentials*. . . . The remarks of our author, however, are directed against superstitious customs solely, and *these* should be abolished, no matter how sacred they may be regarded by the mass of our nation, since all superstition is contrary to the Mosaic Law.[62]

Furthermore, in the section on "immortality," where Johlson concluded on a highly universalist note and expressed a hope for a time of universal peace and brotherhood,[63] Leeser injected an Orthodox note of his own. "What is this period called?" he asked. "The time of the Messiah, who is to be a descendant of King David, and be the means of restoring the people of Israel to their own land, the sacrifices at the temple in Jerusalem, and dispense justice and equity on the earth."[64]

Similarly, in a sermon, "The Consolation of Israel," given at Mickveh Israel on July 27, 1830, just one week before he finished working on *Instruction in the Mosaic Religion,* Leeser reiterated his traditional view of Restoration:

> May we all live to behold the consolation of Israel, the rebuilding of Jerusalem, and the restoration of the worship of the temple, and may we be held sufficiently deserving before our heavenly Father, to receive the crown of glory instead of ashes, and to participate in the joy of those who sincerely mourn for Zion, ardently look forward to the time, when the Lord, whom we seek, will suddenly come to his sanctuary.[65]

Leeser's friend and disciple Mayer Sulzberger went so far as to assert that "for him [Leeser], Palestine was still the country to which Jews had a divine right, which God, in his own good time, would assert—it might be in a day or in a millennium. He believed it necessary to hold one's self in readiness for the call, and this belief doubtless influenced the determination, to which he inflexibly adhered, never to become a citizen of the United States."[66]

Instruction in the Mosaic Religion, Leeser's first published book, was released late in the summer of 1830. He dedicated it "to His Beloved Uncle, Zalma Rehine of Richmond, Virginia." According to Maxwell Whiteman, it was Judah L. Hackenberg (1793–1862) "who was responsible for the publication of Leeser's first work."[67] Hackenberg, a native of Koblenz, Prussia, was a merchant "highly regarded for his many virtues."[68] Later, Abraham Hart (1810–85), a successful publisher and the outstanding lay leader in Philadelphia's Jewish community during the nineteenth century, as well as Hyman Gratz (1776–1857) aided Leeser in his various literary endeavors. Unfortunately, *Instruction in the Mosaic Religion* was poorly received by the public. Leeser later admitted that although intended for "the instruction of the younger part of Israelites of both sexes," the book was "better calculated for the instruction of advanced classes."[69]

Disappointment with the fate of his first book was less troublesome to Leeser than his growing dissatisfaction with the office of hazzan. By the time his first contract was up, he was in open disagreement with the congregation. One complaint regarded his income. On March 25, 1831, he wrote to the congregation that his contract would expire in September and suggested "the propriety of taking such *immediate* steps, as may best comport with the interest of the congregation according to the wisdom of your body."[70] On May 15, 1831, a committee was appointed by the board to meet with Leeser to discuss the renewal of his contract. They offered him a five-year contract at $800 per annum. Nine years later (during another contractual dispute with the congregation) Leeser recalled the difficult summer of 1831. Unsure of his position with Mickveh Israel, he entered into negotiations with Congregation Beth Elohim in Charleston, South Carolina.

> As this amount [$800] was evidently less than I had a right to expect, I did not think myself at liberty altogether to decline to proposals made to me from abroad; yet *I made* such *exorbitant demands* as almost to preclude any idea of their being agreed to; one was *in election without being a candidate,* or going on to be heard beforehand; second, an election for life; third, an absence of three months every year, and lastly to be permitted to stay in this congregation three months after the expiration of my time of service, to enable them to provide a suitable successor. Strange enough, all but the two first demands (and they in a modified degree to correspond with the laws of the above Kahal [congregation]) would have been accepted, if I may put any confidence in the assertions of the heads of the congregation, if in case I had consented to accept office there.[71]

However, because the Charleston synagogue pressed Leeser for an immediate answer, he felt compelled to reject their offer. He decided to remain at Mickveh Israel.

On September 4, 1831, the congregation met to reelect Leeser as its hazzan. They empowered the parnass, Zalegman Phillips, to engage Leeser for five years at a salary of one thousand dollars per annum. The vote was fifteen "ayes" and eight "nayes." Phillips voted against Leeser. One week later, the parnass officially wrote to Leeser and asked if he accepted the terms or whether he desired any modification to the number of years. The hazzan agreed to the new contract as offered by the congregation, but clear battle lines had been drawn, and the wounds on either side would never completely heal.[72]

Besides income and tenure, another area of contention involved the authority of the parnass and the adjunta. The matter came to a head in November 1831, when a member of the congregation, Henry Weil (1793–1853), a native of Hesse-Kassel and a former cavalry lieutenant in Jerome Bonaparte's army, caused a disturbance at Mickveh Israel during services. In the process, he personally affronted Jacob Phillips, a member of the adjunta. Phillips, the *segan* (deputy presiding officer) in the temporary absence of the parnass, brought the matter before the board on November 13. The adjunta placed the offender in *herem* (excommunication) and ordered the hazzan to announce the censure from the pulpit for three consecutive Sabbaths "as a warning to all evil doers."[73]

In America, the use of a partial *herem* by a lay board was already established during colonial times, usually as a way of combating both disruptive behavior in synagogue and religious laxity.[74] An entry in the minutes of Shearith Israel from the year 1757 reads:

> The Parnassim and Elders having received undoubted Testimony that several of our Brethren in the Country have and do violate the principles of our holy religion, such as trading on the Sabbath, Eating of forbidden Meats and other Heinous Crimes . . . therefore whosoever for the future continues to act contrary to our Holy Law by breaking any of the principles command [sic] of the Sinagoge Conferred on him and when Dead will not be buried according to the manner of our brethren.[75]

However, the use of the *herem* as a coercive and punitive measure to combat religious laxity was generally ineffective, especially in post-revolutionary America. It violated the idea of voluntary religious association and thus embodied a mode of religious coercion that was generally unacceptable in republican America. Finally, with the breakdown of the all-inclusive *kehillah,* or synagogue-community, during the Early National Period, it became impossible to enforce a ban of excommunication.

To Leeser, the idea of a lay-imposed *herem* was anathema. He refused to read the censure of Henry Weil in the synagogue. His act of insubordination infuriated the board. They met on February 12, 1832 and

> *Resolved,* That the Parnas inform the Hazan of the great dissatisfaction of the Board, at his not having complied with directions of said resolution, and to enquire of him what reasons, if any, he had for noncompliance with orders of the Board of Managers.
>
> *Resolved,* That this Board will adjourn to meet on Sunday, 11th March, at 10 A.M., at which time the Hazan is required to attend before the Board on the subject of the foregoing resolution.[76]

One month later, the entire board met as planned. Leeser refused to appear before them. Instead, he wrote a letter to the Parnass and openly maintained that he would not "acknowledge the Board of Managers to be [my] constituted Judges." The board, in turn, passed two more resolutions. The first stated that it had "full power and authority to manage the affairs of the congregation and that all officers are bound by the orders of the Board and the directions of the Parnass, and that this Board will exact from the officers of the congregation a strict compliance with all their orders." The second resolution ordered Leeser to make a full report to the entire congregation at their next meeting. On April 8, 1832, the congregation met and reaffirmed the authority of the parnass and adjunta to "control" the salaried officers.[77]

The vote of the congregation was tantamount to a vote of censure. Apparently, Leeser never explained his "motive for refusing to obey a plain duty" to the satisfaction of the congregation. Leeser subsequently discussed the problem of the relationship between the hazzan and the government of the synagogue in the *Occident*. He consistently adhered to a belief in the radical separation of the secular management of the synagogue and its spiritual program. On January 11, 1841, in the preface to his third volume of *Discourses,* he wrote:

> Now it is all well and proper to leave the management of every temporal concern in the hands of the President and his assistants; but the minister should not be in the discharge of duties altogether subservient to the temporal managers, who ought to confine themselves strictly to their branch of duty, and leave the public worship in the proper hands of those elevated to conduct it.[78]

A third source of dissatisfaction for Leeser during his early years at Mickveh Israel was the general conduct of the congregation. On September 28, 1832, less than half a year after being censured, he gave an impassioned sermon, "Obedience and Repentance." "Let me entreat you, brethren," he pleaded, "in this perhaps my last address to you, to forget each of you the peculiar grievances he may have to complain of."[79] He complained not only of factionalism, the withholding of contributions, and a lack of punctuality but of a general laxity in the religious life of the congregation.

> I may, though I hope not to do so, offend by my present remarks; but long since have I felt deeply in spirit for the loneliness which our place of worship presents! 'No one can imagine how much grief it must cause any sincere lover of his religion, to see so little true respect paid to the sacred edicts, which have been the admiration of the heathens even; to see how we, in this free country, where we are at liberty to worship our God according to our holy faith, without molestation, show our stubbornness by seeking every pursuit but that of Heaven, frequent every place but the house of God! Brethren, this ought not to be; let us wipe this reproach from us; let it not be said, and said with truth, that the churches of other denominations are filled with attentive audiences, whilst our Synagogues are nearly empty![80]

Leeser earnestly believed that Judaism could thrive in America. He never abandoned that hope, and he dedicated himself to creating a thriving Jewish religious life in a society where individuals were free to practice or ignore their respective religious traditions. "In many other countries," Leeser reminded his congregation, "the Hebrew is oppressed and despised; here he is upon an equality with other citizens, and is unmolested in the exercise of his religion." He continued,

> In tyrannical countries the Jew has always been a true believer, and a zealot in his faith even to martyrdom. Let us then prove, that in a free country the Jew is no less zealous, no less animated with love of Heaven, although the rod of persecution no longer compels him to seek shelter from the sword of man under the protection of the Almighty.[81]

Leeser was neither naive nor quixotic in his aspirations for Judaism in America. He recognized both the deep inroads that secularization had made in the Jewish community and the way that emancipation had weakened Jewish identity. Secularization, Leeser believed, was basically the product of Enlightenment philosophy and its denial of revelation as the exclusive source of truth in favor of human reason. Thus, he again turned to the manuscript he had prepared in Richmond, *Jews and the Mosaic Law.* With the help of Abraham Hart, the book was finally published in August 1833.[82] Hart, a native of Philadelphia and, since 1832, secretary of Mickveh Israel, was already, at the age of twenty-three, a rising star in the publishing industry.[83]

The completed version of *Jews* and *the Mosaic Law* contained two parts: "A Defence of the Revelation of the Pentateuch, and of the Jews for their adherence to the same," containing twenty-six chapters and an appendix with notes; and "Four Essays on the Relative Importance of Judaism and Christianity," in which Leeser reproduced and elaborated on the letters he first published in the Richmond *Whig* in 1829. Unfortunately, like his first book, this second book was a commercial failure. "The first book I issued made no profit," Leeser wrote in 1837, "and the second caused a considerable pecuniary loss."[84]

For several months after the publication of this work, Leeser was relatively inactive. He only preached twice during the remainder of the year: once during the High Holy Days (on the theme "The Duty of Instruction"), and again on December 12, his twenty-seventh birthday, on "The Selection of Israel," in which sermon he defended the idea of the Chosen People.

It is possible that Leeser had become depressed. Not only was he unhappy as hazzan of Mickveh Israel but he had also suffered a personal setback. Late in 1832, Abraham C. Peixotto, Leeser's host and a friend of Zalma Rehine, asked the hazzan to find a different place to live. Apparently Leeser had fallen in love with one of his daughters and he did not approve. A concerned Zalma wrote to his nephew on December 18, 1832 from Baltimore.

> I wish you to let me know why Mr. Peixotto does not wish to have your letters directed to his care. Should it be on account of Miss Simha, and I think . . . it is on that account from some information I have had . . . let me know it by next Post. I also advise you not to visit too often During the Absent [sic] of Mr. Peixotto at his House. When I receive your answer I shall be more particular, till then I wish you not to say anything to anybody about it, and depend on it I [am] as much interested on your account

> with whatever depends on your Happiness as on any[thing] what Can interest me in this world.[85]

A heartbroken Leeser then found lodging in an apartment sublet by a gentile seamstress, Mrs. Deliah Nash Cozens, at 86 Walnut Street. Some members of Mickveh Israel did not approve of the arrangement. Rumors abounded that Leeser was not eating kosher food and also that he had become fond of Mrs. Cozens' daughter, Ellen. The situation was aggravated by the fact that a previous hazzan, Abraham H. Cohen, whom Leeser knew in Richmond, had married a gentile, Jane Picken.[86]

Late in 1833, while residing at Mrs. Cozens's, Leeser recalled, "I was seized with a fearful malady, which prevented me from continuing my labours till after a long and painful interruption."[87] The "fearful malady" was smallpox, and it left Leeser physically and emotionally scarred for the rest of his life. Rebecca Gratz described Leeser's affliction to her sister-in-law on February 2, 1834:

> There is another evil under the sun that has been making havoc in our city varioloid—poor Mr. Leeser is one of its present subjects, and tho his life and eye sight have been spared I am told his countenance will bear many marks of its ravages—he has always been so sensitive on the subject of personal disadvantages—that his former humility will appear like vanity to his present state—and unless some Desdemona shall arise to see his visage in his mind—all future expectations must be confined to solitary studies.[88]

Mrs. Cozens served as Leeser's nurse. He never forgot her kindness during this trying period in his life and included an annual stipend for her in his will.[89]

Smallpox brought still further grief in its wake. Leeser's younger brother, Jacob, migrated to America early in 1833. Like Isaac, he came to the United States at the request of Zalma Rehine, who had by this time moved from Richmond to Baltimore. Against Isaac's wishes, Jacob went to Philadelphia upon learning of his brother's situation. When he arrived, the hazzan had already slipped into a coma. Little hope was held for his recovery. By a twist of tragic irony, Jacob caught the same disease and died. Leeser, on the other hand, slowly began to recover. With great anguish, he recalled that with his

> being supposed on the point of death my only brother hastened from a distance to my bedside. It pleased our heavenly Father to afflict him with the same disease. Although robust, and to all appearance of that physical construction, as to render his long surviving me almost a matter of certainty, he yet sunk under his sufferings, and tranquil and resigned he breathed out his pure spirit in the hands of Him who gave it, in the twenty-fifth year of his age, on the 14th of March [1834], beloved by many, and hated by none. The recollection of his death is doubly agonizing, because he had to receive from friendly strangers the kindness and attention that ought to have been rendered by his brother, who was kept from his couch of sickness by sufferings of unspeakable intensity and horror.[90]

Less than three months later, Leeser had recuperated to the point where he could preach again. On May 23, 1834, he spoke on "The Duty of Active Benevolence." He began with a prayer of deliverance: "O most merciful One! who sendest succour to the afflicted, and protectest the helpless, grant us thy protection and deliver us from evil, and judge us not according to our unworthy deeds, but according to thy goodness, which is everlasting." In the address itself, he reflected further on the ephemeral nature of human existence.

> We are taught in the books of Holy Writ not to look upon this life as the chief period of our existence; nor upon the goods of earth, the material possessions, as the greatest acquirement; nor lastly, upon sensual pleasures as the highest enjoyment. And seeing that every thing here below is transitory, even the most careless observer is very apt to acquiesce in the idea, that life is short and its pleasures uncertain; yet there are few, indeed, who are led on to a virtuous and godly life through a contemplation of the vicissitudes to which they are subject.[91]

Man, Leeser concluded, should resolve "to exercise charity to the poor, to comfort the afflicted, to love our fellowmen like ourselves, and to keep the festivals of the Lord, and to celebrate weekly with devotion and an abstinence from labour the Sabbath of rest, in honour of our God."[92]

Leeser's spiritual reaction to his illness typifies a basic mode of human religiosity. Fredrick J. Streng, a contemporary student of religion, explains that "when man feels anxiety and pain, religious insight can be awakened. Reflection on who man is . . . wells up from a concern deeper than that for a logically perfect system of philosophy. The question of the meaning of life is experienced as a personal challenge."[93]

Following his recuperation, Leeser felt the challenge of creating a vital Judaism in America grow inside him again. Two years later, in 1836, when he published his first two volumes of *Discourses,* the profound effect of his bout with smallpox was still in evidence.

> The first twenty Discourses were rewritten; because l could not suffer my first attempts to come before the public without a careful revision. The others, however, which were composed chiefly after the chastening hand of the lord had fallen heavily on me, were prepared with more care, and I therefore only corrected them thoroughly, and altered those parts which appeared objectionable or defective.[94]

During the rest of 1834, Leeser continued to recuperate. He spoke once every month (except August) at Mickveh Israel but apparently restricted his other activities in an effort to regain his strength. On June 12, 1834, he again spoke on "The Selection of Israel." During the summer months, he reflected on "The Blessing of Revelation" and "The Permanence of the Law" and thereby was able to contrast the social stability that Torah produced with the severe civil disorders racked Philadelphia that summer. The last sermon he gave that year, "The Jewish Faith," was an attempt to summarize his basic theological position. He began with the premise, in part borrowed from Protestantism, that faith precedes works.

> Without a motive for action, we do not act, and consequently without a motive for religious conduct we would certainly not be religious; and therefore if we wish to be religious, or to speak more properly, if we are anxious to secure that great share of happiness which flows from an obedience to the divine law, we must fortify ourselves previously by an acquisition of such feelings as best conduce to such a desirable consummation; or what is the same, we must endeavor growth of good deeds; for faith alone can be the producer of outward actions, if these actions are to have the least claim to sincerity.[95]

He then listed three basic dogmas:

> In the first place we have, as the foundation of all religion, the belief in the existence of a God; secondly, we are to acknowledge that this God made known to mankind his will for their guidance; and thirdly, that we are accountable to this God for a dereliction from, or to be rewarded by Him for an obedience to, his will as declared to us.[96]

Leeser's list corresponds exactly to that of Joseph Albo, a fifteenth-century Jewish philosopher and preacher, and represented a rejection of Moses Mendelssohn's more universal and rationalist emphasis on the immortality of the soul and free will. On the other hand, Leeser also viewed Moses Maimonides' (1135–1204) "Thirteen Principles of Faith" as the authoritative Jewish creed. Not a systematic thinker, Leeser did not find it necessary to harmonize the positions of the two Judeo-Spanish philosophers, as he believed that they expressed the same "truth" in different manners. His knowledge of both Maimonides and Albo was not based on extensive reading of medieval literature but rather derived from secondary sources. He eventually owned a German translation of Albo (published in 1844), and late in life, he developed a keen interest in Maimonides and even contemplated an English translation of the *Guide to the Perplexed* based on the French work of Solomon Munk.[97]

Leeser's creedal approach to Judaism resolved several problems. First, it put Judaism on a footing similar to that of Christianity and thereby simplified the work of defending Judaism as the "true religion" and demonstrating its reasonableness. Second, it gave Judaism a truly "orthodox" or "right doctrine" character in an age when basic tenets of Jewish belief were being challenged by religious reformers. Third, by drawing on sources from the Golden Age in Spain, Leeser both reinforced Sephardic Jewish identity in the United States and strengthened his case for the historical necessity of revitalizing Judaism in America. Finally, Leeser, who made no claim to being a rabbi, was personally more comfortable discussing Judaism in theological terms than from the perspective of *Halachah* (Jewish law), in which he had little formal training and no authority.

His theology was neither profound nor original. Yet it was representative of Judaism in America during the nineteenth century, especially in its emphasis on dogma and the centrality of the Bible. His fight both with Christianity and Reform Judaism is best understood in this context. His theology did not change significantly over the years. To Leeser, truth was revealed and immutable. The idea of the historical development of religion was simply not a part of his world view. What Leeser learned in Germany and reformulated in Richmond was most fully articulated in Philadelphia from the pulpit of Mickveh Israel.

By the fall of 1834, Leeser was fully recovered from smallpox and was actively at work on a number of projects. It is evident that in general his years as a young preacher were filled with frustration. Relations with the leadership of the congregation started poorly and degenerated into open and mutual hostility. His preaching, very important to him personally, was met with indifference. His publications brought him no glory. Even his meek efforts at romance were hampered by the disapproval of the girl's parents. Finally, illness weakened him and ravaged his already homely appearance.

A person of less inner strength might have been overwhelmed by this sad string of events. Even though he was subsequently subject to occasional periods of depression and despair, Leeser found the resolve to go on with his life and work. He became within a few short years a tremendous intellectual and cultural force in the American Jewish community, broadly recognized by 1840 as the most important American Jewish religious leader of his time. Unfortunately, his relationship with his congregation would not improve. It was to remain a source of personal and professional conflict.

Notes

1. Sam Bass Warner, *The Private* City: *Philadelphia in Three Periods of its Growth* (Philadelphia, 1968), 5.

2. Michael Feldberg, *The Philadelphia Riots of 1844: A Study of Ethnic Conflict* (Westport, Conn., 1975), 12. Also, see his *Turbulent Era: Riot and Disorder in Jacksonian America* (New York, 1980).

3. Warner, *Private City,* 125.

4. Ibid., 49–50, 61.

5. Jacques L Lyons and Abraham de Sola, *A Jewish Calendar for Fifty Years* (Montreal, 1854).

6. Murray Friedman, "Introduction: The Making of a National Jewish Community," in *Jewish Life in Philadelphia: 1830–1940* (Philadelphia, 1983), 2.

7. *WW,* 114.

8. Ibid., 41–42.

9. Ibid., 58–59, 117; *Morais,* 11.

10. *WW,* 76–113; Max Kohler, *Haym Solomon: The Patriot Broker of the Revolution* (New York, 1931); Samuel Rezneck, *Unrecognized Patriots: The Jews in the American Revolution* (Westport, Conn., 1975).

11. *WW,* 121.

12. *Morais,* passim.

13. *BB* I:xx suggests that the kosher food was actually provided by the public committee in charge of the event and not by an ad hoc committee of Philadelphia Jews. See also Morton Borden, *Jews,Turks, and lnfidels* (Chapel Hill, N.C. 1984), 23–51; Jonathan D.

Sama, "The Impact of the American Revolution on American Jews," *Modern Judaism* 1 (September1981): 149–60.

14. On the Phillips family, see Joseph R. Rosenbloom, *A Biographical Dictionary of Early American Jews: Colonial Times through 1800* (Lexington, Ky., 1960); Sama, *Jacksonian Jew*, 1–3; *Morais*, 567; Grinstein, *New York*, passim; Samuel Rezneck, *The Saga of an American Jewish Family Since the Revolution: A History of the Family of Jonas Phillips* (Washington, D.C., 1980).

15. *Morais*, 49.

16. *WW*, 360–71.

17. Ibid., 253.

18. *Morais*, 44, 46.

19. *OCC* 2:314.

20. Quoted in ESC, JRM-L.

21. John Hampden Pleasants to lsaac Leeser, Richmond to Philadelphia, August 27, 1829, D-L.

22. *Morais*, 45–46.

23. Quoted in *JE* 7:663.

24. Isaac Leeser to K.K.M.l., September 7, 1829, quoted in K.K.M.I. Minutebook, typescript, D-L.

25. Zalma Rehine to Isaac Leeser, Richmond to Philadelphia, October 14, 1829, D-L.

26. Isaac Leeser to K.K.M.I., May 15, 1840, D-L and AJA.

27. On Rebecca Gratz see Jacob R. Marcus, *The Arnerican Jewish Woman: A Documentary History* (New York, 1981), 87; Joseph R. Rosenbloom, "Rebecca Gratz and the Jewish Sunday School Movement in Philadelphia," *PAJHS* 48 (1958): 71; and his *And She Had Compassion* (D.H.L. thesis, HUC-JIR, 1957). See also Diane Ashton's Ph.D. thesis (Temple University).

28. Rebecca Gratz to "Maria Gist Gratz, Philadelphia to Lexington, Ky., November 4, 1829, quoted in Letters *of Rebecca Gratz* (Philadelphia, 1929), 108.

29. Rebecca Gratz to Maria Gist Gratz, Philadelphia to Lexington, Ky., April 30, 1830, quoted in Bertram W. Korn, "lsaac Leeser: Centennial Reflections," 132.

30. Rebecca Gratz to Maria Gist Gratz, Philadelphia to Lexington, Ky., August 9, 1831, quoted in Philipson, *Letters*, 132–33.

31. Rebecca Gratz to Maria Gist Gratz, Philadelphia to Lexington, Ky., December 16, 1838, quoted in Philipson, Letters, 257.

32. *OCC* 2:318.

33. Louis Jacobs, "Preaching," *EJ* 13:1002–1006;'Israel Bettan, *Studies in Jewish Preaching* (Cincinnati, 1939).

34. Alexander Altmann, "The New Style of Preaching in Nineteenth Century German Jewry," in his edited *Studies* in *Nineteenth Century Jewish Intellectual History* (Cambridge, Mass., 1964), 65–116. See also Abraham Milgrom, *Jewish Worship*.

35. *DIS* 3:vi.

36. On antebellum Protestantism, see Sydney E. Ahlstrom, *A Religious History of the American People* (Garden City, N.Y., 197S), pts. IV and VI; Winthrop S. Hudson, *American Protestantism* (Chicago, 1961); Martin Marty, *Righteous Empire: The Protestant Experience in America* (New York, 1970). See also Lewis 0. Brastow, *The Modern*

Pulpit: A Study of Homiletic Sources and Characteristics (New York, 1906). On lyceums, see Carl Bode, *American Lyceum: Town Meeting of the Mind* (New York, 19S6); Vern Wagner, "Lecture Lyceum and Problem of Controversy," *journal of the History of Ideas* 15 (1954).

37. *DIS* 1:1–2.

38. *OCC* 20:340–43; and quoted in Berman, Richmond, 42.

39. Maxwell Whiteman, "Isaac Leeser and the Jews of Philadelphia," 213 n. 34.

40. *DIS* 1:1–9. An annotated selection from "Confidence in God" appears in *BB* 2:578–82. Leeser does not explain why his text is neither the regular weekly portion for *Shabbat Naso* (Numbers 4:21–7:89) nor the *Haftarah* Judges 13:2–25). It is possible he meant to give "public instruction" in Judaism and did not view himself as a "preacher" per se at this point in his career.

41. *OCC* 9 suppl.: xiv.

42. *DIS* 1:1–3.

43. Ibid., 9–10.

44. Ibid., x.

45. *DIS* 6:59. See also Robert V. Friedenberg, "Isaac Leeser: Pioneer Preacher of American Judaism," Religious *Communication Today* (September 1983): 22–27.

46. Mayer Sulzberger, "Isaac Leeser," pamphlet (Philadelphia, 1881), S. Sulzberger read this short biography of Leeser before the Young Men's Hebrew Association of Philadelphia, 1881. Copy in Abraham de Sola Papers, AJA, and Mayer Sulzberger, "Isaac Leeser," *American Hebrew* 7 (May 27, 1881): 15–16 and (June 2, 1881): 28–29.

47. *OCC* 25:600.

48. Rosa Mordecai, "Personal Recollections of Rev. Isaac Leeser," AJA, Englander Papers, 1901, 6. Mordecai wrote this highly romaticized biography for the Washington, D.C., section of the (National?) Council for Jewish Women, December 30, 1901. Also, see her "Isaac Leeser," *Appleton's Enyclopaedia*, ed. James Grant Wilson and John Fiske (New York, 1889), 3:676.

49. *BB* 2:279.

50. On the frequency of Leeser's preaching and public speaking activities, see Sussman, "'Confidence in God,'" 266–68.

51. "A Chronological Digest of Isaac Leeeser's Discourses," in Sussman," 'Confidence,'" 240–65.

52. For example, "The Sorrows of Israel," *DIS* 3:10, was delivered on July 24, 1840, during the time of the Damascus Affair, when Jews in Damascus, Syria, and Rhodes were falsely accused of having committed ritual murder.

53. *DIS* 10:313.

54. *DIS* 4:vi.

55. Isaac Leeser to K.K.M.L, March 31, 1830, and April 21, 1831, JRM-L.

56. David Philipson, *The Reform Movement in Judaism* (New York, 1907), 149-SO;JE 7:217–18.

57. Jakob J. Petuchowski, "Manuals and Catechisms of the Jewish Religion in the Early Period of Emancipation," in Altmann, *Jewish Intellectual History*, 48.

58. Isaac Leeser, Instruction *in the Mosaic Religion* (Philadelphia, 1830, 1866), iv.

59. On early Reform Judaism in Germany, see Alexander Guttmann, *The Struggle over Reform Judaism in Rabbinic Literature of the Last Century and a Half* (New York, 1976). See also Gunther W. Plaut, ed., *The Rise of Reform Judaism: A Sourcebook of Its European Origins* (New York, 1968); Philipson, *Reform Movement*.

60. Leeser, Instruction, vii.

61. Ibid., iv.

62. Ibid., 95–96, 99–100.

63. Ibid., 5I-52.

64. Ibid., 46–47.

65. *DIS* 1:62–63.

66. Sulzberger, "Isaac Leeser," 5. See also Maxine Seller, "Isaac Leeser's Views on the Restoration of a Jewish Palestine," *PAJHS* 68 (1968): 118, 135.

67. Whiteman, "Isaac Leeser," 214 n. 39.

68. *Morais,* 52.

69. Leeser, *Instruction,* iii-iv.

70. Isaac Leeser to K.K.M.I., March 25, 1831, D-L.

71. Isaac Leeser to K.K.M.I., May 15, 1840, D-L and AJA; OCC 9:209.

72. *A Review of the Late Controversies Between the Rev. Isaac Leeser and the Congregation Mihveh Israel,* typescript extracts from K.K.M.I. Minutebook, D-L (Philadelphia, 1850), 5–6.

73. *Late Controversies,* 13; *Morais,* 535–36.

74. Sefton Temkin, "Isaac Mayer Wise: A Biographical Sketch," in *A Guide to the Writings of Isaac Mayer Wise,* ed. Doris C. Sturzenberger (Bell and Howell and AJA, 1981), 22; James G. Heller, *Isaac* M. Wise: His *Life, Work* and *Thought* (New York, 1965), 200; *OCC* 8:255–57.

75. Grinstein, *New York,* 334.

76. *Late Controversies,* 13.

77. Typescript extracts from K.K.M.L Minutebook, April 8, 1832, D-L.

78. *DIS* 3:vii.

79. *DIS* 1:342.

80. Ibid., 342–43.

81. Ibid., 344.

82. *Jews and the Mosaic Law.*

83. For a brief sketch of Abraham Hart's life (1810–85), see *Morais,* 53–58. See also Whiteman, "Isaac Leeser," 208 n 3. Several years earlier, Hart was employed by the prestigious Carey and Lea Company at the invitation of Henry C. Carey, a senior member of the firm and a noted political economist. When the firm was divided in 1829, Hart associated with Edward L. Carey, brother of Henry C. Carey. Carey and Hart proved itself to be an outstanding publishing house. It was responsible for numerous important first editions and also printed works of many leading American authors, including Henry Wadsworth Longfellow and James Fenimore Cooper.

84. *DIS* l:xi.

85. Zalma Rehine to Isaac Leeser, Baltimore to Philadelphia, December 18, 1832, D-L.

86. On S. Jane Picken Cohen, see WW, 237–48, 451. On Leeser's relations with Mrs. Deliah Nash Cozens, see Isaac Leeser to Mrs. D. Cozens, Charleston, S.C., to Philadelphia, February 27, 1867, D-L. Emily Solis-Cohen reports on Leeser's relations with three young women: Ellen Cozens, Simha Peixotto, and Louisa Hart, 181–85. Gershon Greenberg reports a conversation he had with Maxwell Whiteman on the "affair" in "A German-Jewish Immigrant's Perception of America, 1853–54," *AJHQ* 67 (June 1978): 325 n. 30. Whiteman informed Greenberg that, in his opinion,

Leeser was involved with a Christian woman: It is true that he lived in the household of Mrs. Ella Cozzens, a respectable Presbyterian lady considerably older than Leeser. She was widowed shortly after Leeser moved in their home for what was to have been temporary quarters. A series of events altered this plan, and when Leeser contracted smallpox . . . he was nursed by her when no one would come near him for fear of contagion. He continued to live there, was constantly chastized but stubbornly refused to move elsewhere. It was only to his uncle, Zalma Rehine, to whom he revealed that he maintained a separate kitchen for kosher food and religious rites and amenities. All of the details of what led to a major controversy have not been brought together. Actually, he was in love with Simha

Peixouo, but the objections of her uncle overruled marriage between the two. Bertrand W. Kam notes, "Leeser never married, and was deprived of the affection and strength that a wife and children can give a man, but he had a huge family of Jewish followers throughout the United States," in "Centennial Reflections," 136.

87. *DIS* 2:34.

88. Rebecca Gratz to Maria Gist Gratz, Philadelphia to Lexington, Ky., February 2, 1834, quoted in Philipson, *Letters,* 193.

89. "The Will of Isaac Leeser," Article 7, December 26, 1867, D-L and AJA. Leeser left Deliah Nash (Cozens) $400 annually as a token of appreciation for caring for him in 1834 when he was suffering from smallpox.

90. *DIS* 2:34. On Jacob Leeser's arrival in America, see Leah Lippman to Isaac Leeser, Denekamp, Holland, to Philadelphia, August (?) 1832, JRM-L. Emily Solis-Cohen also reports that Jacob Leeser came to America in 1832 to join Zalma Rehine. Rehine was then in the process of moving from Richmond to Baltimore.

91. *DIS* 2:35.

92. Ibid., 45–46.

93. Fredrick J. Streng, *Understanding Religious Man* (Belmont, Cal., 1969), 73–74.

94. *DIS* l:ix.

95. *DIS* 2:112.

96. Ibid., 115.

97. OCC 16:347–50, 25:89. Solomon Munk to Isaac Leeser, Paris to Philadelphia, April 4, 1862, AJHS-L.

Jews and Judaism in Philadelphia: A Brief Review

Richard Libowitz

An old joke suggests that if you want three answers, "ask two Jews one question." The rationale behind the jest is Judaism's insistence that prayer is incomplete without study. Two millennia studying holy texts has resulted in many differences of opinion and, traditionally, those differences are examined, discussed, and argued over aloud, with a partner.

"Jews and Judaism": with which does one begin, for they are different yet fundamentally inseparable. Jews are a People (not a race), a nation, like the Irish, the Kurds, or the Zulu. Judaism represents the *evolving religious civilization* of that people. It is a *civilization*, including language,[1] a land,[2] law,[3] social institutions,[4] and culture;[5] facets of any civilization. It is a *religious* civilization, because the religious understandings of Judaism—including the idea of the covenant, a special relationship between God and this People—are central, if not necessarily coextensive, to the civilization. Finally, it is an *evolving* religious civilization, because it has undergone changes continuously throughout a history of more than 3,400 years. The civilization functions in all of its aspects in the State of Israel; in the rest of the world—called by Jews *Galut* (Exile) or "Diaspora" (dispersion)—Judaism is understood as either a religion or a national identity. In Philadelphia, as throughout the United States, it functions as both. Besides synagogues (also called temples or *shuls)*, the Philadelphia Jewish community supports both day and afternoon schools; cultural, social, and athletic centers; summer camps and other youth programs; college student centers; a college; teacher and rabbinical training schools; job training and placement agencies; a Board of Rabbis; retirement and old age homes; hospital and medical facilities; cemeteries; a chaplaincy program; meals programs; a weekly newspaper; and many other charitable activities and institutions here, in Israel, and around the world. Overseeing many of those programs and acting as the primary fundraising arm of the community is the Jewish Federation, a religiously neutral organization that often acts as the public voice of the Jewish community.

Most Americans—Jewish or not—understand Judaism to be a religious faith. Jews maintain beliefs and observe customs and holidays different from those held and practiced by the Christian majority. Primary among the differences, to the general public, is the Jewish understanding of Jesus.

While Jesus as the Christ ("Anointed One") is at the center of Christian faith, he plays absolutely no role in Jewish religious life. Those Jews who consider the relevance of Jesus might understand him as a Jew, possibly a rabbi, who lived and died 2,000 years ago, firmly within the matrix of the Judaism of his time. He was an *apocalyptic*, one who believed the world had become so corrupt that God would end history as people knew it, judge humanity (rewarding the righteous and punishing the wicked), and begin a new age. This was a not uncommon belief at the time, as most Jews were living under the domination of an increasingly strict Roman Empire. Because the area known to the Romans as Judaea was a strategically vital land bridge within the Empire, its masters tolerated little in the way of dissent and appointed strong governors to maintain order, among them, Pontius Pilate. As part of the ending to the status quo, it was believed that the *Messiah* would arrive, drive away the foreign invaders (the Romans) from the land, restore a descendant of David to the throne and repurify the religious rites in the Temple on Mount Zion in Jerusalem. Other Jews shared these ideas but, in the years following Jesus's death, his followers insisted that *he* was the Messiah and eventually ascribed supernatural characteristics to Jesus that mainstream Judaism flatly rejected. As far as most Jews were concerned, Jesus neither defeated the Romans nor reestablished a Davidic kingdom and the idea of an immaculate conception or Jesus as God incarnate were utterly rejected. The first Jews to come to the Philadelphia area may have arrived as early as 1682; it is definite that there were permanent Jewish residents by 1737. The first synagogue in Philadelphia, K.K. Mikveh Israel,[6] was founded about 1740, near its present location at 44 N. Fourth Street. Haym Solomon, one of the fundraisers for the American Revolution, was among its famous members and Benjamin Franklin, who was not Jewish, was one of the donors to its building fund in 1782. The original membership was descended from Jews from Spain and Portugal (known as *Sephardim*); to this day, the congregation follows the *Sephardic* (Spanish) *minhag* (custom) for worship and holiday observances.

Ashkenazic ("German") Jews, who followed the customs developed in Central and Eastern Europe, would not begin arriving in significant numbers until the mid-nineteenth century.[7] The first such wave of immigration began in the late 1840s, when large numbers of Jews from German-speaking portions of Central Europe started arriving.[8] A second much larger wave began in 1882 and lasted until the United States entered World War I, eventually bringing several million Jews from Eastern Europe to the United States. Three other, much smaller, waves of immigrants increased both the national and local Jewish populations. In the 1930s, Jews fleeing the oppression of Nazi Germany sought refuge in America; governmental anti-Semitism blocked many from entry, however. Thousands more, the survivors of the Holocaust, were admitted after World War II, while many Jews seeking to leave the Soviet Union came here in the 1970s and 1980s.

Philadelphia was the locale for the first rabbinical seminary in North America; *Maimonides College* was founded in 1867 but closed several years later, following the death of its founder, Isaac Leeser. *Gratz College*, the first Jewish teacher training school, opened in Philadelphia in 1897 and today offers both undergraduate and graduate degrees in various aspects of Jewish studies. *Dropsie College* opened in 1906, as the first graduate institution for the study of Hebrew language and literature; as the Annenberg Center, it is now part of the University of Pennsylvania. Philadelphia is also the home of the *Jewish Publication Society of*

America, as well as the *National Museum of American Jewish History* (101 South Independence Mall East).

In 2009, the Jewish population within the Greater Philadelphia region was estimated at 215,000. The majority of that population is comprised of descendants of Eastern European immigrants; there are also significant populations from the former Soviet Union and Israeli Jews. Subsets of the population are often defined in terms of religious observance and identification with one of the "branches" of Judaism developed over the past 175 years; in simplest terms, those denominations are known as Orthodox, Conservative, Reform, and Reconstructionist.[9]

Orthodox Judaism

The most traditional groups within Judaism are generally called "Orthodox."[10] Those who define themselves in this way seek to observe as many of the Hebrew Bible's 613 commandments as apply to them.[11] Men cover their heads with a hat or skullcap and the most observant wear an undershirt-like garment with four sets of fringes (*tzitzit*) that are meant to be visible, as reminders of God's commandments. Women dress modestly, in long-sleeved blouses and skirts or dresses that reach to the ankles; many married women within the Orthodox community will cover their hair with scarves or wigs. Orthodox Jews pray three times a day, observe *kashrut*, Judaism's dietary laws, do not perform any of the thirty-nine proscribed manners of work on the Sabbath and holy days, and generally have the largest families within the Jewish world. Only men may become rabbis and only men may be counted in the *minyan*, the quorum of ten adults (age thirteen and over) necessary for a complete worship service.

There are numerous divisions and subdivisions within the Orthodox community, the oldest and most basic being geographic, that is to say, the division between *Ashkenazic* (Central and Eastern European), *Sephardic* (Mediterranean) and *Mizrahi* ("Oriental," Jews from Central Asia). Other Orthodox divisions include "modern Orthodox," *haridim* ("black hats"), and *Hasidim*.[12] They maintain synagogues, day schools, *yeshivot* (rabbinical seminaries), and numerous charitable organizations. Collectively, the various Orthodox groups comprise the fastest growing segment of the Philadelphia Jewish community. Many Orthodox individuals and organizations reject the legitimacy of non-Orthodox rabbis and the practices of non-Orthodox congregations. Among Philadelphia's Orthodox congregations, Mikveh Israel maintains Sephardic practices while B'nai Abraham (521–27 Lombard Street) follows the Ashkenazic tradition.

Reform Judaism

Reform Judaism had its beginnings in several German cities in the early decades of the nineteenth century. It was a movement begun by Jews who were adopting western European ideas and practices and wished to alter some of the rigid strictures of Orthodoxy. While the initial changes—removing repetitious passages in the services, allowing families to sit together rather than separating the sexes, adding an organ, a mixed voice choir, and a sermon delivered in German—may seem mild by contemporary standards, the organized Jewish community, which was a legal entity in most European countries, quickly ordered the reforms halted. There were no such legal restrictions in North America, however, and Reform Judaism, transplanted to the New World by rabbis who began immigrating in the 1840s, soon flourished. Led by Rabbi Isaac Mayer Wise, the first successful rabbinical seminary in America was established (Hebrew Union College), a new prayer book was written, and organizations for both rabbis and congregations were created.[13] The changes in traditional Jewish practices that were advocated and initiated here went far beyond the original European agenda; at the peak of what is referred to as "Classical Reform," the Reform movement abandoned prayer in Hebrew, rejected the notion of exile and the desire to return to a Jewish homeland (Zionism), ended observance of *Halachah* while affirming the moral strictures of the prophets,[14] changed the Sabbath to Sunday, and defined Judaism in a strictly theological manner.[15] Although the extreme changes mandated by the Reform movement in the late nineteenth century have been reversed and many traditional practices restored, Reform remains the most liberal and least traditional of the organized branches or denominations of Judaism. The first female rabbi in North America, Sally Priesand, was trained in a Reform seminary (Hebrew Union College–Jewish Institute of Religion) and ordained in 1973. Most Reform congregations do not require a *minyan* for services. Congregation Rodeph Shalom (615 N. Broad Street) is the oldest Reform Congregation still located within Philadelphia.[16]

Conservative Judaism

Conservative Judaism began to develop in the 1880s, drawing from "left-wing Orthodox and right-wing Reform" to fill the void between the two existing and diametrically opposite forms of Judaism then in existence. Basing its rationale on the teachings of a German rabbi and scholar, Zacharias Frankel, Conservative Judaism tries to allow for modernization of Jewish practice while remaining faithful to the spirit of Jewish law (*Halakhah*). It does so by seeking minority views or finding new interpretations within the discussions of Jewish law in the *Talmud* as well as in later rabbinic writings. This often causes Conservative Judaism to trail behind other non-Orthodox Jewish religious groups in making changes, such as including women in the *minyan* (ca. 1973) and training women to be rabbis. Amy Eilberg[17] was the first woman ordained at the Jewish Theological Seminary[18] in 1985, more than a decade after both the Reform and Reconstructionist seminaries were graduating women. Historically, Philadelphia has been a stronghold of the Conservative movement. Congregation Beth Zion–Beth Israel (300 S. Eighteenth Street) is the largest Conservative congregation in Center City Philadelphia.

Reconstructionist Judaism

Reconstructionist Judaism evolved in the twentieth century from the thought of Rabbi Mordecai M. Kaplan, a professor at the (Conservative) Jewish Theological Seminary in New York. Kaplan believed Jewish tradition should have "a vote but not a veto" when considering change. Influenced by John Dewey, he argued that Judaism should function as a pragmatic democracy, justifying change when the needs of the Jewish people demanded it, even if that change transcended the strictures of traditional Jewish law. Reconstructionist congregations were the first to count women in the *minyan*, in the early 1920s. Kaplan created the *Bat Mitzvah* for girls[19] and changed many prayers within the traditional services.[20] Understood for many years as "the left wing of Conservative Judaism," Reconstructionism became a distinct movement in the mid-twentieth century when it opened the Reconstructionist Rabbinical College in Philadelphia, in 1968.[21] Sandy Sasso (an alumna of Temple University) was the first female graduate of the Reconstructionist Rabbinical College in 1974; Rebecca T. Alpert, now a Dean at Temple, was part of the graduating class in 1976. Leyv Ha-Ir (401 S. Broad Street) is a small Reconstructionist congregation in Center City.

There are several histories of Jewish Philadelphia, some going back to the colonial era, while others concentrate on particular neighborhoods or synagogues. For additional and extensive information, the Jewish Exponent publishes *The Guide to Jewish Greater Philadelphia*, including lists of community agencies, synagogues, and other organizations. The current issue runs the gamut from A (Abrams Hebrew Academy) to Z (Zionist Organization of America).

Notes

1. Whatever other languages Jews speak or have spoken, Hebrew has always been the language of the people. Frozen for nearly 2,000 years as a "holy language," to be used only for prayer and study, it was revived and modernized beginning in the mid-nineteenth century and is the everyday language of the State of Israel with a thriving modern literature.

2. While political borders have been drawn and redrawn over the centuries, *Eretz Yisrael*, the Land of Israel, has been the homeland of the Jewish people for more than 3,200 years. *Zionism* is both an aspect of Jewish religious faith and a political movement seeking, prior to 1948, a modern state for the Jews and, since then, supporting *Medinat Yisrael*, the State of Israel. Traditionally, Jews face in the direction of Israel (and Jerusalem) when praying.

3. Because Judaism does not distinguish between "sacred" (holy) and "profane" (secular) parts of life, Jewish law—in Hebrew, *Halakhah*, literally "the Way"—incorporates all facets of existence, from how one dresses, to the proper order of preparing food, to appropriate prayers for specific occasions.

4. Schools, hospitals, athletic teams, old age homes, cemeteries, and so on.

5. Music, literature, art, and so on.

6. The name means "Holy Congregation, Hope of Israel."

7. Sephardim and Ashkenazim differ in the pronunciation of some Hebrew letters, the wording of certain prayers, as well as customs within both the home and synagogue.

8. They were part of a large wave of German-speaking immigrants who left their Central European homes, either due to the wars being waged in the region or drawn by the 1849 California gold rush. Many of the non-Jewish German speakers settled in the Midwest, giving cities such as Cincinnati, Milwaukee, and St. Louis their distinctive character.

9. These represent the four largest denominations within Judaism. There are others, including ALEPH, an organization for Jewish spiritual renewal, which has been growing in popularity. Many Jews do not identify with any particular religious denomination.

10. The term "orthodox," meaning "straight in belief," is a misnomer. Judaism is far more concerned with behaviors than personal beliefs. "Orthoprax," meaning "straight in practice," is a more accurate, if rarely used, term.

11. No one can observe all 613 commandments. Some are exclusive to men, others to women; some apply only to those of priestly descent, while others refer to agricultural practices in the Land of Israel, and so on.

12. The Hasidim adhere to a movement founded in Eastern Europe in the mid-eighteenth century. Divided into sects devoted to a leader, the *rebbe*, they follow a passionate—some would suggest mystical—form of Judaism. The Lubavitch Hasidim, also known as Chabad, are the largest such group in the Philadelphia region.

13. While few Reform congregations still use the *Union Prayer Book*, the *Central Conference of American Rabbis* and the *Union for Reform Judaism* (originally called the *Union for American Hebrew Congregations*) continue to represent those facets of the Reform movement.

14. *Halachah* (literally, "the Way") is the traditional order of Jewish living derived from biblical law, interpretations developed in the massive commentaries on the Bible known as the *Talmud* and later Rabbinic legal decisions.

15. These changes are contained in a document, the *Pittsburgh Platform*, written in 1885. They were modified in a second document, the *Columbus Platform*, in 1937. A third document, the *Centenary Statement* (1976) reflects the extent to which the Reform movement has reembraced traditional facets of Jewish life that it previously abandoned.

16. While they include members descended from Sephardic and Oriental backgrounds, all of the non-Orthodox religious branches in Judaism developed within the Ashkenazic community and were never duplicated in the Sephardic or Oriental worlds.

17. A native of Philadelphia, her father, Joshua Eilberg, was a Congressional Representative from Northeast Philadelphia.

18. The *Jewish Theological Seminary* is the primary school for Conservative rabbis in the United States. The *Rabbinical Assembly* is the movement's main rabbinic organization, while the *United Synagogue of America* is the congregational association.

19. His daughter, Judith, was the first Bat Mitzvah, in 1922.

20. His first prayer book was burned in public by an Orthodox Rabbinic organization, which declared a ban (*issur)* on Kaplan, his writings, and his followers.

21. Originally based near Temple University, at 2308 North Broad Street, the *Reconstructionist Rabbinical College* is now located in Wyncote, PA. Many of the movement's rabbis are members of the *Reconstructionist Rabbinical Association*, while the school and member congregations recently merged as the *Jewish Reconstructionist Communities.*

Discussion Questions:

1. According to Ashton, why did Rebecca Gratz found the Female Hebrew Benevolent Society? What did it actually do? Whom did it serve?
2. From reading Ashton, how do you think Gratz perceived the future of Judaism in America? Did she advocate or resist assimilation? What did she think of the Christians around her?

Section 6

Catholic Philadelphia

Philadelphia and the German Catholic Community

Jay P. Dolan

The history of German-American Catholicism began more than two hundred years ago. Long before the Revolution of 1776 the Gospel was preached to German Catholics in their mother tongue, especially in Pennsylvania, where two-thirds of the Catholic population in 1757 was German. However, the number of Catholics in colonial America was small, so meager in fact that John Adams observed that in his home town a Catholic was about as "rare as a comet or an earthquake." But if you wanted to find a Catholic in colonial America, and in particular a German-speaking Catholic, a good place to look was Philadelphia.[1]

German-speaking and English-speaking Catholics had worshiped together in St. Joseph's Church and later at St. Mary's Church before the Revolution. Yet the small band of German Catholics was already showing a sense of distinctive group consciousness in the eighteenth century. In 1768 they purchased their own burial ground, and it was evident that the separation of Catholics along lines of nationality was beginning to develop. In 1787 Germans organized the German Catholic Society and informed John Carroll, then Prefect Apostolic of the United States, that in order "to keep up their respective nation and Language" they were "fully determined to build and erect another new place of divine worship for the better convenience and accommodation of Catholics of all nations particularly the Germans under whose direction the building was to be constructed."[2] Two years later, the new church, Holy Trinity, was opened for service. In organizing their own church the Philadelphia Germans gained the distinction of founding the first national parish in the United States; the subsequent history of Holy Trinity illustrates how difficult and contentious such a development would be. From the very beginning German Catholics had to do battle with Church authorities who desired both an American church that knew no national distinctions and a hierarchically structured church that recognized no lay authority in ecclesiastical affairs. The hierarchy lost the battle against the national parish, but they ultimately won the war by gaining control of the system of lay trusteeism.

Throughout the nineteenth century the German American Catholic community increased numerically in both Philadelphia and the nation, principally through large waves of immigration in the 1850s and the 1880s. In 1840 one

Reprinted from "Philadelphia & the German Catholic Community" in *Immigrants and Religion in Urban America*, edited by Randall Miller and Thomas Marzik.

of every ten Catholics in the United States was German (70,592 of 663,000). In the next thirty years, the German Catholic population increased fourteen times, and by 1870 about one of four Catholics was of German stock (1,044,711 of 4,504,000). The Catholic Church had become the single largest denomination in the country, and German Catholics were fast becoming the largest subgroup of church Germans. After the heavy immigration of the 1880s, the number of German Catholics increased to approximately two million by 1890, a 100 percent increase in twenty years.[3] Thereafter, a decline set in as immigration from German-speaking countries ebbed, and the descendants of earlier immigrants became less distinctively German. In 1916 only one of ten Catholics (1,672,670 of 15,721, 815) worshiped in a church that used the German language.[4] Despite the decrease in the German Catholic presence, they had the distinction of being the largest subgroup of church Germans, numbering "slightly less than the total membership of several German Protestant denominations."[5] Within the Catholic Church they were still the largest foreign-language group.

The dominance that German Catholics enjoyed in Philadelphia in the colonial period did not persist into the nineteenth century. By 1842, German Catholics had increased to approximately 12,000, or 20 to 25 percent of Philadelphia's Catholics (about 50,000). Proportionately this was a significant decline from the days when three out of five Catholics in Philadelphia were Germans. By the sheer force of numbers the Irish had gained control of the Church and the Germans had slipped back into second place. In the next fifty years the increase in the German Catholic community was slight. In 1869 they numbered 21,000; by 1892 a rough estimate would put their population at 35,000, or approximately 17 percent of Philadelphia's Catholic population.[6] More significantly, the German Catholic population represented only 3 percent of the city's population in 1890; the entire foreign born German community equaled only 7 percent of the city's population.[7] What had happened is obvious from the hindsight of history. Like other Germans, Catholic Germans had bypassed Philadelphia in the nineteenth century and chose to settle elsewhere, principally in the Midwestern triangle bounded by the cities of Cincinnati, Milwaukee, and St. Louis. The story of German-American Catholicism, which began in Philadelphia in the eighteenth century, had shifted west following the flow of German immigrants.

In the nineteenth century German-American Catholics had become a minority population in Philadelphia. As Catholics they were outsiders in the larger Protestant culture of the city. As Germans they were a minority both in the city and the Church. To preserve their religion in an alien society and to preserve their ethnicity in an Irish church, they followed the patterns set by their colonial ancestors. They formed their own national parishes which, in the mind of one German priest, were "the best means to protect the Catholic immigrants against the loss of their faith, to safeguard them against the inducements and seductions of our adversaries, and to enable them to preserve incorrupt the sacred treasures of religion and to transmit it to their children."[8]

The national parish was the institutionalized attempt of an immigrant group to preserve the religious life of the old country. Among German Catholics it became a distinctive trademark in the nineteenth century. The heart of the issue was language. German Catholic immigrants came from many different countries in Western Europe, but they shared two common traits—language and religion. The two were inextricably joined together. "Language saves faith" was the slogan of German-American Catholics.

Reflecting this mentality, an immigrant guidebook advised newly arrived Germans not to "settle in districts and places where there are no German priests, churches and schools."[9] To settle in an English-speaking parish was "the greatest of all dangers" since "experience teaches that even in places where there are English Catholic churches but no German-speaking priests, German Catholics will become indifferent to the Church within a short time and in due course will be even worse than Protestants and pagans."[10] To this author the English-speaking parish was as great a threat to the faith as a Methodist church. Loss of language meant loss of faith, and it did not matter how you lost the mother tongue, the outcome was inevitably the same. This heightened sense of ethnicity caused one observer to remark that the Germans wanted "everything in German and if they are ever obliged to have Irish or American priests, they complain loudly about this insult."[11]

This fear of the loss of faith, as extreme as it was, appeared to be justified. In Philadelphia, "that irreligious and immoral city," the vitality of religion in the German community was directly connected with the availability of German-speaking parishes. In 1840 the "greater number" of the German community lived in the upper part of the city, where rent was cheaper because of its "distance from the center of the city and because of the poverty of those sections." But the only German parish, Holy Trinity, was located in the lower part of the city. Even under the best of circumstances it could not serve the needs of Philadelphia's 12,000 German Catholics. Thus, many Germans appeared to have "fallen away from the Faith." In 1843 the church of St. Peter's was organized for the German Catholics who lived north of Vine Street in the upper part of the city. From the very beginning the parish began to attract German Catholics from this part of the city as well as from the suburbs of Kensington and North Liberty. According to one writer, the establishment of St. Peter's Church prompted "very many" German Catholics to return to "the one saving faith of their fathers which they had given up either in part or completely."[12] St. Peter's eventually became the showcase of German Catholicism in Philadelphia. By 1848 the congregation numbered 3,000; fifteen years later it was the largest German parish in the city with 10,000 people.[13] The same pattern occurred in the founding of St. Alphonsus Church. Because of trustee troubles, Holy Trinity parish was placed under an interdict and the church was closed. As a result, the Germans of South Philadelphia were without a church, and this caused a "great falling away from the Church."[14] To remedy the situation, the new parish of St. Alphonsus was organized in 1853.

The loss of faith among German immigrants was a serious problem. The most obvious index of this was participation in church services. Only 40 to 60 percent of the Catholic immigrants regularly attended church on Sunday, and many German Catholic immigrants received the sacraments every twenty, thirty, or even forty years. Another less tangible indicator was the decline, or even the absence, of religion itself among the immigrants. German observers noted that their countrymen were not only lax in practicing their religion, but were becoming indifferent as well—"religious only in appearance," as they described it. Others commented that "many had given up the Catholic faith; others were Catholic in name only." The lack of priests and churches deprived them of the support needed to keep the religion of the old country alive. "What else can be expected under such conditions," wrote a German priest, "than that the priceless heritage these people brought from the Fatherland gradually disappears."[15] Church authorities were very concerned about the low level of religious practice and the decline of religious fervor among the immigrants. One means they chose to remedy the situation was the national parish. No one knows how extensive the loss of faith was among German immigrants, but one thing is certain: it would have been considerably greater without the ethnic parish.

Another reason for the establishment of the national parish was the tendency of immigrants to settle in a distinct city neighborhood. By the end of the nineteenth century the majority of German-Americans lived in the city, and this pattern of settlement "put an unmistakably urban stamp upon German-American Catholicism."[16] In Philadelphia "the mid-nineteenth century was *par excellence* the era of the urban parish church."[17] It was a time when Philadelphians were creating their own island communities in a city that was slowly becoming segregated along ethnic, social, and residential lines. Philadelphia Germans were no different from their neighbors. They tended to gather together in distinctively German neighborhoods and to form their own clubs, lodges, and benefit associations. For Catholic Germans the institution that outranked all others in importance was the parish. It was not only the center of both their religious and social lives, but it also was an ethnic fortress which enabled the immigrants to resist the onslaught of the surrounding Protestant culture on their faith and tradition.

For the fifty-three years prior to 1842 there was only one German Catholic parish in Philadelphia. In the next half-century twelve more German parishes were organized.[18] As in other foreign-language groups, the laity played a prominent role in the organization of the parish. Generally they would form a society, raise the necessary money, and purchase the land for their church. They would then petition the bishop for approval of their action and request the assistance of a German-speaking priest. This pattern especially characterized the early years of development, but even in the late nineteenth century German Catholics had to take matters into their own hands if they wanted a new German parish. German Catholics accepted membership in an English-speaking parish reluctantly and only as a temporary arrangement. The Germans, like the Italians and later the Poles, were not satisfied until they had their own church. For them it was as much a cultural institution as it was a center of religion. As Catholics they desired the bishop's blessing on their work, but as Germans they would not wait for him to act. When they finished their work, the bishop had little alternative but to approve their decision.

As a link with the old country, the ethnic parish was the place where Philadelphia Germans recreated the familiar religious customs of the fatherland. According to the theologian, Catholicism was a transnational religion that knew no national distinctions. The Mass, celebrated in Latin in Irish and German parishes, was identical. The devotional life of nineteenth-century Catholicism was also strikingly similar, with special attention rendered to Jesus Christ and Mary. But the Germans, like other ethnic groups, put their own stamp on Catholic piety. They loved pageantry and pomp.

They took obvious pride in elaborate ceremonies which they enthusiastically commented on in the German press. A common religion naturally exhibits similarities of expression regardless of nationality, but in those customs "not essential to Catholic faith and life" German Catholics evidenced a style of their own.[19]

Most striking was the German love of music. The parish choir was an accepted organization in any German parish, and to encourage this development Philadelphia Germans organized a citywide Caecilien Verein in 1882.[20] Every Mass on Sunday, unlike other Catholic parishes, featured music; at the Solemn Sunday Mass an orchestra together with the choir often performed. Parish financial reports indicated that when it came to church music, money was no problem; it was generally the most costly item in the church budget.

Germans loved a parade both in and outside of church. Parish societies, outfitted in their colorful regalia and each displaying its own banner, paraded along the streets of North Philadelphia on special feast days. It was inconceivable for German Catholics to celebrate a religious festival without a colorful procession.

Spiritual confraternities were also common among German Catholics. In addition to these societies, the parish fostered the growth of mutual benefit societies. The majority of Philadelphia parishes had such *Unterstützung–Vereine*. Philadelphia Germans also belonged to the national Central Verein and in 1876 organized this society on a city-wide basis.[21] The rationale behind these benefit societies "which are found in almost every German parish" was not hard to discover.[22] They provided financial assistance in case of sickness or death; they also were a Catholic alternative to similar societies sponsored by the non-Catholic German community. The Church frowned on Catholics joining such non-Catholic vereins since they were a risk to one's "faith and eternal salvation." But a German Catholic newspaper editor argued that Catholic vereins "contribute to one's spiritual end and the good of the church."[23] Such a separatist mentality encouraged the multiplication of a panoply of parish societies for every age group. In the process it reinforced the sense of community in the parish by separating Catholics from their non-Catholic countrymen.

In addition to benefit societies, Philadelphia Germans also organized their own hospital, St. Mary's, and an orphan asylum, St. Vincent's.[24] Both institutions served the city-wide German community. Philadelphia Catholics had other hospitals and orphanages, but here too the Germans felt the need to establish their own institutions. This was especially clear in the organization of St. Vincent's orphanage. Philadelphia had three orphan asylums for young Catholic children when John Nepomucene Neumann became bishop of the diocese in 1852, but these asylums catered to the Irish and the French. Neumann saw the need for another orphanage to care for the increasing number of homeless German children. Benevolent institutions organized along lines of nationality were a common feature of mid-nineteenth-century urban Catholicism. The acute sense of ethnicity, reinforced by the language barrier, demanded it. But another major motivation was to save the children from Protestantism. As Neumann put it, "asylums for our German children are most important and most necessary. These must be regarded as the best and only means of wresting them from the grasp of error, of infidelity and even godlessness."[25] St. Vincent's opened in 1855 in Tacony and eventually became a center of German Catholicism in Northeast Philadelphia.

The fear of children losing the faith also encouraged the founding of parish schools. "By all means," urged a German guidebook, "keep your children away from the public schools which properly ought to be called pagan schools or even worse."[26] Equally essential was the necessity to foster the mother tongue among the children and thus help them preserve the religious heritage of the old country. A dilemma arose, however, because parents also wanted their children to learn English. As a result many parents did not heed the counsel of the clergy and sent their children to public schools. In an attempt to counteract this tendency German parochial schools began to use both English and German in classroom instruction. This bilingual approach became the norm in German schools in the nineteenth century.

In Philadelphia every German parish listed in the German American Catholic Directory of 1892 had a school. St. Peter's, described as "one of the most progressive city parochial schools," was the largest German school, numbering 1,145 students; the Christian Brothers taught the boys and the School Sisters of Notre Dame instructed the girls.[27] As was true in other cities, however, the parochial school could never serve the educational needs of all German children of school age. As Bishop James Wood observed in reference to the parish of St. Boniface, it was obvious "that many do not send their children to the Catholic school."[28] Given this limitation, Philadelphia Germans in particular and German Catholics in general manifested an intense commitment to parochial education. Thus, it is not surprising to discover that in 1914 over 95 percent of the German parishes in the United States had a parochial school.[29]

In building up their ethnic fortress German Catholics set themselves off from other German-Americans. In their desire to preserve their own sense of identity they "displayed fierce antagonisms against any group that infringed upon their rights."[30] Protestant Germans were a frequent object of attack. This hostile attitude was transplanted from Europe, where Protestant and Catholic Germans had been doing battle since the Reformation. "Martin Luther and his latter day followers," noted one historian, "were always the worst of heretics. In 1883, the four-hundredth anniversary of Luther's birth, the Catholic *Volkszeitung* of Baltimore, an arch-conservative paper with a national circulation, noted the occasion with a series of more than sixty articles ripping Luther, the Reformation, and Protestantism to shreds."[31] Club Germans were also objects of Catholic prejudice. Priests warned their parishioners under pain of excommunication to avoid joining such secret societies as the Freemasons, the Red Men, and the Odd Fellows, as well as the popular Turnverein.

German Catholics were also inclined to do battle among themselves. One German priest wrote that "for no other intention is there more need for prayer than for unity among the Germans-not only in the German fatherland, but also here in America."[32] The history of Holy Trinity parish, as stormy as it was, was not untypical. Factions often developed among the people causing a schism in the parish. This would result in the founding of a new parish only a few blocks away from the mother church. This was the case in Philadelphia when conflict in Holy Trinity gave birth to St. Alphonsus parish.[33] As John Hughes, the Archbishop of New York observed, German Catholics were indeed "exceedingly prone to division among themselves."[34]

The most celebrated conflict that German Catholics entered was the struggle against the Irish-American hierarchy during the 1880s and 1890s. This was an intensely heated debate that principally involved the German communities of the Midwest triangle. The Germans of Philadelphia and Baltimore did not appear to be caught up in the issue, though this did not mean that they were unsympathetic to the cause of their Midwestern countrymen.

At the heart of the issue was the German insistence on equal rights in the American Catholic Church. This demand focused on the rights of German Catholics to have their own independent national parish where they could foster the religious heritage of the fatherland. Catholic Germans did not want to be "kept in a position inferior to that of the Irish," wrote Father Peter Abbelen of Milwaukee. "By granting the equal position which we ask," he continued, "no right of the Irish would be impaired, while an injustice and a disgrace would be removed from the Germans."[35] The demand for equality for German parishes was simple enough and not a serious problem, but the hidden agenda advocated a move toward a German church independent of the Irish American hierarchy. The Germans asked Rome to intervene on their behalf. However, the Vatican's inclination to favor the German petition and the Roman proposal to appoint a cardinal protector for German Catholics in the United States aroused the wrath of the more liberal American wing of the hierarchy. The issue was momentarily resolved in 1887, when Rome spoke out in favor of the national parish, but refused to grant further privileges to German-American Catholics.

Three years later the Lucerne Memorial rekindled the debate. The memorial was a document drawn up in Lucerne, Switzerland, in 1890 by the international representatives of the St. Raphael Verein, an immigrant aid society. The document was sent to Pope Leo XIII asking for definite rights for Catholic immigrants. In the United States it was interpreted "as another movement for German particularism." This time the demands were more comprehensive and more explicit. The goal was not just national parishes, but the development of a national clergy, national schools, and "most important of all, proportional representation in the hierarchy for each nationality."[36] The Lucerne Memorial attracted national attention in the United States. It was denounced in the Senate, and President Benjamin Harrison viewed it with concern. To both the politician and the churchman the issue was the same—the interference of foreigners in American affairs. In the 1880s and 1890s the introduction of foreign nationalism in the Catholic Church chiefly meant German nationalism, which was riding high both in the fatherland and in the United States. The reply of Rome once again favored the Americanist position, by stating that the proposals of the Lucerne Memorial were neither opportune nor necessary.

Despite the continued denial of discrimination against the Germans, they did have a legitimate complaint. Germans were not well represented in the hierarchy. In 1869 only 11 percent of the bishops were German (6 of 56). In 1900 after more than a decade of debate on the issue the proportion had increased to only 14 percent (13 of 90). The Irish had gained control of the hierarchy, and by 1900 one out of two bishops was Irish.[37] Bishops were also slow to recognize the demands of the Germans. In Philadelphia one historian observed that Bishop Wood evidenced "an unfriendly attitude toward the

Germans."[38] In other cities controlled by the Irish, people complained that Church authorities "almost ignored the existence of" the Germans."[39] But it is worth noting that when the Germans gained control of the Church, as they did in Wisconsin, they began to act like the Irish in their relations with the recently arrived Polish Catholics. Fearing a German *Kulturkampf* in the Church, the Poles pushed for the same demands that Germans had fought for twenty years earlier. What was one man's cultural pluralism in the 1880s had become another person's nativism in the 1900s.[40]

What happened in Wisconsin reflected the acculturation of German-American Catholics in the years before World War I. The German language was dying out, American habits were being adopted, and the United States was becoming the fatherland for most German-Americans. Immigration of German Catholics had decreased rapidly after 1900, and the use of the German-language newspaper was also on the decline. Only three new publications appeared between 1900 and 1918.[41] In Pennsylvania the same decline was evident, and as early as 1890 "no person who taught elementary subjects in the German language was available in Pennsylvania."[42] In 1911 state law designated English as the only language of the classroom. In the parochial school the last vestige of a commitment to the mother tongue was the use of the German-language catechism.

The national parish was another victim of the gradual Americanization of German Catholics. In 1869 the German Catholic Directory counted 705 churches in which German was the only language used. By 1906 the number had declined to 500; ten years later it decreased to 206. More symptomatic of the times in 1916 was the existence of 1,684 parishes in which both English and German were used.[43]

St. Boniface parish in Philadelphia illustrated the change that was taking place in urban America. Founded as a German parish in 1866, it reached a population of some 1,600 families in the 1890s. In the first decade of the century the parish population declined slightly. In the next decade, according to one observer, "many of the German people began to move north, and to the south and west the colored people came in. At the same time, it became clear that the younger generation did not understand German well enough to derive any real benefit from sermons and instructions in that language. "[44]

Germans were becoming Americanized, and the old nineteenth-century settlement was breaking up as the residential patterns of twentieth-century cities shifted. Germans remained concentrated in North Philadelphia, but the patterns of future change were already emerging. The mother tongue was becoming obsolete, and the nineteenth-century German parish was steadily losing its ethnic constituency as the population of the neighborhood changed. By the end of the 1920s, writes Frederick Luebke, "most German Catholics agreed that the goals of the church could not be served by the preservation of German language and culture."[45] Obviously the anti-German hysteria of World War I hastened the process of Americanization. German-American Catholics were disappearing as a distinctive subculture. The rise of Adolf Hitler and the onslaught of World War II intensified the tendency of German-Americans to bury their ethnicity. Even though 25.5 million Americans identified themselves as individuals of German descent as recently as 1972, the group consciousness of Germans had disintegrated. Only the faintest traces of German ethnic life remained.

In the Catholic community, people of German descent number more than eight million, but the national parish has vanished.[46] No one clamors anymore for German bishops. The Irish are no longer the enemy. In fact, the opposite appears to be the case. If a German Catholic marries outside his group, he will most likely marry into an Irish family.[47] "If you cannot beat them, marry them" seems to be the current strategy of German-Americans.

In the nineteenth century German Catholics struggled to maintain their ethnic identity in the American Catholic Church. To a great extent they succeeded. But history was not on their side as the passage of years weakened the link with the fatherland and encouraged new allegiances to America. In 1900 the issue at stake was the persistence of German-American Catholicism. Today the question no longer is what does it mean to be a German-American Catholic, rather what does it mean to be a Catholic in America?

Notes

1. Francis J. Herktorn, *A Retrospect of Holy Trinity Parish* (Philadelphia, 1914), pp. 6–7.
2. Ibid., p. 22.
3. These figures were calculated by Gerald Shaughnessy, *Has the Immigrant Kept the Faith?* (New York, 1925), pp. 237–238, 251; and also Ernst A. Reiter, *Schematismus der katholischen deutschen Geistlichkeit* (New York, 1869), p. 232.
4. Bureau of the Census, *Religious Bodies* 1916, 2 (Washington, D.C., 1919), 654.
5. Frederick C. Luebke, *Bonds of Loyalty: German Americans and World War I* (DeKalb, Ill, 1974), p. 35.
6. Joseph Salzbacher, *Meine Reise nach Nord-Amerika im Jahre 1842* (Vienna, 1845), p. 112; Reiter, *Schematismus*, pp. 15–17; the 1892 figures are my own estimates based on data in J. N. Enzlberger, *Schematismus der katholischen Geistlichkeit deutscher Zunge in den Ver. Staaten Amerikas* (Milwaukee, 1892), pp. 232–235; *Report on Statistics of Churches in the U.S. at 11th Census 1890* (Washington, D.C., 1894), p. 245; and *Historical Sketches of the Catholic Churches and Institutions of Philadelphia* (Philadelphia, 1895), p. 18.
7. Caroline Golab, "The Immigrant and the City: Poles, Italians and Jews in Philadelphia, 1870–1920," in *The Peoples of Philadelphia*, eds. Allen F. Davis and Mark H. Haller (Philadelphia, 1973), p. 205.
8. *Berichte der Leopoldinen Stiftung*, Oct. 12, 1844, quoted by Joseph White in "German Catholics in the Diocese of Vincennes in the Nineteenth Century" (unpub. seminar paper, Dept. of History, University of Notre Dame, Spring 1975).
9. "Historical Studies and Notes: A Guide for Catholic German Immigrants 1869," *Social Justice Review*, 52 (July-Aug. 1959), 135.
10. John M. Lenhart, O.F.M., "Historical Studies and Notes: Statistical Accounts of Membership of German Catholics in America," *Social Justice Review*, 51 (Jan. 1959), 312.
11. Jay P. Dolan, *The Immigrant Church: New York's Irish and* German Catholics, 1815–1865 (Baltimore, 1975), p. 71.
12. John M. Lenhart, O.F.M., "Historical Studies and Notes: German Catholics in the Diocese of Philadelphia in 1846," *Central-Blatt and Social Justice*, 26 (July-Aug. 1933), 131.
13. *Historical Sketches of the Catholic Churches*, p. 73.
14. Michael J. Curley, C.SS.R., *Venerable John Neumann* (New York, 1952), pp. 222–223.
15. Quoted in *Dolan, Immigrant Church*, pp, 84–85.
16. Luebke, *Bonds of Loyalty*, p. 36.

17. Sam Bass Warner Jr., *The Private City* (Philadelphia, 1971), p. 61.
18. Enzlberger, *Schematismus.* pp. 232–235.
19. Dolan, *The Immigrant Church,* pp. 79–80.
20. Enzlberger, *Schematismus,* p. 325.
21. Ibid., p. 324; these parish societies are listed in *Historical Sketches of the Catholic Churches,* pp. lvii-lviii.
22. "Historical Studies and Notes: A Guide," p. 166.
23. Ibid.; *Katholische Kirchenzeitung,* Sept. 2, 1858.
24. Enzlberger, *Schematismus,* p. 181.
25. Curley, *Venerable John Neumann,* pp. 260–261; see also Francis X. Roth, *History of St. Vincent's Orphan Asylum, Tacony, Philadelphia* (Philadelphia, 1934). On the German Catholics' unhappy experience in public hospitals which led to the establishment of German hospitals see Archives of the Archdiocese of New York, Claims of the Fathers and the Congregation of the Church of the Most Holy Redeemer, New York, to St. Francis Hospital, Fifth Street, New York, July 20, 1868.
26. "Historical Studies and Notes: A Guide," p. 167.
27. Enzlberger, *Schematismus,* pp. 232–235; Thomas J. Donaghy, *Philadelphia's Finest: A History of Education in the Catholic Archdiocese 1692–1970* (Philadelphia, 1972), p. 88.
28. John F. Byrne, C.SS.R., *The Redemptorist Centenaries* (Philadelphia, 1932), p. 193.
29. Richard M. Linkh, *American Catholicism and European Immigrants* (Staten Island, N.Y., 1975), p. 110.
30. Luebke, *Bonds of Loyalty,* p. 36.
31. Ibid., p. 37.
32. Quoted by Sister M. Mileta Ludwig, F.S.P.A., "Sources for the Biography of Michael Heiss, Bishop of LaCrosse, 1868–1880 and Archbishop of Milwaukee, 1881–1890," *Records* of the American Catholic Historical Society of Philadelphia, 79 (Dec. 1968), 210.
33. Curley, *Venerable John Neumann,* pp. 222–224.
34. Archives of the University of Notre Dame, *Scritture Riferite nei Congressi; American Centrale,* vol. 18, letter 1417, John Hughes to Prefect of Propaganda Fide, Mar. 23, 1858, f. 511.
35. Colman J. Barry, *The Catholic Church and German Americans* (Milwaukee, 1953), p. 291.
36. Colman J. Barry, "The German Catholic Immigrant," in *Roman Catholicism and the American Way of Life,* ed., Thomas T. McAvoy (Notre Dame, 1960), p. 199.
37. These figures were calculated from Reiter, *Schematismus,* p. 232 and p. 234; the list of German clergy compiled in Enzlberger, *Schematismus,* pp. 352–381; Bernard J. Code, *Dictionary of the American Hierarchy* (New York, 1940); and the *U.S. Catholic Directory 1900.*
38. Michael J. Curley, C.SS.R., *The Provincial Story* (New York, 1963), p. 161.
39. Dolan, *Immigrant Church,* p. 72.
40. Anthony J. Kuzniewski Jr., "Faith and Fatherland: An Intellectual History of the Polish Immigrant Community in Wisconsin, 1838-1918" (unpub. doctoral dissertation, Harvard University, 1973).
41. Philip Gleason, *The Conservative Reformers* (Notre Dame, 1968), p. 48.
42. Homer Tope Rosenberger, *The Pennsylvania Germans 1891–1965* (Lancaster, 1966), pp. 70–71.
43. Reiter, *Schematismus,* p. 232; Linkh, *American Catholicism,* pp. 108–110.
44. Byrne, *The Redemptorist Centenaries,* p, 188.
45. Luebke, *Bonds of Loyalty,* p. 317.
46. Harold J. Abramson, *Ethnic Diversity in Catholic America* (New York, 1973), p. 19.
47. Ibid., pp. 51–67.

The Philadelphia Bible Riots of 1844

Kathleen Oxx

On a brutally hot night in May of 1844, the most violent urban rioting to that point in American history began. Over the course of the summer, every Catholic church in Philadelphia was attacked, two were burned to the ground, and one was badly damaged. Two libraries, two rectories, a schoolhouse, and multiple blocks of homes were torched. About thirty people were killed, hundreds injured, and over a quarter of a million dollars' worth of damage was done.

The Philadelphia Bible Riots—as they are most commonly called—were caused by a number of different factors: ethnic tensions, clashes between immigrants and native-born Americans, economic and labor strife, disagreement about public institutions, and especially schooling.[1] But most centrally, they were about religion. Religious causes included the historical animosity between Protestants and Catholics; the distinct ways the Bible was translated and how it functioned in those different Christian communities; the common belief that America was (or should be) a Christian country (along with anti-Catholic judgments that Catholics were not Christian); and the religious liberty of Catholics to practice their faith in a Protestant-dominated land.

Philadelphia Context

Catholic visibility increased dramatically in Philadelphia in the first decades of the nineteenth century. In 1789, there were about 2,000 Catholics out of a population of about 30,000; by 1850, they were nearly a quarter of the half million Philadelphians.[2] In 1830, there were four Catholic churches in Philadelphia; by 1840 there were nine.

Anti-Catholics' mistrust and fear of Catholics proceeded apace with the growth of the Catholic population. Institutions devoted to the maintenance of Protestant hegemony proliferated. Political parties provided voters with candidates and platforms that assuaged and even fed their paranoia. Publishing houses produced a steady stream of anti-Catholic materials. Benevolent societies printed and distributed Bibles, textbooks, primers, children's magazines, and other instructional reading material that was explicitly anti-Catholic. The American Sunday School Union, headquartered in Philadelphia and made up of men from different Protestant Christian denominations, published the *Youth's Penny Gazette* for distribution in both Sunday and public schools. Anti-Catholic invectives were printed in most issues, such as one that instructed children: "[A] large portion of the false and foolish constructions which are put upon the Scriptures, to make them speak what 'wicked men and seducers' want to prove, may be traced to the followers of the Pope."[3]

This anti-Catholic and anti-immigrant bigotry is called "nativism," and it was not only evident in the nineteenth century. The contentious process of defining America and Americans has held widespread urgency in many historical periods, when those who considered themselves its "true" citizens attempted to exclude or eliminate outsiders. Though nativism often manifests as prejudice against people who are not U.S. citizens, the ideology encompasses a much broader, symbolic definition of national identity, and its dynamic nature allows it to reoccur and to adjust and adapt to changing contexts.

Though racial, economic, and gender tensions are often intertwined in nativism, the specifically religious aspects of it are crucial—even primary sometimes. Indeed, according to nativist thought, ascribing to a particular kind of Christianity has been a nearly universal requirement for being an American. In the early nineteenth century as immigration and territorial expansion increased Catholic presence, native-born Protestants feared Catholic religious practices more than they disparaged ethnic traditions or foreign languages. They worried about how the Pope—not the King of Germany—would influence American affairs. In their paranoia, they imagined that Catholicism was a "cult" run by a despot and comprised of superstitious and backward people who obeyed the Pope's every word. Some even believed that Catholics aimed to destroy America from within, a plot they were committed to preventing.

Bible Use in Schools

Even though Pennsylvania was famously founded as a haven for religious freedom, it was still in a number of ways a de facto Protestant establishment. In 1834, for example, the Commonwealth made the King James Bible a compulsory textbook in public schools (called "common" schools at the time). The legislature and most citizens believed the Bible should be the basis for morality and the social contract, and in their estimation, the King James—the most common Protestant translation—was the version that should be used.

But Catholics used their authorized translation, the Douay-Rheims Bible, and were not permitted to read the King James. This put Catholic children in a difficult position—should they disobey their teachers or disobey the tenets of their faith and commit a sin? Francis Kenrick, Philadelphia's Catholic Bishop, began to write letters in the Catholic newspaper. He challenged clergy, the laity, and even non-Catholic Philadelphians to "exclaim against this violence offered to the conscience of Catholics."[4] He approached the School Board in November of 1842 and requested Catholic children either be excused from Bible reading or be allowed to use their Douay-Rheims version. He insisted anti-Catholic textbooks—such as those that ridiculed the pope—be removed. And lastly, he appealed for equal rights for his flock and for all religious groups. He did not, as anti-Catholics would later attest, demand the removal of the Bible from schools.[5]

The School Board ruled in 1843 that if Catholic parents were "conscientiously opposed" to the King James Bible their children could read another version "without note or comment." But the ruling ensured the Catholic translation, which had extensive notes and comments, could not be used. Thus, it caused more tension than it dispelled. Not only did it anger many Catholics (and surely their non-Catholic supporters), it confused teachers and school administrators. Some Protestants thought even the request was an outrage and an example of the direct and serious threat Catholics posed to fundamental American religious values.

The May Riots

The mood in Philadelphia in 1844 was tense.[6] Labor strife was on the rise. The economy was unstable. Increasing numbers of immigrants taxed public coffers. Violence was ubiquitous. On top of all that it was an election year, and party platforms were nasty and polemical. Anti-Catholics and nativists grew increasingly paranoid and imagined their very way of life was threatened. Unwilling to relinquish it, they planned action.

On Friday afternoon, May 3, 1844, members of the nativist American Republican Association met at Second and Master Streets in Kensington, a working-class, Irish Catholic neighborhood in the northeast section of Philadelphia "for the purpose of expressing their political opinions." Driven from the site by locals, they gathered elsewhere, and complained about the "flagrant violation" of their right to assemble. They planned to meet the following Monday on the same corner. They publicized the rally to the public and press and claimed their "mistake" on Friday had been not "assembling in force, to beat off the foreign rabble." They invited all Philadelphians to "visit with their indignation and reproach this outbreak of a vindictive anti-Republican spirit, manifested by a portion of the alien population."[7]

On Monday, May 6th, as promised, they returned. When rain began to fall, those assembled took cover inside the neighborhood's central market. The scene quickly became chaotic. Rumors circulated that Irish Catholics were armed and ready to fight off the nativists. Some people retreated; some stood their ground. The chaos turned violent. Words were exchanged, a scuffle ensued, and rocks and bricks were thrown, some at the convent of the Sisters of Charity at Saint Michael's Church at Second and Phoenix Streets. Protestants raided Catholic houses; the Catholics inside returned volleys. An eighteen-year-old Protestant named George Shiffler was shot and killed. He immediately became a symbol—a martyr, even—for the nativists.

One source described the deadly scene:

> Henry Temper . . . received a shot in his side, which glanced off the hip bone and only produced a flesh wound. He received several small shots in the legs. Thomas Ford was struck in the forehead with a spent ball, which did him but slight injury. Lawrence Cox, had his hip seriously injured . . . Patrick Fisher . . . was shot in the face, but not dangerously wounded . . . Nathan Ramsey, received a shot through the breast bone, perforating his lungs, and he was carried to an apothecary store in Second Street, above the junction of Germantown Road. Here he was visited by his wife and mother. The young man is mortally wounded. Another young man,

> named John W. Wright, was shot through the head and killed instantly. He was not participating in the riot.[8]

Nativists started fires. Rumors spread that Saint Michael's Church was going to be attacked, but they proved unfounded for the time. Eventually Kensington turned quiet for the night.

The Native American Party (a larger nativist organization) then held a formal meeting on Tuesday, May 7th, at the State House. They elected leaders and officers, and took up a collection for the family of George Shiffler and other injured Protestants. Some in the crowd of between 2,000 and 3,000 men and women were determined to return to Kensington and enact revenge for the events of the previous day. They headed north, carrying an American flag and proclaiming it was the one that had been "trampled on" after Shiffler was killed. They burned the Irish Catholic Hibernian Hose Company (a fire station) and many more Catholic homes. At least eight men were killed, over fourteen wounded, and as many as thirty buildings burned. Finally, Philadelphia Sheriff Morton McMichael called out the military brigade and the riots ceased for the evening.

Overnight Wednesday a nativist tagged Saint Michael's Church: "POPE PROPERTY." As day broke, nativists again raided Catholic homes, allegedly searching for weapons. The militia, powerless against the force and number of the mob, was distracted from their watch on Saint Michael's by the posse lighting homes on fire. With no soldiers to stop them, the nativists burned the church, its library, and rectory to the ground. The pastor Reverend Donohue's books, papers, and furniture were destroyed, the altar-piece and vestments stolen, the cemetery desecrated. The Sisters of Charity convent and five homes surrounding the church were also burned. Prominent citizen and school administrator Hugh Clark watched his home and valuable library on Fourth and Master Streets go up in flames. Whole blocks were looted, especially the homes of other prominent Catholics.

The rioters marched south after dark where they joined a large crowd already gathered at Saint Augustine's Church on Fourth and Arch Streets. Mayor John Scott arrived and sought calm with a call to "all good citizens" to "preserve the public peace." He was hit by a rock. In a half-hour's time, the church and rectory, along with one of the most valuable libraries in the country, were on fire. As the church began to collapse, an inside wall, remarkably (miraculously, to some) unscathed in the blaze, became visible. According to onlookers, it was painted with a large eye and the eerily damning inscription: "the Lord seeth." Elizabeth West, a young Protestant woman who lived close to Saint Augustine's, described the spectacle:

> [O]ur city is a scene of rioting never was there such a time here before—At 10 o'clock the flames were winding round the steeple. . . . [I]t was most awful but grand. I never saw such a splendid sight: tho' I felt as if it were mockery to look at it.[9]

Pennsylvania Governor David Porter declared martial law on May 10th and authorities arrested rioters. The same day, George Shiffler's funeral was held.

Anti-Catholics marched through the streets, again proclaiming him their martyr and carrying the flag they claimed Catholics had defiled. Elizabeth Cowgill West recorded, " . . . phrenzy has taken hold of men's minds."[10]

On Saturday, May 11th, the *Public Ledger* reported that the "excitement" was "subsiding." Still, many Catholics were camping outside the city for their own protection. Bishop Kenrick suspended all masses that Sunday out of fear of further violence and property damage. And for the first time since the American Revolution, Philadelphia was under military control.

The Grand Jury called after the riots included members of nativist parties and the father of a Protestant wounded during the riot. Not surprisingly, they found Catholics guilty of inciting the riots as well as causing most of the property damage. They were "lawless irresponsible men, some of who[m] had resided in our country only for a short time," according to the jury's report. The nativists, they determined, had gathered to hold a "peaceful exercise."[11]

The July Riots

The end of the May violence was not the end of the Philadelphia Bible Riots, however. Nativist agitators planned to use the July 4th Independence Day parade to visually display their anti-Catholicism and xenophobia for the large crowd. As Susan G. Davis notes, floats and banners commemorated the riots and Shiffler's death. And the King James Bible was featured prominently; on numerous floats it was in George Washington's hands or being read by "Columbia."[12] One banner depicted a Bible in the claw of an American eagle.[13]

Tension again escalated as Catholics anticipated this histrionic display. Even before July 4th, they attacked the Native American Party's tent in Fisher's Woods (now the neighborhood below Snyder Avenue in South Philadelphia) where the parade was staged. With the approval of Governor Porter, they stockpiled weapons nearby at Saint Philip de Neri Church (on Third and Queen Streets) in a nativist neighborhood. When a witness saw the weapons being brought into the church, an angry crowd gathered and demanded their removal. The militia was called out and fired on the crowd, but nativist Charles Naylor threw himself in front of their weapons. He was arrested and held in the church basement.

The following day, the large crowd charged into Saint Philip's de Neri Church and pulled Naylor out. They barraged the building until a wall was breached and then occupied the church. Governor Porter assembled over 5,000 troops from surrounding cities and counties. After two days they restored order, but not until thirteen more Philadelphians were dead and an additional fifty wounded.

By July 8th, Philadelphia was, at long last, quiet. The Bible Riots had ended.

Philadelphia Bible Riots Historiography

As noted above, the riots were the result of many different factors and circumstances, but discrimination against Irish immigrants has most often been cited as their primary cause. Scholars have viewed them as the culmination of conflict that had been increasing between native-born Protestants and Irish Catholics through the early decades of the nineteenth century. The literature then, has highlighted how they were part of a larger pattern of bigotry toward immigrants.

A deeper analysis does not bear out this contention. As Kirby Miller and Michael Carroll have demonstrated, most Irish immigrants weren't Catholic until after refugees of the Great Famine began to arrive at the end of the 1840s.[14] Preeminent Philadelphia historian Gary Nash asks, if the riots were primarily based on ethnicity, wouldn't violence in Philadelphia have dramatically *escalated* in 1850 and beyond, when those tens of thousands of Irish and other immigrants came to Philadelphia?[15] Also telling is that all nine Catholic churches—where people of different ethnicities, classes, and occupations attended—were attacked. In fact, during the riots, Irish Protestants fought Irish Catholics. The rioters themselves belonged to many different religious backgrounds: John Perry and John Gihon (who also served as vice president of the Native American Party) were Unitarian ministers; Walter Colton was a Congregationalist; Lewis Levin was an Episcopalian (and secretary of the Native American Party and editor of the anti-Catholic *Daily Sun)*; Charles Stillwell was a Swedish Lutheran; and William Wright was a Methodist. The two latter men were both killed in the riots.

Aftermath

"Things are quiet and going along smoothly now," Bishop Kenrick recorded in his diary in early 1845.[16] Perhaps. But the Bible Riots left Catholics, Protestants, and the city of Philadelphia altered in significant ways.

Anti-Catholic political parties increased and their members founded fraternal organizations, firemen's societies, clubs, insurance programs, and reading rooms. In the November elections of 1844, nativists won seats in Congress, the Pennsylvania Senate, and numerous county offices. Lewis Levin served three terms as Congressman on the nativist ticket. By 1845, the movement was "in full control" of Philadelphia county.

Catholics varied in their analysis of the riots and the strategies they thought the community should undertake in response. Some advocated full assimilation into Protestant American culture. Some were convinced they could express their faith and demonstrate their "true" American-ness at the same time. Some believed the only way to keep themselves and their children safe was to form separate Catholic institutions (schools, hospitals, banks, political and fraternal organizations, and so on). Others, even more fearful of persecution and violence withdrew entirely from American society; two agrarian Catholic communities were founded in Pennsylvania, for instance.[17] Those who advocated for separate Catholic institutions determined the church's direction for the remainder of the nineteenth and the twentieth centuries in Philadelphia, as so much of the city's early twenty-first century landscape attests.

Protestants were significantly affected by the riots as well. Disagreements over various social, political, and economic issues came to the fore, to say nothing of theological divisions. Some individual Protestants developed more explicit ties to anti-Catholic organizations and created powerful political coalitions. As part of the larger impulse to reform society, many evangelical Protestants continued their benevolent pursuits in the temperance, suffrage, universal education, and other social movements with explicit or implicit intentions to convert Catholics. Others, knowing a just society could never withstand such violence, took aims to ensure the events of 1844 would never be repeated.

The riots also moved the city of Philadelphia to undertake a massive consolidation plan. Civil services were integrated, so that citizens would receive fire or police protection from unaffiliated municipal servants rather than religiously sectarian and politically partisan local groups. Scholars trace the foundation of the contemporary Philadelphia Police Department to the aftermath of the riots; some assert—with evidence in primary sources—that the city made a conscious decision to harness what they thought was the inherently violent Irish immigrant by recruiting them to police other poor and working-class people.[18]

When we understand the riots as primarily triggered by religious difference, we can see how they prefigured crucial questions facing Philadelphians and other urban citizens—indeed all Americans—today. Controversies surrounding the profiling of and discrimination against Muslims and African Americans, violence to mosques and synagogues, the use of inflammatory and racist language and images in the annual Mummers Parade, debates over which religious holidays and clothing are respected, and many, many more civic conflicts and injustices are part of the same struggle the 1844 Bible Riots illustrated. From the beginning of William Penn's "holy experiment," Philadelphians have wrestled with how to achieve this city's promise, how to harness the tremendous power of a critical and diverse mass, how to accomplish together what we cannot alone: attain true equality for each and every citizen of our city. The struggle goes on.

Notes

1. To Michael Feldberg the riots were the result of the economic downturn combined with the cultural differences that undermined class loyalties between Protestant natives and Irish Catholic immigrants. David Montgomery situates them in the context of neighborhood labor conflicts. Vincent P. Lannie and Bernard Diethorn understand the conflict as an early test case for twentieth-century legal battles over religion and education. Tracy Fessenden locates the Bible Riots in the context of the developing understanding of the "metaphor of separation" between church and state. See Michael Feldberg, *The Philadelphia Riots of 1844: A Study in Ethnic Conflict* (New York: Greenwood Press, 1975); Tracy Fessenden, "The Nineteenth-Century Bible Wars and the Separation of Church and State," *Church History: Studies in Christianity and Culture*, vol. 74, no. 4 (December 2005); Vincent P. Lannie and Bernard C. Deithorn, "For the Honor and Glory of God: The Philadelphia Bible Riots of 1844," *History of Education Quarterly*, vol. 8, no. 2 (Spring 1968); and David Montgomery, "The Shuttle and the Cross: Weavers and Artisans in the Kensington Riots of 1844," *Journal of Social History*, vol. 5, no. 4 (1972).

2. The 1789 numbers are for the city core only; the 1850 ones cover the entire urban population, including surrounding districts that remained separate municipalities until 1854. See Randall Balmer and Mark Silk, *Religion and Public Life in the Middle Atlantic Region*, (Lanham, MD: Rowman and Littlefield, 2006), 74; Sam Bass Warner, *The Private City: Philadelphia in Three Periods of Growth* (Philadelphia: University of Pennsylvania Press, 1968), 51, and Philip G. Bochanski, ed, *Our Faith-Filled Heritage* (Philadelphia: Archdiocese of Philadelphia, 2007).

3. "Wresting the Scriptures," *Youth's Penny Gazette*, April 5, 1843.

4. "Common Schools," *Catholic Herald*, April 12, 1838.

5. Hugh J. Nolan, *The Most Reverend Francis Patrick Kenrick, Third Bishop of Philadelphia, 1830–1851* (American Catholic Historical Society, 1948), 198, 212–14, 293–95.

6. The reports of events in May of 1844 vary considerable from source to source. Each religious community had their own printing presses and propaganda. Here, I've reconstructed a sketch of the riots from a number of primary sources, primarily the *Philadelphia Public Ledger*, the city's paper of record at the time. The source of direct quotes is of course cited.

7. *A Full and Complete Account of the Late Awful Riots in Philadelphia* (Library Company, Philadelphia, 1844) 6–7, 10. Available electronically at http://catalog.hathitrust.org/Record/009606697.

8. Ibid.

9. Elizabeth Cowgill West, *Elizabeth C. West Journal of 1844*, Transcribed by Harry F. Langhorne, (Philadelphia: H.F. Langhorne, 1998).

10. Ibid.

11. "Grand Jury Presentment, Kensington Riots." Reprinted in *Records of the American Catholic Historical Society*, "A Selection of Sources Dealing with the Nativist Riots," vol. 80 nos. 2–3, (June–September 1969), 90; and Feldberg, *The Philadelphia Riots of 1844*, 130.

12. "Columbia" and "Lady Liberty" were frequently-used female personifications of America.

13. Susan G. Davis, *Parades and Power: Street Theatre in Nineteenth-Century Philadelphia* (Philadelphia: Temple University Press, 1986), 150–51.

14. Michael P. Carroll, *American Catholics in the Protestant Imagination: Rethinking the Academic Study of Religion* (Baltimore: Johns Hopkins University Press, 2007), xv; Kerby A. Miller, *Emigrants and Exiles: Ireland and the Irish Exodus to North America* (New York: Oxford University Press, 1985), 170, 196–200.

15. Gary B. Nash, *First City: Philadelphia and the Forging of Historical Memory, Early American Studies* (Philadelphia: University of Pennsylvania Press, 2002), 175.

16. Nolan, *The Most Reverend Francis Patrick Kenrick*, 343.

17. Edward T. McCarron, "A Brave New World: The Irish Agrarian Colony of Benedicta, Maine in the 1830s and 1840s," *American Catholic Historical Researches* 105, nos. 1–2 (1994).

18. Noel Ignatiev, *How the Irish Became White* (New York: Routledge Press, 1995) and Roger Lane, *Roots of Violence in Black Philadelphia 1860–1900* (Cambridge: Harvard University Press, 1986).

Suggested Readings

Bruce Dorsey, "Freedom of Religion: Bibles, Public Schools, and Philadelphia's Bloody Riots of 1844" in *Pennsylvania Legacies* 8, no. 1 (May 2008): 12–17.

Discussion Questions:

1. Dolan writes that German Catholics used the motto "Language saves faith." Do you agree that recent immigrants (and their children) are more likely to hold on to their religious faith if worship or religious instruction is conducted in their native language?

2. Dolan writes that the Catholic hierarchy "lost the battle" against "national parishes" (70). Why would the Church oppose national parishes? Do you imagine that, overall, single ethnicity parishes were good or bad for Catholicism in America (think about retention of members, presenting a united front, perception by outsiders, and so on)? Do you think single ethnicity religious communities are a good or bad idea in general?
3. Bishop Kenrick, in his "Address of the Catholic Lay Citizens of the City," wrote: "Under no circumstances is conscience at the disposal of a majority." What do you think he meant by this statement? Why didn't the compromise made by the school board (described by both Oxx and Dorsey) work?
4. Why do you think the "Bible Riots" happened? What were the main causes?

Section 7

Mid-Century Reform

Philadelphia, Reform, and the Second Great Awakening

Elizabeth Hayes Alvarez

The years from the turn of the nineteenth century through the Civil War (1861–1865) were full of hope and optimism that the world could get better. In these decades—years historians call the "era of reform"—Americans worked to build a fairer and more moral society. Their optimism that America would continue to improve grew out of their religious convictions. Many Protestant Christians believed that God was leading people toward a brighter and more just "kingdom of heaven on earth." This sense of Christian progress was ignited by the revivals of the Second Great Awakening.

The "Second Great Awakening" is a term historians use to describe the rapid religious change that happened from about 1790 through the 1830s. Before the Awakening, the majority of Americans were Protestant Christians, mainly Congregationalists (founded by English Puritans), Presbyterians (founded by Scotch-Irish immigrants), and Episcopalians (founded by English immigrants who were part of the Church of England or "Anglican Church.") By the end of the century most Americans were still Christians, but none of these groups dominated. Instead, the majority of Americans were Catholics, Methodists, or Baptists. The increase in Catholics was due to immigration from predominantly Catholic countries like Ireland, Italy, Poland, and Germany; however, the phenomenal growth of Methodists and Baptists came not from immigration but from religious conversions during the revivals of the Second Great Awakening.

The revivals happened everywhere: in the North and the South, in cities and rural communities, and especially in the "burned over" district of New York (which experienced repeated revivals) and the frontier states of Kentucky, Tennessee, and Ohio. These revivals were called "camp meetings" because large numbers of people came from all over to attend them and, because there weren't enough accommodations in homes and inns for them all, many attendees would camp out in the woods. These meetings would be held in local churches or in outdoor tents with chairs or pews and a podium for preachers. Like bands at a music festival today, different Christian preachers would take the "stage" (pulpit) all day long, replacing one another as each grew tired. Preachers came from all over and had different denominational backgrounds. This mixing of backgrounds created a feeling of Christian unity and common purpose. The preaching would go on for hours or days as one minister after another insisted on the importance of true conversion, heart-felt religion, and the rejection of sin and vice. Many preachers denounced *social sins*, encouraging their listeners to renounce greed and consumerism and end slavery and poverty, as well as personal sins such as refraining from soliciting prostitutes, gambling, and drinking alcohol. The passionate preaching and huge crowds (over 20,000 people came to an 1801 revival in Cane Ridge, KY) created an intense, shared experience of public conversions, emotional testimonies, singing, praying, and healing. There were even reports of people spontaneously dancing, fainting, shaking, and barking.

Sometimes ministers would set up an "anxious bench" at the front and encourage people who wanted to be "saved" to come sit there where ministers could talk and pray with them. Often these people were already Christian church-goers or believers, but were not particularly devout and did not yet consider themselves "converted" or "saved." According to the theology of these revivalistic groups, sincere belief and church attendance were not enough to guarantee salvation (forgiveness of sins and eternity in heaven after death). A person must experience a heart-felt conversion with signs of having received God's grace or the presence of the Holy Spirit. These signs were both intangible (hope, a sense of God's presence, an intense desire for holiness) and tangible (a shift toward holy living and away from sinful behaviors). Huge numbers of Americans experienced conversion at these meetings. Many subsequently left their churches to join revivalistic denominations like the Methodists or Baptists while others began attending church for the first time.

Many more women than men converted during the revivals, at a rate of two or three to one. Many African Americans converted as well. Because these meetings were "mixed" (composed of women and men, rich and poor, and, especially, black and white Americans), they were controversial. At some of the revivals, individuals that were typically denied opportunities to speak publicly, like African Americans and women, stood up and testified about their experience of "saving grace" and conversion, encouraged others, prayed aloud, and even preached from pulpits. While many were shocked and offended by this "mixing," some of those who attended felt transformed as racial, class, and gender boundaries were challenged or overthrown, understanding this as evidence of God's powerful presence. Many of them went home to organize reform societies that fought against unfair restrictions on women's rights, sought to end slavery, or to end the sale of alcohol. Many believed that the revivals were a sign that God was at work and that Christian unity, experienced through the shared emotional catharsis of camp meetings, was creating a new, more democratic society where Americans would be on a more even footing.

The more established, structured, and "respectable" Protestant churches objected to the meetings on several grounds: they felt the revivals lacked a clear, accurate theology; that the preaching was emotionally manipulative; that they were led by unlearned men and appealed to the "rabble" of society; and that they threatened the hierarchies that made society stable. Their fear that the revival meetings would challenge and undermine their own cultural authority was legitimate. In 1790, Anglicans (Episcopalians) were by far the largest Protestant group in America while Methodists had about 58,000 members. By 1820, Methodists took the number one spot with over 258,000 members. By 1860, there were over 1,661,000 Methodists in the United States. This represents a growth factor of 28.6, significantly higher than the population growth factor of eight in the same years. This shift in religious affiliation changed the ways the majority of Americans understood themselves as Christians, the identity and role of America as a nation, and a range of social issues. It also represented a real shift in how this group of Americans practiced their faith, what they did and heard in churches, and what they expected their leaders to look and sound like. In short, it was a shift toward populism.

While revivalists came from different backgrounds and had different theologies, they shared "post-millennial" beliefs about the "last days" (how the world would end). Christians then (and now) had a range of ideas about these topics. Post-millennials emphasize that Christians are the body of Christ and carry out God's will on earth. Jesus will come again, they believe, but not until after Christians usher in his return by converting the nations to Christianity and establishing a fair and just society. In contrast, today many revivalist Christians (born-again, evangelical Christians) hold "pre-millennial" ideas. Pre-millenialists believe that the world will continue to get worse and that Christ must return before things get better. (This point of view is presented in the best-selling *Left Behind* series of books by Tim LaHaye and Jerry Jenkins.) While it may seem like an arcane theological distinction, it is important that the revivialists of the Second Great Awakening were post-millenialists because it meant that they believed Christians had the ability and the religious obligation to reform society. They left camp meetings excited about their new-found, or newly-energized, faith *and* optimistic that society could be changed for the better. Their experiences also convinced many of them that the old divisions of denomination, race, and class mattered less than they had thought.

During the Second Great Awakening people became more religious (over 600 religious magazines were founded between 1790 and 1830) and more socially aware. The revivals were a crucial precursor to the woman's rights movement (women should be able to own and inherit property and have access to education among other issues); the woman's suffrage movement (women should have the right to vote); prohibition (alcoholic beverages should be banned because they led to poverty and domestic abuse); and abolition (enslavement and forced labor of all persons should be ended). While these reformist energies flowed out of the revivals, they caught on more broadly. Many Americans who had not participated in the revivals joined or created reform groups, including more traditional Protestants, Catholics, Jews, and the nonreligious, all of whom rejected revivalistic Christianity.

In Philadelphia, reformist impulses led to the founding of many new institutions. In 1800 the Magdalene Society was formed by Episcopal Bishop William White at Race and Schuylkill Streets (now Twenty-first Street) with the intention of housing and reforming "fallen" women; that is, women who were prostitutes, mistresses of married men, or unmarried young women who had been seduced by men. However, the Society refused to admit women who were pregnant, ill with venereal diseases, or African American. The Society hoped that the women they did admit could be transformed by Christian prayer, Bible study, and hard work and could go on to lead respectable lives. It was a restrictive environment; because they did not want the women to influence each other in what they saw as negative ways, they rarely allowed them to converse with each other, gave them numbers instead of names, did not allow them to discuss their pasts, and forbade them from leaving the premises without permission. In exchange for food and shelter, women were confined to the building, working, and reading the Bible for most of the day. Most of the women did not stay long, often choosing to take their chances rather than to abide by the strict regimen, and very few were "rehabilitated" (that is, few found respectable homes and means of income). In time, the group shifted its mission to preventing the sexual exploitation of girls by housing poor and homeless (but not-yet-fallen) girls in a less restrictive and punitive environment. In the twentieth century, the mission changed again to offer underprivileged girls, and later all youth, scholarships and career counseling. This mission continues today in the White-Williams scholarship fund.

Other key Philadelphia institutions created during the Reform Era were the Philadelphia Society for the Relief of Persons Deprived of the Use of their Reason (founded in 1817) which provided care for the mentally ill in a gentle and nonabusive environment; the Female Hebrew Benevolent Society (founded by Rebecca Gratz in 1819) which sought to provide funds and assistance to poor Jews, with special concern for Jewish women and children; and, by 1834, over thirty temperance society chapters with well over 4,000 members.[1] The first National Temperance Convention, with over 400 delegates from all over the country, was held in Philadelphia in May of 1833.

Another important project spearheaded in Philadelphia was prison reform. Eastern State Penitentiary was founded in 1829 by a religiously diverse group of reformers, the Society for Alleviating the Miseries of Public Prisons, which included prominent Philadelphia Quakers and Episcopalians. The first true "penitentiary," the design of the prison and daily life there was intended to induce true penitence: religious reflection, sorrow for misdeeds, and personal transformation. Initially, prisoners were kept in solitary confinement, with their own their personal cells and yards, where they would converse only with overseers or visiting clergy and be given only a Bible to read. Windows in the cells were in the ceilings, so that prisoners only view was of the heavens. While ESP's designers believed that solitude would give prisoners the opportunity to truly reflect and repent, in reality it was psychologically difficult. Charles Dickens famously called ESP's cells "stone coffins" and its prisoners "men buried alive." However, despite the prison's short-fallings, its intention was to transform individuals and society by emphasizing the possibility of redemption rather than the priority of punishment. In this sense, it was like other reform movements of the era.

Reform movements in these years were widespread in their goals and effects. Many had their origins in Christian revivalism, but they invigorated broader coalitions of Americans to embrace change and became secularized (nonreligious) over time. They encompassed ideas that we might now see as progressive (opposing the enslavement of and discrimination against African Americans; opposing the displacement of and discrimination against Native peoples; supporting women's rights; and supporting early labor organizing) and things we might now consider conservative (opposing prostitution, the consumption and sale of alcohol, gambling, and other “vices”). But the division in Americans’ cultural attitudes that we now call the “culture wars” came later. In this period, a profound optimism about human capacity to create a good society that lived out the best intentions of the Creator for humanity led to real and lasting change.

Notes

1. Bruce Dorsey, *Reforming Men and Women: Gender in the Antebellum City* (Ithaca, NY: Cornell University Press, 2006), 115.

Philadelphia, Rufus Jones, and the Reinvention of Quakerism

David Harrington Watt

Quakers such as William Penn (the founder of Pennsylvania), John Woolman (the well-known anti-slavery activist), and Lucretia Mott (the famous nineteenth-century advocate for women's rights) figure prominently in analyses of the history of metropolitan Philadelphia in the years between 1682 and 1880. But after 1880 (the year in which Mott died), Quakers tend to drop out of the story. Few accounts of Philadelphia history in the late nineteenth, twentieth, and twenty-first centuries shed much light on the Society of Friends. That is unfortunate. Philadelphia Quakers did not disappear in 1880.

And they did not stop evolving either. In actuality, Philadelphia Quakers underwent a dramatic transformation in the twentieth century. The sort of Quakerism that is most commonly practiced in Philadelphia today is quite different from the sorts of Quakerism that were practiced in Mott's day. The differences stem in no small part from the work of Rufus Jones (1863–1948): a Quaker writer and teacher who taught at Haverford College for much of his life. Even a cursory examination of Quakers in contemporary Philadelphia reveals a great many signs of Jones's continuing influence.

In the eighteenth and nineteenth centuries Philadelphia was one of the capitals of the international Quaker movement. It still is. Quaker organizations that are headquartered in metropolitan Philadelphia include the Americas Section of the Friends World Committee for Consultation, the Friends Association for Higher Education, and the Friends General Conference. Scores of Quaker congregations are located within the vicinity of Philadelphia. Thousands of men and women belong to those congregations. The region is home to an important Quaker study center called Pendle Hill, three liberal arts colleges with strong connections to the Society of Friends, and dozens of private schools that are said to be committed to Quaker values.[1]

People who are interested in finding out more about Philadelphia Quakers often end up making their way to Friends Center. The center is located just north of City Hall, on a block bounded by Race, Fifteenth, Cherry, and Mole Streets. Quakers have been gathering on this spot since the nineteenth century, and one segment of the center—the so-called Race Street Meetinghouse—dates back to 1856. But from some angles the center looks as if it is simply a modern office complex constructed of brick and glass. Parts of the center were not built until the early 1970s, and the entire center was thoroughly renovated in 2009. In the fall of

2015 a mural designed by Shepard Fairey that protests mass incarceration in the United States was painted on the northern wall of the center.

At present, more than twenty not-for-profit organizations rent space in Friends Center. Three of them are particularly well known. The first of these is the American Friends Service Committee (AFSC). It was founded in 1917 by a group of Quakers who included Rufus Jones (1863–1948) and Henry Cadbury (1883–1974). (Cadbury was a close friend of Jones and also his brother-in-law.) In 1947 the AFSC was awarded the Nobel Peace Prize. Today the AFSC works in Africa, the Caribbean, Asia, and the Americas addressing issues such as the death penalty, militarism, income inequality, and mass incarceration. Some of its activities—its work on behalf of the rights of Palestinians, for instance—have occasioned a good deal of controversy. But the AFSC is nevertheless a highly respected organization, and many Quakers and non-Quakers continue to make generous donations to underwrite its activities. In 2013, the AFSC was able to devote more than 30 million dollars to projects designed to rectify injustices and promote peace.[2]

A second well-known organization whose offices are located in Friends Center is the Philadelphia Yearly Meeting of the Religious Society of Friends (PYM). That organization, which was created in 1955, supports the work of more than 100 Quaker congregations located in Pennsylvania, Delaware, New Jersey, and Maryland. PYM publishes the closest thing Philadelphia Quakers have to an authoritative guide to what Quakers believe and how they should act: *Faith and Practice*. The current edition of *Faith and Practice* presents the history of the Society of Friends in a way that clearly echoes Jones's ideas about Quakerism's origins. It contains numerous quotations taken directly from his writings and those of his colleagues and students. PYM maintains a library that contains a wide range of material that sheds light on the Society of Friends. The library, which is located on the second floor of Friends Center, is named after Henry Cadbury. Its holdings include more than 130 texts written by Jones.[3]

Central Philadelphia Monthly Meeting (CPMM) is another well-known organization that rents space in Friends Center. CPMM is a Quaker congregation established in 1956. At present its membership stands at about 200 persons. Its meetings for worship are generally held on Sundays at 11 a.m. Some Sundays the meetings for worship take place in the center's Rufus Jones Room, which was constructed in the 1970s and can seat scores of people. On other Sundays they are in an enormous room that can accommodate hundreds and dates back to the 1850s. Meetings for worship at CPMM, like those at most Quaker congregations in the Philadelphia region, are "unprogrammed." That means that the services do not follow a set liturgy: at CPMM no one sings, gives a message, or prays aloud until they are convinced that the Spirit is leading them to do so. Sometimes no one feels led to speak. The members of CPMM do not seem to be troubled by meetings that are conducted entirely in silence. Many of them report that they find such meetings to be especially beautiful and particularly meaningful.[4]

Visitors to CPMM who say that they want to learn more about the principles on which Quaker worship services are based are sometimes given a pamphlet, "Quaker Meeting for Worship," written by Douglas Steere (1901–1995). Steere, who studied philosophy at Harvard University and taught philosophy at Haverford College, was one of Rufus Jones's most famous protégés. And visitors who are looking for a more general introduction to the Society of Friends are sometimes handed a pamphlet, written by Jones himself, called "An Interpretation of Quakerism."[5]

Rufus Jones was born on January 23, 1863, at a time when it was not at all certain that the Union was going to win the American Civil War. He died on June 16, 1948, three years after the United States and its allies had achieved a decisive victory in World War II. By then the United States was clearly the most powerful nation in the world. At that point Philadelphia was still the third largest city in the United States. (Only New York and Chicago were larger.)

Within a few days of Jones's death, Philadelphia's leading newspaper ran an article headlined "Rufus Jones: Sage, Seer, Saint."[6] Many of the men and women who read that headline must have thought that it simply restated something they already knew. In 1948 a good many Americans seem to have felt that if there was any Protestant human being living anywhere in the United States who was *both* a true saint *and* a bona fide mystic then Rufus Jones was that person.[7]

During his lifetime Jones was probably the most famous Quaker in the world. His ideas decisively influenced the ways that Quakers in Philadelphia, and in other parts of world as well, thought about what Quakerism is and what it should be. The form of Quakerism that was generally practiced in Philadelphia in the 1940s and still is today—for lack of a better term we might call it Liberal Quakerism—is quite different from the form of Quakerism practiced in William Penn's day. You could make a case that Quakerism was reinvented during Jones's lifetime and that Jones played a larger role in Quakerism's reinvention than did any of his contemporaries.

Like many other famous Philadelphians (Benjamin Franklin, for instance), Jones was born somewhere else. Jones's birthplace was South China, Maine, a small rural village in Kennebec County. Both of his parents were devout Quakers; so were a great many other members of Jones's extended family. As a boy Jones attended schools in rural Maine. In 1879 he left Maine for Rhode Island to attend a Quaker boarding school in Providence.[8]

Jones moved to metropolitan Philadelphia in 1883 in order to study at Haverford College. He did not come from a wealthy family and Haverford, which had been established by Philadelphia Quakers in 1833, offered him a scholarship that covered tuition, room, and board. When Jones studied there Haverford had fewer than eighty students. Most of them were Quakers. All were male. All were white. In many respects Haverford was an unusually insular organization. But compared to the places Jones had been before, Haverford was a fairly cosmopolitan institution and Jones loved studying there. He got along well with his fellow students and he admired his professors immensely. He read widely, did well in his classes, and wrote a graduation thesis on religious mysticism. After graduating from Haverford, Jones traveled in Europe and taught school in Maine, Rhode Island, and New York. In 1888, he married a highly accomplished woman who had recently joined the Society of Friends, Sarah Coutant.[9]

Jones returned to Haverford in 1893 to edit a Quaker periodical and to teach courses at the college. Haverford was his home for the rest of his life. His wife Sarah Jones died in 1899. Three years later he married Elizabeth Bartram Cadbury

(1871–1952). Elizabeth came from one of Philadelphia's most prominent Quaker families and had received her education at Friends Select School and Bryn Mawr College. She was an avid researcher, a careful writer, and a skilled editor. She expended a prodigious amount of labor on various activities to support her husband's work as a writer. It is entirely possible that Elizabeth should be regarded as the coauthor of many of the articles and books that are conventionally attributed to her husband. It is certain that she conducted some of the research on which Rufus's many books and articles on Quaker history were based.[10]

In those books and articles, Jones argued that it was a mistake to see early Quakerism as an offshoot of Puritanism or as nothing more than a protest movement against Anglican beliefs and practices. He said that early Quakerism was a seventeenth-century expression of an ancient human desire. The early Quakers, like countless generations of mystics who had preceded them, wanted to obtain a direct, personal connection to God. The early Friends, he said, were "seekers" who wanted to do more than simply accumulate knowledge about God. They wanted to experience him for themselves. Mysticism was, Jones insisted, at the very heart of early Quakerism. People who did not understand that could not grasp what authentic Quakerism was all about.

The energy that Jones poured into writing about history—and about other topics such as philosophy and theology—was awe-inspiring. Over the course of his lifetime Jones produced hundreds of editorials, book reviews, articles, and book chapters. He wrote more than fifty books. But Jones was not a historian in the strictest sense of that term. Although he took graduate courses at Harvard University, he never earned a Ph.D. in history, philosophy, theology, or any other discipline. His ideas about the methods that should be used when studying the past were not especially sophisticated. When judged by today's modern research standards, they were remarkably naïve. Nevertheless, Jones's arguments about the history of the Society of Friends reached a broad audience and transformed the way both Quakers and non-Quakers thought about the history of Quakerism. The stories Jones told about Quaker history are, to a large degree, the stories that are still told today.

Quakerism, according to Jones's interpretation of it, was a dynamic, forward-looking faith. Quakers should not see the modern era as a time of decay or apostasy. Instead they should regard it with hope and confidence. Quakers should realize that God is just as interested in conversing with human beings in the modern era as he was in communicating with them thousands of years ago. The God Quakers worship is, Jones insisted, "*a living, revealing, communicating God.*" If God ever spoke, He is still speaking." Quakers can be certain that God "is the Great I Am, not a Great He Was."[11]

Quakers, Jones said, should not assume that they and God had nothing whatsoever in common. The differences between a particular human being and God could, he declared, easily be overstated. There was not a vast gulf between them. Quakers ought to realize that "something of God is present in every man."[12] They ought to know that it is possible for human beings to become, in some sense, Godlike. "There is something," Jones said, "so close and intimate between humanity and Divinity that God can express himself in human terms—even in human form—and that man—any man—who receives Him can become like Him."[13]

The Quaker religion, as Jones presented it, was best thought of as a way of life—a life based on careful attention to the inner promptings of God's spirit—rather than a set of doctrines that had to be affirmed. The way of life Quakers were invited to follow was characterized by bravery, unselfishness, and personal integrity. It was also characterized by a determination to "walk the path of peace." Quakers, Jones said, ought to live peaceably even during times of conflict. When their country went to war, Quakers should not take up arms to fight. And Quakers' commitment to peace ought to go far beyond simply eschewing the use of violence. It should also involve them cheerfully taking on their "share of the heavy burden of trying to build a world in which the gentler forms of kindness, love, sympathy and co-operation are put into function."[14]

Through decades of strenuous activity, Jones demonstrated to the world the depth of Quakers' commitment to the cause of peace. During World War I, Jones and other Quakers associated with the AFSC devoted themselves to helping Quakers who refused to fight to find ways of being of direct service to European civilians whose lives had been disrupted by war. After the war ended, Jones and his Quaker colleagues in the AFSC directed their attention to feeding and caring for the inhabitants of countries—Germany, Serbia, Poland, and Russia, for instance—that the war had damaged. In 1938 Jones and two other Philadelphia Quakers traveled to Germany to meet with the Gestapo to discuss the way that Jews in Germany were being treated and to request that Quakers be allowed to offer direct aid to Jews who wanted to emigrate. In the early months of 1948 (the months just before his death), Jones participated in an international effort to establish a "Truce of God" in the city of Jerusalem. Such a truce, he hoped, might lessen tensions between the Jews and Muslims who lived in Palestine and thus prevent needless bloodshed.[15]

Many non-Quakers respected Jones's commitment to peace. And many of them were deeply moved by his explanations of about what it meant to be an authentic Quaker. With assistance from a number of other Friends, Jones succeeding in transforming the way in which non-Quakers thought about the Society of Friends. When Jones began his work, outsiders tended to think of the Society of Friends as a sect that had an unhealthy obsession with preserving its own distinctive modes of speech and dress. They often saw Quakers as quirky, insular, and backward-looking. By the time Jones died, a great many non-Quakers had developed a tremendous respect for the Society of Friends. They came to see it as a progressive denomination that was deeply committed to world peace and as "a great purveyor of devotional wisdom for aspirants of various religious backgrounds." Jones made Quakers seem important and alluring. He persuaded many outsiders to believe that Quakers possessed a profound understanding of a number of universal religious truths that everyone ought to embrace.[16]

Jones's ideas continue to influence the way a great many Philadelphians think about what it means to be an authentic Quaker. There are a number of Quakers in Philadelphia—for example, the Quakers who belong to a congregation located near Temple University called Iglesia Los Amigos Philadelphia—whose interpretations of Quakerism differ sharply from Jones's. But Philadelphians have a tendency to think that people who practice forms of Quakerism that look different from those associated with Jones are somehow not "real Quakers." When they hear someone claim that most of the world's Quakers practice versions of Quakerism that differ sharply from Jones's version of that faith, a puzzled look sometimes crosses their faces. They seem to doubt that such a claim could possibly true. In fact that claim is true. Less than a fourth of the world's Quakers practice a form of Quakerism that is closely related to Jones's. A great many think of themselves as evangelicals or fundamentalists.

In the early twentieth century, a good many of the Quakers who lived in Philadelphia realized that Jones's reinterpretation of Quakerism was quite dramatic. Many of his contemporaries applauded his daring. A few condemned it. Many of today's Philadelphia Quakers have lost sight of the fact that Jones's interpretation of Quakerism really was an *interpretation*. To them his descriptions and analyses of Quakerism often seem to be "self-evidently true."[17] In fact, they are not that at all. They are actually somewhat problematic. That Jones's arguments about Quakerism are now often mistaken for obvious truths is an indication, among other things, of the remarkable influence Jones has exerted—and continues to exert—on Quakerism in Philadelphia.

Notes

1. The author gratefully acknowledges the assistance he received from Alison Anderson, Mary Crauderueff, Sarah M. Horowitz, and Robin Mohr as he was writing this essay.

2. The American Friends Service Committee, *Annual Report 2014*.

3. Philadelphia Yearly Meeting of the Religious Society of Friends, *2014 Directory* (Philadelphia: Philadelphia Yearly Meeting, 2014); and Philadelphia Yearly Meeting of the Religious Society of Friends, *Faith & Practice: A Book of Christian Discipline*. (Philadelphia: Philadelphia Yearly Meeting, 2002), 1–2. Cf. Leigh Eric Schmidt, *Restless Souls: The Making of American Spirituality* (San Francisco: HarperSanFrancisco, 2005), 18 and 235–38.

4. Margaret Hope Bacon, *In the Shadow of William Penn: Central Philadelphia Monthly Meeting* (Philadelphia: Central Philadelphia Monthly Meeting, 2001).

5. Douglas Steere, "Quaker Meeting for Worship" (Philadelphia: Philadelphia Yearly Meeting, [1944]) and Rufus M. Jones, "An Interpretation of Quakerism," (Philadelphia: Philadelphia Yearly Meeting, [1930] 2000).

6. Joseph Fort Newton, "Rufus Jones: Sage, Seer, Saint," *Philadelphia Bulletin*, June 26, 1948.

7. Schmidt, *Restless Souls*, 232–33.

8. Elizabeth Gray Vining, *Friend of Life* (Philadelphia: J.B. Lippincott, 1958), 17–34.

9. Vining, *Friend of Life*, 35–59.

10. My interpretation of Elizabeth's role in the creation of texts attributed solely to Rufus is based on Hugh Barbour, "Jones, Rufus Matthew" *American National Biography Online*, http://www.anb.org.libproxy.temple.edu/articles/08/08-01907.html; accessed September 21, 2015; Mary Hoxie Jones, "Rufus M. Jones, A Biographical Sketch," in *Quakerism: A Spiritual Movement: Six Essays, with a Sketch of His Life*. [written by] Rufus M. Jones and Mary Hoxie Jones (Philadelphia: Philadelphia Yearly Meeting of Friends, 1963), 25; and Vining, *Friend of Life*, 117 and 226.

11. Rufus M. Jones, *A Call to What Is Vital* (New York: Macmillan, 1949), 65.

12. Rufus M. Jones, *Religious Foundations* (New York: Macmillan, 1923), 34.

13. Rufus M. Jones, *A Dynamic Faith* (London: Headley Brothers, 1901), 68.

14. Rufus M. Jones, *The Faith and Practice of the Quakers* (Garden City, NY: Doubleday, Doran, & Company, 1928), 113.

15. Vining, *Friend of Life*, 156–83; 280–93; and 308–11.

16. Schmidt, *Restless Souls*, 230.

17. John Punshon, *Portrait in Grey: A Short History of the Quakers* (London: Quaker Home Service, 1984), 227. Punshon used the phrase "self-evidently true" in a somewhat different context from the one in which it is used here.

Suggested Readings

Muriel Schmid, "The Eye of God: Religious Beliefs and Punishment in Early Nineteenth-Century Prison Reform" in *Theology Today* 59, no. 4 (Jan 2003): 546–558.

E. G. Aderfer, "The Search for Solitude: From Germantown to the Conestoga Frontier" in *The Ephrata Commune: An Early American Counterculture* (Pittsburgh: University of Pittsburgh Press, 1985): 27–37.

Discussion Questions:

1. According to Schmid, what elements of Eastern State Penitentiary were designed to punish (or scare) criminals and potential criminals? What elements of ESP were designed to reform (rather than merely punish) individuals?
2. Which religious traditions shaped or influenced the design and policies of ESP?
3. In our current society, why do we put people in jail? What do we primarily hope to accomplish? Should the state try to "reform" people? Is it more moral to try to reform people or not to try?
4. Many people "find religion" in jail. Why do you think that happens? Do you think people who have that experience stay religious once they leave prison?

Section 8

Philadelphia Sports and Religion

Religion and Sports in Philadelphia

Rebecca T. Alpert

Many Philadelphians explain their love of sport using religious language. Athletes are dedicated to physical training with spiritual intensity; ask anyone who rows on the Schuylkill River at 5 a.m. The euphoria of watching the Villanova basketball team hit a tie-breaking jump shot as the buzzer sounds rivals the exuberant joy of a religious revival; watching their opponents do the same thing may be the equivalent of mourning. People describe trips to Citizens Bank Park as a pilgrimage to "the church of baseball." But Philadelphia is more than a place where sports are seen as a kind of religion. Religious groups have used sports to strengthen their identities and as a medium for the expression of their beliefs. And religious leaders have also come into conflict with sports traditions and values. This chapter will look at the many ways religion and sports intersect in Philadelphia.

Expressing Religious Identity Through Sports

It's no surprise that basketball played an important role for Jews and Catholics to make their mark in Philadelphia. This phenomenon is illustrated by two surprising teams: the South Philadelphia Hebrew Association (SPHAs) in the 1920s and the Mighty Macs Women's team of Immaculata College in the 1970s.

Basketball has religious connections from its beginnings; it was invented in 1891 by James Naismith when he was teaching physical education at the YMCA (Young Men's Christian Association) in Springfield, Massachusetts. His goal was to provide a "wholesome" indoor athletic experience for adolescents during the winter months, in keeping with the values of what is known as muscular Christianity, the nineteenth-century effort to blend the masculine values of sports with Christian piety. Naismith invented a game that requires little equipment and space, so it is ideally suited to the urban setting. Basketball was soon being played in churches, schools, and recreation centers by young men and women alike. (Senda Berenson Abbott, an instructor at Smith College and a Russian Jew, created the rules for the girls game in 1899.) Immigrant ethnic and religious minority communities gravitated toward the sport as a way of becoming socialized into the American environment.

Young Philadelphia Jewish immigrants found the game appealing. When three Jewish students at South Philadelphia High School (Ed Gottlieb, Harry Passon, and Hughie Black) excelled, they wanted to continue to play together after graduation. After losing their sponsorship at the YMHA (Young Men's Hebrew Association) for financial reasons, they became affiliated with the South

Philadelphia Hebrew Association, and the SPHAs were born. Throughout their existence (1918–1950) the SPHAs were among the best semi-professional teams in the United States, winning a half dozen national championships. Their players went on to become important figures in the world of basketball. Eddie Gottlieb, who coached the team after his playing years were over, was the owner of the Philadelphia Warriors (of the newly founded National Basketball Association) and a leading innovator in the NBA. Harry Litwack became the heralded coach of the Temple University basketball team and led that team to championships. Red Klotz became the owner of the Washington Generals, the team that toured with the Harlem Globetrotters.

As a traveling team, the SPHAs faced much anti-Semitism from fans in other cities, especially during the Depression. In spite or because of this they wore their Jewish identities proudly. Their uniforms displayed the Hebrew letters for SPHAs (Shin, Pey, Hay, and Aleph) on the front and the word Hebrews (as Jews preferred to be called in those days) in English on the back. They countered the stereotype of the unathletic Jew, and served as role models and inspiration for Jewish youth. As was the custom in that era the games were followed by social dancing. One of the players (Gil Fitch) played saxophone and was the leader of the band. For young Jews these events afforded opportunities to socialize. Many Jewish Philadelphians claimed to have met their future spouses at a SPHAs game. In 2013, a Pennsylvania Historical Commission marker was erected at the Broadwood Hotel on North Broad Street where the SPHAs played for most of their history to commemorate these local heroes and their contribution to Philadelphia, basketball, and the local Jewish community.[1]

The Jewish young men who meshed their religious identities with basketball had counterparts in the Catholic world. Young Catholic women grew up in Philadelphia playing basketball—with their brothers at home, in recreation centers, Catholic Youth Organization clubs (after 1940), and in Catholic high schools. Ninety percent of Catholic youth in the Philadelphia area were educated in Catholic schools, and the high schools were sex-segregated, creating a comfortable environment in which girls' basketball flourished. The culture of competitive women's basketball was deeply rooted in Catholic life in Philadelphia. The best players went on to play at Immaculata, a Catholic women's college run by the Immaculate Heart Sisters located in nearby Malvern, Pennsylvania. The school's administrators, and especially Sister Mary of Lourdes McDevitt, the president from 1954–1972, were avid basketball fans, and welcomed and supported the game. No men were involved. The team had no priests as chaplains and the coaches and officials were all women. The coaches that revolutionized women's basketball at Immaculata, Jen Shillingford and Cathy Rush, were not even Catholic.

The story of the Mighty Macs is told by Julie Byrne in her book, *O God of Players*. Her thesis is that the experience of these young women (including retired Temple German Professor Margaret Devinney) challenges our notions that Catholic women were always submissive and repressed within the life of the Church, even in Philadelphia, one of the most conservative dioceses in the United States. These young women were not rebels or radicals, and almost all continued a life of faith in the Church, most as wives as mothers, some as nuns and Catholic educators. Byrne argues persuasively that looking at aspects of lived religion like this one gives us a more nuanced understanding of American Catholic life. As she puts it, "And a Catholic is a Catholic not only when she lights votive candles, but also when she plays basketball."[2]

Byrne shows that basketball at Immaculata was Catholic not only culturally but also religiously. She explains that sports, both for girls and boys in mid-twentieth century, are deeply connected to the Thomist values central to American Catholicism. Both men and women are obligated to perfect their immortal souls, and to do so necessitates perfecting the vessels (the human bodies) in which those souls are housed. The moral values that sport encourages—teamwork and leadership, discipline and perseverance—were also in keeping with Thomism, just as they were in sync with the values of muscular Christianity and the religion of sport. Chapter 4 of *O God of Players*, "Praying for the Team," takes a close look at how those beliefs were put into practice through ritual and is the subject of our case study. Byrne expresses an important hope for her book in her Acknowledgments: "If this project conveys just a glimpse of God's hand in these women's lives—and in my life—it fulfills a purpose."[3]

Evangelical Protestants also blend their Christian beliefs with sports. One Philadelphia hero who carried on this tradition was the Hall of Fame defensive end for the Philadelphia Eagles, Reggie White. White's passionate devotion to his religious faith earned him the nickname "the Minister of Defense." White devoted his life to his religious ministry after retirement, and became a controversial figure because of his outspoken antipathy to homosexuality and statements stereotyping racial groups.

Religion and Sports Controversies and Conflicts

Reggie White was not the only Philadelphia example of how religion and sports can generate controversy as well as affirming identity. In 2015, the Eagles brought another famous Christian athlete to Philadelphia, Tim Tebow. To commemorate the occasion, the Philadelphia Pretzel Factory created a "tebowing" pretzel, twisted to look like the signature Tebow pose, kneeling in prayer after a touchdown. Not everyone was moved by the gesture; another pretzel with a "no Tebow" symbol appeared a few days later.[4]

Another case illustrates how religion and sports don't always work together. Caroline Pla, a young girl from Doylestown (a Philadelphia suburb), came from a family of practicing Catholics and passionate football fans. Caroline enjoyed playing football with her brothers, and she was good at it. When she was five she joined a Pop Warner co-ed team and was always one of the star players. At age eleven Carolyn and her friends switched from the Pop Warner league to the local Catholic Youth Organization team. But in the middle of her second year of play Caroline was forced to quit because someone pointed out that the CYO Handbook expressly prohibited girls from playing contact sports with boys. Caroline and her family protested with letters to the Diocese and a change.org petition; Ellen DeGeneres signed the petition and featured Caroline on her TV show. Archbishop Chaput responded to the pressure by permitting Caroline to finish out the season and play the following year as well. But in 2015 when Caroline was no longer in the league the Archdiocese reversed their position and reaffirmed that in the future girls will not be allowed to play football in Philadelphia. Caroline has started another campaign and a new petition. In an opinion article in the *Philadelphia Inquirer* Caroline has made it clear that she was fighting not only for herself, but equality and opportunity for all Catholic girls who want to play co-ed football.[5] Caroline's fight raises important questions about what happens when secular and religious values clash and sports is the venue in which they are expressed.

Are Sports Philadelphia's True Religion?

To get back to where we started: Do sports count as religions? Is it fair to label the joy of rowing or the thrill of a basketball victory as religious? The answer to that question is probably determined by how you define religion. To some people, calling sports religion is, well, a sacrilege. Religions, from this perspective, are about believing in a transcendent power, and expressing that belief through acts of worship. The only phenomena worthy of being called religions are those systems that have been identified as such by scholars: Christianity, Judaism, Islam, Buddhism, Hinduism, and the many indigenous traditions of Africa, Asia, and Latin America. Sports are secular, this-worldly, and therefore the very antithesis of religion.

But some scholars of religion are less interested in limiting religion to those systems. They focus not on what religion is, but on what religion does. They are influenced by the theories of sociologist Émile Durkheim who saw religions as a system of beliefs and practices shared by a community. These scholars emphasize not only believing in and worshiping a higher power but are curious about how those beliefs manifest themselves in a broader range of practices (customs, rituals, stories, laws, ethics, and material culture) and how they create a sense of belonging to a community. What's interesting about religion is how it works in the world to engage human beings in their quest for meaningful lives.

They may also agree with theologian Paul Tillich that religion can be equated with an individual's "ultimate concerns." More and more today scholars are aware that, particularly in American culture, people may form their own personal religions rather than accept the exclusive authority of one recognized system. A growing number of people are identifying as "spiritual, not religious." Often that means that they feel free to pick and choose elements from various world religions to form their own religious practice rather than be limited to only one system. This understanding makes it possible to examine how sports can function like religion in people's lives even if sports are not religions per se.

Sports as Religion in Philadelphia: *Rocky*, Rowing, and the Phillies

Looking briefly at three examples of how sports serve as religion in the lives of Philadelphians (*Rocky*, rowing, and the Phillies) gives us an opportunity to apply this concept. Rocky Balboa may be a fictional character, but he has inspired millions to what could be called religious values including hard work, love, finding purpose in life, and trusting in a higher power. Rowing is a Philadelphia communal tradition that incorporates many religious practices including ritual, material culture, and a storied tradition. The Phillies create a religious community and a sense of belonging for the city of Philadelphia.

It's impossible to be a Philadelphian and not know the story of Rocky Balboa and the central role *Rocky* plays in Philadelphia folklore. The 1976 Oscar award-winning inspirational film starring Sylvester Stallone, not to mention the four sequels and a revival, *Creed*, have become synonymous with Philadelphia. *Rocky* not only connects to the storied history of boxing in the city including Joe Frazier (who makes a cameo appearance and has elements from his life portrayed in the first film), it also exemplifies Philadelphia's Catholic working-class community, their passions and dreams. The story of a boxer who uses discipline and training to go beyond his wildest dreams to succeed fits well into the belief system of the religion of Philadelphia—a city of hard work and hope. What makes *Rocky* even more "religious" beyond the mythic tale is that the character has inspired a series of rituals. The main one, running up what have come to be known as the "Rocky steps" at the Philadelphia Museum of Art is repeated daily by Philadelphians and tourists alike. Running the steps while humming the familiar theme song is an act of hope and exultation that people reenact on special (holy) occasions when they are needing inspiration in their lives. To commemorate the experience it is common to see people taking photographs with the statue of Rocky, a prop from the film that now sits proudly at the bottom of the Art Museum steps. Their trips may be seen as pilgrimages to a holy site.

Rowing may be best known in popular culture as the elite sport of the Winkelvoss twins of *Social Network* fame, but in Philadelphia rowing is at the heart of the city's culture and traditions since the building of the Fairmount Dam in 1821 turned the city's rolling Schuylkill River into a calm lake. The landscape features Boathouse Row, a collection of nineteenth-century buildings that house rowing clubs and their equipment. To highlight the beauty and history of the houses the city has been lighting them at night since 1979, and they remain a popular and venerated public attraction. Boathouse Row hosts five regattas (including the prestigious collegiate races, the Dad Vail) and is home to the boating clubs of three (Drexel, Penn, and LaSalle) of the six universities (Villanova, St. Joseph's and Temple) that have competitive rowing teams. Rowing is so central to university culture in the city that when Temple planned to eliminate its men's and women's crew teams in 2014 the outrage was so great that they had to reinstate them; the athletics director who came from Indiana did not understand that rowing was part of the religion of Philadelphia.

The Boathouses are all on Kelly Drive, named after champion rower John Kelly, Sr., a Philadelphia bricklayer who was denied the opportunity to compete internationally because he was a laborer and not a "gentleman." But Kelly proved his dominance by winning gold in the Antwerp Olympics in 1920, and passed the tradition on to his son, John B. Kelly, Jr., who became a Philadelphia city councilman and participated and medaled in subsequent Olympics. He also won the Henley Regatta from which his father had been excluded.

Thomas Eakins, Philadelphia's best known painter, captured the sanctity and tranquility of the sport in his well-known work, "The Biglin Brothers Racing" in 1872. As the painting suggests, rowing is an optimal site to experience the integration of mind and body in the present moment; a religious experience that is known as "flow," described by psychologist Mihaly Csikszentmihalyi in his groundbreaking work by the same title.[6]

Baseball has often been described as a religion; at least three serious books make convincing and passionate arguments about baseball's sacred qualities and how the "national pastime" functions as America's civil religion because of its rich connections to history, the pastoral setting, the absence of a clock, and its storied saints and sinners.[7] Whether or not you subscribe to that argument in general, it would have been difficult to convince anyone in Philadelphia in October 2008 that the Phillies winning the World Series was anything other than a sacred moment. As thousands turned out for the victory parade dressed in Phillies gear, paying homage to their heroes, a feeling of local pride and euphoria was the dominant emotion. And as the team slid from glory to last place, the city, too, is experiencing a sense of loss or what commentator Frank Fitzpatrick has described as "a spiritually arid summer for Philadelphians." He argues that "sports can provide a municipal safety net. When we feel encouraged about our teams, we feel encouraged about ourselves and the places where we live. Life is better."[8]

Whether or not you subscribe to the religion of baseball, have experienced flow while rowing or the exhilaration of climbing the Rocky steps and thrusting your arms high in the air; even if you don't care about Tim Tebow or Reggie White, or share the passion of Caroline Pla for girls' football; whether or not the SPHAs or Mighty Macs evoke civic pride or religious belonging, it is hard not to recognize that the connections between sports and religion are deeply rooted and richly intertwined in Philadelphia.

Notes

1. To learn more about the SPHAs you may want to read Douglas Stark's *The SPHAs: The Life and Times of Basketball's Greatest Jewish Team* (Temple University Press, 2011).
2. Julie Byrne, *O God of Players: The Story of the Immaculata Mighty Macs* (Columbia University Press, 2003) 11.
3. This section on the Mighty Macs is adapted from my book, *Religion and Sports: An Introduction and Case Studies* (Columbia University Press, 2015).
4. http://www.sbnation.com/lookit/2015/4/23/8482133/tim-tebow-pretzel-war-this-is-a-good-use-of-time-and-dough (accessed May 17, 2015).
5. Caroline Pla, "Let Girls Play Football," *Philadelphia Inquirer*, May 3, 2015.
6. Mihaly Csikszentmihalyi, *Flow: The Psychology of Optimal Experience* (Harper & Row, 1990).
7. See David Chidester, *Authentic Fakes: Religion and American Popular Culture* (University of California Press, 2005); Joseph Price, *Rounding the Bases: Baseball and Religion in America* (Mercer University Press, 2006) and John Edward Sexton, Thomas Oliphant, and Peter J. Schwartz, *Baseball as a Road to God: Seeing Beyond the Game* (Gotham Books, 2013).
8. Frank Fitzpatrick, "A Wasted Summer Can Depress a City," *Philadelphia Inquirer*, May 17, 2015.

Suggested Readings

Julie Byrne, "Praying for the Team" in *O God of Players: The Story of the Immaculata Mighty Macs* (New York: Columbia University Press, 2003): 113-141.

David Chidester, "Church of Baseball, the Fetish of Coca-Cola, and the Potlatch of Rock 'n' Roll" in *Journal of the American Academy of Religion*, 64, no. 4 (Winter 1996): 743–765.

Discussion Questions:

1. Byrne describes how the Mighty Macs reacted to a loss against Queens College (113–114). What was Catholic about their understanding of their loss? Do you imagine someone from another religious tradition would interpret a sporting loss similarly or differently?
2. According to Byrne, what sort of rituals did the team engage in? Why were these rituals important? Were they distinctly Catholic or did they have things in common with other game rituals that an athlete from another religious tradition (or no religious tradition) might engage in?
3. According to Byrne, some players worried about praying to God for a "win." Do you think it is appropriate or inappropriate to pray for the outcome of a sporting event? What about at a public school?
4. Since women's sports had only become popular in the years after Title IX (1974), do you think it was significant for these women that their school took a religious approach to basketball? What do you imagine it meant to these women to be told that God cared about women's basketball?

Section 9

Religion and Civil Rights

Arrival at the Advocate

Paul M. Washington with David McI. Gracie

When I first drove Christine through the neighborhood of the Advocate, around 18th and Diamond Streets, she wept. "Is this where we are going to live?" she asked.

"Yes, this is where we are going to live," I said.

"Paul, there's not even a blade of grass between the concrete slabs," she said through her tears.

But within a few days the tears were dry and her attitude had changed remarkably. Saturday shopping in the neighborhood began the change. Christine found the people to be up-front, honest, warm, and unpretentious. The members of the congregation received us warmly, too, and our children seemed to fit in well at the neighborhood schools.

In those days Philadelphia Police Commissioner Orlando Gibbons had nicknamed North Philadelphia "the Jungle." That name reflected racial prejudice and fear. There was reason for fear because of the explosive combination of social pressures that racism had created here. There was poverty, joblessness, broken homes, overcrowding, and landlord neglect. But there were then, just as there are today, proud blocks with well-tended row houses, churches full on Sunday morning and active in good works during the week, and neighbors who looked out for neighbors. Perhaps North Philadelphia, figuratively speaking, was a jungle. It was indeed a tangled mass of all sorts and conditions of people. It contained every ingredient necessary to make a world.

I began my ministry at the Advocate by taking stock of the relationship between the church and the community. There was a gap to be overcome and we would all have to play a part in overcoming it. I decided that the rectory where we lived, right next door to the church, should have an open-door policy. It was our family home, but no one who needed to see me was going to be turned away from it.

I had heard so many stories of how the poor were treated by welfare agencies and others that were supposed to give services to people in need. So often the needy were treated almost like trash, blamed for being poor, dehumanized, and always kept waiting, waiting. Few realize that if the "haves" are to have, there must be the "have nots." The rich are rich at the expense of the poor. Poverty in our society is systemic.

I decided to give myself—my soul, my time, my resources—to everyone who came to see me. Every person was Christ: "Inasmuch as you have done it unto

---

one of the least of these," Jesus said, "you have done it unto me." So I instructed my family: "When someone rings the doorbell and asks to see me, don't come to me and describe him—clean or dirty, drunk or sober, white or black. Just tell me, 'Someone is at the door to see you.'"

On my first Sunday at the Advocate, my text was not taken from the Bible. I instead quoted an inmate who was in my Bible class at Eastern State Penitentiary. "I searched for my God, but my God I could not see. I searched for my soul, but my soul eluded me. Then I searched for my brother and I found all three." I told the congregation the source of my quote: "This young man, named Isaac, is in prison, banished by a society that includes all of us, and this morning he is saying: 'I am Isaac your brother.'" The Advocate had to become a church that accepted all people as brothers and sisters, particularly the people of the community in the midst of which we sat.

I knew that the church buildings themselves hardly seemed welcoming to those who lived around them. The church proper was such an imposing structure that when our family first entered the huge sanctuary and stood staring up at the one hundred-foot ceiling, Kemah got frightened. "I'm scared, Daddy. This is spooky!" he said. "I want to get out of here."

I was at war with this beautiful church from the beginning. I resented the fact that most people thought of it simply as big buildings that had little real relevance to their surroundings. The church complex had not one but five very big buildings. The church itself looked like a cathedral. The Philadelphia Historical Commission has described it as "the finest specimen of French Gothic architecture in America, a copy, in reduced proportions and with some changes, of the Cathedral of Amiens, France." It had taken seven years to construct (1890–97), at a time when wealthy merchants and professional people lived in North Philadelphia. It is 165 feet in length and reaches 165 feet to its topmost tower, above which stands a magnificent copper statue of the archangel Gabriel sounding his horn. The building can easily hold 1,000 worshippers and in the days of its founder, George W. South (it is the George W. South Memorial Church of the Advocate), it did. I was told by the daughter of the Advocate's second rector how on Sunday evenings there was standing room only in those days.

When I arrived, there were some six hundred members on the rolls. My first Holy Week services were my high-water mark in terms of attendance: 450 on Palm Sunday, five hundred on Easter Day. Of these members, only about one hundred were white, but I was the first black priest ever to serve as rector at the Advocate and I had to feel my way.

It happened that the first pastoral visit I made was to an elderly white parishioner in a hospital. I was uncertain about how she would receive her new pastor, but all went very well. As I was praying with her, she took my hand and tears came to her eyes. I was so impressed that I wrote to Bishop Armstrong to tell him there could not have been a better experience to show me that white people could receive the ministrations of the church from a Negro priest.

If my race was not an issue for the parishioners, my community advocacy would be. The membership of the church was fairly typical for an Episcopal Church at that time: teachers, doctors, city and social workers, and others with "positions." Of course, there were some with just "jobs." It was a fairly class-conscious group of people and they had no great desire to be involved in controversy of any kind. Over the years many would leave because they disagreed with the new course of ministry at the Advocate or simply because they were moving into neighborhoods like Mount Airy and Germantown, where black professionals had become able to purchase some of the fine old homes in neighborhoods some distance from North Philadelphia.

In the congregation there was a group of accomplished bridge players. They participated in tournaments, and every week they played in each other's homes. I recall a bridge tournament at the church on a day when a group had gathered to board a bus for some civil rights demonstration. I did not accompany the demonstrators but said a prayer on the bus before they left. A young man on the bus said to me sarcastically, "You are sending us to the front lines with a prayer, but you will remain here with your real flock—the bridge players." I never forgot that.

At the time when I arrived, the great Selective Patronage Campaign was underway. It was led by a group known as the Four Hundred Negro Ministers, who had been organized by the Rev. Leon Sullivan of Zion Baptist Church. The campaign was a boycott of particular businesses until they agreed to hire and promote more black men and women. The boycott targets were announced from the pulpit by the participating ministers, who had received letters naming the business to be boycotted. One such letter said simply: "Please announce to your congregation that we are not to buy the products of the Tasty Baking Company [one of the major targets] until they agree to hire more Negroes." Those pulpit announcements were very effective, and it did not take long for Tasty Baking or other companies to agree to talk with the leadership group of Negro ministers and with Rev. Sullivan. When I read such an announcement from the pulpit of the Advocate, I was called aside by one of the white vestrymen and told: "We never talk about race in this church."

As a pilot parish in urban ministry, subsidized by the diocese, the Advocate had programs and activities that I had not expected to see. There was a day care center; a community center, open in the evenings for young people; a daily Vacation Bible School for the first two weeks in July, and a summer day camp from mid-July to the end of August. The Advocate had a staff of thirteen for its programs: six in the day care center, five for the community center, and two caretakers. In addition, I had the services of a curate, a full-time secretary, and, of course, the church organist. In all, counting me, we were seventeen.

For some reason, I never felt overawed or inadequate for the very complex and challenging ministry that was now under my direction. But I shall never forget the assistance I received from the curate who was in place when I went there—Jesse Anderson, Jr., now the rector of St. Thomas African Episcopal Church in Philadelphia, the church served then by his father, Jesse Anderson, Sr. Jesse, Jr., had been responsible for starting some of the programs now underway at the Advocate. He introduced me to the staff and labeled about a dozen keys to the Advocate's many doors for my use.

I needed all the help I could get in administering church and community center activities, especially in dealing with the clashes among the various groups that used our facilities. I had hoped for a little time to get acquainted with all the activities before having to deal with conflicts, but that luxury was denied me.

There were two groups using the gymnasium, boys playing basketball and Theater XIV, a very serious and sophisticated group of men and women who regularly presented top-notch plays. The boys resented the theater company using "their" space and preventing them from playing ball. To harass them and drive them out, the boys would identify the cars of the actors and actresses and let the air out of their tires. This was a problem waiting to he solved on my arrival. Fortunately, we had another unused space, an auxiliary chapel. I moved the pews from the chapel into the church proper and gave the chapel over to Theater XIV.

Such problems were interminable. I invited an Alcoholics Anonymous group to hold their meetings at the church a few years after I arrived. They began to meet in the parish hall, but their meetings were invaded by people involved in the Black Unity movement, who preached to them about the need for racial unity and urged them to meet with the Black Unity group upstairs. I had to find another church to provide space for the AA group.

Then there were "the church people" who resented "those other groups" taking over "their space." The Women's Auxiliary had a room that was exclusively for their use, but soon "those outside people" began to congregate there. This conflict was never really resolved, but as time went on a few on the inside began to realize that the outsiders were their raison d'etre. I preached to them constantly that the diocese was not giving its substantial grants to the Advocate just for Sunday services or for church people to do "churchy" things. Without the "outsiders" they could not exist as a church. At the same time, the "outsiders," the community people, were often critical of the church people. I had to get them to understand that were it not for the church people, they would not have a church in which to meet. It was a perfect example of what Episcopalians called in those days MRI, mutual responsibility and interdependence in the Body of Christ.

The Diocese felt proud to have a church with a ministry like ours. The diocesan *Church News* boasted that "that 'rumble' or knifing that you did not read about on 18th Street" may have been due to the outreach ministry that touched and influenced the Advocate neighborhood. That same article quoted me explaining our ministry: "Our job is one of constantly revealing to those who feel they are the unwanted outcasts of God's family that God does care and that his acts of redemption were for all."

I did not come to the Advocate with an agenda for social change. I came to be a pastor and, as always, I tried to listen and learn from the people who turned to me for help. My best teacher was a woman named Jackie, who one day came to my office literally crying for help.

She was extremely distraught, and as she sat in my office crying, I saw in her an incarnation of all the ills of North Philadelphia and of the inner city. She was a product of a home for delinquent girls. She had had seven children, all by different fathers, some of them white. The children had all been placed in foster homes by the Department of Human Services. At that point Jackie had been evicted, and she was hungry.

As I listened to her, I asked God, What will I say to this woman that will soothe her, comfort and help her? I soon stopped listening to her and tried to "prepare my response." Finally her story ended and I began telling her the story of God's love, for even the sparrow that falls to the ground. As I spoke I found that she was not comforted but was becoming aggravated and agitated.

Like a bolt of lightning, she leapt from her seat and exploded before my face. "Listen, mister, you can talk about God's love because obviously he loves you. You live in that big, comfortable house next door, you have food for your children, and you are pastor of this big church. Now you just show me how God loves me!!"

There it was. "Go and *show* John again those things which you hear and see" (Matthew 11:4). "The Word became *flesh*" (John 1:14). At that moment I knew that I had to *show* Jackie how God loved her. The Advocate had to be an incarnation of the Word. I knew from that moment that we had to act out God's love, and it began right there. Christine and I gave her a room in the rectory and she stayed with us until she found work. To this day, twenty-nine years later, she calls at least once a year, thanking me for helping to put her on her feet.

Shortly after my encounter with Jackie, I added to the sign on the church's lawn at the corner of 18th and Diamond, "This church lives the Gospel." For God does not appear in words, but in action. "The Word became flesh."

Into the Streets

PAUL M. WASHINGTON

On October 29, 1963, a riot broke out on Susquehanna Avenue, a block from Diamond Street, where the Advocate was located. I went to the scene to see what was happening. I was simply walking up and down dressed in my clerical attire. And people looked at me and wanted to know: Preacher, what are you doin' here? And it was a sort of joke: I wasn't supposed to be there among "the rioters."

It was lucky for one white motorist that I was there. He had found himself surrounded by hundreds of agitated people on the avenue at the height of the disturbance and was unable to move his car. I called to the crowd, "Open up and let the man get by!" They promptly responded, because they really had no interest in the car and its driver. When I got home I heard that man calling in on Frank Ford's radio talk show to tell how some Negro minister had saved his life from an angry mob. I smiled to think that I was regarded as some kind of hero for simply directing traffic. Can it be that the guilty fear when no man threatens?

More important, because I got out on the streets, I was able to piece together what had really happened to spark the riot. A twenty-four-year-old named Willie Philyaw, Jr., had been shot and killed by police after he allegedly stole a watch from a drugstore. The police said that he had lunged at them with a knife. The district attorney accepted the police account and ruled the killing a justifiable homicide. But from what I learned from eyewitnesses, the police were clearly in the wrong.

Willie was lame. He certainly couldn't run. A policeman must have told him to halt, but he kept hobbling away. Another man who was crossing the street at the time walked between Willie and the policeman. At the moment the officer shot, this man threw up his hand, and the bullet went through his hand into Willie's body. If a man could walk between the policeman and his target, how could the policeman have been in imminent danger of being knifed?

The public statements I made about this incident brought me to the attention of Mayor James H. J. Tate, who invited me to become a member of the Commission on Human Relations of the

City of Philadelphia. I joined the commission in January, 1964, and served until 1971. Sadie Alexander was the chairperson when I joined, and a very strong leader. It was Sadie Alexander who, along with the mayor, summoned me home from a vacation in August, 1964, when a much larger-scale riot broke out on Columbia Avenue (just four blocks south of Diamond Street).

This riot, too, was sparked by a confrontation between police and residents of North

Philadelphia. It began with the arrest of a woman named Odessa Bradford for a traffic violation. A fight with police following her arrest led to large-scale looting and attacks on property on Columbia Avenue. Rumors fed the riot, rumors that the police had killed Odessa and others.

When it was over, the damage was calculated at $3 million, 600 people had been arrested, and nearly 340 had been injured, including 100 police officers. There had been one death, not of Odessa Bradford but of one Robert Green. The newspaper account gave only his name and address and his age, twenty-one, reporting that Green "was shot Sunday night after he attacked an officer with a knife, police said."

In the aftermath, a period of great tension, the Advocate became the scene of many community meetings. Our various programs continued, even as the church became a crossroads where police patrolling the neighborhood could drop in for a cup of coffee and, while they were there, watch rehearsals of the Arthur Hall Dance Troupe. I tried to be a constant presence at the church and in the neighborhood during those troubled days. I joined with other clergy and community leaders in presenting to the city administration a twelve-point plan for easing the tensions in North Philadelphia. We called for job creation, the enforcement of housing codes, the rehabilitation of homes. "Repression through law enforcement is not enough," we said.

Not only was law enforcement not enough, but the police themselves had to be checked. Too often they behaved like an army of occupation and not a protective force. One of the direct action groups that used the Advocate as a base attempted to curb police brutality and illegal arrests by acting as citizen observers. On Friday and Saturday evenings these volunteer members of "Operation Alert" would gather in the parish house to listen to radios that picked up the police band. When they heard of arrests being made, they rushed to the scene in automobiles to observe. It did not take the police long to realize how closely they were being watched. The possession of police band radios by the general public was made illegal in Philadelphia by action of the City Council.

The year of the Columbia Avenue riot, 1964, was also the year when Bishop Armstrong died and a new bishop took his place. The Rt. Rev. Robert L. DeWitt came from Michigan, where for years he had served as a priest to the very wealthy in Bloomfield Hills, a suburb of the Motor City. That wouldn't seem to qualify him for leadership in Philadelphia in such troubled times, but he surprised us all by his willingness to learn. Here's how he describes his early days in our diocese:

> The first day I was on the job as bishop coadjutor of the diocese, several of our clergy were in jail, arrested because they had been involved in demonstrations [for racial desegregation] in that racial powder keg known as Chester, Pennsylvania. In the days, months and years that followed, I was to learn the authenticity of the title of the landmark book by Gunnar Myrdal on racism in America, *An American Dilemma.* Race riots more than a decade earlier in Detroit had been for me a baptism into a consciousness of racism. But Philadelphia was to be my confirmation.[1]

The bishop and I became very close. He came to regard me as one of his instructors in that "consciousness of racism." Bishop DeWitt chose the Church of the Advocate as the site for his service of installation on October 31, 1964. Since the diocese at that time had no cathedral church, the bishop was free to choose where major celebrations were to take place. Choosing the Advocate sent a message that this bishop intended to give priority to issues of racial justice and to the needs of the poor. He selected as preacher for the occasion someone who could put that message into words, Paul Moore, then Suffragan Bishop of Washington, D.C., and well known throughout the Episcopal Church as a champion of civil rights.

The installation service began with a great outdoor procession led by the cadet band and choir from the Valley Forge Military Academy and including eight other Episcopal bishops along with over a hundred vested clergy. What Bishop Moore said in his sermon echoed through the church and was read by church members throughout the Delaware Valley when excerpted in the *Evening Bulletin:*

"Encircling this church are mile after mile of houses in which Negroes are caught in the pressures of ghetto life. Into these streets and houses we must go together, not in a spirit of fear, but in the apostolic spirit of power and love . . . A bishop is without color. When his Negro people are oppressed, so is he, and their fight for freedom is his."

Deeds followed words when, in 1965, Bishop DeWitt gave his backing to demonstrations calling for the racial integration of Girard College in North Philadelphia. The Girard College struggle has been called Philadelphia's Selma, and the bishop would later say that it provided "the most contentious focus the racial issue had in my years in Philadelphia."

Girard College, in reality an elementary- and secondary-level boarding school, was founded in 1848 on what was then forty-three acres of farmland but by 1965 was in the center of black North Philadelphia, entirely surrounded by a ten-foot-high stone wall. The founder was Stephen Girard, one of America's richest men, who has been described as "a one-eyed sea captain, merchant, and opium trader." He stated in his will that the school was to enroll "poor, white, male orphans." The issue in the 1960s was whether such racial discrimination could be tolerated any longer.

From May 1 (Law Day) to December 17, 1965, there were daily demonstrations outside the massive Girard College wall, a structure that became a perfect symbol of continuing segregation and exclusion in our city. Cecil B. Moore, the flamboyant, cigar-smoking criminal lawyer who was president of the Philadelphia Branch of the NAACP, led the marches, assisted chiefly by young people like "Freedom George," "Freedom Smitty," "Freedom Frank," Mary Richardson, Dwight Campbell, and a long list of others whom I came to know and love over the years. A North Philadelphia street gang called the Moroccos also participated, delighting in running along the wall, shouting that they would go over it. Philadelphia police responded brutally at times, on one occasion knocking out Freedom George's front teeth.

But the clergy were present, too, often organized for picket duty by the Rev. Layton Zimmer, who was on Bishop DeWitt's staff as urban missioner. America's best-known clergyman, the Rev. Martin Luther King, Jr., put in an appearance in August, even though Cecil Moore had told him to stay out of town. What need did Cecil or "Cecil's people" have of outside assistance? Moore relented and joined King on a flat-bed truck when he proclaimed, as only Martin Luther King could, that the walls of segregation would come tumbling down.

I took my turn in the marches and pickets, and was proud indeed of my bishop, who resisted great opposition from white clergy and laity who thought that "wills are sacred and inviolable." In 1968 the Supreme Court of the United States found otherwise. The justices ruled against racial discrimination at the school and made it possible for black orphan boys to attend.

When the issue was moved off the streets and into the courts in December, 1965, Bishop DeWitt personally led a service of thanksgiving at the wall.

The bishop felt there was only one moral stand to take. "The issue involved 'our people,'" he said. By that he meant the 18,000 black members of the Diocese of Pennsylvania. But, more than that, he was making a claim of justice, "a claim the church could only ignore at the cost of surrendering its vocation, relinquishing its claim to be the people of God." He paid a price for this stand in the years that followed, in terms of loss of membership in the diocese and reduced giving in support of its programs.

For me, December 17 did not mark the end of the struggle to get Negro fatherless boys into Girard College. The governor of Pennsylvania had appointed William Coleman as a special assistant attorney general for the purpose of preparing a complaint to present in court on behalf of the excluded boys. People to be named as plaintiffs were needed, so when a mother came to tell me she wanted to enroll her two fatherless sons in Girard College, I was advised to bring her to see Mr. Coleman's assistant, a young attorney named Thomas Gilhool, at the offices of the Dilworth, Paxson law firm in downtown Philadelphia. Those offices were on the sixteenth floor of the Fidelity Bank Building.

On the appointed day, I took the mother to Broad and Walnut, where we entered the lobby and stood with others waiting for the elevator. As the doors opened and people stepped in, I nudged her arm and said, "Well, we're almost there." She did not move. Again, I spoke, "This is our elevator." She was frozen, and with eyes cast down to the floor, she said, "I'm afraid of elevators." To which I replied, "Well, it's only sixteen floors, and I can use the exercise." This turned out to be the most arduous segment of the march. Mr. Gilhool received us graciously, and when the last dot was in place, we marched downhill to the first floor, then returned to North Philadelphia. I thought it was a fitting and satisfying end to a long, painful, and at times violent struggle.

Meanwhile, resentments within the diocese toward the bishop continued to be voiced. One expression of opposition came from a secretive lay group that called itself "The Voice from the Catacombs." These disgruntled church members distributed thousands of mimeographed leaflets outside Episcopal churches, handing them to parishioners leaving Sunday services or placing them under automobile windshield wipers. The first set, distributed on June 13, raised concerns about Fr. Zimmer's activities at the Girard Wall as well as concerns about the sanctity of wills. "If the will of Stephen Girard can be broken, the next may be your own," they warned.

Another leaflet asked: "Do you want your money to support the Church of the Advocate?" These leaflets gave no name or phone number, just the name of the group and a post office box. I wrote to the group at their post office number, asking them to identify themselves. "Let us walk together," I asked, "pray together, break bread together." I received no reply.

When complaints came to Church House about my activities, as they often did, Bishop DeWitt would simply say: "He is the rector of a parish, and bishops don't tell rectors what to do." The Advocate was in reality an aided congregation, not a self-supporting parish, so the bishop could very well have told me what to do. He chose instead to honor the leadership that I was providing and to accept as an imperative that we had the right of self-determination.

There were other signs of support from the church. I was elected to serve as a deputy representing our diocese at the General Convention of the Episcopal Church in 1964 and would be almost routinely reelected in succeeding years. This led to my being appointed to a number of committees and commissions at the national level of the church, while in the broader community of Philadelphia over the years I received appointments to the Board of Trustees of Philadelphia Community College and other boards of civic groups and foundations.

Becoming a part of such prestigious bodies in the church and in society, one may be perceived to be an extraordinary person. There is a temptation to be proud of reaching "extraordinary" status, but few realize how deadly and dehumanizing it can be to abandon our given identity and take on the identity of the institutions with which we are affiliated. I have never abandoned the place where God put me nor the personality God chose to give me. Therefore, no matter where I sat, or with whom I sat, everyone was made to know that there was a North Philadelphian in their midst, someone who represented the oppressed.

Mattie Humphrey, who was working then as youth coordinator for the Philadelphia Council for Community Advancement, called me "the legitimizer" for a lot that was going on in the community. Aurelia Waters, educational director for a self-help center at 15th and Diamond, said she could use my name to open doors. That was my goal, that the work that Aurelia and Mattie and so many others were undertaking should go forward. I tried to be in the boardrooms for them and stay in the streets with them, too.

Notes

1. Robert L. DeWitt, "1964–1974: Decade of Crises in a Stormy See," *The Witness*, July, 1984): 6.

When "God in a Body" Lived in Philadelphia: Father Divine and His Peace Mission in the City of Brotherly Love

Leonard Norman Primiano

The streets of any large American city are marked by a number of easily observed structures associated with religious institutions. Not limited to architecture designed for worship—such as churches, synagogues, mosques, and temples—there are also a number of buildings linked to social, educational, and pastoral ministries. In a metropolis like Philadelphia, Pennsylvania, one can see Islamic schools, Catholic hospitals, Young Men's Christian Associations (YMCAs), Jewish Community Centers, Salvation Army recreation centers, Christian Science Reading Rooms, and nondenominational Christian soup kitchens. A drive or walk up the major North-South traffic artery in the city, Broad Street, presents an opportunity to discover many such structures. Not too many blocks south of the Temple University campus, in this North Broad Street area, an imposing structure at Broad and Ridge Avenue is a local landmark. This enormous building is crowned with a striking sign on its roof identifying it as the "Divine Lorraine Hotel." Currently under restoration and restructuring by a private developer for residential and restaurant use, this restructuring will mark the third incarnation of this enormous space. Built in the late nineteenth century as a hotel and residence for nouveau-riche Philadelphians, during the latter half of the twentieth century the Lorraine Hotel began its second embodiment as a distinctive site of social and racial empowerment within the fabric of religious Philadelphia. Reopened in the early 1940s as the "Divine Lorraine Hotel," it was the first integrated lodging of quality in a city where African Americans could not reserve or reside in a room in a fine hotel where, in some cases, they could not even walk through the front door of the building. This "Divine Lorraine" served all people and was a hospitality business owned, administered, and worked by the followers of one of Philadelphia's more distinctive religious communities: the Peace Mission Movement of the Reverend Major Jealous Divine, better known as "Father Divine." While the group did not originate in Pennsylvania, the city of Brotherly Love became the headquarters for Father Divine and his indigenous American Church in the 1940s after he moved his official residence from Harlem in Manhattan where it had been centered since the 1920s. Who Father Divine was, his legacy, and his unique still-practiced system of belief and living are all subjects for consideration in this chapter which invites readers to enter into a conversation with this distinctive, ever resourceful and creative, social justice-oriented and female-dominated empowerment movement.

Father Divine's Peace Mission Movement has been called by some individuals—scholars and nonscholars alike—a "sect." Within American religious studies, especially the sociology of religion, the designation sect refers to a formal structured group of believers that in Christianity are often distinguished from more established Christian divisions known as "denominations." The Peace Mission has also been described by some critics and scholars as a "cult," a more negative expression for a religious community under the domination and influence of a charismatic religious leader whose followers, it is said, show little ability to make clear personal religious judgments for themselves. Terms such as sect and cult have been useful for scholarly writing or teaching about such groups because they offer criteria and terminology that differentiates certain religious communities and structured units of believers from others. Such expressions, however, are not appreciated or used within the religious movements themselves. Their members find such labels as "sect" or "cult" derogatory and degrading.

One person's cult, therefore, is another's religion. When studying the belief system of any religion, it is challenging but important to contextualize religious movements, but at the same time respect their wishes about how they would like to be represented in the classroom or on the printed page. Many believers feel that their religious leader has a unique revelation that is credible, powerful, and worth dedicating one's life to uphold. "Church" or "movement" are preferable terms of reference by scholars and students. It is in this spirit of respect that this chapter discusses Peace Mission and its contributions to American religion and religion in Philadelphia.

Who then was Father Divine? The Reverend M. J. Divine (Major Jealous, ?–1965) was an African American religious leader who began his communitarian religion in Sayville, New York, in 1919. He was a charismatic minister, an influential preacher, a religious entrepreneur, and—for his followers—an incarnation of God on Earth. His origins are a matter of historical speculation. Jill Watts in her 1992 biographical study theorizes that he was born in Baltimore, and that he could have been influenced by a variety of religious traditions during his childhood: his mother's Catholicism; neighborhood Methodism; and the Black storefront churches around him are just three of many possibilities. Another theory is that he was present, at some point between 1906 and 1915, during the "Azusa Street Revival" in Los Angeles, which was the set of religious services that sparked the Pentecostal Christian Movement within American Protestantism. The spirited excitement found in later Peace Mission services could certainly bear a kinship to such Christian revivalist enthusiasm. A final religious influence on Father Divine's thinking and development was a nineteenth-century American movement known as "New Thought." Itself influenced by Transcendentalism and ideas from Eastern religions, New Thought stressed a monistic or single reality and questioned as spiritually divisive dualities that one unconsciously accepts in Western culture, such as good/evil, body/soul, and spiritual/material. One's life in New Thought was to be led in conjunction with the understanding that any negative impulse or even negative thought might somehow create an imbalance between self and the God principle which was the only true reality. Such imbalances led to problems in life from physical illness to emotional instability to economic hardship. In nineteenth-century America, religions including Mary Baker Eddy's Christian Science and the Unity School of Christianity emerged from New Thought, further expressing and elaborating these convictions. Many scholars have noted that Father Divine's religious ideas emerged or were influenced by New Thought generally, and Christian Science and the Unity School of Christianity, in particular.

As Father Divine articulated his theological outlook through the 1930s, Peace Mission followers were paradoxically encouraged to believe in the impersonal principle of Father Divine's deity, while celebrating the experience of seeing God in a particular personal human form. It was the main focus of their belief to maintain a harmonious relationship with the principle of God. That relationship was best sustained through a life of celibacy, abstinence from alcoholic beverages, smoking, swearing, and the preservation of what was known as the "International Modesty Code" within the Movement. Essentially, one best respected what Father called the "divine mind substance" by living a life of respectability, economy, hard work, cleanliness, and self-empowerment.

Father Divine took these principles of balanced consciousness and applied them to the relationship of the individual to government in the 1930s (the years following the Great Depression.) By this time he was a well-established religious figure in Harlem in New York City, as well as an economic and political leader. His "Righteous Government Platform" promulgated in 1936 requested a number of reforms by government officials to accomplish what he interpreted to be the ideals of the American Constitution and its Bill of Rights. In this period, racism in the United States was institutionalized by Jim Crow laws in both the North and the South; thus, Father Divine's insistence on racial and social equality, as well as an end to segregation and lynching, branded him in the eyes of some critics as a dangerous instigator of societal change, as well as a communist or socialist. Such accusations caught the attention of J. Edgar Hoover and the FBI, which maintained an active file on the religious leader. The only description which Father Divine and his followers—many of whom were women and many, but not all, of whom were African American—proudly maintained was that they were "radical and fanatical" about their spirituality, their practice, and their insistence on equality and justice in their everyday lives.

In the Peace Mission, as with so many other belief systems, the religious became intertwined with the personal. To demonstrate what he taught his followers about racial equality, "dark" and "light complected" [sic] followers would room together, and often even slept in the same beds together (words representing race such as white and black are not used within Peace Mission linguistic codes). Men and women lived on completely separate floors and would not sit together while dining, or even ride in the same automobiles to Peace Mission functions. When you lived in Peace Mission environments, your everyday speech was "evangelized," so, for example, one no longer greeted individuals with that word "Hello," which included the negative reference to the home of the "d-v-l," but instead addressed others with the positive statement of "Peace!" Some followers lived "inside" the Peace Mission meaning they worked directly for the Mission in its properties and for its various racially integrated enterprises: hotel work, domestic agency administration, maid service, tax and typing preparation, grocery store establishments, barbershop management, and dry cleaning businesses. Other followers lived "outside" the Peace Mission meaning they worked traditional jobs, but contributed much of their pay to the Mission and spent as much time as possible on weekends, if they lived close to where Father resided, at various services and liturgies.

Father Divine taught that personal and community empowerment was intimately related to economic stability and prescribed wise use of his congregation's massed capital. When Father Divine moved to Philadelphia in the 1940s, many members of his New York Church moved along with him. They collectively brought their financial resources together to purchase buildings throughout Center City. Such real estate entrepreneurship was especially prominent in North Philadelphia around the Temple University campus where the followers purchased inexpensive, older—often Victorian—buildings (not especially prized from the 1930s though the 1970s due to their size and the expense to heat) for use as hotels, residences, grocery stores, garages, and other community functions. The Peace Mission purchased a mansion at Sixteenth and Oxford Streets—once owned by the Disston Saw Manufacturing family—for use as a residence and worship space; a next-door manufacturing building was refurbished as a place to edit and publish the Movement's newspaper, *The New Day*; and an elaborate Victorian mansion on 1430 North Broad Street functioned as a residence for foreign visitors and was christened "the International House." (The Disston Mansion and the International House remain under Peace Mission ownership as of 2016.)

The purchase of buildings to house and feed his followers and others was imperative to Father Divine's alternative economy, as was the establishment of businesses to put individuals to work. This plan for full satisfying employment was a crucial economic move at a time when many African Americans were out of work or labored for those who had no interest in their welfare. Father Divine's followers understood that Father Divine cared for them and would not abandon them, if they remained devoted to him. Father Divine taught them that this Earth right now in their lives was heaven, not some other reality that they needed to die to achieve and experience. He provided the abundance of heaven right here and right now by providing clean safe places to reside and an abundance of inexpensive food. The Peace Mission members helped actualize such abundance by saving their money, but never hoarding it. Father advised them to pay all of their bills in cash and never to pay for any product or service with credit or even a check. They were to make and sell goods of quality and for a fair price. They were not to invest in any sort of insurance for their lives, cars, or homes since they were to "trust in God" as their only insurance. They were never to go on welfare or accept government subsidies because God wanted all men and women to work, to be independent, and to be honest. They were never to accept tips and certainly never bribes. Father Divine asked for federal tax exemption on any property improvements and for legislation to end pollution and uncleanliness. He encouraged free trade and the abolishment of tariffs. He was against the death penalty, and, while pacifism was not a specific tenet of faith, Father Divine stressed the idea of peace and peaceful coexistence constantly.

The everyday lives of followers of Farther Divine balanced two components of their communitarian and celibate tradition: the formality of structured living and the celebration of the freedom of the spirit. All coworkers, for example, adhered to a formal administrative arrangement of the various Peace Mission churches and carried out set duties, whether managing a building's upkeep or cutting vegetables for a Banquet Service. In a Peace Mission hotel, all tasks involved with its operation were handled by Peace Mission followers from twenty-four- hour front desk managers to room maids and from elevator operators to boiler room mechanics. In the Peace Mission cafeterias, which dotted the landscape of Philadelphia until the 1970s with the last such enterprise in University City's Divine Tracy Hotel closing in 2000, the cooks, food preparers, cleaners, cashiers, business managers, and so on were all followers. Though some members maintained employment out of the Mission as nurses, teachers, secretaries, and so on, on Saturdays and Sundays they all spent as much time as they could "around the body of God" as they referred to being in the presence of Father Divine and working in various roles to feed, celebrate, and ritualize Father's message to his congregation about the contagious and positive nature of the "Divine Mind Substance."

After Father "voluntarily gave up his body" and passed out of this consciousness in 1965, his second wife, the "light-complected" Vancouver-born, and much younger Sweet Angel Divine, also known as the second "Mother Divine," took his place as the spiritual leader of the Movement (see Primiano 1999). At the time of their legal union, Father Divine was approximately sixty-eight years of age and Sweet Angel was twenty-one; the first Mother Divine, a dark-complected woman known as Peninnah, had died in the early 1940s. Their inter-racial, celibate, spiritual marriage had to be legalized in Washington, DC because marriages between African Americans and Caucasians were illegal in Philadelphia. Sweet Angel Divine eventually took Father's place as the living exemplar of her husband's ideals (See Mother Divine 1982). Of course, because Father was God, his presence never left the community. In fact, at the Peace Mission's sole liturgical celebration known as a Holy Communion Banquet Service—daily elaborate Eucharistic rituals which continue into the twenty-first century and are spiritualized dinners serving many courses of specially prepared dishes lasting at least three hours—Father Divine's place is always set and he is fed with vegetables, meats, and desserts carefully placed on his plate and then removed for later consumption.

Father Divine's Peace Mission Movement is an indigenous, intentional, celibate, utopian American religious community. It transformed the lives of many Philadelphians, as well as others in places as diverse as New York City, Los Angeles, Australia, Switzerland, England, and Panama. Under the second Mother Divine, the Mission has continued longer without Father's physical presence than it did with him. The membership, however, is presently in rapid decline with few new members. The Peace Mission like another celibate, utopian, communitarian religion founded in the United States—the Shakers of Maine—is facing the reality of extinction in the first half of the twenty-first century. Buildings that the Movement has kept in excellent condition are gradually being sold off, and members are dying after long, work-filled, but satisfying lives. Mother Divine and her followers have spent a great deal of effort to preserve Father Divine's spiritual legacy first by building a tomb for his body on the grounds of Woodmont, Father and Mother's country estate deemed the "Mount of the House of the Lord" in the Philadelphia suburb of Gladwyne. Other buildings which serve representational and preservationist functions were then added to the property including a visitor's center, and most recently a museum and library for the artifacts, papers, and publications of the Movement. Father Divine did not personally write books filled with his thoughts, but as a religion which celebrated oral expression, Father Divine had his sermons taped as soon as the technology was available and practical, and he had his band of secretaries write down his every word for future publication and preservation. The Father Divine Library is especially significant as a research center because it brings together all of this relevant material for those who wish to work on Father Divine's spirituality, societal significance, and cultural influence.

One of the most rewarding ways to study and learn about a religion is by being attentive to the past and present cultural life it has generated. Peace Mission's followers communicated the ideals of their system of belief through a series of dramatic and subtle expressions of personal and community artistry. Their unique vernacular architecture of intention (how they preserved buildings purchased for their unique religious purposes); their colorful use of flowers and floral imagery; their particular system of speech and word use; their effusive song culture; their rich work with photography and photographic arts; their potent styles of cleanliness and order representative of their own unique "Divine Style"; attention to these and other forms of Peace Mission expressive culture leads to a fuller understanding and appreciation of how Father Divine, the Mothers Divine, and their followers crafted the Peace Mission (see Primiano 2004, 2009, 2014). Father Divine's Peace Mission is truly one of the notable "practical" religious movements in a Quaker city resplendent with dynamic conventional and alternative religious communities.

Further Readings on the Peace Mission Movement

Divine, Mother. *The Peace Mission Movement.* (Philadelphia: Imperial Press, 1982).

Primiano, Leonard Norman. "Mother Divine," in *Encyclopedia of Women and World Religion*, ed. Serinity Young (New York: Macmillan Library Reference, 1999), vol. 2, 678–79.

Primiano, Leonard Norman. "Bringing Perfection in These Different Places: Father Divine's Vernacular Architecture of Intention." *Folklore*, vol. 115 (2004), 13–26.

Primiano, Leonard Norman. "'The Consciousness of God's Presence Will Keep You Well, Healthy, Happy, and Singing': The Tradition of Innovation in the Music of Father Divine's Peace Mission Movement," in *The New Black Gods: Arthur Huff Fauset and the Study of African American Religions*, ed. Edward E. Curtis IV and Danielle Brune Sigler, (Bloomington: Indiana University Press, 2009), 91–115.

Primiano, Leonard Norman. "'And as We Dine, We Sing and Praise God': Father and Mother Divine's Theology of Food," in *Religion, Food, and Eating in North America*, ed. Ben Zeller, Marie Dallam, Nora Rubel (New York: Columbia University Press, 2014), 42–67.

Watts, Jill. *God, Harlem U.S.A.: The Father Divine Story* (Berkeley: University of California Press, 1992).

MOVE

Richard Kent Evans

MOVE is a group founded in West Philadelphia in 1972. MOVE people are devoted to the teachings of MOVE's founder, John Africa, whom they considered divine, as recorded in a book called "The Guidelines of John Africa." MOVE was never a particularly large group. At its height, around forty people claimed to follow John Africa's teachings. Even fewer actually joined the group, which mostly involved living communally, wearing their hair naturally and uncombed, eating a raw foods diet, and adopting the surname Africa. In some ways, MOVE was similar to other Black Nationalist religious movements that emerged in the 1960s and 1970s such as the Muslim Mosque Inc., the American Rastafari movement, and the Five-Percent Nation. Like these other groups, MOVE rejected Christianity, including the Black Church, as a vehicle of oppression, looked toward the continent of Africa as a source of both political inspiration and religious imagery, and embraced a culture of self-reliance and physical discipline. MOVE and these other religious groups, while emerging from a centuries-old tradition of religious Black Nationalism, were a direct response to what they perceived as the failures of the Civil Rights Movement in the 1960s to elevate African Americans out of an oppressed social condition.

The 1970s was a tumultuous decade for many Americans. By the beginning of the decade, the Vietnam War had become a deeply divisive political issue. The hopefulness of the counterculture movements of the late 1960s had faded into resigned pessimism. This pessimism was confirmed in 1974 when President Richard Nixon resigned after being caught orchestrating a series of illegal activities including wiretapping, breaking and entering, and other abuses of power in an incident that became known as Watergate. To make matters worse, there was a sustained economic recession throughout much of the 1970s. In 1973, a war pitting Egypt and Syria against Israel led to the suspension of oil exports to the United States. Without oil imports, gas prices skyrocketed, supply of gasoline plummeted, and the American economy stopped growing. Manufacturing jobs, which had long supported America's middle class with comfortable lifestyles, became scarcer in the 1970s due to international competition. As a result, unemployment grew from previous levels, hovering between 5 and 10 percent throughout the decade. Even those with jobs suffered as inflation rose to over 20 percent by the end of the 1970s. In a speech given in 1979, President Jimmy Carter, reflecting on the last decade of American history, noted a "crisis of confidence" that had befallen the nation. Americans, Carter observed, had lost faith in their government and in their hopes for a better future.

America's poor took the brunt of the economic, social, and political tumult. And in the 1970s, few places were as poor as West Philadelphia. The West

Philadelphia neighborhood of Powelton, where MOVE founder John Africa lived, experienced high levels of population loss beginning in the 1950s as many white residents moved out of the city into the suburbs. At the neighborhood's peak in the 1950s, 20,000 people lived in Powelton. By the 1970s, only about 12,000 remained. As residents left, their tax dollars went with them. With lower tax revenues, the city of Philadelphia had fewer resources to provide for maintenance, social services, and crime prevention. This chain of events was not limited to Philadelphia; cities all over the country experienced what historians now call "white flight" during this era.

By the 1970s, West Philadelphia's predominately black population faced dwindling social services, increasing crime, abandoned properties, and high unemployment. To make matters worse, many residents of Powelton risked losing their houses to city redevelopment authorities hoping to convert the neighborhood for the expansion of the University of Pennsylvania and Drexel University. Because many residents of Powelton rented their homes, the city's Redevelopment Authority bought the houses from the landlords, evicted the residents, and bulldozed the neighborhood to clear space for university expansion. Hoping to fight the Redevelopment Authority and save the neighborhood, a group of West Philadelphia residents formed a housing co-op in 1971 called the Powelton Community Housing Project. The co-op pooled its members' money and purchased Powelton houses before the city could purchase them and rented the houses back to the original renters.

It was in the midst of this gentrification crisis that John Africa rose to prominence. John Africa was born Vincent Leaphart in 1931. After serving in the Korean War, Leaphart returned to his hometown of Philadelphia and worked as an interior designer for department stores. In 1961, he married Dorothy Clark who later joined a religious movement called the Kingdom of Yahweh. Though he was uninterested in his wife's religious conversion at the time, he adopted much of the rhetoric and dietary practices of that movement into his own. The marriage ended in 1967. Over the next five years, Leaphart underwent a transformation. When he was married to Dorothy, he was known as a snappy dresser, a smooth talker, and a gentle soul. By the early 1970s, he had become something of an eccentric. Leaphart lived a very simple lifestyle and chose to forego electricity and most technologies. Although he was labeled developmentally disabled and only had a third grade education, he was known throughout his Powelton neighborhood as a street-corner-philosopher who spoke at length on politics, society, and religion. He earned a meager living by walking dogs, selling horsemeat for dog food, and performing carpentry work for the Powelton Community Housing Project.

While working for the cooperative in 1971, Leaphart met Donald Glassey, a white, middle class twenty-two-year-old recent graduate of the University of Pennsylvania's master's program in social work. Glassey was deeply impressed by Leaphart's intellect and helped Leaphart's complete a manuscript containing Leaphart's wide-ranging philosophy, which they titled "The Guidelines." Leaphart began going by the name of John Africa to pay homage to the continent of Africa, which was, in his view, the source of all life. To MOVE people, John Africa was a divine figure. Jerry Africa, who joined MOVE in 1972, was asked to compare

John Africa to Jesus Christ. He scoffed at the comparison. "Jesus Christ, who is he? We're talking about John Africa, a person who is a supreme being who will never die and will live on forever."

In 1972, Glassey began teaching philosophy at Philadelphia Community College. The philosophy he was teaching, however, was the Teachings of John Africa. John Africa invited his sisters Louise James and Laverne Sims to listen to Glassey teach. Soon the group outgrew the confines of the college classroom and began meeting at a house Glassey and John Africa shared in Powelton. Over the next five years, MOVE developed the tenets of their religion. Though MOVE has been categorized as anti-technology, anti-modern, and back-to-nature, John Africa's philosophy was, at its core, an attempt to make sense of the negative effects of modern life. Humans, John Africa argued, thought themselves to be above the laws of nature, more special than any other living thing. All that is built by human hands, all that can be imagined in the human mind, all the art, science, philosophy produced by people is fundamentally corrupt. Only the select few—the MOVE children—who had been raised in the religion could claim to be exempt from the corruption that afflicted all of humanity. Part of the process of transcending humanity involved the physical disciplining of MOVE people, through a strict daily exercise regimen, a special diet, and a lifestyle free of most technology.

In practice, MOVE sought to undo the harm humanity had brought to the natural world. They dug up the concrete sidewalk in front of their home in order to allow plants to regrow. They eschewed technology and formal education both for themselves and the children born into MOVE. The group adopted John Africa's ascetic lifestyle as well. On a typical day, MOVE people woke before dawn, boarded a bus, and drove to the city park where they ran and lifted weights. They returned home to run the dogs, an impressive feat considering that at any given moment there could be dozens of dogs living in the MOVE house. MOVE people adhered to a raw foods diet that was mostly plant-based but sometimes included raw eggs, chicken, and beef. MOVE people were ambivalent about eating meat, arguing that they had to eat some meat because their bodies were used to the high protein diets they ate before joining MOVE and that it would be unhealthy to become strictly vegetarian. MOVE children, many of whom were born into the group, were used to a vegetarian diet and rarely ate meat. MOVE offered classes twice a week in which the public could be taught the "Truth of John Africa." In these early years, MOVE was a welcome addition to West Philadelphia. They rehabbed drug addicts, helped their unemployed neighbors pay the rent, and helped gang members find the straight and narrow. They funded their group by washing cars, pooling their welfare checks, and doing odd jobs around the neighborhood.

MOVE's trouble began when they began protesting public gatherings. From 1973 to 1978, MOVE demonstrated at hundreds of events. They protested both liberal and conservative groups. They hurled obscenities at everyone from Jane Fonda to a group of high school students calling for Nixon's impeachment. They protested other religions, including Buddhists, Quakers, and the Nation of Islam. They were no friend to the Civil Rights Movement. The Philadelphia Zoo and pet stores were also frequent targets. In 1973 alone, they protested Cesar Chavez, nutritionist Adelle Davis, Jesse Jackson, Daniel Ellsberg, Socialists, Communists, the Philadelphia Board of Education, the American Indian Movement, Richie Havens, and many more. Their primary complaint? That the targets of their protests did not know the truth of John Africa.

John Africa calculated all of these protests in order to get media exposure for his religion. While he succeeded in growing MOVE's public profile, the protests also drew the attention of the Philadelphia Police Department's Civil Affairs Unit. From May of 1973, MOVE was the subject of around-the-clock observation, wiretapping, and infiltration. Police observation of religion—particularly black religion—is nothing new. Federal law enforcement agencies including the FBI and the Bureau of Alcohol, Tobacco, and Firearms have a long history of observing black religious movements that continues to the present day. For example, the FBI launched investigations into the Moorish Science Temple and the Nation of Islam well before these groups grew into sizable movements. In fact, some of our best early archives for African American Islam were produced by the FBI. By the mid-1970s, MOVE realized that their phones were being tapped and suspected that their home was bugged. John Africa decided that if the city was interested in arresting MOVE people, he'd give them all the arrests they could handle. In 1974, MOVE began deliberately breaking court injunctions designed to prevent their protests. Their plan was to tie up the Philadelphia court system with an endless parade of uncooperative MOVE people. MOVE's court appearances were carefully orchestrated fiascos. Most of the time, a MOVE person might refuse to stand for the judge as a way of pointing out the disparity between the "unjust" laws of the United States and the wisdom of John Africa. Frequently, MOVE people would ignite courtroom brawls. As the court dates multiplied and the charges piled up, MOVE only grew more defiant toward the judicial system. Over time, they thought, the court system would be drained and might crumble under the weight of the Truth of John Africa, or at least the cost of endless and unproductive trials.

In 1977 the relationship between MOVE and the city of Philadelphia changed dramatically. In May of that year, a group of sheriff's deputies arrived at the MOVE house in Powelton to evict someone who was living inside. MOVE assumed they had come to begin a war that John Africa had foretold. MOVE people, dressed in military garb and brandishing unregistered assault rifles and sawed-off shotguns, stood at attention on the porch. MOVE refused to relinquish their weapons and, as the night wore on, the city's forces swelled to hundreds of policemen. This was John Africa's most dramatic publicity display yet. Mayor Frank Rizzo established a blockade in hopes of starving MOVE out of the house. No one, except for a few trusted religious leaders, was allowed in or out. MOVE was allowed no food and their water was shut off. The standoff lasted for ten months. On April 15, 1978, John Africa's sisters Louise and Laverne hired a lawyer to represent MOVE in negotiations with the city. This decision was a betrayal of the principles of John Africa who condemned the whole legal system and refused to negotiate. Nevertheless, MOVE's lawyer and Mayor Rizzo agreed to end the standoff if the city released the remaining incarcerated MOVE people. In return, MOVE would relinquish their weapons and leave the city. According to the agreement, MOVE people wanted on various minor charges would turn themselves in and the charges would be dropped. The city granted MOVE's demand to leave the Powelton house intact so that they could convert it into a temple, a holy site for their religion. After the agreement was reached, MOVE had ninety days to leave town. However, when MOVE people turned themselves in, the charges were not dropped. Infuriated, John Africa, who was orchestrating the proceedings from another MOVE house in Rochester, New York, ordered MOVE people not to leave the house as planned.

Determined to end the costly and embarrassing blockade, Police Chief Joseph O'Neill surrounded the Powelton house on August 8, 1978 with a small army of police officers and firefighters. The plan was to patiently escalate the situation with tear gas and water in order to force MOVE out of the house. When the smoke cleared hours later, thousands of rounds had been fired into MOVE's Powelton home. A police officer, James Ramp, had been killed and several firefighters, who had been there to flush MOVE out by filling the basement with water, were injured. All fourteen MOVE people in the house were arrested. Television news cameras caught two Philadelphia Police Officers kicking Chuckie Africa and beating him with a police helmet as he tried to surrender. The Powelton House, which the city had agreed to preserve as a religious site for the movement, was bulldozed within hours. Nine MOVE people were sentenced to life in prison for the murder of Officer Ramp. MOVE claims that Officer Ramp was killed by friendly fire. One of the "MOVE 9," Merle Africa, died in prison in 1998. The other eight are still behind bars.

MOVE had suffered a serious blow at the hands of the city, but the ATF hoped to finish them off. After getting arrested on federal weapons charges in 1977, Glassey negotiated a lighter sentence by agreeing to become an informant against MOVE for the ATF. With Glassey's help, the ATF and the FBI built an elaborate conspiracy case against John Africa. They accused MOVE of harboring explosives and firearms and alleged that MOVE was planning to negotiate the release of the MOVE 9 by planting a bomb under a federal courthouse in Rochester, New York. The ATF and the FBI built their case for four years. When the case was tried in 1981, John Africa chose to forego legal counsel and acted as his own lawyer. He was acquitted of all charges.

By 1985, John Africa's religion was beginning to crumble. After the city bulldozed the Powelton House, John Africa and his followers moved into John's sister Louise's house on Osage Avenue in West Philadelphia. In 1983 Louise and her sister Laverne, who had been loyal to their brother since the very beginning, left the movement. Louise decided to leave after she had been badly beaten by her son, Frank Africa at John Africa's instruction. After the trial in Rochester, everyone in MOVE knew that Glassey, once a pivotal figure in transforming John Africa's teachings into a religion, had betrayed his former teacher. As the unpaid bills, health code violations, and neighbors' complaints piled up, the city spent months planning how to evict MOVE once and for all. In the predawn hours of May 13th, hundreds of police officers armed with tens of thousands of rounds of ammunition, explosives, and machine guns surrounded the house. The night before, police evacuated the surrounding block. John Africa, who had returned to Philadelphia after beating the federal charges in Rochester, knew what was coming. This was the war he had foretold years before. Gregor Sambor, the city of Philadelphia's new tough-on-crime police commissioner shouted through a bullhorn at the MOVE house, "Attention, MOVE. This is America. You have to abide by the laws of the United States."

Minutes later, the Philadelphia Police Department and MOVE began exchanging gunfire. In less than an hour, the PPD shot 10,000 rounds of ammunition into the house. The Philadelphia Fire Department used water cannons to spray water into the MOVE house, hoping to fill the basement with water so that MOVE people could not seek refuge there. All the while, television news cameras rolled. The standoff lasted into the afternoon and it was clear that MOVE was not coming out of the house. At 5:30 p.m. members of the Philadelphia Police Department dropped an improvised explosive device from a helicopter onto the roof of the MOVE house. The bomb was made from military-grade C4 that the Philadelphia Police Department bomb squad had obtained from an FBI agent. The explosion ignited a drum of gasoline that MOVE was storing on the roof and within minutes, the MOVE house was engulfed in flames. Mayor Wilson Goode, Police Commissioner Gregor Sambor, and Fire Department Commissioner William Richmond decided to "let the fire burn." And burn it did. By the next morning, an entire city block of West Philadelphia was reduced to ash. Sixty-five homes were destroyed and 240 people were left homeless. The bomb and the fire killed eleven MOVE people. Six adults died: Rhonda, Raymond, Theresa, Conrad, Frank, and John Africa. Five children, ranging in age from nine to fifteen also died: Tree, his sister Zanetta, Delitia, Phil, and Tomaso Africa. Only Ramona Africa, and thirteen-year-old Birdie Africa managed to escape alive.

After the bombing, Mayor Goode appointed a group of prominent community members, including clergy, political leaders, lawyers, and activists, to launch an investigation into the city's handling of the MOVE crisis. The investigation lasted for months and local public television station WHYY broadcasted the hearings live. The MOVE Commission agreed that by the early 1980s MOVE "had evolved into an authoritarian, violence-threatening cult" which was "armed and dangerous," and capable of "terror." But the MOVE Commission also agreed that the mayor, the city manager, and the police commissioner were "grossly negligent and clearly risked the lives of the children" and that the city's actions were "excessive and unreasonable." The MOVE Commission agreed that the plan to drop the bomb was "reckless, ill-conceived and hastily approved." They also accused the Philadelphia Police Department of shooting at MOVE children as they attempted to flee the fire, forcing them to retreat back inside the burning house. Because of this, the MOVE Commission concluded that the deaths of the five MOVE children were "unjustified homicides which should be investigated by a grand jury." The only person who was criminally charged as a result of the MOVE standoff was Ramona Africa, the one adult to escape the bombing alive. She served seven years in prison for assault and conspiracy to riot.

MOVE is still around today. Ramona Africa was released from prison in 1992 and currently leads the organization. In 1996, Ramona Africa, Louise James, and Alphonso Africa sued Police Commissioner Gregor Sambor and Fire Commissioner William Richmond for battery and deprivation of rights.

A U.S. District Court awarded them $500,000 each but ruled that Sambor and Richmond could not be held personally liable. MOVE continues to push for the release of the eight MOVE people who remain behind bars. The group contends that the MOVE 9 are political prisoners who have been sentenced unjustly. MOVE also advocates on behalf of Mumia Abu-Jamal, an activist and journalist who wrote about MOVE sympathetically in the late 1970s. In 1982, Abu-Jamal was sentenced to death for the murder of Philadelphia Police Officer Daniel Falkner a year earlier. MOVE contends that Abu-Jamal is innocent and was not afforded a fair trial in part because he was denied the right to have John Africa represent him in court.

MOVE is an important episode in Philadelphia's religious history because the group unsettles our common definitions of "religion" and "politics." Not everyone agrees that MOVE was a religion. In fact, most people who have studied MOVE consider them an "extremist" *political* group. MOVE has also been called a terrorist group, an environmental protest movement, a Black Nationalist movement, an anarchist group, and a cult. How can one group fall into so many different categories? The answer, in part, lies in our common assumptions about the nature of religion. We often imagine that religions are "rational, respectful of persons, noncoercive . . . [and] agreeable to democracy."[1] MOVE, to many people, did not align with this ideal. Does that mean that they were not a religion? Does this make them a political group? A cult? The history of MOVE is useful for thinking about what—if anything—distinguishes a "political" group from a "religious" one.

Notes

1. Robert A. Orsi, *Between Heaven and Earth: The Religious Worlds People Make and the Scholars Who Study Them* (Princeton: Princeton University Press, 2005), 188.

Suggested Readings

Courtney Lyons, "Burning Columbia Avenue: Black Christianity, Black Nationalism, and 'Riot Liturgy' in the 1964 Philadelphia Race Riot" in *Pennsylvania History: A Journal of Mid-Atlantic Studies* 77, no. 3 (2010): 324–348.

Jordan Stranger-Ross, "Neither Fight nor Flight: Urban Synagogues in Postwar Philadelphia" in *Journal of Urban History* 32, no. 6 (September 2006): 791–812.

Discussion Questions:

1. In Washington's descriptions of his time at the Advocate, what does he say about the relationship between social action and Christian faith? How does he understand his role as a Christian minister in light of the social issues of the city and the nation?
2. From reading Primiano, how do you think urbanity (their location in cities) affected the Peace Mission's religious identity and goals? What similarities and

differences do you see between Father Divine and other religious leaders you have studied in regard to urban mission, social justice, and service to those outside of their religious community?

3. According to Primiano, how did Father Divine approach race? What were the most significant aspects of his teaching and practices on race?
4. After reading Evans, do you understand MOVE to be a religious community/organization? Why or why not? After reading Primiano, do you understand the Peace Mission Movement to be a religious community/organization? What definition of "religion" are you using when you make these judgments?
5. After reading Stranger-Ross, why do you think Rodeph Shalom was tempted to leave North Philadelphia? Why did the congregation choose to stay in the city? Did staying in the city shape or affect how they saw themselves? Are you surprised they stayed (or that they are still here)?
6. How did Rodeph Shalom interact with the surrounding non-Jewish community? Did they try to convert their non-Jewish neighbors? Why or why not? What was their attitude toward racial difference?
7. Both Washington and Lyons discussed the Columbia Ave. riots of 1964. How did ministers and other religious leaders respond to the riots? In your opinion, how should Christian ministers and other religious leaders react to civil rights activism and protests? What if it becomes violent or destructive?
8. Lyons uses the phrase "mediating institution" to describe the Black Church (339). What does she mean?

Section 10

Islam in Philadelphia

Suggested Readings

Katie Day, "Muslims on the Block: Navigating the Urban Ecology" in *Faith on the Avenue: Religion on a City Street* (New York: Oxford University Press, 2014): 159–186.

Aminah Beverly McCloud, "This is a Muslim Home" in *Making Muslim Space North America and Europe,* ed. by Barbara Daly Metcalf (Berkeley: University of California Press, 1996): 65–73.

Discussion Questions:

1. What does Day mean by a "discourse of resistance" (4)? "Resistance" to what? How does this "discourse" manifest in and affect people's lives?
2. What is the "religious code of the street" Day describes (5–6)? How do Christians and Muslims near the Germantown Masjid on Germantown Ave. see each other?
3. Describe what Day means by her statement that at Al Aqsa "there is a culture of crossing boundaries" (8).
4. How did the attacks on September 11, 2001 affect the community at Al Aqsa? How did non-Muslims around them respond?
5. McCloud discusses a sign that some Philadelphians posted on their doors. What is its significance in terms of regulating space? Can you think of other examples of religious individuals/families denoting their religious commitments on or near the entrance of their homes? If so, do you think it functions in the same way?
6. How tied to *urban* life and culture do you think the domestic interiors McCloud describes are? Do you think that Muslim homes in the suburbs had (or have) similar features? Do you live in or have you visited a Muslim home? If so, how does it compare to those described in this article?
7. McCloud describes elements that contributed to this community's unique cultural identity. Cite some of them. Why do you think these elements were important to this community?

Section II

Religious Communities in Philadelphia Today

Korean Churches in Philadelphia

Jacob Kim

The first group of about fifty Koreans came to America in 1885 as a result of political conflicts between Korea and Japan. Korean students, medical professionals, brides, and orphans continued to trickle into the United States until 1964 when the Johnson-Reed Act of 1924 (which limited immigration from Asia) was repealed.[1] Since then, the number of Koreans coming to America averaged about 30,000 people per year. Over a million Koreans currently live in America, making them the second largest group of Asians, behind South East Indians.[2] With about 80,000, Philadelphia has the fifth largest concentration of Koreans in the country.

What is apparent to the interested is the prevalence of Christian churches where Koreans have settled. Though there are several Korean Buddhist temples and a Korean Catholic church in the area, the overwhelming majority of Korean religious gatherings are Protestant churches. It is estimated that 70 percent of Koreans in America self-identify as Christian; this makes the Korean church the center of information for Koreans themselves and for those who study them. In contrast, Christians in South Korea only make up 20–25 percent of the population. This has caused people to wonder why the church attendance rates in America are so much higher than in Korea. Though some Christian believers would like to credit effective ministry methods or the blessing of God, there are other possible factors contributing to the prominence of the church in Korean communities in America.

One contributing factor for the Christian majority in America may be that early Korean migrants to America were predominantly Christian because they were free from many of the traditional Korean customs that held others back. For example, in Korea, first-born sons were traditionally and religiously obligated to oversee and maintain the gravesites of their ancestors. American missionaries in Korea at the time encouraged members of their congregations to make the trip to America. Early Korean migrants established their own churches in America so they could practice their faith in the manner and language they were most comfortable with, away from the scrutiny and discrimination of the surrounding non-Korean population. Later Korean migrants naturally gravitated to these churches, even if they were not Christian, for community and support. People tend to gravitate to the familiar in an unfamiliar environment. Churches quickly became social centers performing functions beyond faith; for example, they helped new immigrants determine the best place to live or location for a business. Adults could be with others sympathetic to the migration transition experience. The advantage of having an ethnic church in America for people who are very community centered was and continues to be significant. In a foreign land that was frequently hostile to Koreans, the church was both a refuge and a network of opportunity.

My own father came to Philadelphia in 1959 to attend seminary; he was later joined by his fiancé in 1963. Many of his former high school students in Korea who subsequently followed him to the area asked their former teacher to start one of the first Korean churches in the Philadelphia area in 1967.[3] When I was a young boy in the late 1960s and early 1970s my father was finishing his doctorate at Temple University while pastoring the church. At the time it was not unusual for my family to get phone calls in the middle of the night from Philadelphia International Airport requesting a ride and a place to stay. We found out much later that the travel agents in Korea were giving travelers our phone number as an initial contact number in America. This social function of the church persists today; extended family members and strangers alike still seek out churches as a kind of ethnic safe space during the transition period from life in Korea to life in America.

A second contributing factor to the popularity of Protestant churches, Presbyterian churches in particular, for Koreans in America might be the church structure or polity. The Presbyterian form of church government, to put it simply, is very similar to the American federal government; it is a representative form of government. Once someone professes faith, that person becomes a voting member and is eligible to hold various offices in the church. Members who are active around the everyday operation of the church are deacons; members who assist in the decision-making process of the church and budget are elders; and those who teach and lead the entire congregation are teaching elders or pastors. Elders and pastors meet annually with pastors and elders of other churches within the same association of Presbyterian churches (denomination) first in the immediate area and then nationally. Leaders are chosen each year from among the attendees at the regional and national levels. Women may participate and receive any of the titles depending on which denomination they participate. This structure easily can be interpreted as a structure of status and influence.

Korean society was and still is a very hierarchical society where seniority and rank influence many aspects of everyday life from family to employment. Within families a person's status is generally determined by age; the older the person, the more authority that person has over everyone else in the family. At a large company the age criteria must be considered but is only secondary to the year a worker begins work at that company. Churches can express hierarchy through both aspects of age and church office. America is largely an egalitarian society where this type of hierarchy might be hard to understand. In the Korean church in America, attitudes, order, authority, respect, courtesy, and even language are often dictated by knowing one's position relative to everyone else in the room. The Presbyterian church structure was readily adaptable to Korean society in such a way that conversion to the Christian faith did not mean cultural norms of hierarchy had to be discarded or overruled.

This structure becomes particularly significant in America where Koreans often feel marginalized and alienated from society. Many scholars in America assert that people often attend church to regain or obtain recognition, status, and self-respect. It is easy to meet Koreans in America who had once enjoyed a life of relatively high social standing in Korea; those Koreans are now helping the family make ends meet, often, through menial jobs. My own mother, for example, was a teacher in the most prestigious girls high school in Korea. Students at the time had to apply to gain entrance to high school, and her school was the most selective in the country. In America she spent many years at what people call a sweatshop today. She often told me, over a pile of dirty dishes, that if she had not come to America and married my father, she would have had servants do all of her chores for her. The church continues to be a place of opportunity for Koreans to rise in social status in a country that frequently does not notice them.

A third factor of the high rates of adherence in America may be the desire to maintain ethnic identity. Koreans have a strong sense of national identity because Korea was often invaded and conquered by other countries throughout its history; it is a peninsula between China and Japan. Most recently it was annexed by Japan in 1910 until 1945, the end of World War II. Korean culture was criminalized and Koreans were ordered to learn and speak Japanese and take on Japanese names. Christians in Korea were also persecuted for their religion when everyone was forced to practice Japanese religion, Shintoism. Although the generation which lived through the occupation is decreasing in number, memories of the suppression of Korean language, culture, and religion resulted in a strong sense of national identity among the earlier waves of Koreans to America. Korean churches in America helped many of them to keep and perpetuate their ethnic roots through Korean language and cultural schools.

As the Korean church community in America matures and grows older, it faces the challenge of justifying its ethnic existence in a society which prefers some process of "Americanization." In other words, many Americans expect people from other countries to make a continuous effort to become "Americans." For example, I, personally, have been accused of discrimination and even racism because our church caters to Korean-speaking Koreans. America generally prefers its inhabitants to speak English rather than people's own native languages. Recent emphasis on globalization might change this expectation in the long run, but for now, anti-immigration attitudes and rhetoric continue to apply pressure to the ethnic identity of the Korean church.

Thus, in addition to teaching the message of Christianity to Koreans living in America, the church must address issues of ethnic identity in a dynamic society. Each church becomes a space of theoretical and theological experimentation on how to live in America as older Koreans die and their children start families of their own. Churches experiment by targeting specific demographic groups; for example, college-aged students, English speaking students, Korean speaking students, or senior citizens. Other churches may start by focusing on a type of program; for example, music programs, afterschool programs, overseas mission work, and social justice programs. Other churches may just focus on young families with children so that children may have friends who are Korean. Each example of experimentation will also adapt the teachings of Christianity to further justify the approach of that church. People who seek a Korean church will shop around until they can find a church that will match with their own expectation of what a church should be and do.

The Korean church in Philadelphia and America will not resolve and answer all of the questions of identity and place anytime soon. Social trends influence the church, which makes maintaining ethnic identity harder or easier. It seems there are more trends that make maintaining the ethnic church easier right now. The increase in the ease of travel between South Korean and the United States make it easier to reacquaint oneself to Asian attitudes and culture. Korean movies and shows are easily viewed through the Internet. Korean contemporary music, K-pop, can sometimes be heard on American top 40 radio stations which motivate people to rediscover their own ethnic pride. Korean consumer products and technology are widely available; raising the perception of Koreans already living in America. These trends in society impact the church so that more experimentation occurs, further increasing the variety and forms Korean churches may take in the Philadelphia area.

Notes

1. The Johnson-Reed Act controlled and restricted migration from Asia through quotas which prevented large numbers of Asians from coming to America. Exceptions were made in the case of diplomats, graduate students, brides, orphans and certain occupational professionals.
2. South Korea currently has a total population of 50 million, so the number is subjectively significant. Current immigration numbers has declined because the standard of living in South Korea has vastly improved.
3. Reverend Sunoon Kim, Ph.D. established "The Korean Presbyterian Church of North Philadelphia" in 1967; the church has since been renamed to "The Korean Presbyterian Church of Huntingdon Valley" when it moved in 1988. The writer is the current senior pastor of that church.

African Spirits in the Holy Experiment: Philadelphia's Botanicas and Odunde Festival

Terry Rey and Ariella Werden-Greenfield

Shortly after Europeans first arrived in what is today Philadelphia, Africans arrived. Like the whites who had enslaved them, they also brought their religions to America. Though over time most Africans and their descendants in the city would quite enthusiastically embrace Christianity (and a smaller number, Islam), today the spirits of Africa are alive and well in William Penn's "Holy Experiment." The majority of those who serve African spirits in the city now are Puerto Rican Santeros (practitioners of the Afro-Caribbean religion Santería), while a minority of African Americans have also reclaimed their faith in ancestral African divinities. Add to this the growing immigrant populations from West Africa, the Caribbean, and Brazil, the present and future of African religions in Philadelphia are assured. This chapter explores the most visible public faces of this influence, the city's botanicas (religious goods stores that cater primarily to practitioners of African-derived religions) and its annual Odunde Festival (the longest continuously performed public African religious festival in the United States).

African Spirit and Spirits in the Holy Experiment

African religions have a long and rich history in colonial America and the United States, beginning with the worldviews and spiritual practices of the first enslaved Africans brought to Virginia in 1619. Within twenty years, Dutch and Swedish settlers had imported African slaves to labor in the Delaware Valley, while later that century Pennsylvania was established as an English colony by William Penn, who was himself a slave owner. Founded in 1682, Penn envisioned a "Holy Experiment" built on Quaker principles of human equality and religious tolerance; within two years Philadelphia was home to roughly 200 enslaved Africans. Thus the African presence and spirit in Philadelphia is nearly as old as the European and African spirits, and have been part of Philadelphia for nearly as long as has Jesus Christ.

And just who are these spirits? Though we do not have accurate information about the specific ethnic groups to which Africans in colonial and early republican Philadelphia belonged, one can say with confidence that many of them were Ashanti, Fon, Kongo, and Yoruba. While the traditional religions of these peoples were and remain distinctive and sophisticated, they share enough in common that we may speak generally here about their ethos. African religions posit that there is a single God behind all existence, and yet this Supreme Being retreated before having finished creating the world, leaving the remainder of that task to a pantheon of spirits who are closely tied to forces in nature. It is with these spirits that most religious commerce in Africa takes place. In addition, African religions are principally concerned with the veneration of ancestors. Devotional service to spirits and ancestors requires rituals or sacrifices aimed to infuse life with sacred energy. Derived from God, this energy is sacramental and in the Yoruba language is called *ashe*.

There is little archaeological or archival evidence of African religion in the city during the colonial era. Yet one can glean its presence and growth from a complaint made by the Philadelphia Council in 1693 "of the tumultuous gathering of the Negroes in the towne of philadelphia, on the first dayes of the weeke."

The Council might well have been referring to communal African rituals in Southeast Square (today Washington Square Park), located at Sixth and Walnut Streets near Independence Hall, which was colloquially known in the eighteenth century as Kongo Square. As one contemporary observer described it, in Kongo Square "could be seen at once more than 1,000 of both sexes, divided into numerous little squads, dancing, and singing, 'each in their own tongue,' after the customs of their several nations in Africa." Their purpose was not lost on this observer: "to honor and celebrate their ancestors, and to leave gifts at the graves of their loved ones."[1] To less informed whites, African religions have long appeared to be "tumultuous," and though the Council members surely did not recognize it at the time, the "gathering" to which they referred was most likely a congregation performing music and dance rituals for the spirits and the dead. As elsewhere in the emergent African diaspora, white officials perceived such African communal ceremonies to be threatening not just culturally but also politically, such that in 1706 a law was passed in Philadelphia that prohibited blacks from gathering, the first of many such prohibitions.[2]

In time, thankfully, abolitionism would shape life in Philadelphia more than slavery. In 1767 Pennsylvania banned the importation of slaves and in 1780 the state passed the first anti-slavery legislation in the young American nation. As the city's black population grew, the memory of African traditional religion faded, however, with most African Americans now being generations removed from the mother continent and firmly entrenched in any number of Christian denominations, including the African Methodist Episcopal, which was founded in Philadelphia by Richard Allen in 1794 as the nation's first independent African American church. This remained the case throughout the nineteenth century, though racial and religious demographics shifted considerably with the Great Migration, which witnessed some 6 million African Americans leave the oppressive segregation of the South for northern cities between 1916 and 1970, many of them settling in Philadelphia. The Migration coincided with the emergence of alternative religions among urban blacks, like the Moorish Science Temple, the Nation of Islam, Father Divine's Peace Mission Movement, and Daddy Grace's United House of Prayer for All People.

By the middle of the twentieth century and the rise of the Black Power movement, some African Americans began seeking more "purely" African forms of religion. In New York there was already a large population of Cubans and Puerto

Ricans practicing Santería, a form of syncretic religion that had first emerged among African and Creole slaves in Cuba. Santería blends Catholicism with West African spiritual traditions, especially those of the Yoruba people, and was the pathway to African traditional religion for many African American seekers in New York at the time. Traditionally Yoruba religion features belief in a single creator God, Olodumare, and a pantheon of spirits, called *orishas*, who are the focus of the religion. Humans are called to live in relationships of reciprocal service with the orishas via insight derived from divination and through personal and communal rituals of sacrifice and praise. In time, many African Americans eschewed the perceivably white elements of Santería as practiced by Latinos, forging their own course by visiting West Africa to be initiated as priests and priestesses of traditional Yoruba religion. They thereby purged their orisha devotion of any lingering Catholic features.

Thus in the United States there are essentially two paths down which African spirits have traveled: one via Cubans and Puerto Ricans who immigrated from Caribbean islands where African religions have thrived since the colonial era, albeit in syncretized form; and the other via an act of spiritual reclamation by African Americans who had become disillusioned with Santería for its Catholic content and for the high percentage of white Latinos practicing the religion. Hence there emerged in the 1950s and 1960s distinctly African American "houses," or congregations, of orisha devotees, with a number of them flourishing in Philadelphia today. Generally African American Yoruba houses reject the term "Santería" as an identifier of their faith and practice. But by far the largest number of practitioners of Yoruba-derived religion in the city are Puerto Ricans, most of whom embrace the term "Santería" or one of its cognates, "Lucumi" or "Regla de Ocha" (lit: "Orisha Rite").

Botanicas in the City of Brotherly Love

After New York City, Philadelphia is home to the largest Puerto Rican community in the United States outside of the island of Puerto Rico. Presently more than 135,000 Puerto Ricans reside in Philadelphia, nearly 10 percent of the entire city population. Their densest concentration is along a roughly ten-block-wide corridor centered on North Fifth Street between Girard Avenue and US Route 1 (Roosevelt Boulevard), spanning the neighborhoods of Kensington, Fairhill, Juniata Park, Olney, and East Oak Lane. A stretch of North Fifth Street at the epicenter of this community is called by locals "El Centro de Oro" (The Center of Gold). El Centro de Oro is home to the city's most important Puerto Rican cultural institution, Taller Puertorriqueño, and to many of the Philadelphia's roughly three dozen botanicas, with several of the others being located along a parallel stretch of North Front Street, four blocks to the east.

It is difficult to gauge the percentage of Philadelphia's Puerto Ricans who practice Santería, but we may look elsewhere in the country for clues. We do know that in South Florida, for instance, an estimated 500,000 Santeros are served by roughly 150 botanicas.[3] This would mean that for every botanica in South Florida there are roughly 2,500 practitioners of Santería. By comparison, if there are, as we estimate, three dozen botanicas in Philadelphia, then there would more than 80,000 Santeros in the city—or the Delaware Valley, as surely many shoppers in Philadelphia's botanicas do not actually reside there. Admittedly, this formula is crude, and it should be underscored that not all clients of botanicas are Santeros. The botanica is, after all, "the public face of a new multicularalism in America that embraces its indigenous, African, European, and Asian heritages and combines them into potent medicines for survival and triumph in the brave new world of the United States."[4] Other shoppers include members of several Vodou congregations in and around Philadelphia, as well as some practitioners of the Afro-Brazilian religion of Candomble.[5] While some customers and clients in Philadelphia's botanicas may have nothing to do with Vodou, Santería, or Candomble, it is safe to say that the vast majority of those who spend money to keep these stores afloat in the City of Brotherly Love do.

Located at Fifth and Cambria Streets in the city's Fairhill neighborhood, the oldest botanica in Philadelphia is Maria Arte Espiritual, which was opened in 1972 by a recently-arrived Puerto Rican woman named Maria Acevedo.[6] It was preceded, however, by at least one "spiritual supply store" founded in the 1960s by an African American conjurer named Bishop Everett. While such "African-American hoodoo drugstores" have been largely supplanted by botanicas in urban America, African Americans continue to make up a significant portion of their shoppers.[7] Botanicas, established and led primarily by priests, priestesses, and/or diviners, are also sacred spaces where one can receive blessings, be cured, or receive spiritual readings; thus, for many of their customers, they are "a beautiful and sophisticated way of encountering a sacred world of power where bodies, hearts, and minds can be transformed."[8] Angel Perez, Acevedo's son who now runs Maria Arte Espiritual, finds that much of the transformation sought by his customers is also material: "They want money, prosperity, open roads."[9]

More than half of Philadelphia's botanicas are located in Fairhill or Kensington, along North Fifth Street and North Front Street. Some of them are named for the orishas, like Botanica Changó, on North Front Street, Botanica Yemaya, near Ninth and Lehigh, and Botanica Obatala, near Front and Westmorland. The first of these is named for the male divinity of thunder and lightning, the second for the female spirit of the sea, and the third for the male orisha of the sky and the creator of human bodies. Like Maria Arte Espiritual, most botanicas have Spanish names, reflecting their service to a majority Latino clientele. Take, for instance, Botanica Corazon de Jesus, at Front Street and Lehigh Avenue, and three others located along North Front Street: La Botanica, Botanica San Miguel, and Botanica El Indio. The last of these three, "The Indian Botanica," reflects the Native American influences in Santería. Meanwhile, Botanica Guadalupe, named for the patron saint of Mexico and located in the Italian Market in South Philadelphia, where a large Mexican population now resides, clearly serves a predominantly Mexican clientele. This makes Botanica Guadalupe unique in Philadelphia, though it would be one of hundreds of such botanicas were it located in Los Angeles. Meanwhile, Botanica 21 Divisions in the city's Olney neighborhood, judging from its name (which reflects a distinctly Dominican form of Vodou), appears to cater primarily to a Dominican clientele.

As the city's Latino population is currently doubling in size every ten years, and as more and more whites and African Americans join religious congregations devoted to the orishas, Philadelphia can expect the number of its botanicas to grow. Whether as destinations to buy candles, incense, dashboard saints, herbs, or beads to mark devotion to the orishas, or as sites for casual reading, spiritual cleansing, or a quick word of advice from a priest or priestess, botanicas are the face of African spirituality in Philadelphia today.

The Odunde Festival

If botanicas are the most ubiquitous sign of the presence of African spirits in Philadelphia, the annual Odunde Festival is the most vibrant. Formerly known by the name of the orisha that it fetes, the Odunde Festival celebrates the most popular of all female divinities in Yoruba religion, Oshun, goddess of fresh waters and all things feminine. As such, Oshun holds a primary position in Yoruba cosmology and her feast day is one of the most significant events in the Yoruba religious calendar. Her original shrine is located in the Yoruba town of Osogbo in western Nigeria, yet she is worshipped throughout the African diaspora. Being "the only female deity present at the creation of the world," her name translates as "the source," for Oshun gives and sustains life and is celebrated as the patroness of civilization and of creativity itself.[10]

Oshun lives in, rules, and is a river—all rivers—and in African religious thought rivers serve as both pathway to and barrier between the two worlds, the world of the living and that of the dead. Being a city that is hemmed in by two rivers, Philadelphia is a natural attraction for Oshun and she feels welcome because she has so many "children" here, as devotees of the orisha are called. One priestess named Iyalosha Oshunguunwa notes the uniqueness of worshipping Oshun in Philadelphia: "in the city, going to the river . . . to talk to Her is a little different. . . . I associate Her with nature . . . [but] I see Her on the city's streets as the consummate businesswoman, or artist. I see so many Oshuns who don't even know they are."[11] Oshun thus takes on distinctly urban and American characteristics in Philadelphia, but she retains her connection to the universal, cosmic river. In Philadelphia, her children visit and venerate her at the banks of the Schuylkill and the Delaware Rivers, enacting locally enculturated practices that draw upon a rich heritage and connect them to a worldwide network of practitioners.

Yoruba traditional religion does not emphasize beliefs but rather "participation in rituals and ceremonial activities."[12] Ceremonial feasts bring the orisha into everyday life, blurring the "boundaries between the sacred and the secular."[13] During festivals, orishas are attracted by the drumming and dancing and thus join the celebration, energizing the event and participants with *ashe*. To the founder of Philadelphia's Odunde Festival, Lois Fernandez, the event is ultimately about knowledge of "what it is to be of African descent, that we are Africans here in America."[14]

Fernandez decided to launch Odunde after sensing that Oshun called her to do so. Traditionally, women who receive a call from Oshun wear ornate jewelry and perfume, mirroring this orisha's own preferences for such niceties. The ornamentation and dress of Oshun devotees in a Yoruba community in New York intrigued Fernandez: "When I met the Yorubas in New York—When I first saw them, I was moved. I felt it in my guts. And I talked to them. And I watched the women with all those bracelets on their arms. I changed my whole dressing style, then finally I changed my whole wardrobe to Africa."[15] Shortly after her initial encounter with Oshun's children, Fernandez visited Nigeria, where she participated in an Oshun festival. After returning to Philadelphia, Oshun asserted herself as Fernandez's *ori*—or spiritual guardian. Fernandez acknowledged Oshun's control of her "head" and destiny, and the orisha made it clear that she wanted to be honored publicly in the city: "We have a river, we are between two rivers. Why don't we do an African American event? Why don't we go to the river?"[16]And once Fernandez received a grant from Philadelphia for city beautification in 1975, the Festival was born.[17]

Today Odunde is one of the largest African American street festivals in the country, attracting up to 500,000 people annually during the second week of June. The Festival grounds, located along South Street between 21st and 23rd Streets, have remained the same since 1975.[18] "Odunde" means "New Year" in Yoruba, and for orisha devotees the Festival promises to ensure a good year. Oshun guarantees as much and succors the festival, as Fernandez observes: "Oshun has sustained us for thirty years and that is why we are here. And the spirit of Oshun is what is felt there—you see it in the peoples' faces. You go up on the bridge, you come down on the bridge and all of these greetings—you get all this feedback. I can't do anything but feel it. It is the power of Oshun that comes down."[19]

The Festival takes place over three days (Oshun festivals in Nigeria traditionally take place over sixteen days), when thousands congregate and process to celebrate Oshun, to infuse their lives with her *ashe*, and to express reverence for her maternal care. Nonpractitioners come to enjoy music, dance, art, food, and the jollity of it all. The first day's events are private and open only to a select few dignitaries from around the world. The second day of the festival begins with a business meeting and a roundtable discussion of African politics and economics. The worldly focus of the day's events segues into the night's otherworldly convergences: At dusk a procession begins in honor of the African ancestors (*engungun*), as the city grows dark, as the realms of the living and the dead and of spirits and humans approach each other. Participants walk in white in honor of and among the ancestors. This concludes with a lively communal dance and drum ritual called a *bembe*.

The third day of the Festival opens with another procession to the Schuylkill River. A Yoruba priest or priestess leads the congregants in *oriki* (praise songs), accompanied in the procession by masked *engungun*. Once atop the South Street Bridge, the faithful drop offerings of fruit, honey, and flowers in the Schuylkill River for Oshun. The presiding priest or priestess then signals the orisha's acceptance of the offerings, allowing the jovial festivities to recommence.

Odunde's centerpiece is an "African marketplace," which celebrates arts from Africa and from throughout the African diaspora. The weekend's best attended event, the marketplace features dance performances, live music, and general revelry. Artisans sell crafts from booths lining city blocks, while live music resounds from the Festival grounds' several stages. Musicians and dancers perform in celebration of the new year, of Oshun, and of Africa.

The Odunde Festival is thus an opportunity for the community to affirm and celebrate its identity and solidarity."[20] For many attendees like Junious Ricardo Stanton, though, something more decidedly religious happens at Odunde: "ODUNDE is like a mystical baptism. The festival there immerses you in a vibratory sea of blackness. You get dipped into a positive spirit of being African and come up revived, energized and feeling good." Odunde is thus both a religious gathering and "a block party" that celebrates Oshun as the "organizing phenomenon of the Yoruba theocentric universe."[21]

Conclusion

Whereas some religions hinge upon a distinction between the sacred and the profane, African religions hinge upon the intertwining of both.[22] Philadelphia's botanicas and its Odunde Festival are cases in point: both are driven by and infused with spirituality and African pride, while also being commercial enterprises. And just as there are many things that bring the faithful to shop or seek guidance and empowerment in Philadelphia's botanicas, there are many ways to participate in the Odunde Festival, which is at once a street fair that strengthens communal bonds, an event that bolsters African Americans' and Puerto Ricans' connection to Africa, a celebration of African culture, and communal worship ceremony for Oshun. And so is the botanica, a hallmark of African spirituality in the United States and a moving testimony to the endurance of the spirits of Africa in and beyond Philadelphia's Centro de Oro. The Holy Experiment continues, alas, and the orishas are an important part of it.

Notes

1. John Fanning Watson, in Willis P. Hazard, ed., *Annals of Philadelphia, and Pennsylvania, in the Olden Time* (Philadelphia: E. S. Stuart, 1891), 265. For an interesting relevant discussion, see John Davies, "Vodou in the Early Republic: More Questions than Answers." http://usreligion.blogspot.com/2013/11/vodou-in-early-republic-more-questions.html; accessed October 24, 2015. We thank John Davies for bringing this important text to our attention.

2. Ibid., 13.

3. José Antonio Lammoglia, "Botanicas: Presence in Miami, Absence in Cuba," M.A. thesis, Latin American and Caribbean Center, Florida International University, 2001. On Haitian botanicas in Miami, see Terry Rey and Alex Stepick, *Crossing the Water and Keeping the Faith: Haitian Religion in Miami* (New York: New York University Press), 2013.

4. Joseph M. Murphy, *Botánicas: Sacred Spaces of Healing and Devotion in Urban America* (Jackson: University Press of Mississippi, 2015), 8.

5. The Vodou congregations that we have identified in the city were not founded by nor are they run by Haitians, though some Haitians do attend services there. Our impression is that the vast majority of the 30,000 Haitians in the Philadelphia area are Protestants, judging by the dozens of storefront churches that they have opened in the city.

6. Frederick R. Wherry, *The Philadelphia Barrio: The Arts, Branding, and Neighborhood Transformation*(Chicago: University of Chicago Press, 2008), 78. A journalistic source claims that Acevedo emigrated from Spain, not Puerto Rico, but this could be mistaken. Theresa Stigale, "In the Heart of Gold," *Hidden City Philadelphia*, August 20, 1913. http://hiddencityphila.org/2013/08/in-the-heart-of-gold/; accessed October 30, 2015.

7. Murphy, *Botánicas*, 20.

8. Ibid., 8.

9. As cited in Kia Gregory, "A Shop Customers Believe in: Faithful Base Keeps Phila. Store Going." *Philadelphia Inquirer*, February 7, 2010.

10. Diedre L. Badejo, "The Pathways of Osun as Cultural Synergy," in *Òrìsà Devotion as World Religion: The Globalization of Yorùbá Religious Culture*, ed. Jacob K. Olupona and Terry Rey. (Madison: University of Wisconsin Press, 2008), 191–202.

11. Rachel Elizabeth Harding, "'What Part of the River You're In': African American Women in Devotion to Oshun," in *Oshun Across the Waters: A Yoruba Goddess in Africa and the Americas*, ed. Joseph M. Murphy and Mei-Mei Sanford . (Bloomington: Indiana University Press, 2001), 165–188.

12. Jacob K. Olupona, *Kingship, Religion, and Rituals in a Nigerian Community: A Phenomenological Study of Ondo Yoruba Festivals* (Stockholm: Acta Universitatis Stockholmiensis, 1991), 14.

13. Diedre Badejo, *Oshun Seegesi: The Elegant Deity of Wealth, Power and Femininity*. (Trenton: Africa World Press, 1995), 54.

14. Thomas B. Morton, Lois Fernandez, and Debora Kodish, "We Shall Not Be Moved: Thomas Morton's Photographs of 30 Years of ODUNDE." *Works in Progress* vol. 18, nos. 2–3 (2005), 14.

15. As cited in Morton, Fernandez, and Kodish, "We Shall Not Be Moved," 17.

16. Helen Schenck, "'ODUNDE': An African American Festival on South Street, Philadelphia." *Expedition* vol. 41, no. 3 (1999), 42–43.

17. ODUNDE 365, an organization that grew out of the Festival, works year round to encourage cultural education and artistic expression in the Philadelphia community. http://www.odundefestival.org/; accessed October 30, 2015.

18. City officials asked Fernandez to change the festival's location to Penn's Landing but she refused. The original location, she reasoned, was deeply ingrained with the history of Philadelphia's African American community and thus it should not be changed.

19. Morton, Fernandez, and Kodish, "We Shall Not Be Moved," 17.

20. Badejo, *Oshun Seegesi*, 134.

21. Schenck, "ODUNDE," 1. David O. Ogungbile, "Eerindinlogun: The Seeing Eyes of Sacred Shells and Stones," in *Oshun Across the Waters: A Yoruba Goddess in Africa and the Americas*, ed. Joseph M. Murphy and Mei-Mei Sanford. (Bloomington: Indiana University Press), 2001, 189–212,.

22. Émile Durkheim, *The Elementary Forms of Religious Life*. Trans. Karen E. Fields (New York: Free Press, [1912]1995); Mircea Eliade, *The Sacred and the Profane: The Meaning of Religion*. Trans. Willard R. Trask. (New York: Harcourt [1957]1987 1957).

Section 12

Religious Freedom

Joan DelFattore • "The Myth of Madalyn Murray O'Hair" in *The Fourth R*

The Myth of Madalyn Murray O'Hair

Joan DelFattore

The day that this country ceases to be free for irreligion it will cease to be free for religion—except for the sect that can win political power.

—*Justice Robert Jackson*

Among the many misconceptions that plague discussions of school prayer is the widespread belief that a wild-eyed atheist named Madalyn Murray O'Hair single-handedly—or single-footedly—kicked God out of the public schools. In truth, by the time her case reached the Supreme Court so many other school-prayer lawsuits were in progress that the outcome would almost certainly have been the same without her. Indeed, the Court did not even hear her case separately but joined it with a similar action filed by a Unitarian family in Pennsylvania. All the same, her extravagant speech, open antagonism toward religion, and association with the Communist Party caused her to be regarded as the flesh-and-blood embodiment of hostility to prayer. As recently as 1999, when she had been missing for four years, she was rumored to have "gone off to die quietly so Christians wouldn't pray over her" (Katie Fairbank, "O'Hair Allegedly Was Killed," [Wilington, Delaware] *News Journal*, May 28, 1999, p. A17): (In fact, she had been kidnapped and murdered by an employee who stole her money; her remains were identified in March 2001.) The *Washington Post* described her as "that vilified and idolized secularist war-horse" (Paul Duggan, "The Root of All Evil," August 17, 1999,· p. C1), and a lawyer who paid $12,000 for her personal papers echoed her own belief that she was "the most hated woman in America" (Associated Press, "Papers of Missing Atheist Go for $12,000," [Wilmington, Delaware] *News Journal*, April 22, 1999, p. A18).

Birth of a Legend

Madalyn Murray, who later remarried and became Madalyn Murray O'Hair, entered the history—and folklore—of church/state disputes in the fall of 1960. Her older son, William, was a seventh-grader in a Baltimore public school, and Murray demanded that he be excused from the daily prayers and Bible-reading.

Their accounts of the basis for her protest differ: William, now a born-again Christian and a leading school-prayer advocate, claims that he was used as a tool of his mother's hostility toward religion, whereas Murray asserted that she went to the principal only because William asked her to do so.

When the principal refused to excuse William from the morning exercises, Murray unsuccessfully sought help from school officials and advocacy groups. William stopped going to school, and two weeks later a local newspaper reported the story after Murray wrote to the editor about it. William then returned to class accompanied by reporters, and for days the school administrators struggled to keep the journalists corralled and to prevent William from staging a demonstration. Meanwhile, Murray entertained the journalists with vivid language and anti-religious rhetoric, calling the principal "the Buxom Bitch," describing religion as organized insanity, and accusing the post office of stealing her mail. She also claimed that her neighbors had called the police about her barking dogs because the dogs were atheists. On the advice of the attorney general of Maryland, the Baltimore school board instituted an opt-out policy, but by then Murray was determined to eliminate religious exercises from the public-school program. Once again, she sought help from advocacy groups, but none of the organizations she approached was willing to represent her after an attorney provided by the American Civili0J Liberties Union, who had acted on her behalf during the early stages of the controversy, declined to continue doing so. Both then and in her later writings, she accused the ACLU of hostility toward atheists, since all its school-prayer cases included some religious plaintiffs. The ACLU responded that it had already filed so many lawsuits that were essentially the same as Murray's that her case would not have been a good use of its resources. Her former attorney also implied that she had proved to be a more colorful and impulsive client than lawyers prefer to have when they are trying to set precedents in constitutional law.

Having given up on the ACLU, Murray accepted the help of a lawyer who had ties to the Communist Party. She claimed to have met him through a Fuller Brush salesman, known only as "Bob," who, she said, had come to her door and identified himself as a Communist after reading news stories about her case. Murray had traveled to the Soviet Union and had allegedly tried to give up her U.S. citizenship and defect to Communism, but the true nature and extent of her Communist ties were never entirely clear. Nevertheless, they were widely discussed because, despite the popular linkage of Communism with school-prayer protests, she was the only plaintiff in any of the Supreme Court cases who was shown to have any such connections. The Communist issue was also raised in early news stories about William, whose history teacher had scolded him in front of the class for writing a pro-Soviet essay. His schoolmates subsequently called him a "Commie" and beat him up whenever they could catch him. Recalling these incidents in his 1995 book, *Let Us Pray,* he sided with his tormentors. "We lived in an ethnic working-class neighborhood," he wrote. "Many of our neighbors were Polish and Hungarian Catholics who had escaped the violence of Communist countries. Our family wanted to replace the democracy they had sought in America with the same godless totalitarianism that they had escaped from. Some had lost loved ones to Communist gulags. In my eagerness to please my mother and her Marxist friends, I was ignorant of the pain I caused my neighbors" (p. 19).

When it became known that Murray's lawyer had represented Communists, she first denied having been aware of it and then retracted that statement. The attorney bowed out, and she engaged Leonard Kerpelman, a Baltimore lawyer with no experience in constitutional law. She became his client because he was the only lawyer willing to represent her without charge, but her estimate of him was not high. "With him as our counsel," she later wrote, "it meant that we were *really* on our own" (O'Hair, 1989, p. 153). Kerpelman's opinion of her is not recorded.

The Murrays filed their lawsuit, *Murray v. Curlett,* in the Maryland state courts; the first-named defendant, John Curlett, was president of the Baltimore City school board. Their complaint challenged not only the practices at William's school but also a school board policy that, in conformity with Maryland state law, provided for "'the reading, without comment, of a chapter in the Holy Bible and/ or the use of the Lord's Prayer. The Douay version may be used by those pupils who prefer it. Appropriate patriotic exercises should [also] be held as a part of the general opening exercise of the school or class"' *(Murray v. Curlett,* 228 Md. 239 [1962], pp. 241–42). The board responded with a short document called a "demurrer," asking the court to dismiss the case without a trial. The court did so, declaring that public schools may and should advance religion because failing to do so would establish atheism. Like many of the state court decisions discussed in Chapters Three and Four [of *The Fourth R*, DelFattore], this one asserted that sectarian practices would be impermissible but that the Bible is nonsectarian. "The inference that the Holy Bible is either sectarian or partisan," the decision stated, "is a rather startling and novel thought." The court also found no merit to the Murrays' claim that believers and nonbelievers should be treated equally. In its view, the religious freedom of believers would be curtailed if religious exercises no longer took place in public schools, but "Just how the religious liberty of a person who has no religion can be endangered is by no means made clear" *(Murray v. Curlett,* unpublished opinion of the Superior Court of Baltimore City, April 27, 1961, p. 9). The decision also suggested that if nonbelief were accorded equal status with belief, some of America's most cherished traditions might be excluded from the public schools. "It is even possible," the court speculated, "that United States currency would not be accepted in school cafeterias because every bill and coin contains the familiar inscription, 'IN GOD WE TRUST"' (p. 17). When this ruling was upheld by Maryland's highest court, the Murrays turned to the U.S. Supreme Court.

The Supreme Court had handed down *Engel v. Vitale* shortly before agreeing to hear *Murray v. Curlett,* and the Murrays' brief followed the reasoning of that decision closely. They asserted that they had no objection to the use of religious texts in secular instruction, "including the Bible in all or any of its versions, when such material is presented and discussed as literature or history." What they opposed, they explained, was exactly what the Court had struck down in *Engel:* "favor for religion as opposed to non-religion, and . . . the conduct of religious teachings, whether such teachings be called sectarian or whether they be called non-sectarian" (Brief of the Petitioners, December 10, 1962, p. 9). In arguing that the recently adopted opt-out policy did not adequately resolve the dispute, they relied heavily on the Court's ruling that school-sponsored religious observances are unconstitutional even if dissenters are excused.

Engel was, of course, very bad news for the school officials, whose case had until then been based on the assertion that nonsectarianism and an opt-out policy were sufficient to render school-sponsored prayer constitutional. In an attempt to find new groun4 ground on which to stand, their brief alleged that the opening exercises in the Baltimore schools were not merely nonsectarian but entirely nonreligious. While conceding that the Bible and the Lord's Prayer are religious in origin, the brief contended that they "are not used in the challenged opening exercises as a form of religious instruction or as a religious service. Rather, these materials are utilized as a source of inspirational appeal to inculcate moral and ethical precepts of value in a salutary and sobering exercise with which to begin the school day" (Brief of Respondents, January 8, 1963, p. 4). Unable to find any comparable distinction between Maryland's opt-out policy and the one struck down in *Engel,* the school officials had little choice but to ask the Court to reconsider its ruling on that point.

The Other Shoe Drops

While the Murrays and the Baltimore school officials were preparing their briefs, the Supreme Court agreed to hear another school-prayer case, *Abington v. Schempp. Abington* was an ACLU-supported Pennsylvania lawsuit that O'Hair often mentioned when castigating the organization for declining to represent her. Although the background of *Abington* was considerably less dramatic than that of *Murray,* the two appeals raised the same issues, and the Supreme Court heard them together and handed down a single decision covering both. At issue in *Abington* was a 1949 Pennsylvania statute mandating that "'At least ten verses from the Holy Bible shall be read, or caused to be read, without comment, at the opening of each public school on each school day, by the teacher in charge. . . . If any school teacher, whose duty it shall be to read the Holy Bible, or cause it to be read, shall fail or omit so to do, said school teacher shall, upon charges preferred for such failure or omission, and proof of the same, before the board of school directors of the school district, be discharged'" *(Schempp v. Abington,* 177 F. Supp. 398 [1959], p. 399, n. 3). Although the statute did not mention the Lord's Prayer, Abington officials confirmed that it was recited as a matter of tradition throughout the district.

The oldest of the Schempps' three children, Ellory, was a junior at Abington High School when he concluded from his study of the Bill of Rights that the daily Bible-reading and prayer were unconstitutional. With his parents' approval, he stopped participating in the devotionals, and his homeroom teacher sent him to the vice-principal for refusing to rise for the Lord's Prayer. In a recent interview with Robert Alley, a prominent opponent of state-sponsored school prayer, Schempp recalled that the vice-principal was "flabbergasted by my behavior" (Alley, 1996, p. 94). The boy was referred to the guidance counselor, who, Schempp quipped, eventually concluded that he was sane and allowed him to spend homeroom period in her office each day. A new principal later rescinded that arrangement and required Ellory to participate in the prayers, but by then he had already contacted the ACLU. In February 1958, ACLU attorneys filed suit in federal court on behalf of the Schempp family, which included two younger children who would continue to attend the Abington public schools after Ellory graduated. On the advice of his lawyers, Ellory complied under protest with the requirement to take part in the morning exercises, as did the younger Schempp children.

The Abington school officials' refusal to establish an opt-out policy even after the lawsuit was filed was one of the few elements distinguishing the Schempp case from *Murray v. Curlett,* and it arose because they maintained all along that the exercises were not religious. They described the daily Bible-reading not as worship but as an educational exercise designed to familiarize students with a seminal text that has played a major role in American history, as well as influencing literature throughout the western world and promoting generally accepted moral norms. Since the Bible-reading was not being conducted as a religious exercise, they asserted, no student had any basis for demanding to be excused as a matter of religious freedom. The Schempps retorted that the state law's repeated references to the "Holy" Bible and the reverential manner in which the daily readings were conducted suggested otherwise. They challenged their opponents to provide another example of secular instruction that consisted of requiring all students to rise from their seats for the reading of archaic and complex language to children as young as six with no explanation or discussion. And where else in the curriculum, they inquired, did teachers face dismissal for failing to use exactly the same text and teaching method from the first grade through the senior year of high school? Further, the Schempps maintained, the Bible-reading was not only religious but sectarian. As Unitarians, they asserted that their beliefs conflicted with such biblical doctrines as the Immaculate Conception, the Trinity, the divinity of Christ, and the anthropomorphic nature of God. They also objected to stories of blood sacrifices, uncleanness, leprosy, and a vengeful Deity. And, they added, there could be no secular justification for demanding that all students stand to recite the Lord's Prayer every day. Accordingly, they sought not an opt-out policy but the removal of Bible-reading and the Lord's Prayer from the official school program.

Since the facts of the morning exercises were not in dispute, both sides relied heavily on expert witnesses to explain their significance. The Schempps' expert was a rabbi and scholar, Dr. Solomon Grayzel, who concentrated on making the point that the daily Bible-reading was both religious and sectarian. "I don't want to step on anybody's toes," he testified, "but the idea of God having a son is, from the viewpoint of Jewish faith, practically blasphemous" (trial transcript, August 5, 1958. p.44). Similarly, he denied the school board's assertion that the readings took place without comment, since the KJB contains Christocentric chapter headings, epigraphs, and other explanatory material suggesting, among other things, that the primary purpose of the Hebrew scriptures/Old Testament is to foretell the coming of Jesus. He also asserted that Jewish students were harmed by the use of certain verses, notably the one in which the Jews cry out to Pontius Pilate, "His blood be upon us and upon our children." "And I submit to you," he testified, "that this verse, *this* exclamation has been the cause of more anti-Jewish riots throughout the ages than anything else in history. And if you subject a Jewish child to listening to *this* sort of reading, which is not at all unlikely before . . . Easter, I think he is being subjected to little short of torture" (p. 53). Indeed, he asserted, such passages do more harm when read without any clarification other than the KJB notes than they might do if accompanied by a cultural or historical explanation.

To counter Dr. Grayzel's remarks, Dr. Luther Allan Weigle, dean emeritus of Yale Divinity School, testified that neither the Bible nor the practice of reading it without comment is sectarian. The Bible, he argued, has "great value, it seems to me, to the perpetuation of those institutions and those practices which we ideally think of as the American way of life, because the Bible has entered vitally into the stream of American life" (p. 154). He added, "I see nothing in the Lord's Prayer that is sectarian. Everything in that prayer can be paralleled in Jewish literature, in the Holy Scriptures of the Jewish people" (p. 155)·. Nevertheless, when the Schempps' attorney asked him, "When you said 'non-sectarian,' did you mean as among the various Protestant sects?" he replied, "I meant among the various Christian bodies" (p. 161).

Weigle's Christocentric view of the Bible probably did not help the school officials' case, but it made little real difference because the main issue was not whether the Abington morning exercises were sectarian but whether they were in any way religious. And even that turned out to be a pointless distinction, since the federal district court that heard the case declared that public schools were prohibited not only from promoting sectarian tenets but also from advancing religion in general over nonbelief. While agreeing with the school officials that the secular use of the Bible as an instructional tool would be constitutional, it rejected their contention that such was the case here. "In our view," the decision stated, "inasmuch as the Bible deals with man's relationship to God and the Pennsylvania statute may require a daily reminder of that relationship, that statute aids all religions. Inasmuch as the 'Holy Bible' is a Christian document, the practice aids and prefers the Christian religion" (p. 405).

Try, Try Again

At the time this decision was handed down, the Supreme Court had not yet ruled in *Engel* that opt-out provisions are insufficient to render state-sponsored prayer constitutional. Consequently, the Pennsylvania school authorities thought that if they established a provision for excusing individual students, they might be able to preserve the morning devotionals even if the courts continued to deem them religious. Thus, the Pennsylvania statute was amended to say: "Any child shall be excused from such Bible reading, or attending such Bible reading, upon the written request of his parent or guardian" *(Schempp v. Abington,* 201 F. Supp. 815 [1962], p. 817). School officials then asked the court to reverse its ruling and dismiss the case on the ground that the opt-out policy had resolved the conflict between the Schempps and the school district. When the Schempps reiterated that what they wanted was not an opt-out policy but the termination of the religious exercises, the court ordered a new trial.

Ellory Schempp was in college when the second trial took place in 1961, but his siblings, Roger and Donna, were still in the Abington public schools. They had chosen not to take advantage of the new opt-out policy, and despite a barrage of objections from the school board's attorneys, their father was allowed to explain why. "We originally objected to our children being exposed to the reading of the King James version of the Bible," he testified, "which we felt was against our particular family's religious beliefs, and under those conditions we would have theoretically liked to have the children excused. But we felt that the penalty of having our children labelled as 'odd balls' before their teachers and classmates every day in the year was even less satisfactory than the other problem" (trial transcript, October 17, 1961, p. 214). Moreover, although there had been no suggestion that his family had Communist connections, Schempp worried about the popular perception that opponents of school prayer were atheists, and atheists were Communists. As he pointed out, children excused from the prayers would also miss the Pledge of Allegiance, thus further confusing the issue of exactly what they were dissenting from. The school board's lawyers tried to counter his testimony by arguing that a particular family's choice not to use the opt-out policy did not detract from its effectiveness in protecting the rights of dissenters, but the court was not persuaded. In its view, the morning exercises were school-sponsored religion, and the opt-out policy neither made that sponsorship constitutional nor eliminated coercion to participate.

Following its second loss in the district court, the school board turned to the U.S. Supreme Court, which agreed to hear an appeal. (The title of the case then changed from *Schempp v. Abington,* as it had been when the Schempps were suing the Abington board, to *Abington v. Schempp,* indicating that the board was now initiating the legal action.) By this time, the Supreme Court's decision in *Engel* had been announced, and in an effort to prevent that precedent from dooming their case, the school officials' attorneys raised a novel argument. In order to be truly neutral toward religion, they asserted, the courts must not change the way anything has been done in the past. "Does not the religious neutrality required by the First Amendment mean that neither the religious nor the nonreligious may use the government to improve their respective positions?" they asked. Pointing out that the Court had rejected attempts to add new religious exercises to public schools in *McCcollum* and *Engel,* they asserted that neutrality required it to uphold the existing practices of the Pennsylvania schools. Otherwise, if courts could halt the introduction of new religious observances while removing the old ones, the result would not be religious neutrality but "a policy that required the government to remove from public life all of the admittedly existing religious leaven and in its place establish an absolute nonreligious state. Such a policy could not be considered by reasonable men to be anything other than one of hostility toward religion as a matter of law" (Brief for Appellants, January 4, 1963, p. 39). The Schempps retorted that whenever their opponents said that "the government" should be neutral in religious matters, they invariably meant only the judicial branch. "This is a curious and ingenious argument," their brief suggested. "Its initial fallacy is the equation of this Court with 'the government.' It blithely ignores the obvious fact that what [the Schempps] are complaining about is that 'the government' in the person of the legislature of Pennsylvania has not observed the 'neutrality towards religion' which [the school officials] so rightly commend. In such a situation to urge this Court to be 'neutral' by not interfering is to be oblivious to the very function of the judiciary and, because one branch of the government is induced to remain supine, the non-neutrality of the other is allowed to continue. This is neutrality with a vengeance!" (Brief for Appellees, February 1r, 1963, p. 22).

Schempp Meets Murray

On February 27, 1963, the Supreme Court heard oral arguments in *Murray v. Curlett* and *Abington v. Schempp*. The first speaker was the Murrays' lawyer, Leonard Kerpelman, who denied his opponents' assertion that school prayer was acceptable as a matter of tradition. "'Well I don't think, if Your Honors please, that we can repeal the Constitution by this particular means," he said. "A matter which is once unconstitutional does not become constitutional by being allowed to persist" (transcript of the oral argument in *Murray v. Curlett,* p. 4). The justices, as is their custom, interrupted frequently. Justice Potter Stewart, the lone dissenter in *Engel,* was particularly persistent in challenging Kerpelman about the rights of the students who wanted to pray and about the use of a demurrer instead of a trial in the Maryland courts. His point was that because no trial had taken place, there was no testimony or other evidence to show how the school had conducted the prayers and enforced the opt-out policy.

The school board's lawyer, an experienced advocate named Francis Burch, had an even worse time, albeit for different reasons. When he claimed that Bible-reading had a calming effect on the students, one of the justices said, "You could just give them tranquilizer pills, if that's—if that's the purpose" (p. 22). Later, in an effort to demonstrate that the Bible was not being read for religious reasons, Burch speculated that the people of Baltimore might be equally willing to have their children read the Koran, the Veda, or a Buddhist text. The Court's response appears in a parenthetical notation in the transcript: "[Laughter]." When Burch tried again to make that point, Justice Black cut in. "It seems to me," he observed, "like you'd do better if you'd face the issue. I don't know what's the answer to it, but how can you assert seriously or argue or ask us to consider seriously this is not a religious ceremony based on the Bible and the Lord's Prayer? Those who are strongest for it I doubt, would not hesitate to say that" (p. 27).

Following the oral argument in *Murray,* the Court heard from attorneys representing the Abington school board and the Schempps. The board's attorney, Philip Ward, disagreed with the Schempps' contention that the opt-out provision harmed dissenters by marking them as "different." On the contrary, he suggested, the policy was a celebration of individuality that contrasted with the bleak enforced orthodoxy of dictatorships. In response to one justice's suggestion that his advocacy of opt-out policies sounded like the separate-but-equal doctrine of racial segregation, he declared, "'That's the glory of the country: they can be separate, they have the right to be separate. There are only two places where they would all be the same. One, of course, would be a totalitarian state where we couldn't be different; and two would be some sort of big togetherness state where we never did anything unless everybody wanted to do that very same thing" transcript of the oral argument in *Abington v. Schempp*, p. 14). Shortly afterward, Justice Black asked Ward about the use of the Koran as a source of moral precepts, and Ward quipped, "The one thing I know about the Koran is it says that you should have no more than four wives." Using his joke as an illustration, he told Black that the Baltimore schools would not use the Koran "because we don't consider the Koran the supreme source of morality that we consider the Bible." "Why?" asked Black. Because, Ward said, it is better to use a familiar book that teaches morals of which everybody approves. Black said, "Everybody?" (pp. 19–20) and Ward conceded that he meant the majority, but he continued to maintain that the reason for using the Bible was not that it is a religious text.

The Schempps' attorney, Henry Sawyer, ridiculed Ward's claims about the Bible as a source of moral instruction by quoting several scriptural passages involving actions that would not be morally acceptable today. His main point, however, was not to critique the Bible but to argue that state-sponsored religious practices are unconstitutional. "The question is," he said, "is it a constitutional right, under the free exercise clause, to have the state conduct the prayer, or 'to pray,' in other words, under the aegis of the state? And I think clearly not. Even if the overwhelming majority so feel, I think it probably has nothing to do with the question of majorities" (p. 29). This mention of majorities led Justice Stewart to ask whether Bible-reading would be acceptable if the students themselves voted overwhelmingly to have it, and Sawyer's response reflected the distinction between government and private action that would later become a dominant element in school-prayer lawsuits. If, he said, the students in Stewart's hypothetical situation were acting entirely on their own, that would be fine; but if the Bible-reading were conducted over the public address system when the students were gathered for other school purposes that would involve school sponsorship and would be unacceptable regardless of the majority vote. "But isn't it a gross interference with the free exercise of the religion," Stewart asked, "of those, in my imaginary case—those 98 percent of the student body who say our religious beliefs tell us that this is what we want to do?" "Well, they have a right to do it, Your Honor," Sawyer replied, "but they haven't got a right to get the state to help them" (p. 30). Later, the Court raised the question of America's religious heritage, and Sawyer responded with an impassioned speech. "I think tradition is not to be scoffed at," he said, "but let me say this very candidly: I think it is the final arrogance to talk constantly about the religious tradition in this country and equate it with this Bible. Sure, religious tradition. Whose religious tradition? It isn't any part of the religious tradition of a substantial number of Americans. . . . And it's just, to me, a little bit easy and I say arrogant to keep talking about our religious tradition. It suggests that the public schools, at least of Pennsylvania, are a kind of Protestant institution to which others are cordially invited" (p. 46).

Decision

In an 8-r 1 decision, the Supreme Court found in favor of the Schempps and the Murrays. To Madalyn Murray's fury, the cases were listed in that order, and the decision is so commonly referred to as "Abington" that few nonlawyers realize that it also covered her case. She later alleged that although the Court had received her appeal first, given it a lower file number, and heard it first, "so great was the onus against [atheists] that in the historical recording of the case it was titled Abington School District vs. Schempp rather than to let the name of Atheists *(Murray v. Curlett)* be reported out in any official United States legal reports!!" (O'Hair, p. 277).

The opinion, written by Justice Tom Clark, was based on an early version of a concept that was later expanded into the so-called *Lemon* test (see Chapter Fourteen [of *The Fourth R*, DelFattore]). In determining whether a school prayer law is constitutional, Justice Clark wrote, "The test may be stated as follows: What are the purpose and the primary effect of the enactment? If either is the advancement or inhibition of religion then the enactment exceeds the scope of legislative power as circumscribed by the Constitution. That is to say that to withstand the strictures of the Establishment Clause there must be a secular legislative purpose and a primary effect that neither advances nor inhibits religion" *(Abington v. Schempp,* 374 U.S. 203; 83 S.Ct. 1560 [1963], p. 222). On the basis of that standard, the Court declared that the morning exercises in the public schools of Abington and Baltimore were unconstitutional because the advancement of religion was their primary purpose and effect. Moreover, far from improving the situation, the opt-out policies merely provided further evidence that the activities were religious.

In response to the argument that eliminating Bible-reading and the Lord's Prayer from the public schools would show hostility toward religion, the decision stated, "We agree of course that the State may not establish a 'religion of secularism' in the sense of affirmatively opposing or showing hostility to religion. . . . We do not agree, however, that this decision in any sense has that effect." The Court also clarified, as it had done in *Engel,* that "Nothing we have said here indicates that [literary or historical] study of the Bible or of religion, when presented objectively as part of a secular program of education, may not be effected consistently with the First Amendment. But the exercises here do not fall into those categories. They are religious exercises, required by the States in violation of the command of the First Amendment that the Government maintain strict neutrality, neither aiding nor opposing religion" (p. 225). Similarly, the Court rejected the school board's contention that terminating state-sponsored religious observances would violate the religious freedom of the majority. "[W]e cannot accept," the decision stated, "that the concept of neutrality, which does not permit a State to require a religious exercise even with the consent of the majority of those affected, collides with the majority's right to free exercise of religion. While the Free Exercise Clause clearly prohibits the use of state action to deny the rights of free exercise to *anyone,* it has never meant that a majority could use the machinery of the State to practice its beliefs" (pp. 225–26).

As he had done in *Engel,* Justice William O0. Douglas wrote a concurrence arguing for the elimination of all government funding for religious purposes. The lone dissent in *Abington,* as in *Engel,* was written by Justice Stewart, although in this case he stopped short of saying definitively that the morning exercises were constitutional. The reason for his indecision was that *Murray* and *Abington,* as presented to the Court, did not include what he considered adequate factual information. Unlike his colleagues, Stewart thought that opt-out policies were capable of providing adequate protection for dissenters, but because there was no evidence showing how they were applied in the Baltimore and Abington schools, he did not declare outright that the practices of those schools were acceptable. Instead, he stated as a general principle that the only obligation the government owes dissenters is "that of refraining from so structuring the school environment as to put any kind of pressure on a child to participate in those exercises; it is not that of providing an atmosphere in which children are kept scrupulously insulated from any awareness that some of their fellows may want to open the school day with prayer, or of the fact that there exist in our pluralistic society differences of religious belief" (pp. 31r6–1r7). On the other hand, "if the exercises were held during the school day, and no equally desirable alternative were provided by the school authorities, the likelihood that children might be under at least some psychological compulsion to participate would be great. . . . [But] I think we would err if we *assumed* such coercion in the absence of any evidence" (p. 318). Ideally, he suggested, religious exercises might be held before or after school or when students were free to engage in any one of several activities. More than twenty years later, after he had retired from the Court, a version of that plan passed Congress overwhelmingly under the title of the Equal Access Act, which the Court subsequently upheld (see Chapters Eleven and Twelve [of *The Fourth R*, DelFattore]).

Go Thou and Do Likewise

Naturally, *Abington* had a marked impact on other school-prayer cases making their way through the courts. Notable among these was *Chamberlin v. Dade County Board of Public Instruction,* which went through the Florida state courts in conjunction with another case, *Resnick v. Dade County.* The plaintiffs were agnostic, Jewish, and Unitarian parents who objected to such activities as Bible-reading (with and without comment), the Lord's Prayer, after-hours Bible classes, religious films and symbols, holiday services, a religious census of the students, and religious tests for the employment and promotion of school personnel. They also sought to prevent the Gideons from distributing Bibles in the school and to remove a sign erected on the school lawn by a local church. Despite an opt-out policy covering some of these practices, the plaintiffs wanted all of them terminated.

The trial court upheld most of the disputed practices, including Bible reading and the Lord's Prayer. The Florida State Supreme Court affirmed this decision, declaring that the U.S. Supreme Court's distorted interpretations of the Constitution were undermining the rightful authority of the states and threatening the "long established and accepted customs of the vast majority of the American people" *(Chamberlin v. Dade County,* 1r43 So. 2d 21r [1r962], p. 30). The Florida court also objected to what it saw as the misuse of the Constitution to bestow special privileges on minorities. *Chamberlin,* it contended, was "just another case in which the tender sensibilities of certain minorities are sought to be protected against the allegedly harsh laws and customs enacted and established by the more rugged pioneers of the Nation. In the instant case we are told that the primary objects of solicitude are the children of the plaintiffs, atheists, Unitarians and Jews, which children, although not required to be present at the time, will, so it is said, suffer some supposedly irreparable emotional stress if their classmates are permitted to hear the Bible read" (pp. 31–32). Indeed, the court found, the opt-out policy itself was evidence of special treatment for minorities, since students could not ordinarily pick and choose which parts of the state-approved school program they wished to attend. "The plaintiffs assume," said the court, "inferentially at least, that minorities enjoy a peculiar susceptibility to psychological and emotional trauma and compulsions and are entitled to some peculiar and fatherly protection against the strange ways of the ordinary American citizen. But such is not the case. The minority is entitled to enjoy the same privileges and the same justice as are enjoyed by people generally as an inherent right. The minority and the majority are both denied the privilege of disrupting the lives of others because of some hyper -sensitivity or fractious temperament" (p. 32).

Chamberlin was appealed to the U.S. Supreme Court, which vacated the decision of the Florida Supreme Court and sent the case back with instructions to reconsider it in light of *Abington.* The Florida court subsequently affirmed its earlier ruling on the ground that Florida's Bible-reading statute had the explicit secular purpose "'of good moral training, of a life of honorable thought and good citizenship."' More significantly, the court declined to comply with *Abington* because it felt that "the establishment clause of the Constitution was never designed to prohibit the practices complained of" *(Chamberlin v. Dade County,* 171 So. 2d 535 [1965], pp. 537, 538). Once again, the plaintiffs appealed to the

U.S. Supreme Court, which struck down Bible-reading and the recitation of the Lord's Prayer in the Florida schools but did not address the plaintiffs' other claims because they were not presented in a way that would allow a federal court to decide them.

Although the Supreme Court elected to make *Abington* rather than *Chamberlin* its test case on Bible-reading and prayer in the public schools, one of the issues raised by the Florida lawsuit deserves mention because of its relevance to later school-prayer controversies. The *Resnick* plaintiffs' attorney, Leo Pfeffer, was a renowned First Amendment litigator and scholar who had, among other things, written amici curiae briefs in *Engel* and *Abington* on behalf of the Synagogue Council of America and the National Community Relations Advisory Council. As a lead attorney in *Resnick,* he framed the case in terms of the Free Exercise Clause, whereas *Murray* and *Abington,* like most school-prayer lawsuits of that time, emphasized the Establishment Clause. This distinction is important because the Establishment Clause defines what the government can and cannot do: in particular, it cannot favor or disfavor any religious view. By contrast, the Free Exercise Clause focuses on the right of individuals, including students, to practice their religion as they see fit. In Pfeffer's view, prescribing certain religious observances for use in the public schools not only represented an establishment of religion by the government but also impinged on the students' personal right to free exercise of religion. Ironically, Pfeffer's approach had a great deal in common with that of Justice Potter Stewart, the only member of the Supreme Court who wanted to uphold state-sponsored prayer in *Engel* and *Abington* as long as dissenters were offered a sufficiently attractive way to opt out. Both Pfeffer and Stewart sought to emphasize not the school officials' behavior but the students' religious rights. T1he reason they disagreed so completely about whether state-sponsored school prayer is permissible is that Stewart discussed free exercise in terms of the right of the majority to have its prayers, whereas Pfeffer thought that the Free Exercise Clause was meant to protect religious minorities from state interference with their religious practices (as by trying to engage them in religious observances other than their own). Nevertheless, each of them maintained in his own way that school-prayer lawsuits should focus not on school officials but on students. Had the Supreme Court elected to decide *Chamberlin/ Resnick,* with its emphasis on the Free Exercise Clause, rather than *Abington,* based primarily on the Establishment Clause, the case law regarding school prayer might well have evolved differently, or at least at a different rate of progression. As Chapters Eleven and Twelve [of *The Fourth R*, DelFattore] demonstrate, the student-focused approach advocated in different ways by Pfeffer and Stewart eventually became the dominant model for resolving school-prayer disputes, although arguably later than it might otherwise have done.

Second Generation

As the Florida State Supreme Court's remarks suggested, some states and school districts were loathe to comply with *Abington,* and the inevitable result was more lawsuits. As an example, New Jersey Attorney General Arthur Sills sued two recalcitrant school boards in his state, one of which had also been sued a decade earlier in *Doremus v. Board of Education of Hawthorne,* a school-prayer case dismissed by the Supreme Court because the plaintiffs' child had graduated (see Chapter Four [of *The Fourth R*, DelFattore]). The outcome of *Doremus* had left Hawthorne's religious practices intact, and despite the Supreme Court's subsequent ruling in *Abington,* the school board refused to terminate them. In *Sills v. Board of Education of Hawthorne,* both the Superior Court of New Jersey and the State Supreme Court ruled against the Hawthorne officials, who thereupon reluctantly complied.

In contrast to the Hawthorne board's open defiance of *Abington,* the school board in Netcong, New Jersey, tried a less direct approach. Over Sills's objections, it established morning exercises in which students read and reflected on the sections of the *Congressional Record* in which the prayers of the House and Senate chaplains are reported. When this stratagem was brought to the attention of Congress, Representative Richard Roudebush (R-Indiana) applauded "the ingenious idea of reading Chaplain prayers from the *Congressional Record* each day as a substitute for regular prayer services outlawed by the Supreme Court." Realizing that the chaplains' prayers might be difficult for younger students to understand, he and some of his colleagues began reading children's prayers into each week's *Record.* "I hope this plan catches on like wildfire," Roudebush said, "and that schools across the Nation will turn to the pages of the *Congressional Record* for a source of children's prayers inserted to provide a legal remedy to the tragic Supreme Court decision" *(Congressional Record,* October 2, 1969, p. 282–84).

Bolstered by such support, the Netcong board defied Sills's order to terminate the readings, and he once again went to court. The dispute became so unpleasant that the trial court reproved pro-prayer activists for describing those who differed with them "as 'Anti-God,' 'Anti-Christ' or 'Communists.' Telegrams and letters were sent to the court . . . which clearly and depressingly set forth the temper of the community and the eagerness of certain 'citizens' to create division, diversion and prejudice" *(State Board of Education v. Board of Education of Netcong,* 108ro8 N.J). Super. 564; 262 A. 2d 21 [1970], p.571). Similarly, the court chastised the board for using "intemperate and unwarranted adjectives" to describe the Supreme Court, and it cited several early school-prayer decisions to refute the assertion that *Abington* was "a recently concocted, ultra-liberal construction of our Federal Constitution" (p. 580). Not surprisingly, the court also rejected the argument that reading what the Netcong board described as "remarks" from the *Congressional Record* was a secular exercise. In its view, "To call some of the beautiful prayers in the *Congressional Record* 'remarks' for a deceptive purpose is to peddle religion in a very cheap manner under an assumed name. This type of subterfuge is degrading to all religions" (p. 583). This decision was upheld by the New Jersey State Supreme Court, and when the U.S. Supreme Court declined to hear an appeal, Representative John Hunt (R-New Jersey) protested, "it is extremely difficult to comprehend how this innocuous exercise . . . violates the spirit oftheof the Constitution. In my estimation, it is the denial of this right that is a gross distortion of the ideals and aspirations of our Founding Fathers" *(Congressional Record,* December 3, 1970, p. 39853).

The Other Way Around

Whereas both New Jersey cases were filed by state officials against local boards, in other instances it was the state authorities themselves who were sued for defying *Abington.* Such a lawsuit took place just across New Jersey's southern border, where the attorney general of Delaware, David Buckson, ordered school officials to ignore the Court's ruling. Delaware's two school-prayer statutes, adopted in 1953 to codify much older practices, required the reading of at least five Bible verses daily and forbade all religious exercises other than Bible-reading and the recitation of the Lord's Prayer. Teachers who failed to comply faced a twenty-five-dollar fine for the first offense (a substantial part of a week's salary in 1953) and the revocation of their teaching credentials for any subsequent offense. The Lord's Prayer, permitted but not required by law, was commonly recited following the Bible-reading. Although the statutes did not specify any particular version of the Bible, school officials stated that they purchased only the KJB and, as far as they knew, no other translation was used in the schools.

Attorney General Buckson told Delaware school officials to continue these practices after *Abington* because, he claimed, state laws took precedence over Supreme Court rulings. The president of the ACLU of Delaware, Irving Morris, retorted that unless Delaware had seceded from the Union, it was subject to the rulings of federal courts. He also told a reporter for the local newspaper that the ACLU-DE would provide legal representation to any parents who wanted to challenge Buckson's order. Morris later explained that the organization had been asked several times to file a school-prayer lawsuit but had declined to do so because its resources were stretched to the limit by a school-desegregation fight that was then raging. Nevertheless, he wrote in a magazine article, "I was not at all prepared to have the chief law enforcement officer in Delaware abandon the rule of law, which is the essence of the social compact. . . . Attorney General Buckson' s opinion set an example for the people of the State of Delaware to follow, which, I thought, would have put us on the road to anarchy; I would have none of it" (Morris, 1986, p. 8). More prosaically, he acknowledged that the case was such an easy win that it required little effort. Indeed, the complaint he filed consisted of little more than a reference to *Abington*.

The plaintiffs on whose behalf Morris filed the lawsuit were W. Harry and Anne Johns of Dover and Garry and Mary De Young of Middletown. Each couple had children in the Delaware schools, and Mary De Young taught second grade at Middletown School No. 60Go. Nevertheless, Buckson denied that either family had standing to sue. As he framed the argument, Delaware's school-prayer laws could be challenged only if they promoted a religion with which the plaintiffs disagreed. The Johns's, he said, were Presbyterians who could hardly claim that reading the KJB and reciting the Lord's Prayer contradicted their religion. Garry and Mary De Young were agnostics, and Buckson argued that it is impossible to violate the religious convictions of people who do not know what their convictions are. Had he prevailed, the often-repeated accusation that anyone who opposes school prayer must be an atheist or at least a non-Christian would have become reality, since only those whose views were demonstrably incompatible with the Bible would have been able to challenge traditional public-school devotionals.

The lawsuit, *Johns v. Allen* (Robert Allen was the first-named member of the state school board), was heard by a three-judge panel of the federal district court headed by Chief Judge John Biggs, Jr., of the Court of Appeals for the Third Circuit. Judge Biggs, who had presided over a similar panel in *Abington,* had written the decision that had subsequently been upheld by the Supreme Court. Delaware's school-prayer statutes were almost identical to the Pennsylvania law struck down in *Abington,* and Biggs, whom Morris described as "tall, autocratic, powerful" (p. 13), did not look favorably on Buckson's open defiance. Moreover, as Buckson pointed out with a laugh during an interview for this book, the opposing candidate he had defeated for the post of attorney general had been none other than John Biggs III. Obviously, Buckson knew that he had no chance of success; as he explained in the interview, he was hoping to run for governor and did not want to appear to be cooperating too tamely with a Supreme Court ruling that most Delawareans disliked. An interview with Morris elicited roughly the same idea from a different perspective: "What'd he have to lose? If he won, he was a miracle worker. If not, well, at least he would've put up a fight" (January 16, 1997). Other elected officials, from the governor on down, followed Buckson's lead in emphasizing that the threat to the popular religious exercises emanated from the federal courts, not from them. Since Delaware's schools were embroiled in an intensely controversial court-ordered program of racial desegregation, the federal judiciary was an easy target for public wrath.

At the trial, the Johns's echoed the sentiments expressed by a fellow Presbyterian, Samuel Thayer Spear, almost a century earlier (see Chapter Four [of The Fourth R, DelFattore]). In Harry Johns's view, "[T]o establish that the King James version of the Bible is read in our schools surely must prejudice [children] to feel that this is the authorized Bible in the public schools, and I feel that is wrong." As a member of the Protestant majority, he said, "I feel I have a greater responsibility under the American concept of religious freedom to protect those who do not read my Bible at home or do not read any Bible." Anne Johns added that school prayer "is damaging to [children's] development as citizens of our country because we teach them to admire and respect certain ideals that our country stands for, like religious freedom and equality. But when they get to school they find out that priority is given to Protestants. And I think that this demonstrates a double standard in our attitude" (trial transcript, January 27, 1964, pp. 123, 130, 154)·. Mary De Young's testimony was similar to that of the Johns's, but Garry DeYoung proved to be a much more inflammatory witness. Among other things, he said that all Catholic nuns and priests are sexual perverts, and he testified at length about a book of iconoclastic, erotic poetry that he had published at his own expense. Morris later confessed that he had been unaware of his client's more exotic views and was horrified when a front-page story in The next day's newspaper left the impression that he himself shared them.

The trial was further enlivened by a celebrity witness, Episcopal Bishop James Pike of California, a well-known advocate of state-sponsored school prayer. He denied that Delaware's school-prayer laws favored Christianity because, he said, Jesus was "a first-century rabbi' and the Lord's Prayer is "the summation of Jewish piety" (trial transcript, March 30, 1r964, p. 250). He added that nothing in the Bible conflicts with Jewish beliefs when read without comment. "[H]earing what the New Testament says in a literary way about Jesus Christ," he said, "no Jew could say is not so, that is, the Bible does say it and it is part of the literature of our culture that these beautiful words have been written, and any Jew knows that" (p. 275). Similarly, he stated that the rights of agnostics and atheists were not being violated "because it is not being read devotionally; it is being read like five verses of Shakespeare" (p. 257).

Following the trial, the Middletown School Board announced that it would not renew Mary De Young's teaching contract for the following year. Morris offered to represent her in a suit against the school district, but she declined. The De Youngs moved to another state, which forced them to withdraw from the case before the decision was issued. To no one's surprise, that decision, written by Judge Biggs, struck down Delaware's school-prayer laws not only because Bible-reading and the Lord's Prayer were religious but also because the exclusion of any other form of worship favored a particular religious tradition. Governor Elbert Carvel announced that the state would appeal to the Supreme Court, but Buckson dissuaded him because such an appeal would have been costly, time-consuming, and unsuccessful. Having made his points—political, personal, and legal—he told the school officials to obey the court's order. As Morris would have it, Delaware was back in the Union.

In the Public Arena

In addition to generating a series of lawsuits, *Abington* unleashed a flood of public and political protest. Nevertheless, although this decision affected far more schools than did *Engel,* the reaction to it lacked the note of startled hysteria that had greeted the Court's first intervention in school-prayer matters. Among other things, the news media, which had helped to exaggerate the effect of *Engel,* was better prepared to deal with shades of meaning in *Abington.* University of Virginia law professor Robert O'Neil, who was Justice William Brennan's law clerk when *Abington* was decided, recalled seeing a headline saying, "Supreme Court Bans Devotional Use of the Bible in Schools." The qualifying term "Devotional," he felt, marked an improvement over the frenzied coverage of *Engel,* which had suggested that no mention of God was permitted in public schools (interview, December 10ro, 1999). Like the media, some religious leaders responded in a more measured way to *Abington* than they had to *Engel.* Among these was the dean of the Episcopal Cathedral in Chicago, who told a reporter for *Time* magazine, '"Unlike last year when I reacted emotionally, illogically, and non-intellectually, this decision doesn't disturb me'" (Fenwick, 1989, p. 139). Methodist Bishop John Wesley Lord also supported the Court, suggesting that the real tradition of religious freedom in America was better served by *Abington* than it would have been by the continuation of school prayer. '"We accept the declaration of the Court,"' he said, '"in full recognition of the historic spiritual value the decision seeks to preserve.'" Similarly, the 1963 assembly of the United Presbyterian Church declared, "Now that the Court has spoken, responsible Americans will abide by its decision in good grace"' *(Congressional Quarterly,* June 21, 1963, p. r1oo002).

Clearly, religious people who agreed with the Court were more outspoken and received more public attention after *Abington* than they had after *Engel.* Ironically but predictably, this indication that not all God-fearing Americans supported state-sponsored worship galvanized some school-prayer advocates into redoubling their efforts to make the Court's actions appear extreme. '"God pity our country,"' said evangelist Billy Graham, '"when we can no longer appeal to God for help"' (Beaney and Beiser, 1964/1993, p.419). Similarly, Bishop Fulton J. Sheen, a popular television evangelist known for his anti-Communist rhetoric, offered the bewildering but emotionally stirring prediction that the Court's next anti-prayer decision "will be a repetition of article 124 of the Soviet Constitution, which reads: 'The Soviet Union recognizes freedom of religious worship and freedom of antireligious propaganda.' If a court says, 'Thou shalt not pray,' because it will offend the atheists, then is not the next step to give to the atheists rather than to God-fearing men the right to propaganda? The next decision logically will be that one which affirms that antiprayer and antireligion in school have the support of law in education. America has reached a critical hour where its citizens must once again hear the words that Washington spoke to his soldiers at Valley Forge: 'Put only Americans on guard tonight"' *(Congressional Record,* March 11II, 1964, p. 50105oro).

Bishop Sheen's association of Abington with atheistic Communism was shared by several members of Congress and from there it was but a short step to the assertion that prayer is a fundamental right of American schoolchildren because this is a Christian nation. Senator Willis Robertson (D-Virginia), for instance, deploring what he saw as "disrespect for the Bible and for the fact

The Myth of Madalyn Murray O'Hair

"That we are a Christian Nation," asserted that "the most inherent distinction between our representative democracy and communism is our belief in God and the acceptance of the Bible as His Holy Word" (*Congressional Record*, June 19, 1963, pp. m4311143, m4511145). Among the most often used to justify this Christian Nation position was a book by Justice Joseph Story, who was appointed to the Supreme Court in 1811r8n. Although he was a child when the Constitution and the Bill of Rights were drafted, he was so close to the Framers' generation and such a prominent constitutional expert that his statements about their intentions are given great weight. Story wrote (1833/1987),

> Probably at the time of the adoption of the constitution, and of the [first] amendment to it . . . the general, if not the universal, sentiment in America was, that Christianity ought to receive encouragement from the state, so far as it is not incompatible with the private rights of conscience, and the freedom of religious worship. An attempt to level all religions, and to make it a matter of state policy to hold all in utter indifference, would have created universal disapprobation, if not universal indignation . . . . The real object of the amendment was, not to countenance, much less to advance Mahometanism, or Judaism, or infidelity, by prostrating Christianity; but to exclude all rivalry among Christian sects, and to prevent any national ecclesiastical establishment, which should give to an hierarchy the exclusive patronage of the national government. (pp. 700–701m)

Without necessarily challenging Story's analysis of the Framers' intent, foes of the Christian Nation theory vigorously denied that eighteenth-century social views should dominate current interpretations of the Constitution. As Justice Brennan observed in his concurring opinion in *Abington,* what the First Amendment protects is the concept of religious freedom, not the specific way in which it was put into practice two hundred years ago. By way of comparison, Christian Nation opponents noted that many Founders deemed "All men are created equal" compatible with slavery and with the denial of equal rights for women. Since then, they asserted, cultural evolution and the Fourteenth Amendment have caused the freedoms enjoyed by any demographic group to be shared by all, thus rendering the Founders' privileging of Christianity incompatible with the present-day understanding of religious freedom.

Civil Disobedience

As the Christian Nation rhetoric suggests, pockets of determined resistance to *Abington* continued in some areas, led by fiery political officials. Governor George

Wallace of Alabama, who had once blocked the entrance of the state university to impede court-ordered integration, announced, "I don't care what they say in Washington, we are going to keep right on praying and reading the Bible in the public schools of Alabama" (Alley, 1994, pp. 122–23). Similarly, Senator Olin Johnston (D-South Carolina) spoke out in favor of the kind of defiance exhibited by the Hawthorne and Netcong school districts in New Jersey and by the attorney general of Delaware. "Despite the Supreme Court ruling," he said, "I am urging schoolteachers and schools to continue the reading of the Bible and to continue praying in classrooms. There is no statutory provision to penalize the school officials for defying the Supreme Court. They can continue to pray and read the Bible in schools until a court injunction is issued in each individual and every case, restraining them from continuing the practice in defiance of the Supreme Court" (*Congressional Record,* June 19, 1963, p. 110rro90).

Amid all the political speeches and lawsuits, it was reasonable to ask whether most schools were in fact complying with the Supreme Court's ruling. Among those who sought to answer this question was education scholar H. Frank Way, Jr., who distributed a questionnaire to randomly selected teachers throughout the country. On the basis of their self-reports, he concluded that "with the exception of the South, the [religious] practices had largely disappeared in public elementary schools by the academic year 1964–65" (Way, 1968/1992, p. P-457).[1] A different methodology led to quite different results in a case study of four midwestern communities reported in *The School Prayer Decisions: From Court Policy to Local Practice* (1971). Its authors, Kenneth M. Dolbeare and Phillip E. Hammond, used interviews, public records, and on-site observation to support their assertion that relatively little change took place in communities where public pressure to retain the status quo was strong. While a few school officials openly defied the Court, they noted, far more found ways to engage in inaction, denial, conflict avoidance, and what the authors called "substantial cognitive deflection about actual local practices" (p. 68), resulting in inaccurate claims of being in compliance with the Court's rulings. The lawsuits discussed later in this book, filed as recently as the late twentieth and early twenty-first centuries against continuing school-sponsored prayers, tend to bear out Dolbeare and Hammond's conclusion that decisions such as *Engel* and *Abington* were merely "the opening of a long struggle in which lower level power holders often have the last word" (p. 153). As they further observed, compliance with the Court's rulings is likely to be enforced only when, and if, at least one resident or public official is willing to go to court. Understandably, people who see nothing wrong with school-sponsored prayer are frustrated to find that even if an overwhelming majority of residents want it to continue, their wishes can be overridden by anyone who chooses to sue. Accordingly, opponents of *Engel* and *Abington* initiated what became a decades-long effort to reverse the Court's rulings and reinstate traditional public-school devotionals.

Notes

1. Additional early scholarly studies on responses to *Engel* and *Abington* are summarized in Boles, 1967.

Section 13

Temple University

James Hilty • "Temple University: 125 Years of Service to Philadelphia, the Nation, and the World"

"Temple University: 125 Years of Service to Philadelphia, the Nation, and the World"

James Hilty

Temple University did not spring from the generosity of a captain or the munificence of a financial wizard. Unlike other multipurpose universities of today, Temple was not the creation of the state or the beneficiary of federal land grants. Neither did it have roots extending back scores of decades with connections to America's aristocracy; nor was it the vehicle of a religious order or an offshoot of a training institute, as were so many colleges founded in the latter part of the nineteenth century during America's Gilded Age.

Indeed, Temple's founding was principally the work of one man—not a captain of industry, but a captain of erudition, an educational entrepreneur who sought to democratize, diversify, and widen the reach of higher education. He challenged prevailing values and norms regarding the purposes of higher education and who should benefit. Rather than serve America's affluent classes, he provided deserving working men and women right of entry to an education otherwise denied them by circumstances of birth or life's station. Rather than provide only the esoteric classic curriculum, he prepared students for life's vicissitudes and for success in the modern world.

Universities are among the Western world's oldest and most stable institutions with continuous histories. Only the Roman Catholic Church, the law courts of certain European countries, some army regiments, and a few town and craft corporations can claim similar longevity. But, once Temple was begun, its survival and growth were far from certainties. Over the 125 years of its existence. Temple has faced many precarious moments, considerable adversity, and more than its share of financial difficulties.

In those 125 years, as it has grown physically and intellectually, Temple has evolved the ideals and purposes of its founder into a simple, compelling mantra: "Access to Excellence." By access we mean maintaining allegiance to the founder's pledge to serve deserving students from all stations in life, keeping an open mind on academic issues, and maintaining diversity in the student body, faculty, and staff. By *excellence* we mean providing the highest-quality education possible, advancing and disseminating knowledge and new discoveries through research and scholarly inquiry, developing and applying new approaches to learning, and sustaining an unshakable commitment to serve the community, the city, and the world.

The Man and the Vision

Russell Herman Conwell's life story and his aspirations for Temple University resonate with the personal life narratives of Temple University's students, faculty, staff, and alumni. He is connected to us all. Conwell played many roles—as an actor, showman, brilliant orator, journalist and editor, lawyer, minister, educator, real estate speculator, promoter, entrepreneur, and founder of Temple University. Most compellingly, Conwell grasped the meaning of his time, understood the moving forces of his generation, and demonstrated the courage to capture and control those forces and, in effect, bend history. His greatest contribution was the 'Temple Idea"—the conviction that a great university must do more than discipline the mind and conscience, expand knowledge, and prepare students for the workplace. It must also serve its community, uplift its people, and be a vehicle for social justice.

Conwell was a complex man, a mingling of myth and reality, and details of his early life remain unclear despite several biographies and despite Conwell's many autobiographical insertions in his lectures and writings. For whatever reasons, Conwell embellished significant episodes in his young adult life. Perhaps Professor J. Douglas Perry explained it best: Conwell understood intuitively that "to gain support for a cause or an institution, one must give to people an image on which they would look with wonderment, yet one with which they also could identify."

Born February 15, 1843, Russell Conwell was reared on a 350-acre hardscrabble subsistence farm in the Berkshires in western Massachusetts, near South Worthington, about fifteen miles from Westfield, Massachusetts. He attended Wilbraham Academy for two years and then taught school in South Worthington. Alas, most of Conwell's descriptions of his early adult life cannot be independently corroborated or verified through written records, although several historians have put considerable effort into the task.

Piecing together major elements of Conwell's early life, we learn that at a young age he developed exemplary elocutionary skills and a wondrous capacity for extemporaneous speaking, combined with an exceptional ability to attract attention. Conwell left home in 1861 to enroll at Yale University, where he planned to study law. To earn money for tuition he held several jobs near campus but apparently spent only a few months actually enrolled in classes. In later years Conwell freely admitted that he felt humiliated by the Yale students, many of whom mocked his shabby clothing, rural manners, and ungentlemanly resort to menial labor in a New Haven hotel.

When Civil War broke out, Conwell returned to Massachusetts, where he proved a persuasive recruiter for the Union cause, giving rousing patriotic speeches that made young men enlist on the spot. Credited with recruiting an entire company of volunteers, though only nineteen, he was elected captain, Company F, Forty-sixth Massachusetts Volunteer Militia. His men presented him with a fancy dress sword inscribed *Vera Amicitia Est Sempiterna* ("True friendship is eternal"). Company F was mustered out in July 1863, after seeing light action. Conwell reenlisted in August and was commissioned captain of Company D, Second Regiment, Massachusetts Heavy Artillery.

Conwell's personal orderly was a slight young man and a neighbor of the Conwell family named Johnny Ring. Johnny greatly admired Russell Conwell, served as his personal servant, and shared his tent. A staunch Christian, Ring read the Bible daily and nightly, to the great annoyance of Conwell, who, even though raised in a devout Methodist home, boasted of being an atheist.

According to Conwell, Ring sacrificed his life for him during a Confederate attack when the unit was overrun and Ring ran across a burning bridge and through enemy fire to retrieve Conwell's ceremonial sword from his tent. In Conwell's various versions of the story, Ring's last full measure of devotion evoked an epiphany, bringing Conwell to kneel in prayer at the side of Johnny's cot when the young man died a few days later. Conwell pledged to work sixteen hours a day from then on—"eight hours for myself and eight hours for Johnny Ring who died for me." He repeated the story in sermons, books, and a motion picture script.

Unfortunately, war records indicate the place and circumstances of Ring's death were not as Conwell later described them. Nor was Conwell even present. Records reveal instead that Conwell was absent from his post during the attack, subsequently court-martialed (later expunged by President Ulysses S. Grant), and separated from the service on May 20, 1864. Conwell claimed to have served beyond that date, telling biographers that a private, unrecorded high-level arrangement allowed the twenty-one-year-old to remain in the service to serve on General James McPherson's staff as a lieutenant colonel. Conwell maintained that he was severely wounded at the Battle of Kennesaw Mountain on June 27, 1864, but no evidence exists of his presence on McPherson's staff or at the battle, other than his word. One simply does not know what to make of the contradictions. Conwell possessed photographs of himself in the uniform of a lieutenant colonel, and in speeches he frequently referred to his role as a staff officer in the war. Later in life, according to several sources, Conwell sought treatment for a recurring war wound that could not have been imagined.

Conwell often said he was so moved by Johnny Ring's devotion to duty and to his God that he decided to devote his life to being a minister. The decision to enter the ministry, however, was not confirmed until 1876. In the meantime Conwell lent his hand to journalism, filing a series of graphic stories depicting the horrors of war that earned him a position as a reporter and a round-the-world trip as correspondent for the *New York Tribune* and *Boston Traveler.* In 1869 he revisited the Civil War battlefields and described the battles in a series of reports and vignettes later assembled by Temple professor Joseph C. Carter and published as a book.

One thing is certain about Conwell's Civil War service: He never abandoned his love of books and learning. He carried books with him everywhere, studying the law and the classics every spare moment. Conwell earnestly believed that "there are no real scholars but those who have fought with circumstances while they studied books." Returning home, Conwell read the law with a local lawyer, entered law school at the University of Albany, and earned a bachelor of laws in the spring of 1865.

That summer he married Jennie P. Hayden, his childhood sweetheart, moved to Minneapolis, and was baptized in the First Baptist Church. He practiced law, worked as a correspondent for the *St. Paul Press,* published two weekly newspapers, ran a real estate business, and served in a host of local civic organizations. When a devastating fire burned his home and all of his possessions, including his voluminous library, Conwell, his wife, and their two small children returned to the Boston area and settled in Somerville, where he practiced law, served as a Baptist lay preacher, and wrote articles for the *New York Tribune*. In 1872 Conwell's wife, Jennie, died suddenly. The stricken Conwell immersed himself in theological studies, mission work, and his law practice.

Two years later Conwell married Sarah F. Sanborn, a devout Baptist and member of a patrician Boston family. They formed a strong, purposeful union, melding common sense and duty with the virtues of their faith. Meanwhile, Conwell's law practice thrived. He was admitted to the bar and served as counsel to banks and railroads. Yet these successes gave him small satisfaction. In 1876 he formally committed to the ministry, becoming the full-time pastor of a frail Baptist church in Lexington, Massachusetts, immediately reviving it and putting it on its feet financially. Conwell was formally ordained in 1879 at the Newton Seminary.

Many elements contributed to his decision to enter the ministry, but Conwell frequently singled out Johnny Ring's devotion and sacrifice as the reason for his decision, pledging to rededicate his life in compensation for Ring's death. Conwell retold his version of the Ring story countless times. It became officially enshrined in Temple University's lore in 1964 when a statue of Ring sculpted by Boris Blai, founding dean of the Tyler School of Art, was placed in a garden just north of Mitten Hall, thereafter to be called Johnny Ring Garden.

In November 1882 Russell Conwell accepted the pastorate of the Grace Baptist Church in Philadelphia and moved his family into the parsonage at 2004 North Park Avenue (now the site of Peabody Hall). The congregation was small, with only ninety persons, and it carried a heavy debt from a new building at Berks and Mervine streets, where the courtyard of Gladfelter Hall now stands. Conwell's energy, organizational skills, and gifted oratory attracted many new parishioners, and soon there was not enough room to accommodate all who wished to worship at the church and to listen to the brilliant, entertaining, and motivating pastor. He had barely arrived before the parishioners were discussing the need to build yet another, larger church.

The Speech

By the time Conwell arrived in Philadelphia he had gained fame as a lecturer on the Chautauqua circuit, a traveling tent show that visited towns in America's heartland, presenting musical performances, plays, political speeches, and spellbinding orations, such as Conwell's "Acres of Diamonds" lecture, part sermon, part dramatic recitation, part autobiographical recounting, and always entertaining. By Conwell's count he gave the speech 6,152 times, a fact included in *Ripley's Believe It or Not*. Tirelessly delivered in conversational style, "Acres of Diamonds" was a morality tale of the value of education, devotion to the Protestant ethic, and the importance of family and community service.

In 1870, while traveling near Baghdad along the Tigris river in what is modern-day Iraq, Conwell heard the tale of a wealthy Persian farmer, Ali Hafed, who spent years wandering in search of a mythical field of diamonds. Ali Hafed died far from home a disillusioned pauper. Soon after, the acres of diamonds were discovered in his own land. "Your diamonds are not in far distant mountains or in yonder seas," Conwell concluded, "they are in your own back yard, if you but dig for them."

Conwell molded the tale of Ali Hafed to fit modern times and urged listeners to "do what you can with what you have where you are today." Greatness, he insisted, "consists not in holding some office; greatness really consists in doing some great deed with little means, in the accomplishment of vast purposes from the private ranks of life . . . . To be great, one must be great here and now in Philadelphia. He must give to this city better streets and sidewalks, better schools, more colleges, more happiness, more civilization, more of God."

Conwell believed that Christian living would surely yield material success. Money, Conwell often repeated, was not evil, only the love of money was. "I say you ought to be rich; you have no right to be poor. To live in Philadelphia and not be rich is a misfortune, because," as he put it, "Philadelphia furnishes so many opportunities . . . . Money is power, money has powers; and for a man to say, 'I do not want money,' is to say, ' I do not wish to do any good to my fellowmen."'

Conwell's speech reinforced much of the contemporary wisdom of the day. He endorsed the doctrine of the secular calling, the obligation to serve both God and community through a chosen profession or simply through hard work. He also espoused the then-fashionable tenets of the "Gospel of Wealth," as articulated by Andrew Carnegie, the steel-magnate-turned-philanthropist who urged that wealth not be passed on to heirs but be used, instead, to accomplish great things for the common good. He promoted the ideas of democratic capitalism and the theory of the self-made man made popular by Horatio Alger's "rags to riches" novels. Truly great people, he said, were simple, approachable people of common origins. Mixed in with all of these beliefs was an unabated sense of progress and national destiny.

Conwell's message had a larger purpose transcending contemporary wisdom. The pathway to personal success, he stressed, was largely education. Educated persons, in turn, were obligated to serve the less fortunate and to help them realize their full potential. Further, it was the duty of all to meet the needs of the community. "We must know what the world needs first," said Conwell, "and then invest ourselves to supply that need, and success is almost certain." To meet those needs Conwell initially used his church to reach out to all peoples of North Philadelphia—many of them poor and many of them recent immigrants—offering spiritual sustenance, recreation, social life, economic assistance, and instruction in basic life skills. Gradually he channeled his energies into meeting what he considered the foremost of those needs, namely education.

Conwell's Philadelphia

Conwell arrived in 1882 to a thriving, throbbing Philadelphia, known then as the Workshop of the World. Philadelphia and the United States were in the midst of a huge industrial expansion. Philadelphia's expansion differed from that of other large industrial centers whose huge plants produced mass quantities of steel. The city focused instead on mid-sized industries engaged in flexible specialization, relying on batch and custom operations rather than mass production.

At the heart of this specialized production process was the skilled worker, making hats, glass, linoleum, pianos, or other custom goods; cutting fabrics; rolling cigars; stitching baseballs; working in a machine shop; assembling locomotives and ships; brewing beer; or tanning leather. Conwell's new church lay near what amounted to the western border of an industrial village that housed a large segment of working-class Philadelphia; the areas east of the church teemed with industry and with the homes of skilled workers and their families.

Textiles was the city's largest industry, with 60,000 jobs and 800 mills at its peak. Broad and Lehigh was the textile center of the United States. Frankford and Kensington housed mills and factories of varied descriptions. The Baldwin Locomotive Works, at one time the region's largest single employer, was located at Broad and Spring Garden streets. The Baldwin production process did not rely on mass production techniques; instead the company used skilled craftsmen to build and assemble each part of the locomotive, relying on an apprentice-training program to enlarge skill levels for custom work. Henry Disston & Son Saw Works was at Front and Laurel streets. John B. Stetson operated the nation's largest nonunion hat business at Fourth Street and Montgomery Avenue. Nicetown was home to the Midvale Steel Works. All were within walking distance of Grace Baptist Church.

'Philadelphia was called a paradise for skilled workmen whose abilities were highly respected.

Most of the skilled workers were of northern European, Irish, or Anglo descent, with ancestors who immigrated to America generations earlier. The worst jobs, the most dangerous and deadening unskilled industrial jobs, went to the "new" immigrants from southern and eastern Europe, who received the lowest pay and the least respect. Between the time of Conwell 's arrival in Philadelphia in 1882 and the onset of World War I in 1914 approximately one million "new" immigrants arrived in the United States each year.

By 1920 Philadelphia was the third-largest metropolis in the United States, with two million people. However, it never became the center of new immigrant life comparable to New York or Boston. Unlike New York, Philadelphia did not concentrate its population in tenements or high-rise multi-family buildings. Known as The City of Homes for its proportion of single-family and owner-occupied homes, Philadelphia possessed relatively inexpensive land and accessibility that permitted the construction of low-rise housing and single homes. It also featured the row house, which multiplied prodigiously after the Civil War.

In the late nineteenth and early twentieth centuries the areas around Conwell's church (and the future Temple campus) blended the best and the worst of living conditions. The industrial village stretched from around Tenth and Berks streets eastward toward the Delaware River into Northern Liberties and Kensington to the mills, shops, and factories that served as the backdrops for block after block of workers' row houses. Westward, however, the scene changed dramatically to one of elegant row houses and impressive, well-constructed town houses with brick facades, mansard roofs, and granite stoops, such as those buildings still standing on Temple's campus along Park Avenue (now Liacouras Walk). Just beyond lay the grand tree-lined boulevard that was North Broad Street, home until the 1920s of Philadelphia's new business and professional classes and many nouveau riche entrepreneurs.

When Conwell arrived, the old-money Philadelphia elite lived in a pocket of grandeur around Rittenhouse Square. In the 1870s center city congestion, combined with the demand for larger showcase homes of conspicuous consumption, brought new-money classes to build magnificent mansions and palatial four-story town houses along North Broad Street. Two of Philadelphia's richest men, the street railway and trolley car magnates P.A.B. Widener and William Elkins, lived at Broad and Girard in splendid mansions across the street from each other. Henry Disston, who owned the mammoth saw works in Tacony, built a mansion at Broad and Jefferson. In 1892, as a sign of his growing status and success, Conwell moved to a larger, more luxurious home at 2020 North Broad Street (across the street from where Johnson-Hardwick Hall currently stands).

Russell Conwell's relationships with the wealthier classes and the working classes are critical factors in understanding the contexts within which Temple University originated. Conwell arrived in Philadelphia in the midst of a redefining moment in the city's social and cultural history. The huge Centennial celebration had just concluded, and cultural institutions were preparing for the 1887 Constitution Centennial, just as immigrants poured into the city. Philadelphia's affluent classes promoted an image of the city as a cosmopolitan center of cultural and historical importance; they were wedded to its historical imagery, to its importance to the national character and the nation's meta-narrative. In those days the belief was widespread, as historian Gary Nash revealed, that "historical memory would nourish sacred values, that remembrances of the dead white heroes would sustain a country of immigrants." Such images benefited and sustained the identity and importance of Philadelphia's dominant white majority and its cultural and political leaders.

In reality, though, such images and remembrances resonated weakly among immigrants and the working classes, because they stood in marked contrast to the stark reality of the industrial city, differing as they did with the desperation and starkness of the lives of the working-class families, new immigrants, and migrating Southern blacks, the city's working-class backbone.

Conwell found himself caught in the tension between Philadelphia's old elite—the remnants of the founding Quaker oligarchy and the old established commercial crowd that dominated Philadelphia economic and cultural life for more than a century—and the new, defiantly un-elite class of working men, skilled craftsmen, and immigrants striving for ascendancy. Conwell was philosophically and sentimentally aligned with the working classes, yet reliant on the elites for donations and social acceptance. For the working classes, his sermons on the "success gospel" fed their dreams and aspirations; for the affluent classes, those same words were taken as license or rationalizations for keeping what was theirs.

Conwell donated the proceeds from his "Acres of Diamonds" lectures to Temple College and spent his remaining years appealing to the affluent elites, beseeching them for money and approval. Conwell proved marvelously adroit at fund-raising among the middle and business classes, but he was not nearly as successful with the truly super rich and the old-line Philadelphia elite. He won their personal appreciation and esteem, but rarely their ultimate approval in the form of institution-shifting, large-scale philanthropic gifts. His hopes for substantial gifts to the college, he often said, were pegged on elevating Temple's students into the middle class, where they in turn would help their alma mater.

Temple College

One Sunday evening in 1884, Charles M. Davies, a young printer, approached Conwell to ask for advice on preparing for the ministry. Davies had little money or formal education. Conwell offered to teach him. Davies brought along six friends, and Conwell tutored them all in his study. Shortly after, the number grew to forty. Conwell found volunteer teachers and moved classes from his study into the church basement. Extensive tutorials or short courses continued until the fall of 1887, when Conwell announced from the pulpit the official formation of Temple College and set a formal schedule of classes.

Oddly enough, given all that transpired later, the name *Temple College* was not Conwell's idea. According to a reliable account provided many years later by Orlando T. Steward, one of the first students to seek tutoring in Conwell's study and later the secretary of the Baptist Union of Philadelphia, it was the students who first suggested that what they were experiencing ought to be thought of as "college." As Steward remembered, "We began to call it a 'college' and felt it should have a name." They decided to name the college after the new church building, which, although not yet built, they knew would be called The Temple. And for this reason, said Steward, "the name 'Temple College' was selected." Conwell suggested another name, but "[h]e finally yielded to our desire," said Steward, "and Temple College it was called."

With the aid of pamphlets prepared by Davies, word was sent throughout center city and the working-class neighborhoods describing Grace Baptist Church and Temple College as within "easy walking distance to factories employing 30,000 workmen" and within a half hour's ride by horse car from where "180,000 working men and working women" were employed. Two hundred prospective students signed up in the first month.

A temporary board of trustees, drawn mostly from the membership of Grace Baptist Church, elected Conwell president. Conwell then invited representatives from Philadelphia's thirty-two Baptist churches to join the effort. However, they insisted on restricting admission to Baptist men and to limiting the courses to preparation for the Baptist ministry, which Conwell rejected. He did not envision a college based exclusively on Christian principles like so many of America's existing sectarian liberal arts colleges. Conwell doubted that instruction based exclusively on Christian ethics and piety could sustain colleges if they failed to prepare young people for success in the real world. Sensing the temper of his times, realizing what motivated and concerned young working-class people, Conwell set out to create a non-denominational college to open the way for social and economic advancement and awaken the untapped talents and potential of all citizens, especially those for whom higher education was otherwise beyond reach.

On May 14, 1888, Temple College was chartered and incorporated by the state. Its stated purpose was "the support of an education institution, intended primarily for the benefit of Working Men." In 1891 the charter was amended to read "primarily for the benefit of Working Men; and for men and women desirous of attending the same." "The regular tuition," according to the college catalogue, "is free." Moreover, "No special grade of previous study is at present required for admission, as the purpose of the faculty is to assist any ambitious young man, without especial reference to previous study." Free tuition and open enrollments attracted more than the basement of the Grace Baptist Church could accommodate. Some classes were moved to the two houses next to the church on Mervine Street, one rented and one owned by the church.

No distinct legal connection existed between Temple College and Grace Baptist Church, but they were closely linked. The church publicly acknowledged taking a "special interest" in Temple College. Indeed, the college could not have survived in its early years without the support of the church. But within just three short years of Conwell's arrival, both the college and the church were in desperate need of space. Together they resolved to meet those needs.

The Temple (aka the Baptist Temple)

Conwell's popularity as a mesmerizing lecturer and sermonizer was so great and the crowds so large that the congregation resorted to printing tickets for Sunday services. The Grace Baptist Church simply could not hold all who wanted to attend. The church wanted to move from Berks and Mervine to Broad and Berks streets, up on the main thoroughfare and nearer to the center of residential wealth and influence, but it lacked money enough.

Ever the innovator and opportunist, Conwell contrived several ingenious methods to raise funds for the new church. The most often cited example of that prowess is the story of Hattie May Wiatt. One Sunday, as Conwell tells it, he encountered Hattie outside the church. She had been denied entrance into the Sunday school because it was filled. Children were being turned away. Conwell said, "I took her up in my arms, lifted her to my shoulder, and then as she held on to my head—an embrace I never can forget—carried her through the crowd in the hall." The next day, according to Conwell, he met Hattie on the street and told her, "Hattie, we are going to have a larger Sunday school room soon," one "large enough to get all the little children in."

Hattie May Wiatt died soon after. She had saved fifty-seven pennies in a small purse, which Hattie's mother gave to Conwell after the funeral. Conwell auctioned off each of the pennies, raising $250, which was used to buy the house next door to the church on Mervine Street to serve initially as a Sunday school and eventually as the place where Temple College first organized. When fifty-four of the pennies were returned to Conwell, he persuaded the owner of the lot at Broad and Berks to accept the fifty-four cents (along with other funds and collateral) as a down payment on the lot.

In 1886 the land was acquired, and a year later Thomas P. Lonsdale was selected as the architect. Ground was broken in 1888. William Bucknell, a prosperous real estate and utilities investor, contributed $10,000 to the campaign on condition that the building would not be dedicated as a church until the mortgage was paid. To comply with Bucknell's wishes, Conwell designated the new building as simply "The Temple," and until the mortgage was paid it was technically only the meetinghouse of Grace Baptist Church. The power and simplicity of the name *The Temple* appealed to Conwell, and so, even after the mortgage was paid, he declared, "It will always be known as The Temple."

Conwell intended The Temple to be a multi-purpose spiritual, educational, and community facility where "entertainments" could be held for the "mutual and spiritual advantage" of the people of Philadelphia and also for help in paying off the mortgage. He was once warned: "Russell, you'll never make a success of this Temple as a religious and educational institution." To which Conwell the showman replied, "If we don't make it a success as a Temple, we'll turn it into a theater."

The building opened March 2, 1891, to a joyful and spectacular day of services, addresses, and musical performances. The *Philadelphia Inquirer* reported that 15,000 people flocked to the church for one or another of the services held throughout the day. Considered an architectural marvel of its time, The Temple sanctuary was designed with four support columns and the balconies were hung by cables, thus affording clear sight lines to the choir loft and pulpit from virtually every one of the 4,108 seats. With the addition of camp chairs the total seating capacity could be expanded to 4,600, giving The Temple the largest seating capacity among Protestant churches in the United States.

The building's exterior is a fine example of the Romanesque Revival style in America. The most prominent feature of the front, or west-facing, facade is the stained-glass half-rose window, thirty feet in diameter. Beneath the window, THE TEMPLE is carved in relief. By 1894 the building was commonly referred to as Grace Temple (Baptist). Sometime thereafter (date uncertain but after Conwell's death), the carving of THE TEMPLE on the front of the building was covered over by a metal sign reading The Baptist Temple, which was how the building came to be known to almost everyone. In 2008 the metal sign was removed, restoring the original appearance.

The Temple soon became a Philadelphia landmark, a popular and frequent venue for major civic meetings, musical performances, and cultural events, including Russell Conwell's delivery of "Acres of Diamonds" for the 6,000th time on October 25, 1921. The Temple attracted visitors and tourists; its likeness even appeared on postcards and travel circulars.

The Temple was Conwell's personal showcase. Sunday services were extravaganzas with Conwell at center stage. The productions featured the huge, booming Robert Hope-Jones organ and a spirited choir (sometimes with a hundred or more trained voices), framed in theatrical lighting, with every element of the program produced and directed by Conwell. Conwell's majestic stentorian baritone resonated throughout the hall in this pre-loudspeaker era. His large physical presence and animated antics charmed and captivated congregants. "He was a big man," Kathryn F. Bovaird, a church member, recalled, "large of frame with rather unruly black hair, which stayed black until he was an old man . . . . His voice was rich and deep." Conwell's granddaughter, Jane Conwell Tuttle, later wrote that the baptismal ceremony in particular "was something no one ever forgot." Her grandfather, she said, had a special hold on the audience: "Personally, I have always felt he was a combination of psychiatrist, magician, and hypnotist."

The Temple met the needs of the Grace Baptist Church, but what of Temple College? The church had already provided temporary space for classes, raised money to aid the college, loaned money to meet the monthly payroll, and paid Conwell's salary. Prodded by Conwell, the church offered to sell its old building at Berks and Mervine to Temple College. But the college, still in its infancy, lacked the funds and the credit to follow through on the purchase. The church needed to recover some of its investment in the old building, and so it sold the original church at Berks and Mervine streets to the Christian Church. Again encouraged by Conwell, the church purchased land on Broad Street immediately south of The Temple and deeded it to the college corporation as a site for its own building.

The Temple (aka the Baptist Temple and Grace Baptist Temple) also became a regular venue for Temple College events, including the first commencement in 1892 and all thereafter until 1932, when the graduating classes became too large for the church auditorium to accommodate and commencement exercises were transferred to the Municipal Auditorium. Even then, mid-year commencements, convocations, and other special events were held in the Baptist Temple well into the 1960s.

In 1951 the Chapel of the Four Chaplains was installed in the west end of The Temple's lower level. The multi-denominational chapel was constructed to honor the heroism of four World War II army chaplains of different faiths (one of whom was the son of Grace Baptist Church pastor the Rev. Daniel K. Poling) who gave up their life vests to save others on a sinking army transport ship, the USAT *Dorchester*, which had been torpedoed off the coast of Greenland. The chapel was officially dedicated in 1951 by President Harry Truman. It remained until the 1980s, when the officers of the chapel decided to end their relationship with Temple University and move away, first to Valley Forge, Pennsylvania, and subsequently to the naval yard in South Philadelphia.

Over the years many distinguished figures visited the Baptist Temple, including President Franklin D. Roosevelt, General Dwight Eisenhower (when he was president of Columbia University), the Rev. Martin Luther King Jr., the Rev. Billy Graham, presidential candidate Senator George McGovern, anthropologist Margaret Mead, and Anne Sullivan and her famed pupil Helen Keller. Alistair Cooke and Edward R. Murrow delivered commencement addresses at the Baptist Temple.

By the 1970s the congregation of Grace Baptist Church had dwindled, and in 1972 the church trustees voted to relocate to Blue Bell, Pennsylvania. In 1974 they sold the building to Temple University for $550,000. The university continued to use the building as an auditorium and for academic offices for another few years. However, in the 1980s the truss system supporting the roof failed, causing a great deal of water damage to the building's interior. Scaffolding and emergency repairs paid for by the commonwealth stabilized the building, but it was effectively condemned and unusable thereafter. A 1983 university planning study recommended renovating the building and converting it to a performing arts center. In 1984 the Philadelphia Historical Commission certified the Baptist Temple as a historic building.

Two years later the board of trustees voted to demolish the building, citing the high cost of renovation, finding no clear reuse for it, and declaring its inadequacy as a performing arts space. The Historical Commission denied the demolition request. In 1998 the university performed further work to stabilize the building. Shortly after his arrival at Temple, President David Adamany declared in his 2001 "Self-Study and Agenda" that "this historically important and aesthetically fine building should be carefully studied both for potential University uses and for historic preservation." Major repairs to fix the roof and facade and to correct structural deficiencies were begun in 2002. Plans were once again developed for the restoration and adaptive reuse of the building as a performing arts center. In 2003 the American Institute of Architects designated the structure a landmark building, recognizing its historical significance, its contribution to the architectural character of North Broad Street, and the work of its architect, Thomas Lonsdale.

Exciting new plans call for $29 million in expenditures to resurrect and completely renovate the building, expected to reopen in 2010 with room for a 100-piece orchestra and flexible seating for as many as 1,200 people. When completed, The Temple will again take its place as one of Philadelphia's premier venues for arts and cultural productions, international speakers, and symposia. As a northern anchor of Philadelphia's Avenue of the Arts, the new Temple will reclaim its place as a magnificent setting for education and entertainment, reviving and restoring Russell Conwell's grandest aspirations.

The "Temple Idea"

Temple College was more than a place, more than just a gathering of teachers and students: It was a bold new idea, a transforming concept. "The Temple Idea," Conwell explained, is to educate "workingmen and workingwomen on a benevolent basis, at an expense to the students just sufficient to enhance their appreciation of the advantages of the institution." Benevolence, said Conwell, "was the motive when 'the Temple College idea' was conceived and from its foundation to its present fame every step has been governed by this one central idea."

When Conwell saw a need, he stepped forward to fulfill it. He understood that the skilled crafts necessary to propel the Workshop of the World and to move Philadelphia's commerce depended on continuing education. He also knew that the aspirations of the working classes for themselves and their children could ultimately be met only through more education. "Everywhere the call for some useful education to aid in the daily toil of the people was loud and sincere. Into that duty," wrote Conwell, "the Temple College rushed with promptness and care."

The gist of the Temple Idea was summarized in an early advertisement, which stated, "Temple College is the pioneer in the work of providing an education for working people. In the evening from 7:45 to 9:45 it provides thorough instruction in all branches of practical education." The advertisement summarized the mission of Temple College thusly: "Temple College does not exist as a private enterprise for the purpose of gain but as a 'Peoples' University' to give all possible help to those who enter its walls."

Open admissions and free tuition brought increasing numbers into Temple's walls but cost the college the respect of the state accrediting agencies. But like many of his entrepreneurial breed who risked all to realize their visions, Russell Conwell accepted the risks and operated with little regard for government or public opinion. In many respects, as one historian noted, higher education during the Gilded Age was the "ultimate unregulated industry." In 1891 Conwell bypassed the state education agencies and went to the Court of Common Pleas, which granted Temple College the authority to award degrees. The first commencement was held in June 1892. Eighteen graduates of Conwell's class in oratory were awarded the bachelor of oratory. Four women were among those receiving degrees. The college also received authority to award honorary degrees, and one of the earliest recipients was Conwell, who received doctor of divinity and doctor of laws degrees.

By 1893 the Temple faculty had grown to forty, almost all of whom were personally recruited from students and recent graduates of the University of Pennsylvania, the Philadelphia school district, or area businesses. Early in Temple's history the majority of faculty members were volunteers. Very few, if any, during the college's infancy relied exclusively on Temple for employment. Conwell called them "self-sacrificing philanthropists." Faculty salaries were very low, no more than token honorariums. Moreover, Temple's chronic financial problems meant the faculty members were underpaid and sometimes not paid at all. There was no gradation in faculty ranks; all faculty members were "professors." None were recognized as noted scholars, but all were able teachers. Because of negative public opinion about evening schools and Temple's non-accredited status, highly credentialed, well-published, and accomplished faculty trained at accredited universities shied away. The majority of classes were conducted on weekday evenings, and most of the faculty taught classes after working at their day jobs. Governance and the setting of academic policy were strictly the purview of Conwell and the board of trustees and did not involve faculty.

As enrollments increased and Conwell's ambitions for the college grew, he needed help managing its affairs. Conwell was not a detail person, and so the position of dean was created to recruit and manage the faculty, keep records and accounts, solicit funds, and prepare reports. The dean was expected to arrive early and attend to administrative duties from 3:00 to 5:00 P.M. before teaching evening classes. Five deans came and went between 1888 and 1891. When Conwell threatened to resign in 1891, the board of trustees changed the dean's job description to shift more of the administrative burdens away from Conwell. Dr. Frank Lambader accepted the position under those terms, joined by James M. Lingle, the business manager, and a bright-eyed, young Philadelphia schoolteacher named Laura Carnell, who took care of just about everything else.

The range of academic programs offered in the early years of Temple College ran the educational gamut. No curricular planning was evident. Courses were developed on the basis of need and interest. Laura Carnell was under orders from Conwell to provide classrooms and teachers for any group of six or more students who wished instruction in any subject, no matter what it was. This approach required a remarkable amount of flexibility and energy. Conwell himself offered classes on an astounding array of subjects, including Greek, Latin, French, German, rhetoric and logic, surveying, newswriting, English composition, and Bible training.

By 1891 the outlines of a liberal arts program appeared, along with the first day classes. To earn a baccalaureate degree, students were required to pass examinations in the following subjects: Greek (Homer's *Iliad* and Xenophon's *Anabasis),* Latin (Cicero's *Oration,* Virgil's *Aeneid* and *Bucolics),* German or French (general written correspondence), logic (a comprehensive review), composition (a comprehensive review), geography and history (ancient and modern), elocution (general examination), geometry (plane and solid), and hygiene. Clusters of theology and business courses were added in 1893. A group of education courses were organized into a kindergarten training department in 1894. That same year a ladies' department opened with Mrs. Sarah F. Conwell as principal; this led to a department of household science that offered courses in cooking, embroidery, millinery, and dressmaking.

By 1893, close to 3,000 students of all grades, kindergarten to college, attended Temple College. Enrollment increases meant additional demands for classroom space. After the Grace Baptist Church was sold, the college moved some classes into The Temple basement and also rented row houses at 1831–1833 Park Avenue (now Liacouras Walk). Still growing, it rented two large halls, one at 1235 Columbia Avenue (now Cecil B. Moore Avenue) and one at 2107 North Broad Street. When those spaces proved insufficient, the only alternative was to build on the lot next to The Temple. And so Conwell again hired Thomas Lonsdale as the architect and launched the first capital campaign for Temple College. Unable to secure a large lead gift from a benefactor, Conwell gladly accepted any and all contributions, regardless of size. Two of the largest came from John B. Stetson (owner of the hat company) and Charles E. Hires (maker of root beer); they each gave $1,000 toward the total building costs of $100,000.

College Hall was dedicated on May 3, 1894, with the governor and other dignitaries in attendance. The building contained thirty-five classrooms, a large lecture hall known as the Forum, and a gymnasium in the basement. A passageway above the street connected the building via a bridge to The Temple. In fairly short order the Forum was taken over by the Library, where it remained until 1936. The opening of College Hall encouraged Conwell to think again of expanding the Temple Idea.

Conwell, like his counterparts in industry and big business, sought always to expand. He proposed to extend the Temple Idea to create a totally comprehensive educational institution with instruction from kindergarten through professional schools. In business parlance, he sought to "vertically integrate," from the bottom to the top, and thus control a significant portion of the market. A bold step was taken in 1894 when he opened "Temple Academies" spread across the region—to the west on Lancaster Avenue, to the east on Frankford Avenue, to the south on South Broad Street, Wharton Street, and Pine Street, and to the north at Twentieth and Tioga streets—enrolling approximately 2,000 students in rented classroom facilities. The academies were basically high school-level evening programs for adults. The intention, as Conwell explained, was for the academies "to act as feeders for the college," receiving any person of any grade. Conwell once considered placing a Temple academy in each of the city's wards, thus creating a kind of shadow secondary school system to supplement the school district.

Conwell's exuberant haste to fill an education need with the Temple Academies was one instance in which he should have taken greater care before rushing in, for the demand on Temple College was too great. Tuition was too low (five dollars per year) and the costs too high for the college to support. With no alternative, Conwell closed the academies. Still, his experiment with them demonstrated the existence of a huge demand among immigrants and working adults to commence or complete their high school educations. Moreover, Conwell's initiative brought the city school district to respond to those needs by opening the first evening schools.

Conwell's experiment in secondary education left Temple with "a most dangerous debt," which, according to Conwell, was paid by "some enthusiastic friends" who "gave all their property to enable the college honorably to draw out of the academies and pay all bills." Conwell also had no other option than to begin raising tuition. Tuition started at five dollars per year for the evening division (for those employed during the day) and at fifty dollars for the day division. By 1907 those fees increased respectively to forty dollars and seventy-five dollars "for the whole year of nine months."

In founding Temple College, Conwell had hoped to strike a blow, as Douglas Perry wrote, "to free higher education from the fetters of the aristocratic ideal." Conwell worried that unless the working classes "could be educated further, the wealthy classes alone would form an educational aristocracy dangerous to our American democracy." Yet, in many respects Conwell's association with Philadelphia's working class bound him and the college to a mission resisted by the wellborn and moneyed classes. The large, spectacular philanthropic gifts thrust at other institutions eluded Temple for all its early history.

Looking back, Conwell regretted that there were "no large donations in the first thirty years of the college life." But he regretted most "the gifts that never came," the pledges of prospective donors that were not kept. Conwell's neighbors who lived in the mansions and luxury town houses along Broad Street may have occasionally worshipped in Conwell's church, but by and large they sent their children and their money to other colleges.

At times Conwell seemed to doubt whether Temple College could be more than a momentary social experiment, a seed for others to cultivate and nurture to fruition. He ignored taunts that Temple was a "sham" college, and he stoically dismissed those who called it "Conwell's Folly." But at various times when facing dire financial straits he attempted to coax others into assuming Temple's responsibilities and debts. Among others, he tried offering Temple College to the Baptists, the Philadelphia School Board, and the Commonwealth of Pennsylvania.

Conwell desperately tried to persuade men of great fortunes to endow Temple College with enough funds to guarantee its continuation. He and his fellow captains of erudition—William Rainey Harper (University of Chicago), David Starr

Jordan (Stanford), G. Stanley Hall (Clark), Andrew White (Cornell), Seth Low (Columbia)—all became "honorable beggars" in search of large-scale philanthropic gifts. By 1900 most major donors became less inclined to undertake the building of a new campus; there was recurrent worry that American higher education had become overextended with too many immature institutions. The super rich sought new strategies to influence higher education; one such means was the philanthropic foundation.

All of this must have been greatly frustrating to Conwell because he knew many men of means capable of such gifts. For example, he spent years attempting to bring the like-minded, seemingly sympathetic John Wanamaker to support Temple College with a large gift. Wanamaker, the creator of the modern department store and a civic activist and philanthropist, sometimes attended Conwell's services, even though he was a Presbyterian. Conwell wrote a flattering biography of Wanamaker, who spoke glowing praise for Conwell's church and educational work, but to Conwell's disappointment, Wanamaker never offered a substantial gift.

Anthony J. Drexel, head of Drexel & Company, so appreciated Conwell's idea of serving the unmet educational needs of the city and was so moved by Conwell's passionate advocacy of the Temple Idea that he decided to emulate it. Drexel put more than $2 million toward establishing the Drexel Institute of Art, Science and Industry, now Drexel University. On the one hand, Drexel's decision was a great symbolic victory for the Temple Idea, but on the other hand, it was yet another rebuke by the affluent establishment.

Fellow Baptists John D. Rockefeller and William Bucknell were at the top of Conwell's prospect list. Rockefeller contributed $35 million to revive the University of Chicago, but he ignored two decades of appeals and detailed proposals from Conwell. Finally, he sent Conwell a check for $1000 as a personal gift. When Conwell sent Rockefeller a note acknowledging the gift on behalf of Temple University, Rockefeller sent another $1,000 check, pleading, "Won't you keep this for yourself this time?"

William Bucknell's large donation saved the University at Lewisburg from financial ruin in 1881, and so in 1886 the Lewisburg trustees changed its name to Bucknell University. In 1889 Conwell offered to change the name of Temple College to Bucknell University of Philadelphia if William Bucknell would assume Temple's debts. Bucknell contributed $10,000 to The Temple, but his death in 1890, with nothing bequeathed to Temple, ended the matter.

Temple also suffered by comparison with the University of Pennsylvania. A preeminent university during Revolutionary times, Penn had declined in stature. Except for its Medical and Law schools, still among the most prestigious in the country, Penn had slipped, and by 1870 it was described as hardly more than a "parochial academy for the more conservative Old Philadelphians." But in

1872 Penn purchased part of the Andrew Hamilton estate (the Woodlands), sold its center city campus at Ninth and Chestnut, and moved to its current location in West Philadelphia, experiencing a brilliant "academic blossoming" with new buildings and inspired leadership, plus a huge infusion of donations.

Conwell and all of his Temple successors have since faced inevitably unflattering comparisons of their school with the powerful Ivy League university "across the river." However, one seminal study of the distinctions between American colleges and universities in the 1880 to 1910 era indicates that prospective students may not have differentiated between Penn and Temple in terms of a hierarchy of prestige. Affordability was an issue but not reputation. American higher education had not yet crystallized into "universities versus colleges." Back then, Philadelphia students behaved as consumers who opted for one program over another for varied, pragmatic reasons, rather than differences in reputation and prestige. Temple's rise to university status in 1907 both helped attract more students and contributed to a rise in status.

Until 1910, when interest in and demand for college admission increased, few universities (Temple included) did much planning; when demand increased, universities (Temple included) simply admitted more students. Some universities instituted entrance (more properly placement) exams to screen applicants and place them in majors, but few applicants were turned away. As the lure of collegiate life descended on America's middle class, entrance exams began to be used to exclude applicants. It is at this point that the hierarchy of prestige among American colleges

took hold; thereafter the reputational differences between Temple and Penn were more often noticed and asserted.

By World War I the most materially successful colleges, such as Penn, catered to the urban Protestant upper and upper-middle classes, drawing on their new wealth to build institutions for them. These colleges successfully positioned themselves to place students on the path to the most desirable professional opportunities in business, medicine, and law. Temple University found itself struggling to compete in that market. But one sweet, ironic consequence Conwell observed from offering a "thorough university training" to "busy people" was that "many sons of wealthy men who could not be spared" from their offices or businesses found it convenient to enroll at Temple in the evening. "So that the institution which was founded for the poor," Conwell said with undisguised satisfaction, "soon became a university for all classes."

Looking at Temple within the broader context of American higher education leaves one all the more impressed by Russell Conwell's daring. Founding a college in nineteenth-century America, according to one distinguished historian of American higher education, "required courage and vision, if not foolhardiness." No European precedent existed for creating small institutions of higher education; this was truly an American enterprise. Many colleges, however, were doomed to fail or become secondary schools. Temple's situation was more precarious than most since it benefited from neither the Morrill Act, which fostered the establishment of the great land-grant universities (Cornell, Penn State, Michigan), nor large-scale philanthropy, yet Conwell somehow managed to keep Temple afloat. The future was by no means guaranteed and the most difficult of times lay ahead, but Conwell had plans to make Temple College into Temple University.